Readings
in Urban Analysis

Readings in Urban Analysis

Perspectives on Urban Form and Structure

Edited by
Robert W. Lake

Copyright 1983, Rutgers, The State University of New Jersey

All rights reserved.

Published in the United States of America
by the Center for Urban Policy Research
Building 4051 - Kilmer Campus
New Brunswick, New Jersey 08903

Library of Congress Cataloging in Publication Data
Main entry under title:

Readings in urban analysis.

  Bibliography: p.
  Includes index.
  1. Cities and towns — United States — Addresses, essays, lectures. 2. Urban economics — Addresses, essays, lectures. 3. Human ecology — United States — Addresses, essays, lectures. 4. Housing — United States — Addresses, essays, lectures. I. Lake, Robert W. II. Rutgers University. Center for Urban Policy Research.
HT123.R38   1983   307.7'64'0973   82-19723
ISBN 0-88285-082-2

Contents

Acknowledgments vii
Introduction ix

I. THE NEO-CLASSICAL TRADITION

1. A Theory of the Urban Land Market
   William Alonso 1
2. The Spatial Structure of the Housing Market
   Richard F. Muth 11
3. The Journey-to-Work as a Determinant of Residential Location
   John F. Kain 27

II. HUMAN ECOLOGY

4. Human Ecology
   Robert E. Park 53
5. Toward a More Human Human Ecology:
   An Urban Research Strategy
   Harvey L. Molotch 65
6. Growth, Politics, and the Stratification of Places
   John R. Logan 73
7. Men Without Property: The Tramp's Classification
   and Use of Urban Space
   James S. Duncan 86

III. CONFLICT AND INSTITUTIONAL CONSTRAINTS

8. Local Interests and Urban Political Processes in Market Societies
   Kevin R. Cox 103
9. Locational Conflict and the Politics of Consumption
   David Ley and John Mercer 118
10. Urban Social Theory and Research
    Ray E. Pahl 143

11. The Role of Institutions in the Inner London Housing Market: The Case of Islington
   Peter R. Williams 157
12. Large Builders, Federal Housing Programmes and Postwar Suburbanization
   Barry Checkoway 173

IV. MARXIST APPROACHES

13. The Urban Process under Capitalism: A Framework for Analysis
   David Harvey 197
14. Capital Accumulation and Urbanization in the United States
   Richard Child Hill 228
15. Class-Monopoly Rent, Finance Capital and the Urban Revolution
   David Harvey 250
16. Toward a Theory of Gentrification: A Back to the City Movement by Capital, not People
   Neil Smith 278

Suggestions for Further Reading 299

Index 308

Acknowledgements

I am grateful to the contributing authors and publishers for their kind permission to reprint these articles. My sincere appreciation goes to Joan Frantz, Lydia Lombardi, and Arlene Pashman for their invaluable assistance in manuscript preparation, and to Mary Picarella for guiding this book through publication.

Introduction

OBJECTIVES

The objective of this book is to bring together a range of perspectives in contemporary urban analysis. If one thing characterizes the field of urban analysis in the 1980s, it is the multiplicity of approaches, philosophies, and methodologies employed in the examination of urban structure and urban problems. This fragmentation of perspectives is not simply a reflection of the multifaceted and complex nature of the city as subject matter. Nor is it a function of the variety of disciplines—geography, planning, economics, history, and sociology, at the very least—represented under the rubric of urban analysis. Cross-cutting all of these topical issues and disciplinary allegiances has been the emergence in recent years of a vociferous debate on fundamental issues of philosophy, ideology, and basic assumptions underlying the analysis of urban form and structure. The readings that follow have been selected to illustrate the range of perspectives that has emerged as part of that debate.

Urban Analysis

The notion of urban analysis embraced in this book focuses on the spatial structure of the city, its causes and its consequences. At issue is the city as a spatial fact: a built environment with explicit characteristics and spatial dimensions, a spatial distribution of population and land uses, a nexus of locational decisions, an interconnected system of locational advantages and disadvantages, amenities and disamenities.[1]

An all-too-common conceptualization of urban analysis views the "urban" as largely coincidental. Such an approach treats of politics, economics, and a panoply of "problem" issues (e.g., poverty, unemployment, pollution, transportation, municipal finance, etc.) that sometimes take on an urban locus. The implication is that urban analysis is the study of whatever one fortuitously finds located in cities.[2] In contrast, the conception of urban analysis adopted here takes the city itself as the focus of concern: What is its spatial form and structure? What factors account for the particular structure of the urban built environment and the spatial distribution of people and land uses? How, why, and under what conditions do these patterns and distributions change over time? What are the consequences and implications of the constituent processes? The attempt to answer these questions is what we comprehend as urban analysis. Within this framework, the investigation of urban problems such as the distribution of poverty and the efficiency of transportation systems is no less important than in the more aspatial versions, but here their analysis is tied explicitly—in terms of both cause and consequence—to the spatial structure of the city.

A Fragmentation of Perspectives

Much like the city itself, beset by demographic shocks, economic obsolescence, and political impotence, the field of urban analysis has recently come under attack from all directions. Throughout the 1960s, perhaps the heyday of both popular and academic concern for urban issues, urban analysis was marked by the widespread adoption of quantitative methods, a relative unity of perspective, and a sense of cumulative growth of understanding about cities. The past decade has seen the introduction of competing, indeed often incompatible methodologies, philosophies and assumptions and the debunking of earlier models in a process of fragmentation that appears endemic to each of the subfields contributing to the endeavor.

From within sociology, for example, Manuel Castells answers negatively to his query, "Is there an urban sociology?," arguing that what traditional researchers thought of as "urbanism" is but a manifestation of industrial capitalism and that consequently the latter must replace the former as the focus of analysis.[3] A "new urban history" burst upon the scene in the mid-1960s, overthrowing earlier work through the promised application of social science methodology to urban historical analysis, but this too has largely succumbed to a loss of direction and purpose and a persistent current of self-doubt.[4] Indicative of the general trend, the new urban history is itself under criticism for its inability to absorb or respond to more recent work within a Marxist framework.[5] In a similar manner, urban geography emerged from a period marked by the preeminence of quantitative analysis—the *pax quantitas*—into a fragmentation of approaches and philosophies that Brian Berry has characterized as a "new tribalism" in which the potential for cumulative growth and innovation has "degenerated into license."[6] Even urban economics, heretofore the most sacrosanct branch of urban analysis,

Introduction

has been subjected to critiques at various levels ranging from a questioning and extension of simplifying assumptions[7] to a more far-reaching and potentially damaging charge of ideological naivete.[8]

The debate, in short, centers on questions of philosophy, ideology, and methodology, questions aimed at specifying the fundamental essence and purpose of urban analysis. Perhaps ironically, the very volume of criticism, questioning, and self-examination is itself testimony to the vibrancy and significance of the field: such an abundance of comment and critique is rarely levelled at a moribund discipline. Periodic cycles of fragmentation following consensus appear commonplace in the evolution of a discipline.[9] The present malaise is far more in the nature of a recurrent refrain than a requiem.

Perhaps the greatest contribution of the current debate is the achievement of a wider sensitivity to assumptions, a more vigorous questioning of basic premises. The introduction of alternative ways of looking at the world has forced a reappraisal of basic assumptions that theretofore had been uncritically accepted. Regardless of the relative efficacy of the alternative viewpoints, the mere suggestion that radically different perspectives are available prohibits the phrasing of questions and the selection of methodology in an unselfconscious and uncritical manner. The types of questions being asked and the way they are formed is clearly preliminary to and more significant than the answers being provided.

For the student initially approaching the study of urban issues, a common intention is to seek explicit answers and information from a set of readings. The substantive content—the concrete information that can be "learned" about how cities work—is most important. While the readings that follow do indeed provide substantive content, attention to the *questions* being asked is at least as if not more important than the answers supplied. In undertaking these readings, the emphasis should be less on what information is provided than on what information is being sought. The critical question is: why has the author defined the research issue in this particular way? What is the conceptual framework that has led the author to define a particular type of information as important? Does this perspective potentially conceal other information by defining it as less important or by failing to direct analytic attention to it? Would an alternative framework spotlight other information that may prove to be significant but that would not have been uncovered by the initial approach because of how the research question was defined? What are the basic assumptions underlying each perspective? These questions should be kept in mind in assessing the respective contributions of the authors represented in this book.

A basic objective of this reader is thus to inspire a healthy skepticism in the student. In a developing and dynamic field, no one work should be regarded as a definitive statement. Answers are still forthcoming, understanding is still being refined. Appreciation of a variety of perspectives may be a more fruitful and rewarding posture than the search for or adherence to a rigid orthodoxy. A particular work, then, is best comprehended within its full intellectual context, where an author's approach can be understood as either alignment with or reaction to earlier work in the field. Informed evaluation requires recognition of the perspective within which the author approaches the issue at hand, for that perspective delineates the way the problem is phrased, the type of evidence that is collected, and the way in which the evidence is interpreted.

Selection of Articles

The profusion of approaches to urban analysis has itself been the subject of considerable attention, especially when viewed in the context of the philosophical and methodological debates infusing the parent disciplines. At the most basic level, a fundamental dichotomy separates positivist approaches from those that have arisen in response to the perceived shortcomings of positivism. Without venturing into a complex discussion here, positivism (or logical positivism or realism) connotes a philosophical system which (1) holds that the material world exists independently of the observer; (2) grants primacy to positive empirical data that (in principle) can be directly perceived by the senses; and (3) seeks to identify relationships within such empirical data in the form of universal laws. Wittingly or unwittingly, this is the philosophical basis for practitioners of spatial science, spatial analysis, regional science and related schools who have pursued the quantitative analysis of empirical data in a hypothesis-testing format in search of universal laws and relationships.

In opposition to the positivist approach in urban analysis (and in the social sciences generally), there is an assortment of philosophical approaches including idealism, humanism, structuralism, and materialism.[10] Each of these conceptual systems challenges the assumptions and premises of positivist spatial science at a very basic and fundamental level.[11] In addition, other approaches, such as behavioralism, have been developed that attempt to correct for the perceived deficiencies of positivist spatial analysis but without altering the basic philosophical premises of positivism.[12]

Most recent discussions of perspectives in urban analysis treat both the fundamental and marginal departures from positivist analysis. Thus, for instance, Johnston describes "spatial science" as premised on the belief that the spatial organization of activity results from universal processes, identification of which will yield universal laws.[13] Among alternatives to this approach, Johnston identifies the behavioralist emphasis on the decision-making process ("positivism in another modelling framework"); the humanist's insistence on a subjective viewpoint (the attempt "to study human behavior 'from the inside'"); and the structuralist concern for the broad scale context of constraints governing individual action.[14] Similarly, Neil Smith quickly passes over the "mild-mannered criticism" offered by the behavioralist approach to consider several variants of what he terms "post-positivist" modes of explanation that developed as part of the broader critique of positivism in the social sciences.[15] Perhaps the most accessible survey of current approaches is that provided by Bassett and Short, which has the added advantage of considering the direct application of a range of perspectives to the specific question of housing and residential structure.[16] Included in their overview are the essentially positivist approaches of the Chicago school of human ecology and neo-classicial economic land use models, behavioral and spatial interaction models, power and conflict approaches that introduce a political dimension into economic models, institutional and managerialist versions of constraint-oriented analysis, and Marxist or political-economic analysis.

Reflecting these surveys of current urban analysis, the articles reprinted in this reader have been selected to illustrate the following basic perspectives in urban analysis:

1. neo-classical economic land-use theory;
2. human ecology;
3. political approaches to locational conflict;
4. institutional influences and urban managerialism; and
5. Marxist or political-economic analysis.

The basic dimensions of these approaches are outlined briefly in the following section. At the risk of establishing boundaries where none exist, the first two categories represent substantially positivist approaches (at least in their classical formulations), the political and institutional perspectives attempt to correct for earlier deficiencies, while political-economic analysis represents a fundamentally different philosophical system and mode of inquiry. Several additional points need to be made in clarifying the selection of articles in terms of these categories. First, the boundaries between categories are at best indistinct. Political conflict factors have been introduced into studies originating in a human ecology framework. Institutions and urban managers can be and have been analyzed from a Marxist perspective. The blurring of distinctions appears to progress in step with the development and maturation of a perspective, as later work fuses with concepts from other approaches in a hybridization process. Secondly, the categories delineated above themselves subsume yet other approaches which one could easily argue deserve independent standing. For instance, James Duncan's analysis of the definition and partitioning of urban space, included here under the rubric of human ecology, could equally be categorized under a behavioralist or a humanist heading. In short, this reader is meant to be illustrative of the range of perspectives currently in evidence in the urban analysis literature, rather than a definitive encyclopedia of all of them.

Each of the selected perspectives is introduced by a major article setting forth the basic theoretical position: in many cases this was the seminal statement that introduced the perspective to the field. This initial piece is then followed by several articles that illustrate, develop, or critique the original essay. The intention throughout has been to include both classical statements and new departures; as a consequence, the readings span nearly fifty years of work in this continually developing field. Both the introductory and the illustrative articles represent the multi-disciplinary character of the endeavor. Represented among the authors are economists, sociologists, geographers, and political scientists. The collection should thus prove useful as a text in a range of courses in these and the closely-related disciplines of urban planning, American studies, and public administration, and should be of interest to that broad readership that shares a concern for the status of knowledge and understanding of urban form and structure.

OVERVIEW OF SELECTED APPROACHES

The common thread connecting all the articles which follow is the basic substantive issue: how are we to understand the spatial structure of the city? As we have seen, the attempt to answer this question takes a variety of forms resting on different philosophical premises, methodological techniques, and types of data. Each of these approaches offers advantages and disadvantages over its alternatives and is thus subject to its own particular criticisms. This section provides a brief overview of the aims and objectives of each of the selected perspectives, and summarizes the principal criticisms that have been raised.

The Neo-Classical Tradition

The neo-classical tradition in urban analysis represents the application of neo-classical economics to the examination of urban land markets. Neo-classical economics is that body of economic thought (today's "mainstream" economics) in which the distribution of scarce resources is seen as organized in the market where prices are determined by the intersection of demand and supply functions in accordance with consumer preferences and marginal productivities. The application of economic theory to the urban land market was motivated by a belief that land values, and associated land uses, could be explained in terms of universal laws or regularities, and that the operation of the urban land market could be predicted in terms of such laws. This search for nomothetic laws was itself motivated by a reaction against earlier idiographic (i.e., descriptive) approaches that accented the uniqueness, rather than the generality, of observed phenomena.

The discovery of generalizable statements about cities, most preferably reducible to the terms of a mathematical relationship, was thus the *sine qua*

Introduction

non of neo-classical spatial analysis. As expressed by Brian Berry in a seminal article:

> The symbolic models of interest are those which provide idealized representations of properly formulated and verified scientific theories relating to cities and sets of cities perceived as spatial systems.[17]

As illustration of the potential of this approach, Berry was able to show through a series of mathematical relationships that the distribution of population by density within a city is related to that city's position within a system of cities organized by population size. Thus, with a series of simple but elegant statements, the approach succeeded in discovering a substantial element of order and regularity in what theretofore had appeared as an anarchic and chaotic assemblage of unique and idiosyncratic urban places.

William Alonso's contribution in the article reprinted here (Chapter 1) was to apply this approach to derive a general model relating land value and land use to location within the city (i.e., distance from the city center). Although Alonso's paper adopts a general framework introduced by von Thunen more than a hundred years previously, his work was significant precisely because the model he presented provides a parsimonious yet elegant framework applicable to all land uses in all cities. The following two chapters constitute empirical applications and tests of the principal implications of Alonso's model. Richard Muth (Chapter 2) confirms through a series of statistical tests that the population density gradient predicted by the Alonso model is best approximated mathematically by the negative exponential function. In short, Muth's paper contributes yet more rigorous specification of the form of the Alonso model. In Chapter 3, John Kain empirically describes some of the implications of this distance-density relationship for households differentiated by sex, occupation, size, and race. In so doing, he provides a measure of empirical validation for Alonso's theoretical model, while at the same time offering significant substantive findings regarding home-workplace trips for such groups as working women and minorities.

Evidencing its origins in neo-classical economics, this "spatial science" approach to urban analysis is constrained both in assumptions and ideology to a market perspective. As Alonso readily notes, his is an "economic model: it speaks of economic men, and it goes without saying that real men and social groups have needs, emotions, and desires which are not considered here." This disclaimer by necessity opens the Alonso model (and its extensions) to all the critiques directed at neo-classical economics in general, with its roots in assumptions of consumer sovereignty and utility (or profit) maximizing behavior. These critiques will be summarized below in introducing alternative approaches that developed in part as a means of offsetting them.

A potentially more damaging form of criticism addresses the narrowness of the neo-classical perspective in its adherence to market explanations. For instance, Alonso considers the paradox of the poor crowded on expensive land near the city center while the rich live on cheap land near the periphery. His explanation, resting on the poor's relative inability to absorb commuting costs in exchange for cheaper land, lies entirely within the operation of market processes: the question of *why* the market works in this fashion is beyond the scope of his analysis. Similarly, Muth is concerned with "the forces which determine the distribution of population within urban areas," but his analysis is restricted largely to market forces. Finally, Kain's analysis reaches the "tentative conclusion that the observed distribution of housing quality is the result of the long-run operation of [the] market." This conclusion is in large degree foreordained by the exclusion of such "non-market" factors as political influence, institutional behavior, and developer decisions from his analysis. These shortcomings provide the rationale for some of the perspectives developed subsequently and described briefly below.

Human Ecology

The approach of human ecology initiated by Robert Park and the Chicago school of urban sociology in the 1930s developed independently of, and in parallel to the work of the later economists.[18] The two approaches nonetheless exhibit several striking similarities. Both, for instance, arrive at a similar end result: Park (Chapter 4) observes that, from the CBD, "land values decline at first precipitously and then more gradually toward the periphery of the urban community," with these land values determining the location within the city of land uses and residents. Park's explanation for this pattern is found in the Darwinian concepts of competition, dominance, and succession—but as in the economic model, competition in classical human ecology is defined in terms of ability to pay. Finally, just as in neo-classical spatial analysis, Park's human ecology was an attempt to define a nomothetic (i.e., abstract, law-giving) understanding of urban processes.[19]

The notion of order applied by Park to the urban community was derived from the Darwinian model of plant and animal communities. The interdependence of parts is the hallmark of the ecological model: change in one component of the community affects all other components and the community as a whole. Not only does this model provide a dynamic encompassing competitive interaction among the constituent species (plants, animals, population groups), but just as importantly, "the community itself, i.e., the system of relations between the species, is likewise involved in an orderly process of change and development." The biological analogy, translated for the urban community into a language of economic competition, provided Park with a systematic model describing not only the pattern of population distribution within the city but also the process by which that pattern and the community as a whole changed and developed over time.

Introduction xvii

The analogy with the biological community that provided the central focus of Park's formulation also generated early and persistent criticism. Milla Alihan in 1938 challenged the overly mechanistic "biotic" concept of competition held to apply in the human as in the biological community, and Walter Firey in 1945 argued for greater recognition of "sentiment and symbolism" as influences on residential patterns.[20] More recent commentaries have extended these early critiques in updating the human ecology approach for the study of the contemporary urban community. For Harvey Molotch (Chapter 5), the fundamental difference between human and plant or animal communities is that the former can engage in organized instrumental action to alter the conditions of competition in their favor. While Park's concern was largely with the distribution of population groups within the city, Molotch carries the discussion an important step further by stressing the feedback implications of that distribution. His insight is that the dynamic forces do not cease once a spatial distribution has been achieved: "the difficulty is that once people of the metropolis relate themselves to a certain area, their fortunes and futures become dependent upon the fate of the geographical unit to which they have become attached." A consequence of this realization by residents is organized activity "devoted to enhancement of a certain land area" and manifested in the form of block clubs, neighborhood improvement associations, chambers of commerce, and the like. Molotch thus introduces a change in the form and dimensions of competition implied in the ecological approach. Competition is not only operant among population groups seeking advantageous locations, but also, and perhaps more importantly, "urban spaces are competing for certain kinds of people and land users."[21] True to the ecological model, Molotch retains the notion of interdependence of parts, so that successful mobilization for growth or development in one area of the city suggests decline or deterioration in another less fortunate area—an important message for those concerned with planning and policy implications.

The notion that competition among places feeds back on the competition among groups is expanded and developed in John Logan's discussion of the explicitly political dimensions of the process (Chapter 6). Where Molotch calls for a "more human human ecology," Logan seeks a "more political human ecology" focusing on the "continuing collective effort to influence the pattern of development among places through political action." Logan develops explicitly what was implicit in Molotch's suggestion—that political, social and economic inequality among places is not only the result of spatial differentiation and stratification but also the cause. From this perspective comes the "general orienting concept... of places as collective actors" and the consequent notion of an organized political dimension of ecological competition.

Logan's concept of group control over place is articulated by James

Duncan (Chapter 7) as the "moral order" sustained by a group in a place. Where Logan and Molotch are concerned with overt political action to control the development of places for competitive ends, Duncan carries the discussion a step further and asks how places are defined by groups within the competitive process. The answer lies at the broadest level in the central ideology pervading the social system and at the level of specific places in the moral order established there. For Duncan, "the moral order of an area is the public order . . . It stipulates what people under what circumstances are allowed to engage in what activity in what places." Duncan here has moved from the plane of organized political action (à la Logan and Molotch) to the level of the subtle formal and informal cues for behavior supported in a place.[22] In addition to formal political influence, such cues are provided through routine social interaction, agents of social control such as police and the courts, and the design of the built environment. Central to this perspective is the recognition that the meaning of places and the populations and behaviors accommodated in a place are socially constructed rather than fixed, objective characteristics of the place.[23]

Consistent throughout all of this later work is the basic ecological concept of interdependence among places (neighborhoods, areas) within the city. The more recent work on political, organizational, and symbolic dimensions of that interdependence has added significantly in offsetting the overly simplistic economic determinism of the original formulations.

Conflict and Institutional Constraints

Common to both neo-classical spatial analysis and the ecological approach in its original formulation are several basic assumptions stemming directly from roots in neo-classical economics. Primary among these is an emphasis on consumer demand as the basic dynamic. For both perspectives, residential patterns represent the end-product of consumer choice operating within the housing and land markets. Two somewhat related approaches have developed motivated in part by dissatisfaction with this demand-oriented viewpoint. The power/conflict approach views the spatial pattern of population groups and land uses not as a result of individual consumer decisions but as the outcome of political interest groups and power differentials played out in a context of locational conflict. A second approach replaces demand-oriented considerations with an emphasis on institutional influences viewed as supply constraints defining the range of options available to the consumer.

The political conflict approach developed by Kevin Cox and his associates examines the relationship between market processes and local political processes in urban areas.[24] At issue is the explicit linkage between economic and political factors in the determination of urban structure (Chapter 8). Cox's thesis is this: housing markets structure the flow of investments and residents among urban neighborhoods and municipalities, since market conditions (e.g., housing prices) affect the ability of areas to attract desirable residents and activities and price out undesirables such as the poor. Market processes thus affect the welfare of local groups and as a consequence, such groups (via residents associations, etc.) resort to local political involvement aimed at influencing and directing housing market flows to their advantage. Cox observes, however, that such political involvement is much more prevalent in the U.S. than Britain, and thus asks under what conditions housing market processes have local welfare implications of the sort that would motivate local political intervention. His response rests on the nature of residential preferences for social homogeneity, and on the extent of municipal dependence on locally-raised sources of revenue for public education and municipal services. In Britain, where a substantial share of local revenue needs are provided by the central government, maintenance of the local tax base is a much less pressing concern than in the U.S., and local exclusionary pressures are accordingly less in evidence.

Where recent work in human ecology has recognized that places become politicized within the sphere of competition for dominance in the urban community, the power/conflict perspective seeks an explicit understanding of the political process and its influence on places. David Ley and John Mercer (Chapter 9) take as their starting point the political nature of locational conflict, and pursue the issue of identifying the underlying motivations for the positions taken by groups active in the process. Their discussion represents a brief for the importance of "consumption lifestyles" or symbolic lifestyle preferences and values as guiding ideologies underlying political action, and traces out the influence of one such value structure on land use decision-making in Vancouver in the mid-1970s. This emphasis on the variety of lifestyle values contrasts with both the neo-classical economist's oversimplification of consumer preferences and with the Marxist derogation of preferences to a secondary and derivative position (see below).

The issue of value-orientations motivating the forces influencing urban structure is central also to the institutional approach to urban analysis. The basic point of departure for the institutional approach is an emphasis on the role of "urban managers" and institutions (e.g., developers, financial organizations, governmental units) in controlling and directing the access of individuals and groups to scarce resources such as housing, amenities, and advantageous locations within the city. This constraints-oriented approach stands squarely in contrast to the demand-oriented approach characteristic of neo-classical spatial analysis. As Ray Pahl suggests in his initial statement of the institutional approach (Chapter 10), the crucial question then reduces to one of identifying the values and ideologies of these urban managers and institutions. Within this framework, it is then possible to address the sources and determinants of the institutional value structure, the institutional and managerial goals derived from these values, and the ways in which institutional goals influence the distribution of scarce resources. In sum, "we need to know how the basic decisions affecting life chances in urban areas are made."

A substantial literature on urban managerialism and institutional analysis has developed subsequent to Pahl's formulation.[25] Among the issues debated in this literature are the relative emphasis on private versus public sector institutions[26] and the extent to which institutional ideologies are rooted in the capitalist economic system.[27] Bassett and Short summarize much of this recent literature in terms of a typology of institutions including those involving land and housing production (builders, developers, landowners), consumption (financial institutions, insurance agents, mortgage brokers), and exchange (real estate agents, appraisers, assessors).[28]

Peter Williams's analysis (Chapter 11) of the role of institutions in the inner London housing market provides an illustration of the approach. His intention "is to provide a counter to the viewpoint which sees consumer choice as being the fundamental mechanism in the housing market." Instead, "factors of supply, of control, and of constraint are of equal if not greater importance." Williams illustrates this perspective by examining the role of thrift institutions ("building societies" in Britain), real estate agents, attorneys, and the local housing authority in redefining a declining London neighborhood as attractive for investment, rejuvenation, and gentrification. Most importantly, Williams shows how the interests and attitudes of these institutional actors are interrelated, such that institutions provide a context not only for consumer choice but also for other institutions. A similar set of interrelationships is identified by Barry Checkoway's account of the role of large builders in post-war U.S. suburbanization (Chapter 12). In examining the "decision process and institutional context by which suburban places were established and developed," Checkoway uncovers the extensive intersection of interests between large builders, realtors, and government programs that resulted in a suburban development boom of massive proportions. This concordance of interests created a vortex of forces in the face of which the influence of consumer preference fades to insignificance.

Marxist Approaches

The perspectives and approaches discussed thus far represent variations within the general positivist frame of spatial analysis. Where critiques and alterations have been introduced, their genesis has been largely in the context of correcting for perceived deficiencies of neo-classical economics while remaining within a unified notion of market forces. In contrast, Marxian analysis represents an entirely new starting point—a restructuring of basic assumptions, conceptual framework, and mode of analysis. It is therefore

Introduction

helpful to consider the political economic approach first in terms of its critique of the neo-classical model and then on its own terms as a theoretical framework for analysis.

Three fundamental points of disagreement can be identified.[29] First, neo-classical economics is individualistic. It assumes a society of independent individuals, each of whom enters the marketplace armed *a priori* with an established set of tastes and preferences obtained through some psychological process prior to entry into the economic arena. Marxist analysis, in contrast, argues that individual tastes and preferences are structured by the broader social and economic context, a context that at any given time is the historically specific outcome of the current stage of development of the mode of production. It follows, then, that analysis of the mode of production must precede analysis of the mode of consumption.

Second, neo-classical economics focuses on exchange, where individuals confronting one another in the marketplace create the foundation setting the terms of social interaction. The basic social dynamic in Marxist analysis is centered in production, where classes are defined in terms of capitalists who own the means of production and workers who own labor power that is sold to capitalists in production. Finally, neo-classical economics views market exchange as a "natural" process encompassing relationships among things (e.g., resources, labor, capital, products), while Marxist analysis insists that these market processes are but surface manifestations of class relationships among people.

The cornerstone of Marx's analysis of capitalism, the labor theory of value, holds that value is created within production through the application of labor, and that the value of any commodity is equal to the amount of labor time required to produce it.[30] Since labor itself is a commodity, the value of labor power is equal to the amount of labor time required to provide for the reproduction of the laborer (i.e., the survival of the worker and the worker's family). The capitalist purchases labor power as a commodity to use for a specified period of time, the working day. For part of the working day, the worker's labor time is used up creating value equal to the value of goods and services necessary to provide for the reproduction of the laborer (i.e., provide for the worker's survival). The value created by the worker during the remainder of the working day is surplus value that is appropriated by the capitalist. The accumulation of surplus value is the *raison d'être* of the capitalist, for as David Harvey asserts in Chapter 13, "accumulation is the means whereby the capitalist class reproduces both itself and its domination over labor."

Harvey pursues this theme of accumulation in tracing out the cyclical pattern of investment in the urban built environment, employing Marx's distinction between the primary and secondary circuits of capital. Periodic crises in the primary circuit of capital (direct investment in the immediate productive process) force switching of capital into the secondary circuit (investment in long-term fixed capital and infrastructure only indirectly keyed to the productive process). Thus, the flow of capital into formation of the built environment for both production and consumption is a function of a surplus of capital relative to investment opportunities in the primary circuit. The switching of capital into the secondary circuit is facilitated by institutional structures such as the capital market, intermediary financial institutions, and governmental programs designed to organize and guarantee the long-term, large-scale investments characterizing development of the built environment. Since such investment is motivated by crisis in the primary circuit, however, capital switching is only a temporary solution; there is a limit to the productivity of switching and at some point the investment in the secondary circuit will become unproductive as well. At this point, Harvey argues, the physical resource of the built environment becomes devalued (i.e., becomes "devalued capital"), clearing the way for successive rounds of a new cycle of reinvestment and renewed accumulation.

Various points in this conceptual framework are examined and illustrated in the following articles. Richard Hill (Chapter 14) focuses on the essential linkage between developing urban form and changes in the mode of production, and sketches in more detail the relationship between urban evolution and the demands of capital accumulation. In Chapter 15, Harvey pursues the concept of capital switching between primary and secondary circuits to account for the role of rent as a payment to land ownership, and develops the implications of class-monopoly rent extracted as a result of manipulating land scarcity to maximize return on this form of investment. Finally, Neil Smith (Chapter 16) applies the notion of the cyclical devaluation of the urban built environment as the fundamental process underlying neighborhood revitalization and gentrification. These latter articles, focusing on the role of landlords, investors, developers and financial institutions, represent essentially "managerialist" or institutional analyses placed squarely within a Marxian framework, where the requisite of capital accumulation provides the context for, and explanation of, institutional behavior.

SUMMARY

The variety of approaches to understanding urban form and structure encompasses a broad range of assumptions, questions, and methods. To a degree this may be anticipated by the imprudence of expecting a unicausal explanation of complex events and processes. Beyond this, however, the various approaches are more than contemporaneous alternatives each seeking answers to one particular piece of the puzzle. An incompatibility of assumptions, ideologies, and methods of verification militates against their easy interchangeability. In the face of this grim prognostication, however, at least two observations hold out the possibility of synthesis.

First, a basic agreement in systems-wide, contextual analysis underlies each of these approaches. Compare, for instance, the following two statements, the first written from a neo-classical and the second from a Marxist perspective:

> The most immediate part of the environment of any city is other cities . . . For systems of cities, the most immediate environment is the socio-economy of which they are a part.[31]

> A particular city cannot be divorced from the encompassing political economy within which it is embedded and through which it manifests its particular functions and form.[32]

The understanding of urban systems can be substantially advanced by focusing on the nature of the linkages suggested in both of these statements. The danger lies in the disintegration of this endeavor into a sterile debate on the nature of the socio-political economy in which both the city and its linkages to the broader setting disappear from view.

Secondly, there remains a substantial need for pursuing the interstices between the various perspectives to achieve a fully rounded understanding of urban processes. Replacement of neo-classical economics with Marxism serves little purpose if we only exchange an individualistic model devoid of structural context with a rigidly structural model that denies the complexity of individual variability. Continuing research is needed on the ways in which individuals respond to structural and contextual imperatives, and similarly, on the ways in which socioeconomic structures are molded and formed by individual decisions and actions. Focusing the analysis of these issues within the urban setting will help to further our understanding of the as yet imperfectly comprehended city.

NOTES

1. As Allen Scott has recently argued, "it is precisely out of the peculiar logic and dynamics of the urban land nexus as an assembly of dense, polarized, land-contingent events that the urban question *par excellence* arises." Allen J. Scott, *The Urban Land Nexus and the State* (London: Pion, Ltd., 1980), preface.

2. For instance, James Heilbrun, *Urban Economics and Public Policy* (New York: St. Martin's Press, 1981); Matthew Edel and Jerome Rothenberg, *Readings in Urban Economics* (New York: Macmillan, 1972); Alfred Page and Warren Seyfried, *Urban Analysis* (Glenview, Illinois: Scott Foresman, 1970).

3. Manuel Castells, "Is there an urban sociology?" in *Urban Sociology: Critical Essays* edited by C.G. Pickvance (New York: St. Martin's Press, 1976), pp. 33-59.

4. John B. Sharpless and Sam Bass Warner, Jr., "Urban History," *American Behavioral Scientist*, Vol. 21 (December 1977) 221-244.

5. James A. Cronin, "The problem with urban history: reflections on a recent meeting," *Urbanism Past and Present*, No. 9 (Winter 1979-80) 40-44.

6. Brian J.L. Berry, "Creating future geographies," *Annals of the Association of American Geographers*, Vol. 70 (December 1980) 449-458.

7. H.W. Richardson, *The New Urban Economics* (London: Pion, Ltd., 1977).

8. Michael Ball, "A critique of urban economics," *International Journal of Urban and Regional Research*, Vol. 3 (September 1979) 309-330.

9. Whether or not the episodes of fragmentation qualify as a paradigm shift is an open question. See Thomas Kuhn, *The Structure of Scientific Revolutions* (Chicago: University of Chicago Press, 1970). For an assessment of how well the paradigm model applies in one discipline, see R.J. Johnston, *Geography and Geographers* (New York: Halsted Press, 1980).

10. An overview of each of these philosophical systems is well beyond the scope of this Introduction. For excellent discussions, see Russell Keat and John Urry, *Social Theory as Science* (London: Routledge and Kegan Paul, 1975); Anthony Giddens, *New Rules for Sociological Method* (London: Hutchinson, 1976); and Derek Gregory, *Ideology, Science, and Human Geography* (New York: St. Martin's Press, 1978).

11. For discussion of these approaches, see the sources cited in footnote 10 above. Additional useful references include M.P. Smith, *The City and Social Theory* (New York: St. Martin's Press, 1979); David Ley and Marwyn Samuels (eds.), *Humanistic Geography: Prospects and Problems* (Chicago: Maaroufa Press, 1979); and Peter Saunders, *Social Theory and the Urban Question* (New York: Holmes and Meier, 1981). For a partial response, see Alan M. Hay, "Positivism in human geography," in *Geography and the Urban Environment*, Vol. II, edited by D.T. Herbert and R.J. Johnston (New York: John Wiley, 1979), pp. 1-26.

12. See, for instance, Gary T. Moore and Reginald G. Golledge, "Environmental knowing: concepts and theories," in Moore and Golledge (eds.), *Environmental Knowing: Theories, Research, and Methods* (Stroudsburg, PA: Dowden, Hutchinson, and Ross, 1976), pp. 3-24.

13. Ronald J. Johnston, "On the nature of explanation in human geography," *Transactions, Institute of British Geographers*, Vol. 5, No. 4 (1980) 402-412.

14. Ibid.

15. Neil Smith, "Geography, science, and post-positivist modes of explanation," *Progress in Human Geography*, Vol. 3 (September 1979) 356-383.

16. Keith Bassett and James R. Short, *Housing and Residential Structure: Alternative Approaches* (London: Routledge and Kegan Paul, 1980).

17. Brian J.L. Berry, "Cities as systems within systems of cities." *Papers and Proceedings of the Regional Science Association*, Vol. 13 (1964) 147.

18. For the basic literature in classical human ecology as well as early critiques, see George A. Theodorson (ed.), *Studies in Human Ecology* (New York: Harper and Row, 1961). A collection of Robert Park's writing is found in Ralph A. Turner (ed.), *Robert E. Park on Social Control and Collective Behavior* (Chicago: University of Chicago Press, 1967). For a contemporary version of the classical formulation, see Brian J.L. Berry and John Kasarda, *Contemporary Urban Ecology* (New York: Macmillan, 1977).

19. J. Nicholas Entrikin, "Robert Park's human ecology and human geography," *Annals of the Association of American Geographers*, Vol. 70 (March 1980) 43-58.

20. Theodorson, *Studies in Human Ecology*.

21. Molotch has extended his discussion of these concepts in several articles. Harvey Molotch, "The city as a growth machine: toward a political economy of place," *American Journal of Sociology*, Vol. 82 (September 1976) 309-332; and "Capital and neighborhood in the United States: some conceptual links," *Urban Affairs Quarterly*, Vol. 14 (March 1979) 289-312.

22. Erving Goffman, *Relations in Public* (New York: Harper and Row, 1971).

23. David A. Cornwell, "The management of tensions between conflicting usages of a public place," *Sociological Review*, Vol. 21 (May 1973) 197-210; James Duncan, "Landscape tastes as a symbol of group identity," *Geographical Review*, Vol. 63 (July 1973) 334-355; Sean Damer, "Wine alley: the sociology of a dreadful enclosure," *Sociological Review*, Vol. 22 (May 1974)

Introduction

221-248; Peter Hugill, "Social conduct on the golden mile," *Annals of the Association of American Geographers*, Vol. 65 (June 1975) 214-228; Elihu M. Gerson and M. Sue Gerson, "The social framework of place perspectives," in Gary T. Moore and Reginald G. Golledge (eds.) *Environmental Knowing: Theory, Research, and Methods* (Stroudsburg, PA: Dowden, Hutchinson and Ross, 1976), pp. 196-205.

24. Kevin R. Cox (ed.), *Urbanization and Conflict in Market Societies* (Chicago: Maaroufa Press, 1978); Kevin R. Cox and David Reynolds (eds.), *Locational Approaches to Power and Conflict* (New York: John Wiley, 1974); Kevin R. Cox and Jeffrey McCarthy, "Neighborhood activism in the American city: behavioral relationships," *Urban Geography*, Vol. 1 (January-March 1980) 22-38.

25. An early suggestion focusing attention on institutional analysis is found in William A. Form, "The place of social structure in the determination of land use: some implications for a theory of urban ecology," *Social Forces*, Vol. 32 (May 1954) 317-323; see also William L.C. Wheaton, "Public and private agents of change in urban expansion," in Melvin M. Webber *et al, Explorations into Urban Structure* (Philadelphia: University of Pennsylvania Press, 1964), pp. 154-196.

26. Ray E. Pahl, *Whose City?* (second edition) (New York: Penguin, 1975).

27. Michael J. Boddy, "The structure of mortgage finance: building societies and the British social formation," *Transactions of the Institute of British Geographers*, Vol. 1 (1976) 58-71.

28. Bassett and Short, *Housing and Residential Structure: Alternative Approaches*, chapter 6.

29. This section borrows heavily from Bassett and Short's excellent summary: *Housing and Residential Structure*, pp. 171-172.

30. For an excellent introduction to the vocabulary and basic concepts of Marxist analysis, see Matthew Edel, "Capitalism, accumulation, and the explanation of urban phenomena," in Michael Dear and Allen J. Scott (eds.), *Urbanization and Urban Planning in Capitalist Society* (New York: Methuen, 1981), pp. 19-44.

31. Brian J.L. Berry, "Cities as systems within systems of cities," pp. 160-161.

32. Richard Child Hill, chapter 14 in this volume.

I
The Neo-Classical Tradition

1
A Theory of the Urban Land Market

William Alonso

The early theory of rent and location concerned itself primarily with agricultural land. This was quite natural, for Ricardo and Malthus lived in an agricultural society. The foundations of the formal spatial analysis of agricultural rent and location are found in the work of J. von Thunen, who said, without going into detail, that the urban land market operated under the same principles.[1] As cities grew in importance, relatively little attention was paid to the theory of urban rents. Even the great Marshall provided interesting but only random insights, and no explicit theory of the urban land market and urban locations was developed.

Since the beginning of the twentieth century there has been considerable interest in the urban land market in America. R. M. Hurd[2] in 1903 and R. Haig[3] in the twenties tried to create a theory of urban land by following von Thunen. However, their approach copied the form rather than the logic of agricultural theory, and the resulting theory failed to consider residences, which constitute the preponderant land use in urban areas.

Yet there are interesting problems that a theory of urban land must consider. There is, for instance, a paradox in American cities: the poor live near the center, on expensive land, and the rich on the periphery, on cheap

---

From *Papers and Proceedings of the Regional Science Association,* Vol. 6 (1960), pp. 149-157. Reprinted by permission of the Regional Science Association.

land. On the logical side, there are also aspects of great interest, but which increase the difficulty of the analysis. When a purchaser acquires land, he acquires two goods (land and location) in only one transaction, and only one payment is made for the combination. He could buy the same quantity of land at another location, or he could buy more, or less land at the same location. In the analysis, one encounters, as well, a negative good (distance) with positive costs (commuting costs); or, conversely, a positive good (accessibility) with negative costs (savings in commuting). In comparison with agriculture, the urban case presents another difficulty. In agriculture, the location is extensive: many square miles may be devoted to one crop. In the urban case the site tends to be much smaller, and the location may be regarded as a dimensionless point rather than an area. Yet the thousands or millions of dimensionless points which constitute the city, when taken together, cover extensive areas. How can these dimensionless points be aggregated into two-dimensional space?

Here I will present a non-mathematical overview, without trying to give it full precision, of the long and rather complex mathematical analysis which constitutes a formal theory of the urban land market.[4] It is a static model in which change is introduced by comparative statics. And it is an economic model: it speaks of economic men, and it goes without saying that real men and social groups have needs, emotions, and desires which are not considered here. This analysis uses concepts which fit with agricultural rent theory in such a way that urban and rural land uses may be considered at the same time, in terms of a single theory. Therefore, we must examine first a very simplified model of the agricultural land market.

AGRICULTURAL MODEL

In this model, the farmers are grouped around a single market, where they sell their products. If the product is wheat, and the produce of one acre of wheat sells for $100 at the market while the costs of production are $50 per acre, a farmer growing wheat at the market would make a profit of $50 per acre. But if he is producing at some distance—say, 5 miles—and it costs him $5 per mile to ship an acre's product, his transport costs will be $25 per acre. His profits will be equal to value minus production costs minus shipping charges: 100-50-25=$25. The relation may be shown diagrammatically (see Figure 1). At the market, the farmer's profits are $50, and 5 miles out, $25; at intermediate distance, he will receive intermediate profits. Finally, at a distance of 10 miles from the market, his production costs plus shipping charges will just equal the value of his produce at the market. At distances greater than 10 miles, the farmer would operate at a loss.

In this model, the profits derived by the farmers are tied directly to their location. If the functions of farmer and landowner are viewed as separate, farmers will bid rents for land according to the profitability of the location.

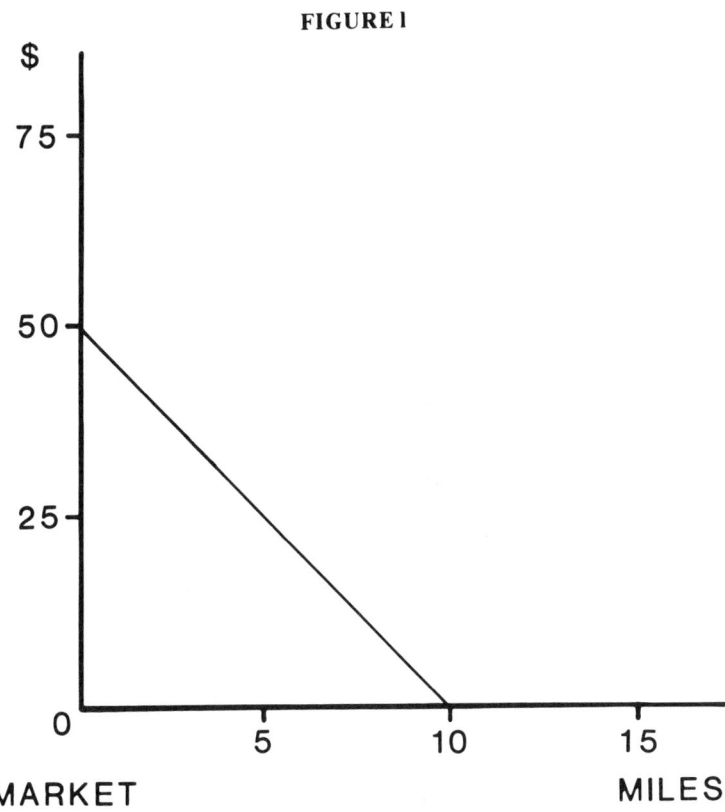

FIGURE 1

The profits of the farmer will therefore be shared with the landowner through rent payments. As farmers bid against each other for the more profitable locations, until farmers' profits are everywhere the same ("normal" profits), what we have called profits becomes rent. Thus, the curve in Figure 1, which we derived as a farmers' profit curve, once we distinguish between the roles of the farmer and the landowner, becomes a bid rent function, representing the price or rent per acre that farmers will be willing to pay for land at the different locations.

We have shown that the slope of the rent curve will be fixed by the transport costs on the produce. The level of the curve will be set by the price of the produce at the market. Examine Figure 2. The lower curve is that of Figure 1, where the price of wheat is $100 at the market, and production costs are $50. If demand increases, and the price of wheat at the market rises to $125 (while production and transport costs remain constant), profits or bid rent at the market will be $75; at 5 miles, $50; $25 at 10 miles, and zero at 15 miles. Thus, each bid rent curve is a function of rent vs. distance, but there is a family of such curves, the level of any one determined by the price of the produce at the market, higher prices setting higher curves.

FIGURE 2

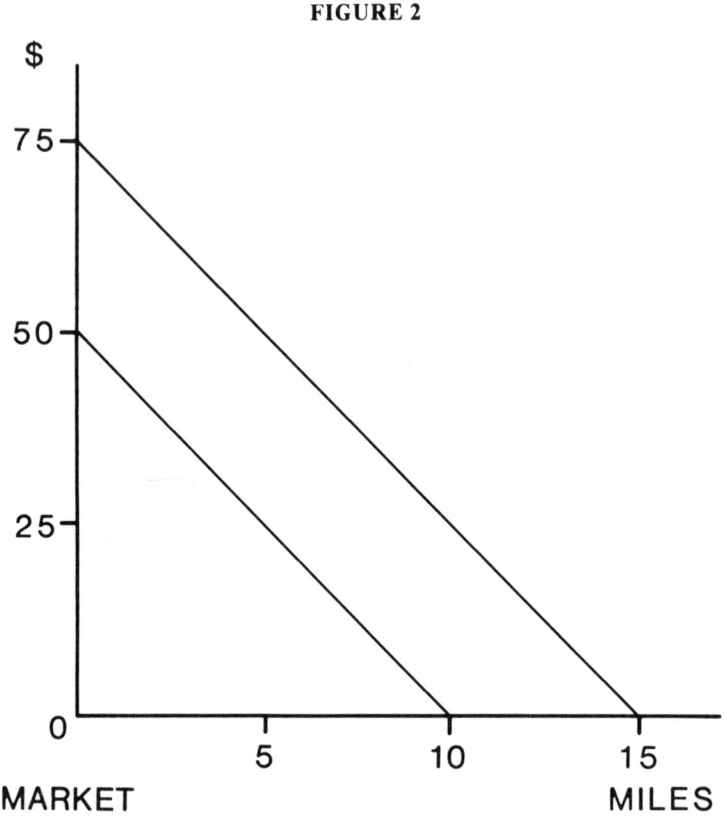

Consider now the production of peas. Assume that the price at the market of one acre's production of peas is $150, the costs of production are $75, and the transport costs per mile are $10. These conditions will yield curve MN in Figure 3, where bid rent by pea farmers at the market is $75 per acre, 5 miles from the market $25, and zero at 7.5 miles. Curve RS represents bid rents by wheat farmers, at a price of $100 for wheat. It will be seen that pea farmers can bid higher rents in the range of 0 to 5 miles from the market; farther out, wheat farmers can bid higher rents. Therefore, pea farming will take place in the ring from 0 to 5 miles from the market, and wheat farming in the ring from 5 to 10 miles. Segments MT of the bid rent curve of pea farming and TS of wheat farming will be the effective rents, while segments RT and TN represent unsuccessful bids.

A Theory of the Urban Land Market

FIGURE 3

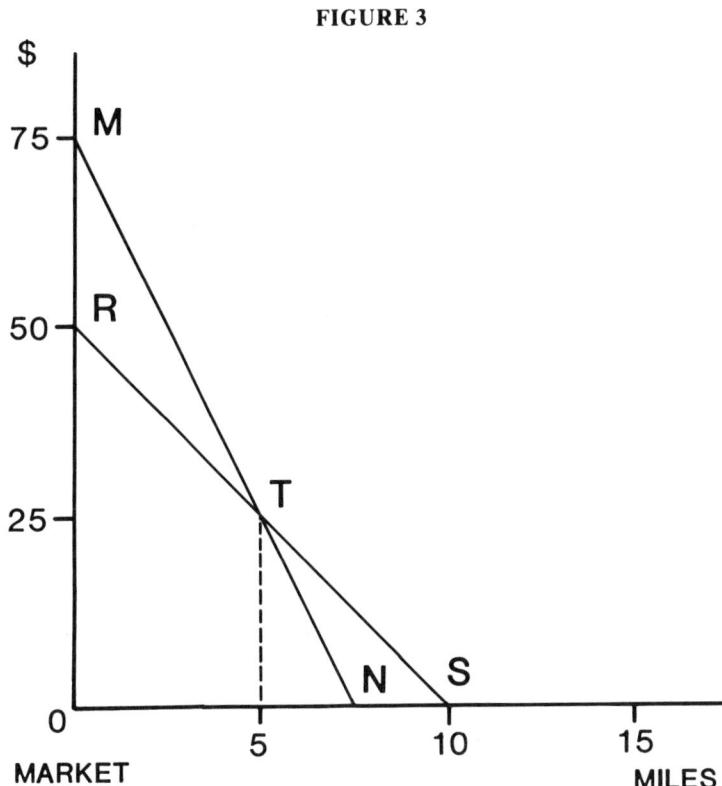

The price of the product is determined by the supply-demand relations at the market. If the region between zero and 5 miles produces too many peas, the price of the product will drop, and a lower bid rent curve for pea farming will come into effect, so that pea farming will be practiced to some distance less than 5 miles.

Abstracting this view of the agricultural land market, we have that:

1. land uses determine land values, through competitive bidding among farmers;
2. land values distribute land uses, according to their ability to pay;
3. the steeper curves capture the central locations. (This point is a simplified one for simple, well-behaved curves.)

Abstracting the process now *from* agriculture, we have:

1. for each user of land (e.g., wheat farmer) a family of bid rent functions is derived, such that the user is indifferent as to his location along any *one* of these functions (because the farmer, who is the decision-maker in this case, finds that profits are everywhere the same, i.e., normal, as long as he remains on one curve);

2. the equilibrium rent at any location is found by comparing the bids of the various potential users and choosing the highest;
3. equilibrium quantities of land are found by selecting the proper bid rent curve for each user (in the agricultural case, the curve which equates supply and demand for the produce).

BUSINESS

We shall now consider the urban businessman, who, we shall assume, makes his decisions so as to maximize profits. A bid rent curve for the businessman, then, will be one along which profits are everywhere the same: the decisionmaker will be indifferent as to his location along such a curve.

Profit may be defined as the remainder from the volume of business after operating costs and land costs have been deducted. Since in most cases the volume of business of a firm as well as its operating costs will vary with its location, the rate of change of the bid rent curve will bear no simple relation to transport costs (as it did in agriculture). The rate of change of the total bid rent for a firm, where profits are constant by definition, will be equal to the rate of change in the volume of business minus the rate of change in operating costs. Therefore the slope of the bid rent curve, the values of which are in terms of dollars per unit of land, will be equal to the rate of change in the volume of business minus the rate of change in operating costs, divided by the area occupied by the establishment.

A different level of profits would yield a different bid rent curve. The higher the bid rent curve, the lower the profits, since land is more expensive. There will be a highest curve, where profits will be zero. At higher land rents the firm could only operate at a loss.

Thus we have, as in the case of the farmer, a family of bid rent curves, along the path of any one of which the decision-maker—in this case, the businessman—is indifferent. Whereas in the case of the farmer the level of the curve is determined by the price of the produce, while profits are in all cases "normal," i.e., the same, in the case of the urban firm, the level of the curve is determined by the level of the profits, and the price of its products may be regarded for our purposes as constant.

RESIDENTIAL

The household differs from the farmer and the urban firm in that satisfaction rather than profits is the relevant criterion of optional location. A consumer, given his income and his pattern of tastes, will seek to balance the costs and bother of commuting against the advantages of cheaper land with increasing distance from the center of the city and the satisfaction of more space for living. When the individual consumer faces a given pattern of land costs, his equilibrium location and the size of his site will be in terms of the marginal changes of these variables.

A Theory of the Urban Land Market

The bid rent curves of the individual will be such that, for any given curve, the individual will be equally satisfied at every location at the price set by the curve. Along any bid rent curve, the price the individual will bid for land will decrease with distance from the center at a rate just sufficient to produce an income effect which will balance to his satisfaction the increased costs of commuting and the bother of a long trip. This slope may be expressed quite precisely in mathematical terms, but it is a complex expression, the exact interpretation of which is beyond the scope of this paper.

Just as different prices of the produce set different levels for the bid rent curves of the farmer, and different levels of profit for the urban firm, different levels of satisfaction correspond to the various levels of the family of bid rent curves of the individual household. The higher curves obviously yield less satisfaction because a higher price is implied, so that, at any given location, the individual will be able to afford less land and other goods.

INDIVIDUAL EQUILIBRIUM

It is obvious that families of bid rent curves are in many respects similar to indifference curve mappings. However, they differ in some important ways. Indifference curves map a path of indifference (equal satisfaction) between combinations of quantities of two goods. Bid rent functions map an indifference path between the price of one good (land) and quantities of another and strange type of good, distance from the center of the city. Whereas indifference curves refer only to tastes and not to budget, in the case of households, bid rent functions are derived both from budget and taste considerations. In the case of the urban firm, they might be termed isoprofit curves. A more superficial difference is that, whereas the higher indifference curves are the preferred ones, it is the lower bid rent curves that yield greater profits or satisfaction. However, bid rent curves may be used in a manner analogous to that of indifference curves to find the equilibrium location and land price for the resident or the urban firm.

Assume you have been given a bid rent mapping of a land use, whether business or residential (curves $brc_{1,2,3}$, etc., in Figure 4). Superimpose on the same diagram the actual structure of land prices in the city (curve SS). The decision-maker will wish to reach the lowest possible bid rent curve. Therefore, he will choose that point at which the curve of actual prices (SS) will be tangent to the lowest of the bid rent curves with which it comes in contact (brc_2). At this point will be the equilibrium location (L) and the equilibrium land rent (R) for this user of land. If he is a businessman, he will have maximized profits; if he is a resident, he will have maximized satisfaction.

Note that to the left of this point of equilibrium (toward the center of the city) the curve of actual prices is steeper than the bid rent curve; to the right of

FIGURE 4

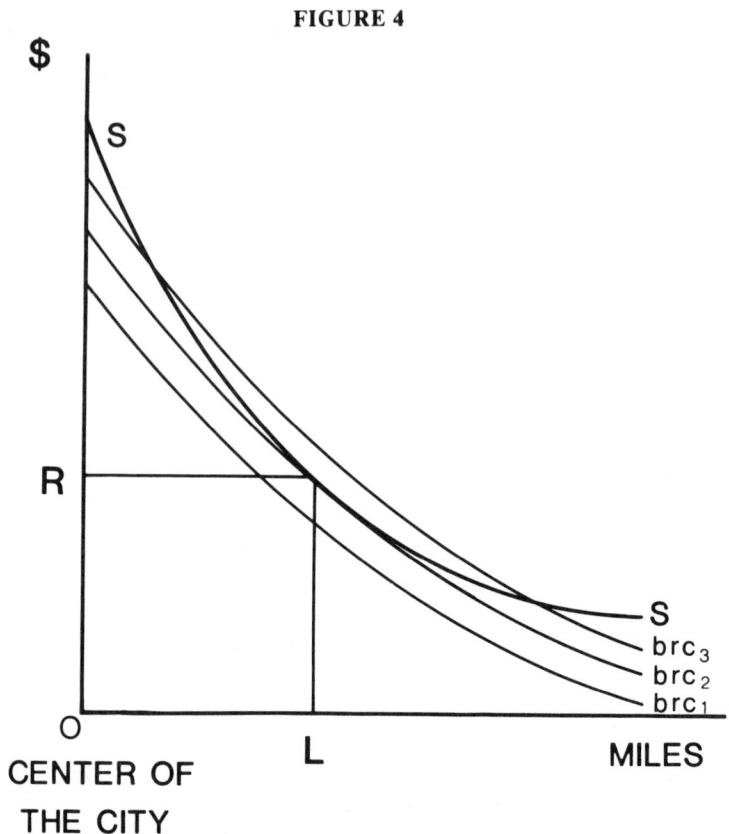

this point (away from the center) it is less steep. This is another aspect of the rule we noted in the agricultural model: the land uses with steeper bid rent curves capture the central locations.

MARKET EQUILIBRIUM

We now have, conceptually, families of bid rent curves for all three types of land uses. We also know that the steeper curves will occupy the more central locations. Therefore, if the curves of the various users are ranked by steepness, they will also be ranked in terms of their accessibility from the center of the city in the final solution. Thus, if the curves of the business firm are steeper than those of residences, and the residential curves steeper than the agricultural, there will be business at the center of the city, surrounded by residences, and these will be surrounded by agriculture.

This reasoning applies as well within land use groupings. For instance, it can be shown that, given two individuals of similar tastes, both of whom prefer living at low densities, if their incomes differ, the bid rent curves of the wealthier will be flatter than those of the man of lower income. Therefore, the poor will tend to central locations on expensive land and the rich to cheaper land on the periphery. The reason for this is not that the poor have greater purchasing power, but rather that they have steeper bid rent curves. This stems from the fact that, at any given location, the poor can buy less land than the rich, and since only a small quantity of land is involved, changes in its price are not as important for the poor as the costs and inconvenience of commuting. The rich, on the other hand, buy greater quantities of land, and are consequently affected by changes in its price to a greater degree. In other words, because of variations in density among different levels of income, accessibility behaves as an inferior good.

Thus far, through ranking the bid rent curves by steepness, we have found the relative rankings of prices and locations, but not the actual prices, locations, or densities. It will be remembered that in the agricultural case equilibrium levels were brought about by changes in the price of the products, until the amount of land devoted to each crop was in agreement with the demand for that crop.

For urban land this process is more complex. The determination of densities (or their inverse, lot size) and locations must be found simultaneously with the resulting price structure. Very briefly, the method consists of assuming a price of land at the center of the city, and determining the prices at all other locations by the competitive bidding of the potential users of land in relation to this price. The highest bid captures each location, and each bid is related to a most preferred alternative through the use of bid rent curves. This most preferred alternative is the marginal combination of price and location for that particular land use. The quantities of land occupied by the land users are determined by these prices. The locations are determined by assigning to each successive user of land the location available nearest the center of the city after the assignment of land quantities to the higher and more central bidders.

Since initially the price at the center of the city was assumed, the resulting set of prices, locations, and densities may be in error. A series of iterations will yield the correct solution. In some cases, the solution may be found by a set of simultaneous equations rather than by the chain of steps which has just been outlined.

The model presented in this paper corresponds to the simplest case: a single-center city, on a featureless plain, with transportation in all directions. However, the reasoning can be extended to cities with several centers (shopping, office, manufacturing, etc.), with structured road patterns, and other realistic complications. The theory can also be made to shed light on the effects of economic development, changes in income structure, zoning regulations, taxation policies, and other. At this stage, the model is purely theoretical; however, it is hoped that it may provide a logical structure for econometric models which may be useful for prediction.

NOTES

1. Johan von Thunen, *Der Isolierte Staat in Beziehung auf Landwirtschaft und National-ekonomie.* 1st vol., 1826, 3d. vol. and new edition, 1863.

2. Richard M. Hurd, *Principles of City Land Values.* N.Y.: The Record and Guide, 1903.

3. Robert M. Haig, "Toward an Understanding of the Metropolis," *Quarterly Journal of Economics,* XL: 3, May 1926; and *Regional Survey of New York and its Environs,* N.Y.: New York City Plan Commission, 1927.

4. A full development of the theory is presented in William Alonso, *Location and Land Use,* Cambridge: Harvard University Press, 1964.

2

The Spatial Structure of the Housing Market

Richard F. Muth

This paper is devoted to an analysis of the forces which determine the pattern of intensity of residential land-use in urban areas. It is especially concerned with the question of why some cities are more "spread-out" than others. While the tendency for the outlying parts of metropolitan areas to grow more rapidly than their inner zones has been widely noted, there has been little combined theoretical and empirical investigation, at least by economists, of the forces which determine the distribution of population within urban areas.[1]

I shall first outline a simple theory of the spatial structure of the housing market. One of the implications of my analysis is a negative-exponential decline of residential population densities with distance from the city center. Such a tendency was first noted by Colin Clark about ten years ago,[2] but there has never been a careful evaluation of the negative-exponential hypothesis. Therefore, in the second section of this paper I consider the goodness-of-fit of the negative-exponential density function to data for 46 U.S. cities in 1950. The density gradient, or the slope of the regression of log density on distance, yields a natural measure of the spread of urban populations. Finally, in section three I discuss the results of a regression analysis of the differences in density gradients among U.S. cities.

From *Papers and Proceedings of the Regional Science Association,* Vol. 7 (1961), pp. 207-220. Reprinted by permission of the Regional Science Association.

I

The model of residential land-use described in this section is a very simple one, embodying only what I believe are the most important elements of the problem. While this model might obviously be generalized in several directions, I need hardly defend the proposition that simple models can be very useful in themselves. Likewise, it does not seem worth while to complicate matters before determining whether the analysis has any empirical relevance.

I assume that a market exists at some point in space and that land of homogeneous physical characteristics extends in an infinite distance in all directions. This land is used only for residential purposes; all transactions involving the production and sale of commodities other than housing take place at the market.[3] Associated with each point surrounding the market is some transport cost for consumers locating there. It seems quite reasonable to assume as I do that transport costs increase at a decreasing rate with distance from the market. I shall also assume that transport costs are independent of direction from the market, although this is hardly true in a descriptive sense.

For any pattern of residential location to be an equilibrium one, for each consumer at his optimal location the saving in housing costs from a small change in distance must exactly equal the change in transport costs.[4] In symbols,

$$-qp'(k) = T'(k), \tag{1}$$

where q is the household's consumption of housing, $p(k)$ the price per unit of housing and $T(k)$ transport costs, both a function of distance from the market, k. It is therefore obvious that housing prices must decline with distance. Likewise, it can be shown that price must decline at a decreasing rate with distance.[5]

Equation (1) has two implications of interest to us. First, if the marginal costs of transport fall, at the old equilibrium location the savings in housing costs from a move a unit distance further from the market would now exceed the increase in transport costs. In such a situation all households would have an incentive to move further from the market. This would result in a bidding up of housing prices in more distant locations relative to central locations, so that in the new equilibrium the rate of decline of price with distance would be smaller. Second, anything such as an increase in income or a fall in construction costs which increases the consumption of housing per household increases the savings in housing costs resulting from an increase in distance, given the price-distance structure. With transport costs unchanged, all households would thus have an incentive to move further from the market, with a resultant decline in the rate of decrease of housing prices with distance.

If one assumes, as I shall, that all households are identical—the same size and with the same tastes and incomes—then all households must be on the same indifference curve in equilibrium, regardless of their location. It follows that the per capita consumption of housing increases with distance, and its change per unit distance depends upon the real-income-constant price elasticity of demand for housing and the change in price per unit distance.

I turn now to a consideration of the locational equilibrium of producers.[6] Producers of housing combine land and non-land factors in production in such a way as to maximize their income; I assume that all have identical production functions, are competitive, and that the price per unit of the composite bundle of non-land factors is the same everywhere. Under these conditions, the rent per unit of land must fall with distance from the market if the price of housing does.[7] For if rents were everywhere the same but price declined with distance, firms, say, four miles from the market would earn lower incomes than firms only two miles away. It would be in the interest of the former to offer more for land two miles away than the existing users pay, so that the rent of land centrally located would be bid up relative to rents at distant locations.

Given the decline in land rents with distance from the market, the output of housing per unit of land declines with distance as firms substitute land for non-land factors so as to maximize their incomes. The change in output per unit of land with distance depends upon the elasticity of substitution of land for non-land factors and the rate of change in rent per unit distance.

Thus, my model implies that the price per unit of housing, rent per unit of land, and output of housing per unit of land all decline, and the per capita consumption of housing increases with distance from the market. However, data relating to those magnitudes are difficult to obtain and interpret, for reasons I won't enumerate here. Data on population densities, however, are less troublesome in these respects. Gross population density, or population per unit of land, is equal to the output of housing per unit of land divided by the per capita consumption of housing, so my model implies that gross density declines with distance from the market. Making what are probably the simplest possible assumptions about the functional form of the model's fundamental relationships,[8] namely that:

1. The price-distance function declines negative-exponentially with distance,
2. The per capita demand function for housing is linear in the logarithm of price, and
3. The production function for housing is logarithmically linear and exhibits constant returns to scale,

it can be shown that gross population density, D, declines negative exponentially with distance from the market.[9] In symbols,

$$D = D_0 \exp.(-gk) \text{ or } \ln D = \ln D_0 - gk, \qquad (2)$$

where D_0 is central density or density extrapolated to the city center, and g the density gradient. The latter is equal to the price gradient multiplied by a constant which depends upon the real-income-constant price elasticity of housing demand and the exponents of the housing production function.

II

The model described in the preceding section, under certain special but not unreasonable assumptions, implies that urban residential densities decline exactly negative-exponentially with distance. Now, one can think of many reasons why this result might not hold. Some of these would produce a scatter about a negative-exponential regression line, while others might work to change the form of the regression line. The only way to appraise the model is to see how well it fits data drawn from the real world.

Existing estimates of the pattern of urban residential densities are deficient in at least two respects. First, estimates have been made for relatively few U.S. cities, although we are fortunate to have data for several different years in some cases.[10] But more important, the basic data for most estimates are average densities in concentric rings at progressively greater distances from the city center. Such measures hide virtually all the variation about the regression line and are too few in number to test for deviations of the observed pattern of decline from that expected to prevail.

For these reasons I have used data on average (gross) density for census tracts, more specifically for a random sample of 25 census tracts in each city.[11] All told I used data for 46 U.S. cities in 1950. Starting with the list of all tracted cities in the continental U.S., I had to eliminate those for which the central business district tracts could not be identified.[12] I also eliminated three urbanized areas with more than one central city of 50 thousand or more—New York, Minneapolis-St. Paul, and San Francisco-Oakland—because of certain estimation difficulties. The 46 cities studied have urbanized area populations ranging from about 100 thousand to almost 5 million.

Population data for the tracts included in the several samples were obtained from the census tract statistics of the 1950 population census.[13] To obtain densities, the population figures were divided by the areas of the census tracts; in most cases the latter were measured with a polar planimeter using the census tract maps given in the tract statistics reports.[14] The line-of-sight distance from the geometric center of the central business district, the empirical counterpart of my model's market, to the geometric center of the census tract was measured with a ruler; the location of the centers were estimated by eye. Repeated measurements made on the same characteristic suggest to me that measurement errors in the distance variable are small relative to those inherent in the area measurements and, hence, the density variable.

TABLE I

Summary of Density-Distance Regressions, 46 U.S. Cities, 1950

City	D_0	g	r^2	Linearity F^a	Curvature
Akron, Ohio	38	0.84	0.72	1.0	
Atlanta, Ga.	22	0.48	0.43	0.13	
Baltimore, Md.	69	0.52	0.53	0.19	
Birmingham, Ala.	9.4	0.20	0.35	0.23	
Boston, Mass.	78	0.30	0.35	0.66	
Buffalo, N.Y.	29	0.19*	0.16	3.6'	+
Chicago, Ill.	60	0.18	0.47	0.12	
Cincinnati, Ohio	120	0.69	0.67	4.2'	+
Cleveland, Ohio	22	0.13***	0.048	5.2''	−
Columbus, Ohio	10	0.19	0.43	0.50	
Dallas, Texas	26	0.48	0.47	4.5''	−
Dayton, Ohio	18	0.32	0.22	0.67	
Denver, Colo.	17	0.33	0.41	0.094	
Detroit, Mich.	19	0.098	0.30	4.7''	−
Flint, Mich.	26	0.73	0.42	0.14	
Fort Worth, Tex.	17	0.42	0.73	0.14	
Houston, Texas	14	0.28	0.58	8.7'''	−
Indianapolis, Ind.	9.2	0.18	0.30	0.47	
Kansas City, Mo.	13	0.26	0.33	0.059	
Los Angeles, Calif.	14	0.078*	0.20	2.6	
Louisville, Ky.	29	0.47	0.30	1.2	
Memphis, Tenn.	14	0.22	0.46	0.52	
Miami, Fla.	14	0.24	0.22	7.2''	+
Milwaukee, Wis.	61	0.44	0.70	0.044	
Nashville, Tenn.	9.3	0.071***	0.022	3.0'	−
New Haven, Conn.	46	0.99	0.74	0.35	
New Orleans, La.	35	0.41	0.69	1.3	
Oklahoma City, Okla.	16	0.43	0.64	0.21	
Omaha, Nebraska	18	0.38	0.46	3.0'	+
Philadelphia, Pa.	86	0.40	0.50	0.38	
Pittsburgh, Pa.	17	0.091***	0.022	2.0	
Portland, Ore.	11	0.16*	0.18	0.48	
Providence, R.I.	14	0.41	0.50	1.5	
Richmond, Va.	41	0.82	0.49	0.078	
Rochester, N.Y.	43	0.64	0.54	9.5'''	−
Sacramento, Calif.	15	0.36	0.38	0.010	
St. Louis, Mo.	47	0.28	0.27	2.7	
San Diego, Calif.	18	0.39	0.62	17'''	−
San Jose, Calif.	21	0.46	0.24	1.0	
Seattle, Wash.	25	0.31	0.57	0.61	
Spokane, Wash.	5.9	0.34	0.31	0.45	
Syracuse, N.Y.	48	0.92	0.45	0.026	
Toledo, Ohio	6.1	0.20	0.42	0.17	
Utica, N.Y.	51	1.2	0.46	2.1	
Washington, D.C.	20	0.27	0.43	0.49	
Wichita, Kansas	19	0.53	0.36	12'''	−

a With 1 and 22 degrees of freedom.
*** Not significantly greater than zero at the 0.10 level.
* Not significantly greater than zero at the 0.01 level.
' Significant at the 0.10 level.
'' Significant at the 0.05 level.
''' Significant at the 0.01 level.

For each city two least-squares regressions were computed with the natural log of density as dependent variable, one linear and one quadratic in distance. The results of these are summarized in Table I. The first three columns show central density, D_0, the density gradient, g, and the coefficient of determination as estimated from the linear regression. The fourth column shows the F-ratio for testing the significance of the second degree term in the quadratic regression, and the fifth the sign of the second degree term where it is significant.

In all but 6 of the 46 cities the density gradient shown in Table I is significantly greater than zero at the 0.01 level, and in all but three at the 0.10 level. The coefficients of determination, r^2, ranged from about 0.02 in Nashville and Pittsburgh to 0.74 in New Haven, the median being about 0.45. Thus, on the average, distance alone explains a little less than one-half the density differences among census tracts. There is no significant tendency for the goodness-of-fit of the linear regressions to vary with city size or region of the country. Spearman's rho for r^2 and urbanized area population is -0.099. The Kruskal-Wallis H for testing the significance of regional differences, computed from the ranks of the r^2's is significant only at about the 0.50 level.

TABLE II

Mean Rank of r^2 By Region

Region	Number of Cities	Mean Rank
Northeast	11	21.2
North Central	11	23.2
South	12	20.7
West	12	28.8
Total	46	23.5

$H = 2.70$; Probability ≈ 0.5.

Turning now to the quadratic regressions, in 12 of the 46 cities an F-ratio significant at the 0.10 or smaller level was observed, indicating too much deviation from linearity to attribute to chance variation alone in those particular samples. Now, of course, we would expect some significant results purely by chance in 46 samples. Table III indicates, however, that overall too many deviations from linearity were observed to attribute to sampling variation. However, there is no tendency for departures from linearity to be associated with city size or region. Spearman's rho for F and urbanized area population is +0.15, significant at about the 0.40 level, while the H statistic for testing the significance of regional difference in the F's was significant only at the 0.98 level.

TABLE III
Distribution of F-ratios, Observed and Expected on the Hypothesis of Linearity

F	Probability	Observed	Expected
<1.00	>0.5	25	23.0
1.00-2.94	0.5-0.1	9	18.4
>2.94	<0.1	12	4.6
Total	...	46	46.0

$X^2(2) = 16.9$, Probability <0.001.

TABLE IV
Mean Rank of F by Region

Region	Number of Cities	Mean Rank
Northeast	11	23.1
North Central	11	25.3
South	12	23.0
West	12	22.8
Total	46	23.5

$H = 0.256$; Probability ≅ 0.98.

Also, among the regressions summarized in Table I there is no significant tendency for departures from linearity to result in predominantly positive or negative curvature in the relationship between log-density and distance. Nor is there any tendency for the sign of curvature to be associated with city size or region. Of the 12 samples with significant F's curvature was positive in 8 cases; on the null hypothesis of equally numerous positive and negative departures, the probability of a divergence from expectation as great or greater than observed is about 0.40. Likewise, for all 46 samples curvature was positive in 28 cases, but this is significant only at the 0.20 level. Table V indicates almost identical distributions of curvature for large, medium and small cities. While the distribution of curvature differs among regions, these differences are significant only at about the 0.30 level, as shown by Table VI.

In sum, then, it would seem that the negative exponential function is the best simple approximation to the pattern of population density decline with distance from the city center in urban areas.

TABLE V
Relation of City Size to Direction of Curvature

City Size (Rank)	Curvature	
	Positive	Negative
>650 thousand (1-16)	10	6
365-650 thousand (17-31)	9	6
<365 thousand (32-46)	9	6
Total	28	18

$X^2(2) \cong 0$; Probability $\cong 1$.

TABLE VI
Relation of Region to Direction of Curvature

Region	Curvature	
	Positive	Negative
Northeast	9	2
North Central	5	6
South	6	6
West	8	4
Total	28	18

$X^2(3) = 3.9$; Probability $\cong 0.3$.

III

One of the most striking features of the data summarized in Table I is the great variation in the estimated density gradients. While the majority of the gradient estimates range from 0.2 to 0.5, they vary all the way from about 0.07 in Nashville to 1.2 in Utica.[15] This section is devoted to a regression analysis of factors responsible for differences in density gradients among cities.[16]

The analysis of the first section of this paper suggests that the lower transport costs and the greater the average per household consumption of housing, the smaller the rate of decline of housing prices with distance and, hence, the smaller the density gradient. Transport costs, however, are very difficult to measure, and the best I can do is to use some surrogates for this variable.

The Spatial Structure of the Housing Market

From data supplied by the American Transit Association I have computed miles of line of local transit systems per square mile of the urbanized area, X_1, and vehicle miles operated per mile of line, X_2.[17] One might expect that the greater either of these measures the smaller are transport costs, so both should be negatively related to the density gradient.

Two aspects of age were also included, the number of decades since the SMA of which the central city is a part first attained a population of 50 thousand, X_3, and the proportion of the SMA's growth that took place during the period 1920 to 1950, X_4.[18] The older the city on either of these measures, the less adapted I would expect the street system to be for motor vehicles and the greater transportation time and cost. Hence, I would expect X_3 to be positively and X_4 negatively related to the density gradient.[19] It might also be argued that the greater X_4 the more nearly adjusted is the actual pattern of densities to the equilibrium one for the auto era. The latter would also imply a negative relation between X_4 and the density gradient. A final surrogate for transport cost is car registrations per capita, X_5. I would expect that where the costs of private automobile transport are low relatively more people would own autos, and I would predict a negative relationship between X_5 and the density gradient.

The most important variable affecting the average per household consumption of housing in a metropolitan area is income. Thus, as X_6, I included the median income of families and unrelated individuals of the urbanized area in the expectation that it would be negatively associated with the density gradient.

Relaxing the assumption made earlier that all transactions other than those involving housing take place at the city center suggests including other variables as well. In general one would expect that the more dispersed are employment centers throughout the area, the less the premium people would pay for locations close to the city center and the smaller the price and density gradients. To the extent that the spatial distribution of retail sales affects the distribution of population, rather than the reverse, one would expect dispersion of shopping centers to have an effect similar to that of employment centers. Thus, as independent variables I include the proportion of SMA manufacturing employment inside the central city, X_7, and the proportion of SMA retail sales within the central business district, X_8.[20] I would expect both to be positively associated with the density gradient if they are significant at all.

In addition to the considerations discussed above, it might be argued that the prices consumers will pay for housing in different parts of the city are influenced by tastes and preferences proper. To the extent that, say, a relatively higher proportion of dwelling units near the city center are dilapidated than elsewhere and consumers have an aversion to living near such residences, the premium they would offer for living close to the center would be smaller than otherwise. Hence, price would decline less rapidly with distance and the density gradient would be smaller than it would otherwise be. In an attempt to account for the influence of tastes, I have included the following variables, which one might expect to be negatively related to the density gradients: X_9, a measure of the condition of central city dwelling units, X_{10}, a measure of industrialization, and X_{11}, a measure of crowding. In addition, X_3 might be interpreted as a taste variable, in which case one would expect a negative association with density gradients.

Finally, as X_{12}, I have included a measure of size in one of the regressions.[21] Casual inspection of Table I suggests a negative relationship between size and g, but size is rather strongly inter-correlated with several of the other independent variables—income, for example. I included X_{12} primarily to see if its relation with g is due to these inter-correlations, as I can think of no very convincing reason why density gradients should be negatively related to size itself. A significant partial correlation between X_{12} and g, like the presence of serial-correlation in the computed residuals from time-series regression, would suggest to me that some important variable has been omitted from the analysis.

In all my regressions I used the logarithm of the estimated density gradient as the dependent variable. Logs were used for two reasons. First, scatter diagrams indicated that the simple regressions between g and the independent variables described above are on the whole more nearly linear if the logs of the g's are used. And second, since the estimated variances of the g's tend to vary directly with the estimated gradients, the scatter about the regression line appears to be more nearly homoscedastic when using the logs of the g's.

The results of my regression analysis of differences in the g's are summarized in Table VII. In all cases, the regression results are based upon data for the 36 cities for which measures of all the independent variables described above are available. The first column on Table VII shows the simple correlation coefficient between the log of g and each of the independent variables. Columns two through four show partial correlation coefficients when different combinations of the independent variables are included in the regression equation. Those coefficients which are significant and of the sign expected on *a priori* grounds are designated with asterisks. The last row of the table gives the coefficient of multiple determination for each of the three multiple regression equations.

The results shown in Table VII indicate some tendency for density gradients to be smaller the lower are transport cost and the greater median incomes, in line with the implications of my analysis. The simple correlation coefficient and all three partials of X_2 are negative, although none of the partials is significant at the 0.10 level. The proportion of SMA growth from 1920 to 1950, X_4 is significantly negatively correlated with g, except when size

TABLE VII

Simple and Partial Correlation Coefficients, Logs of the Density Gradients with Various Independent Variables, 36 Cities, 1950

Independent Variable[a]	Simple Correlation Coefficient	Partial Correlation Coefficients, Equation		
		(1)	(2)	(3)
X_1	0.31	0.28	0.26	0.17
X_2	-0.23*	-0.18	-0.21	-0.21
X_3	-0.066	-0.15	-0.11	0.23
X_4	-0.30**	-0.38**	-0.30*	0.0060
X_5	-0.14	-0.22	-0.38**	-0.43**
X_6	-0.24*	-0.18	-0.31*	-0.15
X_7	0.28**	0.44***	0.48***	0.41**
X_8	0.41***	-0.016	0.025	-0.26
X_9	0.0041	...	-0.43**	-0.37**
X_{10}	0.033	...	0.31	0.29
X_{11}	-0.22*	...	-0.094	-0.089
X_{12}	-0.63	...	...	-0.50
R^2	...	0.47	0.59	0.69

* Significant at the one-tail 0.10 level.
** Significant at the one-tail 0.05 level.
*** Significant at the one-tail 0.01 level.

a Definition of Independent Variables Used:

X_1 Miles of line of local transit systems per square mile of the urbanized area, 1950. Data on miles of line and vehicle miles operated (X_2 below) were compiled from data for individual companies or public authorities located in a given urbanized area which reported to the American Transit Association on operations for 1950. These were taken from American Transit Association, *Transit Operating Reports--1950*, Part I (New York: American Transit Association, 1951). Miles of line were divided by the area in square miles of the urbanized area from U.S. Bureau of the Census, *1950 Census of Population*, Vol. 1 (Washington, D.C.: U.S. Government Printing Office, 1952), Table 17.

X_2 Vehicle miles operated per mile of line, local transit systems, 1950. (See above.)

X_3 Age of the SMA in 1950. Number of decades since the SMA first attained a population of 50 thousand, from Bogue and Harris, *op. cit.*, Appendix Table I, p. 73.

X_4 Proportion of SMA population growth in the period 1920-1950. Computed from data given by Donald J. Bogue, *Metropolitan Growth and the Conversion of Land to Nonagricultural Uses* (Oxford, Ohio: Scripps Foundation, 1956), Appendix Table II, pp. 28-32.

X_5 Car registrations per capita in principal SMA counties, 1950. Car registrations data are from Automobile Manufacturers Association, *Automobile Facts and Figures*, 31st ed. (Detroit, Mich.: Automobile Manufacturers Association, 1951), pp. 24-25, while the population data are from U.S. Bureau of the Census, *1950 Census of Population*, Vol. II (Washington, D.C.: U.S. Government Printing Office, 1952), Tables 4 and 5.

TABLE VII (CONTINUED)

X_6 Median income, families and unrelated individuals, urbanized area, 1949. From *ibid.*, Part 1, Table 93.

X_7 Proportion of SMA manufacturing employment in the central city, 1947. Computed from data in Evelyn M. Kitagawa and Donald J. Bogue, *Suburbanization of Manufacturing Activity within Standard Metropolitan Areas* (Oxford, Ohio: Scripps Foundation, 1955), Appendix Table A-1, pp. 132-38.

X_8 Proportion of SMA retail sales in the central business district, 1954. From *1954 Census of Business, Central Business District Statistics, Summary Report, op. cit.*, Table 4.

X_9 Proportion of central city dwelling units substandard (in need of major repair and/or lacking running water), 1950. Computed from data in *1950 Census of Population*, Vol. III, *op. cit.*, Table 3.

X_{10} Proportion of urbanized area manufacturing employment (male) in manufacturing, 1950. Computed from data in *1950 Census of Population*, Vol. II, *op. cit.*, Table 3.

X_{11} Average density of the central city, 1950. Population per sq. mile of land area, from *1950 Census of Population*, Vol. 1, *op. cit.*, Table 17.

X_{12} Log of urbanized area population, 1950. From *ibid.*

is added. In equations (2) and (3), car registrations per capita are significantly negatively correlated with g. The simple correlation of income with g and the partial in equation (2) are both significantly negative, though the partial is not when size is added in equation (3).

X_7 and X_8, the variables relating to the spatial distribution of employment and shopping centers, are quite interesting. Except for the size variable, none of the independent variables is more strongly and consistently correlated with g than X_7, the proportion of SMA manufacturing employment inside the central city. The retail sales variable, however, while showing a highly significant and positive simple correlation with g, becomes insignificant when other factors are held constant. These results indicate that the spatial distribution of employment is a very important factor in determining the spatial distribution of population in urban areas. But, in line with central place theory, the spatial distribution of retail sales appears to be a result rather than a cause of urban population distribution.

Of the three taste variables, only dwelling unit condition, X_9, exhibits a significantly negative partial correlation with g. This correlation is consistent with the hypothesis that people prefer outlying residential locations in part because of the dwelling unit characteristics of the central city. But adding X_9 alone increases R^2 only from 0.47 to 0.53, so the condition of dwelling units would appear to have a much weaker influence on the spatial distribution of population than is often ascribed to it.

Finally, the size variable is significantly negatively correlated with g, even when all the other independent variables are included in the regression. This result suggests to me that there are other factors not included in this analysis which have a significant influence on the slope of the density-distance function.

IV

The empirical analysis of this paper shows a strong and highly significant tendency for urban population densities to decline with distance from the central business district. While too many departures from the negative-exponential pattern of decline were noted to be attributable to sampling variability, there was no significant tendency for the log density-distance regressions to exhibit predominantly positive or negative curvature. Hence, the negative-exponential function is probably the best simple approximation to the pattern of urban residential densities in U.S. cities in 1950.

Great variation in the density gradients for 1950 was found and analyzed. The results suggest a significant tendency for density gradients to be smaller or cities more spread out where transport costs are low. If anything it appears that the greater the average income in an area, and hence the average per household consumption of housing, the smaller the density gradient. One of the strongest factors affecting the gradient is the spatial distribution of employment, X_7 being consistently and positively correlated with g. The larger the proportion of central city dwelling units which are substandard the more spread out is population within the city, a result consistent with the hypothesis that poor-quality housing leads some consumers to seek out residences at greater distances from the center than they otherwise would. Finally, even when all other variables are included in the regression equation, there is a strong tendency for cities to have smaller density gradients the greater their size.

APPENDIX

The purpose of this appendix is to demonstrate the assertion that, if certain simple assumptions are made about the price-distance, demand, and production functions, population densities decline negative-exponentially with distance.

Assuming that housing firms have identical log-linear production functions which exhibit constant returns to scale, the first-order or necessary conditions for firm equilibrium are given by:

$$Q^* = a_0^* + a_1 L^* + a_2 R^*, \ a_1 + a_2 = 1$$

$$L^* = a_1^* + p^* + Q^* - w^* \qquad (3)$$

$$R^* = a_2^* + p^* + Q^* - r^*$$

where X^* stands for the natural logarithm of X. Substituting the second and third of these into the first yields

$$r^* = \text{const.} - \frac{a_1}{a_2} w^* + \frac{1}{a_2} p^*. \tag{4}$$

Equation (4), which gives the maximum rent firms offer for land as a function of non-land cost and price, when substituted into the third of equations (3), gives:

$$\left(\frac{Q}{R}\right)^* = \text{const.} - \frac{a_1}{a_2} w^* + \frac{a_1}{a_2} p^*$$

or
$$\tag{5}$$

$$\frac{d}{dk}\left(\frac{Q}{R}\right)^* = \frac{a_1}{a_2} \frac{dp^*}{dk}.$$

Assuming that price declines negative exponentially with distance,

$$p^* = p_0^* - ck, \quad \frac{dp^*}{dk} = -c, \tag{6}$$

so

$$\frac{d}{dk}\left(\frac{Q}{R}\right)^* = -\frac{a_1}{a_2} c. \tag{7}$$

Likewise, if the per capita demand for housing is

$$\left(\frac{Q}{P}\right) = \text{const.} \times p^{A_1}, \tag{8}$$

where A_1 is the real-income-constant price elasticity,

$$\frac{d}{dk}\left(\frac{Q}{P}\right)^* = A_1 \frac{dp^*}{dk} = -A_1 c. \tag{9}$$

Since density, D, equals (Q/R) divided by (Q/P),

$$\frac{dD^*}{dk} = \frac{d}{dk}\left(\frac{Q}{R}\right)^* - \frac{d}{dk}\left(\frac{Q}{P}\right)^* = -\left(\frac{a_1}{a_2} - A_1\right) c = -g. \tag{10}$$

Equation (10) says that the log of density declines at a constant rate with distance, and this rate of decline depends upon the price gradient, the real-income-constant elasticity of demand, and the exponents of the production function. Integrating equation (10), we find:

$$D = D_0 \exp(-gk), \text{ where } D_0 = \frac{Pg^2}{2\pi}, \tag{11}$$

the constant D_0 being evaluated by equating the integral of density over the land area used for housing with total population, P.

NOTES

1. For a summary of the evidence relating to the spread of population within urban areas see Philip M. Hauser, "The Changing Population Pattern of the Modern City," in *Cities and Society*, 2nd ed., eds. Paul K. Hatt and Albert J. Reiss, Jr. (Glencoe, Illinois: The Free Press, 1957), pp. 157-74. The most complete study of urban population distribution I have seen is Donald J. Bogue and Dorothy L. Harris, *Comparative Population and Urban Research via Multiple Regression and Convariance Analysis*. (Oxford, Ohio: Scripps Foundation, 1954).

2. "Urban Population Densities," *Journal of the Royal Statistical Society*, Series A, CXIV (Part IV, 1951), 490-96. The essentials of my analysis were worked out before I became aware of Clark's empirical observations. Hence, I am more confident of the predictive power of this analysis than I would have been had it been constructed for the expressed purpose of yielding a negative-exponential density decline.

3. Throughout this paper, when I speak of housing I mean the bundle of consumer services supplied both by structures and by the land on which they are located.

4. Likewise, for the equilibrium location of a household to be at a finite distance, the savings in housing costs must not increase more rapidly than transportation costs as distance increases.

5. The condition that the net saving on housing and transport cost per unit increase in distance not increase with distance implies that:

$$p''(k) \geq \frac{-1}{q} \left\{ p'(k) \frac{\partial q}{\partial k} + T''(k) \right\}$$

In the neighborhood of the optimal location real income is constant but $p'(k) < 0$, hence $(\partial q/\partial k) > 0$. Thus, if $T''(k) < 0$, $p''(k) > 0$.

6. Throughout I treat owner-occupants as producers of housing selling housing services to themselves as tenants.

7. Letting π be the "profits" of a firm producing housing, Q its output, L and R nonland and land, and w and r their respective prices,

$$\pi = pQ - wL - rR$$

Differentiating,

$$d\pi = (Qdp - Rdr) + (pdQ - wdL - rdR).$$

The second parenthesis is zero, from the first-order conditions of profit maximization. Hence,

$$d\pi = 0 \text{ implies } r'(k) = (Q/R)p'(k) < 0.$$

8. The negative-exponential price-distance function is to my knowledge the simplest one for which price declines at a decreasing rate with distance. The logarithmically linear approximation is the simplest form of the production function with declining marginal physical productivities. It has been widely used in empirical work. I have found that either a linear or logarithmically-linear housing demand function is a workable approximation in using national data; see my "The Demand for Non-Farm Housing," in *The Demand For Durable Goods*, ed. Arnold C. Harberger (Chicago: University of Chicago Press, 1960).

9. A proof of this assertion is given in the appendix.
10. See Clark, *op. cit.*
11. In each case I omitted tracts in the central business district and any tract with fewer than 100 residents from the population of tracts sampled on the grounds that in these land is devoted almost entirely to other than residential uses. Likewise, for uniformity the population sampled included only tracts in the central city, since the outlying parts of metropolitan areas are not tracted in all cases.
12. Central business district census tracts are listed in U.S. Bureau of the Census, *1954 Census of Business, Central Business District Statistics, Summary Report* (Washington, D.C.: U.S. Government Printing Office, 1958), pp. APP1-6.
13. U.S. Bureau of the Census, *1950 Census of Population,* Vol. III (Washington, D.C.: U.S. Government Printing Office, 1952), Table 1.
14. *Ibid.* For two cities, Los Angeles and Cleveland, measures were taken from larger tract maps obtained through the census tract key persons in those cities. In all cases, three measurements of area were made and averaged. If one of the three differed from the average of the other two by as much as one-third it was discarded and another measurement made. For three cities already available area measurements were used. For Boston these were taken from unpublished measurements supplied by the Research Division, United Community Services; for Chicago from Chicago Community Inventory, "Gross Land Area and Gross Population Density of Census Tracts and Community Areas for the City of Chicago, 1950," (Unpublished, November, 1952); for Philadelphia from Philadelphia City Planning Commission, "Population Densities in 1940 and 1950 by Census Tracts-Philadelphia," (Unpublished, August, 1954).
15. The median of the g's in Table 1 is about 0.35.
16. Since the g's are but estimates, part of the reason for differences among them is sampling variability. However, study of the estimated variances of the gradient estimates suggests that sampling variability accounts for only about 10 percent of the variance of the estimated gradients among the several cities.
17. These measures cover only those local transit companies and public companies and public authorities which reported to the Association on their operations for 1950, and are available for only 37 of the 46 cities for which I computed density gradients. The compilations of the Association permit one to calculate passengers carried per vehicle mile operated as well for all but four of these cities. To avoid running too short of degrees of freedom, however, I did not include this variable.
18. The sources for all data used in this part of the analysis are given at the foot of Table VII.
19. The relation of X_4 to density was first suggested to me by an unpublished manuscript of Lowdon Wingo.
20. Data on SMA retail sales were not available for one of the 37 cities for which I have data relating to local transit systems.
21. This is the log of the urbanized area population. Use of logs for this variable resulted in a more nearly linear scatter.

3

The Journey-to-Work as a Determinant of Residential Location

John F. Kain

This study presents some empirical evidence on the manner in which transportation costs influence the household's choice of a residential location. It also describes a residential location model which considers the problem of residential location somewhat differently than have models available elsewhere in the literature.[1] This model makes it easier to understand the empirical tests offered in this paper. The central hypothesis, suggested by this and similar models, is that households substitute journey-to-work expenditures for site expenditures. This substitution depends primarily on household preferences for low-density as opposed to high-density residential services.

THE MODEL

The model deals with the locational choice of a single household. It is assumed that this household's transportation costs increase monotonically with the distance it resides from its workplace. The reasonableness of this assumption may be seen if the household's monthly expenditure for transportation is broken into its component parts. These outlays may be expressed as the sum of the costs of the journey to work, of obtaining residentially oriented services within the immediate residential area, i.e., groceries, elementary school, etc., and of obtaining other services available only outside the residential area. Included are both dollar expenditures for transportation and dollar valuations of time spent in travel. Unless the distinction is explicitly made, transportation costs here will refer to these combined costs.

The household's monthly transportation costs, T, may then be expressed as the sum of its expenditures for those services obtainable within the residential area, t_r, those which vary with the residence's distance from its workplace, $t(w_1), t(w_2), t(w_3), \ldots, t(w_n)$, and those which vary with the residence's distance from other points outside the residential area, $t(o_1), t(o_2), \ldots, t(o_m)$, where n equals the number of workplace destinations for the household and m equals the number of other destinations outside the residential area. The household's total monthly transportation cost for each residential site may thus be expressed:

$$T = t_r + t(w_1) + t(w_2) + t(w_3) + \cdots + t(w_n) + t(o_1) + \cdots + t(o_m) \qquad (1)$$

For our purposes it may be assumed that t_r is invariant with the household's choice of location. The level of t_r may vary with the kind of residential area the household chooses, i.e., low-density versus high-density, but there is no reason to expect a significant variation between areas of similar characteristics.

If the costs of residentially provided services—retailing, medical services, schools, etc.—may be considered as invariant, the accuracy of our assumption depends on the relative weights placed on the trips to workplaces and on the trips made to other points outside the residential area. It is my contention that for the majority of urban households the sum of transportation costs to points other than work or within the immediate residential area is small, and that the costs to any one other single point are almost always trivial. The journey-to-work costs, by way of contrast, are large and significant. Thus, if these contentions are correct, no serious violence is done in most instances by considering only journey-to-work costs in our residential location model.

It is not at all difficult, however, to find exceptions to the rule I have proposed. For example, there is the large and probably increasing population of households without a member in the labor force. For such households the worktrip term in our equation is equal to zero. For these households the location of other destinations may be of considerable importance. Many retired people desire to live near their children and grandchildren. Single persons and young married couples may make frequent trips to major cultural and recreational centers. The monthly travel costs of these households may vary significantly with the distance from these centers.

Despite these exceptions to the rule, it is my belief that the assumption used in this model is approximately correct for a very large proportion of the population, perhaps for as many as 80 or 90 percent of households having a member in the labor force.

The data in Table 1 illustrate the importance of the journey-to-work in the household's travel budget. Nearly half of all trips from home are made to work. Of the remainder, some portion of social-recreation trips and personal business trips are made to other destinations outside the residential area. The destinations of these trips may be spatially quite separated. Furthermore, many will be to points nearby the workplace, since a large proportion of cultural, recreational, personal business, and other destinations are likely to be nearby employment concentrations.

TABLE 1
Purpose of Trips Originating in the Dwelling Unit in 38 Cities

Trip Purpose	Percent	Trips per 1000 Dwelling Units (Hypothetical)
Work	43.9	1010
Business	6.8	155
Social-Recreation	21.4	490
Shopping	11.9	275
School	4.8	110
All Others	11.2	260
Total	100.0	2300

Source: Robert E. Schmidt and M. Earl Campbell, *Highway Traffic Estimation*, The Eno Foundation for Highway Traffic Control, 1956, Table II-4

These trips made to the same destinations may be added to the trips made to the workplace. If a small proportion of the population makes large numbers of these trips, the averages shown in Table 1 overstate the importance of those trips for the remainder of the population.

The Market for Residential Space

It is also assumed that the household is an atomistic competitor in the market for residential space. That is, it is assumed that there is a market for residential space and that the price a single household must pay per unit for space is given. Residential space is defined as the urban land utilized by the household in its residential activities. For single-family dwelling units this would be closely approximated by lot size. For multiple units it would be some proportion of the total amount of land utilized by the structure. (I am glossing over, at this point, a number of complex relationships among the lot layout, overall neighborhood densities, and substitutability between capital and land and residential space.)

I am assuming that the price the household must pay per unit of residential space varies from one location to another. This price is an economic rent which landlords can obtain from households for more accessible sites. The rents on more accessible sites arise because of households' collective efforts to economize on transportation expenditures. For this model, I am assuming that these rents, which I will refer to hereafter as location rents, decrease with distance from the household's workplace. Specifically, I am assuming that the unit price the household must pay per unit of residential space *of a stated quality and amenity* decreases monotonically from its workplace. Of course, the magnitude of the location rents is significant only when there is a significant concentration of employment.

It is possible, as Alonso, Wingo, and others have done, to obtain this second result using only the first assumption.[2] Since I am unable to improve on their solutions in what I consider to be the most important directions, i.e., adequate and explicit treatment of time, depreciation, obsolescence, quality, and other problems of housing market dynamics, I am instead offering this as a provisional hypothesis. Common sense, the excellent theoretical works cited above, and fragmentary evidence support its acceptance; arrayed against it is the opinion of a number of knowledgeable institutional real estate economists and other urban researchers. A really adequate empirical verification or rejection of the hypothesis has yet to be accomplished or even attempted.

The Household's Consumption of Residential Space

It is further assumed that residential space is not an inferior good and that the household chooses its residential location and its consumption of residential space by maximizing the utility obtainable from given income. Thus, the quantity of residential space the household will consume depends on the household's income, the price of residential space, and its preference for residential space. These, along with the assumptions about location rents and journey-to-work costs, are the basic components of the model presented in this paper. It will be seen that, if the household's workplace and transportation costs per mile are taken as given, its residential location can be expressed as a function of its space consumption. Similarly, then, the household's residential location may be expressed as a function of its income, space preference, and the price of residential space. These are the nature of the hypotheses to be tested later in this paper. First, however, it is necessary to spell out the implications of our key assumptions more completely. These key assumptions are (1) the assumption that the household's transportation cost function increases with distance from its workplace, (2) the existence of a market for residential space in which the price per unit a household must pay for residential space of a given quality decreases with distance from its workplace, (3) a fixed workplace, (4) utility maximization on the part of households, and (5) the assumption that residential space is not an inferior good.

The Location Rent Function

The location rent function or schedule of location rents, i.e., the function which describes the decrease in location rents with distance from the household's workplace, describes the savings per unit of residential space the household may achieve by moving farther from its place of employment. What is of interest to the household in making a locational choice, however, is not this amount but its total savings at various distances. If rents per unit of space decrease as the household moves farther from its workplace, the absolute amount of savings possible through longer journeys-to-work depends on the amount of residential space consumed by the household. Since the household's space consumption has not been specified, the decline in total location rents with distance is described by a family of iso-space curves similar to the economist's iso-quants. Each curve in Figure 1, for example, illustrates the decline in location rents with distance for a given quantity of residential space. From Figure 1, it can be seen that the absolute dollar savings obtainable by a longer journey-to-work clearly become larger as more residential space is consumed. By way of contrast, the household's transportation costs per mile, $t(d)$, are invariant with the amount of residential space consumed.

FIGURE 1
Total Iso-Location Rent Curves

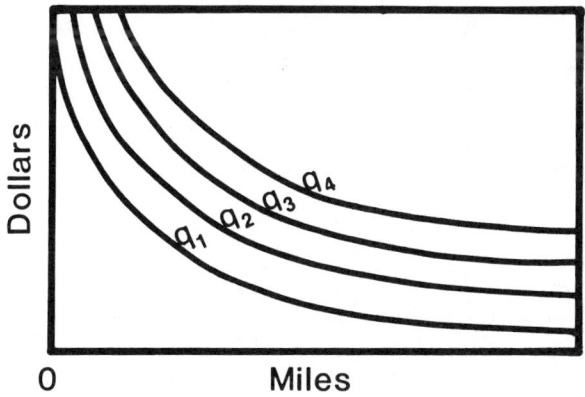

It is, however, the combined outlay for transportation costs and location rents that ought to concern the household in selecting a residential site. Since a given dollar spent for transportation or rents has the same disutility, the household's utility maximization combination of the two is included in the set which minimizes the combined outlay for rents and transportation costs for each quantity of residential space.

Marginal Savings in Location Rents and Marginal Increases in Transportation Costs

The characteristics of the solution we seek can perhaps be more easily understood if we use functions which describe the changes in each of these substitutable costs with the household's distance from its workplace. Figure 2 illustrates the incremental savings in location rents obtained by commuting an additional unit of distance for each quantity of space. The area under each curve is equal to the total location rents that would have to be paid by the household if it were to reside at its workplace and if it were to consume the quantity of space specified by a given curve. Since this function describes the

FIGURE 2
Marginal Location Rent and Transportation Cost Functions

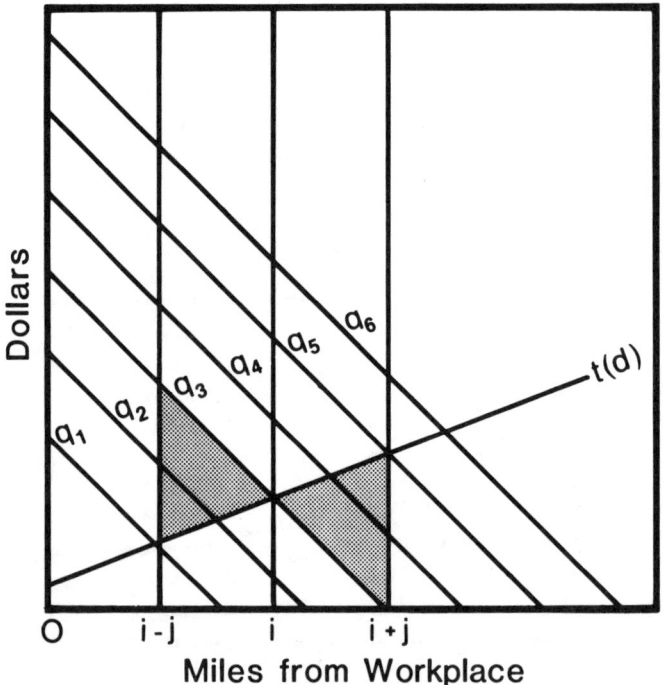

The Journey-to-Work

manner in which total location rents decrease, the area under each curve to the right of *oi* equals the total monthly location rents that must be paid to locate at *i* for each quantity of residential space. For example, the area under q_3 to the right of *oi* is paid for the quantity of residential space represented by the curve q_3.

Marginal Transportation Costs

The incremental increase in transportation costs can be illustrated in the same manner. The line *t(d)* in Figure 2 shows the incremental increase in transportation costs with distance. The area under the curve *t(d)* to the left of *oi* is equal to the expenditures for the journey-to-work required to reside at *oi*.

The minimum cost location for each quantity of residential space is given by the intersection of the marginal cost of transportation function and each of the marginal location rent savings functions. For q_3 the minimum cost location is at *oi*. For larger quantities of residential space, the minimum cost location is farther from the household's workplace; for smaller quantities, nearer.

This solution can be easily verified by using Figure 2. Locations farther from the workplace, say *oi + j*, add the area between *oi* and *oi+j* under the *t(d)* curve to the household's transportation costs. Its savings in location rents amount only to the area under q_3 between *oi* and *oi +j*. Thus, the household's total location costs for the quantity of residential space q_3 are increased by the shaded area under *t(d)* between *oi* and *oi + j*.

Similarly, if the household locates closer to its workplace, say *oi - j*, it reduces its transportation costs by the area under the *t(d)* curve between *oi - j* and *oi*. At the same time, it increases its rental expenditures by the quantity under the q_3 curve between *oi - j* and *oi*. Thus, the household consuming the quantity of residential space q_3 and residing at *oi - j* rather than *oi*, makes uneconomic expenditures for location which equal the shaded area between *oi - j* and *oi*.

Thus, we have obtained those locations which minimize the household's locational costs for each quantity of residential space. In addition, we have obtained the household's required expenditures for each quantity of residential space. This is all the information needed to obtain a unique locational solution for each household.

Total location costs divided by the quantity of residential space is the price the household must pay per unit for residential space. With this price information the household's locational solution is straightforward. Given the price of all other goods and services, the household's preference for residential space, its preference for all other goods and services, and its income, the household's consumption of residential space is uniquely determined. Knowing its consumption of residential space, we have uniquely determined its residential location.

EMPIRICAL TESTING

At the beginning of this paper, I stated that the purpose of this model is to provide some testable hypotheses. The variables employed in the model are location rents at each site and transportation costs per mile, from which we obtained a third variable, the price of residential space; incomes; preferences for residential space; and preferences for all other goods and services. I have already stated my willingness to specify the shape of the location rent function. Money costs of transportation are fairly straightforward. The valuation of time is complex. In the empirical tests presented here it is assumed that similar households place the same valuation on time per mile. Preferences are always difficult to quantify, but we can offer some propositions about the relative space preferences of various classes of households. It is reasonable to assume, for example, that larger households, such as those with children, have higher preferences for space than do smaller households. Since I assume that residential space is not an inferior good, the consumption of residential space will increase with income.

Data for the empirical tests presented here were obtained from the origin and destination study conducted in 1953 by the Detroit Area Traffic Study. The data consist of the origins and destinations of worktrips, information on the characteristics of the workers making these trips, information on the characteristics of the households to which the trip-maker belonged, and certain attributes of the trips themselves, for a stratified random sample of approximately 40,000 Detroit households.

The Location Rent Surface for Detroit

For empirical testing of the residential location model, the Detroit metropolitan area is divided into concentric distance rings, numbered from one to six from the center outward, around the central business district. It is assumed that location rents for a unit of residential space of a given quality and amenity successively decrease from ring to ring outward from the center, with rents very high near the center and very low near the outer circumference. The rate of decrease is assumed to be substantial in the inner rings and very slight in the outer. The surface in the outer rings is assumed to be quite flat, and to decrease only moderately with distance from the central business district.

These assumptions about the shape of the location rent surface are obtained from our premises about the determinants of the surface. It was stated earlier that location rents result from the competition among many workers for residential space near the same workplace or other workplaces nearby. The number of workers employed within each ring may be thought of as representing the number of demanders for residential space within the ring, and the number of acres within the ring as the supply of residential space. Ring 1 includes only 0.2 percent of the available space within the study area, but provides jobs for nearly 11 percent of Detroit's workers. Detroit has 60 percent of its employment located within six miles of the central business district, but only 10 percent of the land within the study area is located there. This indicates a substantial excess demand for space within the close-in rings, and a substantial lessening of demand for space in outer rings. The relatively low level of demand for urban use in the outermost ring is indicated by the large proportion of land which is not in urban use within the ring. A full 68 percent of the available land in Ring 6 is vacant; if land devoted to streets and alleys were subtracted, this figure would be even higher.

Thus it is reasonable to expect that location rents in the central business district and nearby would be very high, while in Ring 6 they would be very low. The high level of demand for residential space in inner rings is indicated by the high employment—and, for that matter, high residential densities. The low level of demand for residential space in outer levels is indicated by low employment densities, low residential densities, and the large quantities of vacant land within these rings.

The Analysis

If workers stratified according to income, sex, race, family size, residential density, or structure type have a common workplace, i.e., the same location rent function, the residential location model would predict different distributions of residence around this workplace for each of these groups. At the same time, the model would predict differences in the residential distribution of the same class of worker, if the workers are employed at different workplaces, i.e., have different location rent functions. For the empirical tests presented in this section, the residential distributions of different classes of workers employed within the same ring, having by assumption the same location rent function, are compared with distributions expected *a priori* from the model. In addition, the residential distributions of workers belonging to the same class but employed at different workplaces, i.e., having different location rent functions, are compared for consistency with the expected relationships.

The first finding which supports the appropriateness of the residential location model is a well-known one. The journey-to-work is predominantly from outer residential rings to inner workplace rings. Furthermore, the proportion of a ring's workers residing within the same or adjacent rings increases with the workplace ring's distance from the central business district.

In terms of the model described above, equal transportation costs are incurred with movement in any direction. Reductions in location rents are to be found only away from the central business district. As a result, the minimization of location rents is always obtained in the direction of the periphery regardless of the household's space consumption. Secondly, as the schedule of location rents flattens out toward the periphery, the space consumption of households becomes less of a constraint and higher proportions of the workplace's employees live nearby. The model's only justification for a journey-to-work is to reduce the household's total expenditures for location rents. If, as hypothesized for Rings 5 and 6, total location rents do not decrease as the household makes a longer journey-to-work, or decrease only slightly, there is little incentive to make a journey-to-work, at least to economize on rents. Thus, the direction of the journey-to-work is from residences in outer rings where location rents are low to workplaces in inner rings; and larger proportions of worktrips are made to nearby rings as the workplace's distance from the central business district increases.

The distribution of elapsed time spent by workers employed in each ring in reaching work also exhibits the expected relationship. The fewest short trips are made by workers employed in the central business district. Few workers employed in Rings 5 and 6 make long trips. For example, 49 percent of workers employed in the central business district make trips more than one-half hour long. By way of contrast, only 17 percent of those employed in Ring 6, where the location rent surface is hypothesized as being nearly horizontal from the workplace, make trips of longer than a half-hour. The proportion is even lower for Ring 5: 14 percent. If it is assumed that the distribution of travel time valuations, money costs of transportation, incomes, space preferences, etc., are similar for each workplace ring, the model would predict longer journeys-to-work by workers employed in inner rings than for those employed in outer rings. The longer journeys-to-work made by Ring 6 workers are explained by the fact that much of Ring 6 is rural. Workers employed in isolated establishments within the ring may have to make substantial journeys-to-work to obtain an adequate selection of housing.

These results may seem trivial as tests of the appropriateness of the residential location model. It should be noted, therefore, that the empirical results for nonwhites, who because of housing market segregation are unable to compete freely in the market for residential space as we defined it, are exactly the opposite. The longest trips by Detroit nonwhites are made by those employed in outer rings and the shortest by those employed in inner rings. Similarly the journey-to-work pattern of nonwhites employed in outer rings is from residences in inner rings to workplaces in outer rings. If this economic model lacked relevance, or if residential location resulted entirely from some socioeconomic clustering as many urban sociologists and real estate market analysts have suggested, these regularities would not have to

The Journey-to-Work

exist. Distributions similar to those observed for nonwhites might be the rule rather than the exception.

Male-Female Differences in Work-Residence Patterns

The work-residence patterns of all workers conceal important differences among the various classes of workers. An understanding of these differences is important for a satisfactory explanation of the relationships between the journey-to-work and the selection of a residential location. Among these is a significant difference in the ring-to-ring movement of male and female workers. Table 2 compares the proportions of males and females residing in each distance ring, by ring of employment.

TABLE 2
Proportion of Males and Females Residing in Each Distance Ring by Ring of Employment

Employment Ring	Sex	Distance Ring						Total
		1	2	3	4	5	6	
One	Male	4.8%	9.9%	25.0%	26.8%	23.2%	10.2%	100%
	Female	2.6	15.6	38.0	25.8	12.9	5.0	100
Two	Male	1.0	19.1	31.2	22.9	17.1	8.6	100
	Female	0.8	23.2	39.2	20.9	11.0	4.6	100
Three	Male	0.8	11.3	36.9	24.0	16.9	10.1	100
	Female	0.4	9.7	46.9	25.3	12.5	5.1	100
Four	Male	0.5	6.4	21.0	32.2	24.2	15.7	100
	Female	0.0	4.0	23.0	44.0	19.8	9.2	100
Five	Male	0.4	2.1	10.2	16.6	50.8	20.0	100
	Female	0.0	1.9	8.7	16.6	53.8	18.9	100
Six	Male	0.5	2.0	6.9	10.1	22.4	58.0	100
	Female	0.2	1.6	3.8	6.1	16.6	71.8	100

From Table 2 it is evident that the residential distribution of males around their workplaces is flatter than that of females. Higher proportions of female workers consistently reside in nearby residential rings than do the proportions of male workers.

The tighter locational pattern of female workers is, in terms of the residential location model, consistent with at least three different hypotheses. The first inference that might be drawn is that the direction of causation assumed in the model is wrong for women workers. It might plausibly be argued that the residence is selected for some unspecified reason, and that the wife and mother has a greater need to find a convenient job near the home. Such an argument would correctly point out that many females, if not most, are secondary wage earners. As such, they tend to seek nearby jobs to augment the family budget, with a more casual attitude in job seeking than that of the primary wage earner. As a result, the place of employment generally has less effect on the choice of a residence. This view suggests that women's selection of a place of employment is more conditioned by the selection of residence.

The second interpretation is that females make shorter journeys-to-work because their workplace is the same as or nearby to that of their husbands. Such households have a stronger incentive to shorten the journey-to-work because the combined journey-to-work costs are higher than for households having only a single wage earner.

Finally, it is likely that a disproportionate number of female wage earners belong to households having lower space preference, i.e., to one- or two-person households. For these households both the greater numbers of working wives and the lower space preferences work in favor of shorter journeys-to-work.

OCCUPATIONAL DIFFERENCES IN RESIDENTIAL DISTRIBUTIONS

The model would postulate that if households had the same location rent

FIGURE 3
Proportion of the Central Business District's Low-, Medium-, and High-Income Workers Residing in Each Residential Ring

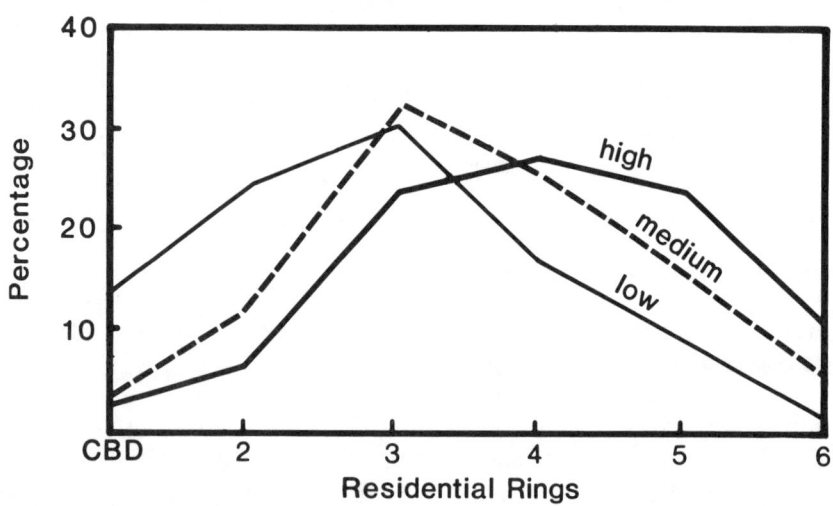

function, the same transportation cost function, the same space preference, and the same valuation of time, but different incomes, the length of the households' journey-to-work would increase as an increasing function of income. The Detroit origin and destination study did not obtain household income, but the occupations of wage earners can be used as a crude measure of household incomes.

Figure 3 shows the proportion of high-, medium-, and low-income central business district workers residing in each residential ring. Clearly, lower-income workers have the tightest residential pattern; the highest income workers, the most dispersed.

Analysis of the Data for Occupations Ranked by Median Income

Similar residential distributions were obtained for Employment Rings 1, 2, and 3, using eight occupational classifications. For workers employed in Ring 4, however, these relationships show signs of weakening. The hypothesized relationships have all but disappeared for Rings 5 and 6—an expected result. Since the location rent function is very flat from workplaces located in Rings 5 and 6, space consumption provides less of a justification for a journey-to-work. Additionally, the lower-income workers retain their tight adhesion to the workplace observed for inner rings. Of the service workers employed in Ring 6, 77 percent reside within the same ring. The proportion is nearly as large for male service workers—75 percent.

The relationships between occupational earnings and the proportion of each occupation residing in each ring may be subjected to a more rigorous test. The proportion of workers employed in each occupation residing in each ring may be ranked by size. Table 3 illustrates these rankings for workers employed in Ring 2. If the hypothesis is correct, the ranks of the proportions residing in that ring should have the opposite order from those of the median earnings of each occupation. A perfect inverse ranking would show that in all cases, as the median income increases, the proportion of the occupation residing in a residence ring would decrease. This represents the expected pattern for rings near the workplace, where rents decrease significantly with distance from the workplace. A perfect ordering in the opposite direction is expected for Rings 5 and 6. The proportions of the occupation's members residing in Ring 6 should decrease as the average income of the occupation decreases.

It can be seen in Table 3 that although the order generally accords with the hypothesis, it is not perfect, the imperfection being that lower percentages of sales workers and clerical workers reside in inner rings than their incomes would lead us to expect. By contrast, a higher proportion of operatives and craftsmen resides in inner rings than is consistent with their income rankings. The ordering is also very good for residence Rings 5 and 6. If the above two

TABLE 3
Ranked Residential Distributions for Occupational Groups Employed in Ring

Occupation	Median Income	Residence Ring								
		2		3		4		5		6	
		%	Rank	%	Rank	%	Rank	%	Rank	%	Rank
Managers	$4516	10.6	8	28.8	7	28.8	2	27.4	1	8.5	4
Professionals	4099	12.0	7	27.0	8	29.5	1	22.0	2	8.6	2.5
Craftsmen	3715	19.1	4	29.6	6	24.2	3	16.0	4	10.6	1
Operatives	3002	24.9	3	37.9	1	16.8	7	13.1	6	6.4	6
Salesworkers	2792	15.4	6	33.5	4	24.1	4	18.4	3	8.6	2.5
Clerical	2706	18.0	5	36.3	3	23.2	5	15.3	5	6.5	5
Laborers	2690	34.3	2	30.5	5	18.1	6	6.8	7	6.2	7
Services	2262	35.0	1	36.5	2	15.4	8	6.1	8	2.6	8

pairs of occupations were exchanged, the order of occupational incomes and the rank of the percentage residing in Ring 5 would be identical. This is a systematic discrepancy for all workplace rings. The operatives group is consistently out of order. Only operatives of the four highest income occupations reside in inner rings at higher-than-average proportions and outer residential rings at below-average proportions. This apparent discrepancy can be largely explained in terms of differences in female participation by occupation mentioned earlier. For this reason we will present results both for all workers and for males only. For the analysis of ranked data which follows, the data for each of the six workplace rings are arranged as in Table 3.

The Spearman Coefficient of Rank Correlation provides a powerful and efficient tool for evaluating the degree of association among these ranked relationships. The Spearman Rank Order Correlation Technique is interpreted in a way similar to that applied to the usual correlation technique. For the relationships among these sets of ranked data to be consistent with our *a priori* expectations, the following relationships would have to be exhibited.

The inner employment rings best satisfy the assumptions about the schedule of location rents set forth in the model; therefore, in the innermost three rings, the proportion of an occupation residing in a given ring should be negatively correlated with income. For outer residential rings there should be a high positive correlation between these occupational groups ranked according to median income and ranked according to the proportion of each residing in the residential ring. As the workplace's distance from the urban center increases, the relationship should deteriorate. This would be observed empirically by a decrease in the size of the coefficient of rank correlation for both inner and outer residential rings, and perhaps a nonuniform change of sign in many cases. Where the ring of employment and ring of residence are

The Journey-to-Work

the same, it is expected that the relationship would always be negative, because low-income workers are small space consumers and thus make shorter journeys-to-work. Tables 4 and 5 give the coefficients of rank correlation between occupation and the percentage of that occupation residing in the ring for all six employment rings, for all workers and for males.

TABLE 4
Rank Order Coefficients Between Occupations
Ranked by Income and Occupations
Ranked by Rate of Residential Selection,
for All Employment and Residence Rings: All Workers

Employment Ring	Residence Ring				
	2	3	4	5	6
CBD	-0.86*	-0.74*	0.69	0.83*	0.98*
2	(-0.81)*	-0.67	0.83*	0.89*	0.71*
3	-0.50	(-0.64)	0.76*	0.88*	0.76*
4	-0.57	-0.71	(-0.48)	0.88*	0.89*
5	-0.47	0.04	0.29	(-0.33)	0.19
6	-0.33	0.21	0.42	0.90*	(-0.61)

Note: Figures are in parenthesis where residence and employment rings are the same.
* Differs significantly from zero at the 0.05 level.

TABLE 5
Rank Order Coefficients Between Occupations
Ranked by Income and Occupations Ranked by Rate of Residential Selection,
for All Employment and Residence Rings: Male Workers Only

Employment Ring	Residence Ring					
	1	2	3	4	5	6
CBD	(-0.69)	-0.81*	-0.74	0.57	0.95*	0.95*
2		-0.50	-0.55	0.88*	0.88*	0.90*
3		-0.76*	(-0.95)*	0.95*	0.86*	0.83*
4		-0.88*	-0.57	(-0.17)	0.48	0.19
5		-0.43	0.29	0.29	(-0.38)	0.38
6		-0.40	0.36	0.36	0.81	(-0.40)

Note: Figures are in parenthesis where residence and employment rings are the same.
* Differs significantly from zero at the 0.05 level.

The coefficients in Tables 4 and 5 are generally as expected. Reading the tables from left to right, i.e., from inner residential rings to outer residential rings, the coefficients change from high negative correlations to high positive correlations. Reading from top to bottom, i.e., from inner workplace rings to outer, the relationship tends to weaken. Where the residence and workplace rings are the same, the figures are in parenthesis; these are the diagonal elements in Tables 4 and 5. The expected pattern for these rings also materializes; lower-income workers reside in above average proportions in these rings, i.e., the journey-to-work typically becomes shorter as income falls.

The overall consistency of the pattern indicates that the locational selections of household by occupation are generally consistent with the model of residential location.

Family Size by Residence Ring

The relationships between family size and residence are neither as uniform nor as simple to interpret as those between sex and residence and occupation and residence. Family size is employed at this point as an indicator of household space preferences. Larger families undoubtedly spend a greater proportion of their time in the home, using it for a far broader range of social and recreational activities. As a result, it is expected that these households, *ceteris paribus*, would manifest a greater preference for residential space.

At the same time, residential space beyond minimum requirements is to some extent a luxury. When families reach a very large size, the greater desire to consume space is probably partially offset by a lower per capita income. The minimum levels of food, clothing and other necessities require a larger

TABLE 6
Cumulative Percentages of Ring 1 Workers Residing in Rings 1 Through 6, by Family Size

Family Size (No. Persons)	Residence Ring					
	1	2	3	4	5	6
1	26.1%	55.6%	86.0%	97.8%	98.5%	100%
2	2.5	14.8	50.3	76.2	93.4	100
3		9.7	39.8	69.3	90.5	100
4	0.4	10.2	38.8	68.8	90.8	100
5		9.8	35.7	67.3	89.5	100
6		11.2	52.0	77.0	93.4	100
More than 6		15.9	46.8	70.7	92.1	100
All	3.7	16.1	46.8	72.9	91.4	100

Source: Tabulated from Detroit Study Deck.

The Journey-to-Work

proportion of the household budget. Thus, there appears to be some tendency for the space consumption of households to fall off as family size increases beyond a certain point.

The Family-Size Residence Pattern for Inner Employment Rings. Tables 6 and 7 show the cumulative percentages of those employed in Rings 1 and 2 who reside in Rings 1 through 6. From Table 6 it can be seen that the proportion of one-person families residing in inner rings is substantially higher than that of any other family unit size. The cumulative percentages residing in Rings 2, 3, 4, and 5 fall as family size increases, until a family size of five persons is reached. For families of six or more, the relationship reverses itself. The proportion of six-person families residing in inner rings exceeds the proportions for all family groups except those having more than six persons or unrelated individuals.

TABLE 7
Cumulative Percentages of Ring 2 Workers Residing in Rings 1 through 6, by Family Size

Family Size (No. Persons)	Residence Ring					
	1	*2*	*3*	*4*	*5*	*6*
1	9.7%	59.7%	87.1%	94.6%	98.9%	100%
2	0.8	22.6	56.4	79.8	93.0	100
3		16.7	51.1	74.7	93.3	100
4	0.1	15.8	48.9	73.5	91.2	100
5	0.1	17.3	48.3	70.7	89.4	100
6		19.2	53.6	75.0	89.7	100
More than 6	1.4	21.6	58.6	79.2	90.8	100
All	1.0	21.1	54.2	76.6	92.2	100

Source: Tabulated from Detroit Study Deck.

The decreasing proportion of central business district workers residing in inner rings, as family size increases, is consistent with a higher space preference on the part of these households. A higher space preference, *ceteris paribus*, leads to a greater consumption of space and a longer journey to work.

The reversal of the relationship for households having more than five members is consistent with their lower per capita income. Beyond a certain size, the greater space preference is offset for many very large families by an income constraint. Household demand for other needed goods and services causes them to forego higher space consumption.

Table 7 shows that these relationships hold for Employment Ring 2 as well, with only one unimportant difference: from Rings 3 through 6 the cumulative percentage of families having more than six persons falls below that of six-person families. The percentage still exceed all but those of one- and two-person families, however.

Family Size by Ring of Residence—Outer Employment Rings. In the outer employment rings, we should expect either a reversal of the pattern observed in Rings 1 and 2 or no discernible relationship between family size and residential location. Table 8 shows that one- and two-person families employed in Ring 5 tend to reside in inner rings in the highest proportions of all family-unit sizes. Because of the lower space requirements, living closer to the central business district is less costly for them than for those having higher space preferences. To state that the higher location rents are less of a constraint for these households fails, however, to provide any reason that smaller families should be more willing to pay higher location rents or make a longer journey-to-work in order to reside nearer the center. The more incomplete specification of the transportation costs of these households provides such an explanation.

TABLE 8
Cumulative Percentages of Ring 5 Workers Residing in Rings 6 through 1, by Family Size

Family Size (No. Persons)	Residence Ring					
	1	*2*	*3*	*4*	*5*	*6*
1	100%	89.1%	78.3%	52.3%	32.6%	10.0%
2	100	99.8	96.6	83.9	63.6	20.9
3		100.0	98.3	85.6	67.8	19.7
4		100.0	98.0	89.2	72.0	23.1
5		100.0	98.8	92.5	72.5	21.2
6		100.0	99.2	88.8	73.1	27.1
More than 6		100.0	97.6	86.6	70.9	26.6
All	100	99.5	97.2	86.2	67.4	22.5

Source: Tabulated from Detroit Study Deck.

It is logical to expect that many of these households make above-average numbers of trips to social and recreational centers located in or near the central business district. Their locational choices, therefore, would be heavily weighted by these trips. This should be true for one-person families as well. Unfortunately, one-person households employed in Ring 6 exhibit the tightest locational pattern of all families but those having more than five persons. One-person households employed in Ring 5 exhibit the expected behavior. From Table 8 it can be seen that only 33 percent of those employed in Ring 5 reside either in it or in Ring 6. By contrast, 64 percent of two-person households and 73 percent of six-person families reside in one of these two rings.

The Journey-to-Work

Also, it is likely that a large proportion of two-person families have a second wage earner. If the second member of the household is employed in an inner ring, this provides an added incentive for the household to live closer to the center. It should be remembered, for all family sizes, that only small proportions of those employed in Rings 5 and 6 live in Rings 1, 2, and 3.

The final relationship exhibited by Tables 8 and 9 is an increase in the proportion of a ring's employees residing nearby the workplace as family size increases. This finding is also consistent with the lower per capita incomes of larger families. When changes in total location rents with distance are slight, minimization of transportation costs results in the minimization of total locational costs. Households with lower per capita incomes may be more sensitive to small differences in transportation costs.

TABLE 9
Cumulative Percentages of Ring 6 Workers Residing in Rings 6 Through 1, by Family Size

Family Size (No. Persons)	Residence Ring					
	1	2	3	4	5	6
1	100%	93.7%	84.3%	81.1%	79.0%	66.8%
2	100	99.7	96.5	88.0	76.1	56.3
3		100.0	98.7	92.3	81.7	62.7
4		100.0	93.8	93.1	83.5	58.4
5		100.0	97.8	93.4	85.5	62.6
6		100.0	99.6	92.9	90.0	66.4
More than 6		100.0	99.4	95.1	87.3	66.7
All	100	99.6	97.6	91.4	82.2	61.0

Source: Tabulated from Detroit Study Deck.

Family Size by Ring of Residence—Rings 3 and 4. Above-average proportions of the very large and very small households employed in Rings 3 and 4 reside in rings near the center. Families with three to six members reside in higher proportions in Rings 5 and 6. The closeness in locational patterns of one- and two-person families employed in Rings 3 and 4 is even more reasonable than is that of the same size families employed in Rings 5 and 6.

Suburban living must be far less attractive to the young married or the childless couple than to those with children; their social and recreational activities are to a much greater degree directed outside the home. For the unattached person, residence in a suburban neighborhood far from the center of activity is even more unsatisfactory.

No adequate explanation in terms of the model can be offered for the locational choices of the very large families. In the case of Employment Ring 4, the divergence is great enough that a larger proportion of its workers reside in Ring 3 than in Ring 5. Even so, more workers reside in the two rings away from the central business district than reside in those nearer the central business district.

Space Consumption by Residential Ring

The model of residential location postulates that where location rents are a significant factor, households consuming larger quantities of space will, *ceteris paribus*, make longer journeys to work than those consuming lesser quantities. The distance the household resides from its workplace is expressed in the model as a function of the quantity of residential space consumed. The relationship between space consumption and length of the journey to work, like that between income and the length of the journey, should deteriorate for outer employment rings, where the schedule of rents decreases only slightly or not at all around the workplace.

TABLE 10
Percentage of Inner Employment Ring Workers Residing in Each Ring, by Structure Type

STRUCTURE TYPE	Residence Ring						
	1	2	3	4	5	6	Total
Percentage of Ring 1 (CBD) Workers							
One-family	-	5.4%	22.1%	29.8%	28.9%	13.8%	100%
Two-family	-	13.1	46.7	32.8	5.8	1.5	100
Multiple	2.4	29.5	50.2	14.7	2.1	1.1	100
All	3.8	12.6	31.1	26.3	18.4	7.8	100
Percentage of Ring 2 Workers							
One-family	-	8.7%	25.5%	28.1%	25.1%	12.5%	100%
Two-family	0.2	26.2	46.8	21.4	4.0	1.4	100
Multiple	1.2	43.6	43.4	9.3	1.7	0.7	100
All	1.0	20.1	34.1	22.4	15.6	7.7	100
Percentage of Ring 3 Workers							
One-family	-	5.3%	27.0%	29.7%	24.1%	13.9%	100%
Two-family	0.1	13.8	60.0	21.4	3.7	1.0	100
Multiple	0.8	25.2	59.9	11.2	2.0	0.8	100
All	0.7	10.9	39.3	24.3	15.9	0.9	100

Source: Tabulated from Detroit Study Deck.

In this paper, structure type is employed as a measure of space consumption. This is an admittedly inadequate index, especially for single-family dwelling units, where the index fails to differentiate between very significant differences in lot size. Regardless of these deficiencies, structure type undoubtedly represents a dimension of the space consumption relationship. It is probably roughly correlated with the measure of space consumption we would wish to employ. For this reason, we will look at the relationships between residential location and occupancy of single-family, two-family, or multifamily dwellings.

The Residence-Space Consumption Pattern for Inner Employment Rings. Table 10 shows the percentages of workers occupying each type of dwelling unit in each residence ring, for Employment Rings, 1, 2, and 3. As might be expected, those choosing higher density structures—two-family dwelling units and multiple dwellings—reside in well-above-average proportions in the close-in residential rings. For example, 30 percent of central business district workers who live in multiple dwelling units reside in the adjacent ring. In contrast, the adjacent ring is selected by only 5 percent of those choosing single-family structures and 13 percent of those selecting two-family structures. This pattern persists through Ring 3, where 50 percent of all central business district workers who live in multiple dwelling units reside. Ring 3 also provides dwellings for 47 percent of those residing in two-family units, as opposed to only 22 percent of those residing in one-family units.

The proportion of those residing in multiple and two-family units in Residence Rings 5 and 6, on the other hand, is very low. Less than 2 percent in each case live in Ring 6.

The Residence-Space Consumption Pattern for Outer Employment Rings. The differential pattern of residence by structure type for outer workplace rings is also in basic conformity with the model. These patterns are shown in Table 11. A large proportion of these residents of all three structure types reside in their workplace rings or adjacent rings. Employment Ring 6 encompasses the residences of 64 percent of all single-family households, 40 percent of the two-family households, and 52 percent of households choosing multiple units, who work in that ring. Where the rent schedule is relatively flat, as in Ring 6, we would postulate a short journey to work regardless of space consumption. In the case of Employment Rings 4 and 5, a similar pattern exists: the residential distribution is tighter than for inner rings, but less tight than for Ring 6. Figure 4 illustrates the contrast in those distributions for Rings 2 and 6. In terms of the model, households employed in Ring 6 tend to live nearby, regardless of space consumption. Those employed in Ring 2, by comparison, tend to live nearby only if they consume limited quantities of residential space. They tend to make a journey to work from outer rings if they consume larger quantities of residential space. Very few of those consuming small quantities of space live in Rings 4, 5, and 6.

TABLE 11
Percentage of Outer Employment Ring Workers Residing in Each Ring, by Structure Type

STRUCTURE TYPE	Residence Ring						
	1	2	3	4	5	6	Total

Percentage of Ring 4 Workers

One-family	-	2.6%	13.4%	34.2%	30.7%	19.1%	100%
Two-family	-	8.2	39.4	42.8	7.1	2.5	100
Multiple	-	21.5	43.2	25.5	5.1	4.7	100
All	0.5	6.0	21.4	34.5	23.3	14.4	100

Percentage of Ring 5 Workers

One-family	-	.7%	6.0%	16.3%	51.8%	25.1%	100%
Two-family	-	5.2	27.0	31.8	30.2	5.9	100
Multiple	-	12.9	34.4	24.2	17.9	10.5	100
All	0.3	2.2	10.5	18.4	46.8	21.8	100

Percentage of Ring 6 Workers

One-family	-	.8%	3.4%	7.3%	24.0%	64.5%	100%
Two-family	-	3.2	21.2	25.7	10.2	39.8	100
Multiple	-	9.8	18.2	10.3	9.5	52.2	100
All	0.4	2.0	6.2	9.2	21.2	61.0	100

Source: Tabulated from Detroit Study Deck.

Somewhat larger proportions of those employed in Ring 6, and consuming small amounts of space, reside in interior rings.

Income and Substitution Effect

It was pointed out previously that in terms of the way the problem is formulated in this paper, the price of residential space is determined by location rents and transportation costs. As a result, the households employed in inner rings, confronted by higher and steeper schedules of location rents, must pay a higher price for residential space than must be paid by those employed in outer rings. If the assumption of similar incomes, tastes, and transportation costs for those employed in each successive ring is reasonably

FIGURE 4
Percentage of Ring 2 and Ring 6 Workers Residing in Each Ring, by Structure Type

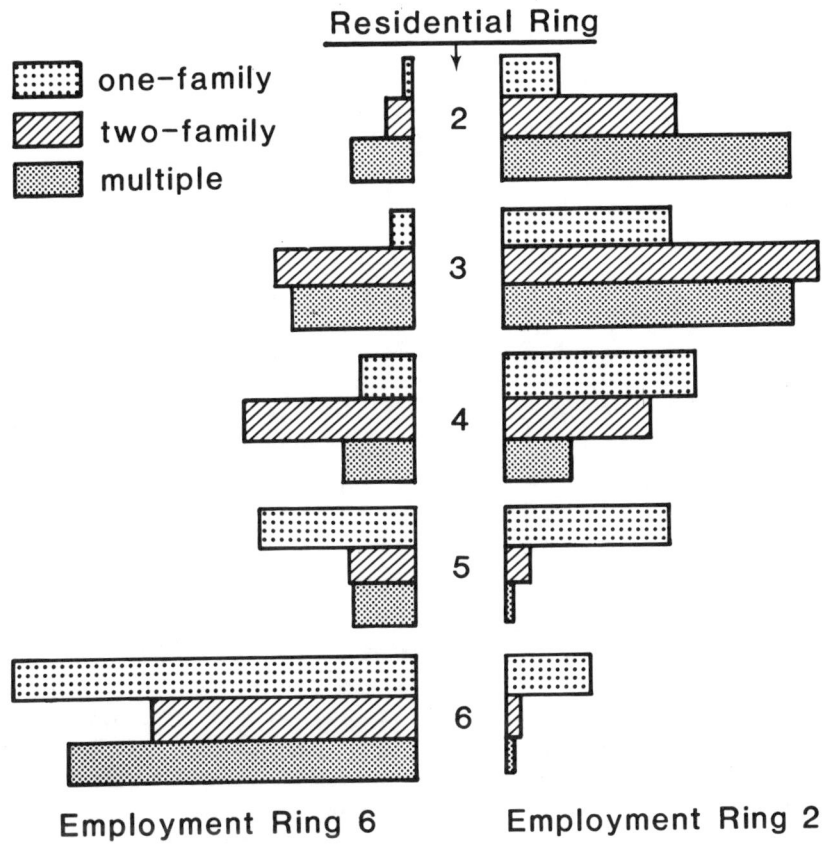

adequate, it would be expected *a priori* that the relatively lower price of residential space for those in outer rings would lead to higher space consumption.

From Table 12 it can be seen that this pattern generally holds. A smaller proportion of central business district workers and those employed in Ring 2 reside in single-family units. A larger proportion select two-family and multiple units. The proportion employed in Rings 5 and 6 living in one-family structures in turn exceeds those for Rings 3 and 4. Similarly, the proportion residing in multiple and two-family living quarters is smaller.

TABLE 12
Percentage Residing in Each Structure Type, by Employment Ring

STRUCTURE TYPE	Employment Ring					
	1	2	3	4	5	6
One-family	58.4%	56.9%	60.6%	69.0%	79.2%	78.1%
Two-family	18.2	21.7	20.8	18.4	11.8	10.4
Multiple	17.4	17.2	15.4	10.4	6.9	7.5
Other	5.9	4.2	3.2	2.4	2.2	4.0
Total	100.0	100.0	100.0	100.0	100.0	100.0

Source: Tabulated from Detroit Study Deck.

DERIVED DEMAND FOR RESIDENTIAL SERVICES

There is one final question which should be considered briefly. A large number of researchers have emphasized the role of good schools and public services, and the supply of new and high-quality dwelling units, in determining residential location.

It is an empirical fact that the mean quality level of the housing stock, and most likely of government services, increases with distance from the central business district. My intuition, based partially on the findings presented here and those of related research, is that an explanation of residential location in these terms is at best an oversimplification and at worst may be basically incorrect. It is my belief that housing quality is less of a determinant of residential choices than are collective residential choices a determinant of the quality of housing services and of the quality of governmental services. Among other things, the theory developed in this paper predicts a spatial distribution of demand for residential space by different income groups. If the demand for housing quality and quality of governmental services is a derived demand, the distribution of quality predicted by my model and to some extent supported by the evidence presented in this paper would be very similar to that observed empirically. This leads me to the tentative conclusion that observed distribution of housing quality is the result of the long run operation of an admittedly imperfect market, but one which is possibly less imperfect than often supposed.

There is one major exception to my remarks: racial discrimination represents a major market imperfection which distorts the spatial demand for residential space by both whites and nonwhites.

CONCLUSIONS

This paper presents a simple economic theory of residential location and evaluates this theory with data on residential distributions for Detroit whites employed in six concentric rings around Detroit's central business district. These same six distance rings are also used as the residential subareas in the analysis. I have hypothesized that workers employed in each ring face different housing costs, transport costs and trade-offs than workers employed in every other ring. These differences arise from the fact that the schedule of prices per unit of urban space in each differs with distance and direction from the workplace. As a result, differences in the length of the journey to work and in the locational choices of workers employed in each ring may be understood only when the characteristics of the metropolitan schedule of location rents is specified. For Detroit, it is reasonable to assume that the surface of location rents tends to decrease with distance from the central business district, and that the rate of decrease is greatest near the center and least near the periphery.

In addition, although housing quality was not explicitly included as a variable in the empirical work, I offered some conjectures about the relationships between the distribution of housing quality and the selection of residential locations by households.

The empirical findings are generally in conformity with those expected *a priori* from the model of residential location. This model would predict that, where the market for residential space has the characteristics ascribed to the inner rings in Detroit, households will locate at varying distances from their workplaces according to their transportation costs, space consumption, space preferences, and incomes.

The empirical analysis revealed that the commuting pattern was largely from residences in outer rings to workplaces in inner rings, that the average length of the journey-to-work decreased with the workplace's distance from the central business district, and that the proportion of a ring's workers residing in the same or nearby rings increased as the workplace ring's distance from the central business district increased.

Workers employed in higher-income occupations and working in inner rings tend to make longer journeys-to-work and reside in outer rings. When employed in outer rings they make much shorter journeys-to-work and live within the same ring and adjacent rings at very high rates. Low income workers make short journeys-to-work and reside within the workplace ring and in nearby rings regardless of the location of workplace.

Family size as an indicator of space preference has a similar effect on residential location. The smallest and largest families make the shortest journeys-to-work. For the smallest families, I attributed this to low space preferences; the shorter journeys-to-work by the largest families I attributed to a per capita income constraint.

Structure type is used as a measure of the household's space consumption. The longest journeys to work are made by those residing in one-family units and the shortest by those residing in multiple units. A marked difference between the locational choices of males and females was discovered. Female workers, regardless of workplace ring, make shorter journeys-to-work than male workers and reside within the workplace ring and nearby rings in much higher proportions. Finally, it was determined that the proportion of workers residing in low-density structures increased as the workplace ring's distance from the central business district increased.

All the relationships summarized above are very clear cut for rings near the central business district, where the location rent function with distances from the workplace is believed to be very steep. For peripheral workplace rings, where the function is probably very flat, the relationships are much weaker.

In summary, the evidence presented in this paper bears out the appropriateness of the theoretical framework employed. The findings are generally consistent with our *a priori* views on the problem as obtained both from this model and similar models by Alonso, Wingo, and others. The issues evaluated in this chapter are still far from settled, however, and will remain so until we are able to take into account more explicitly the dynamics of the housing market both in our models and our empirical work.

NOTES

1. See, for example, Edgar M. Hoover and Raymond Vernon, *Anatomy of a Metropolis* (Cambridge, Mass.: Harvard University Press, 1959); William Alonso, "A Theory of the Urban Land Market," in *Papers and Proceedings of the Regional Science Association* (Philadelphia, Pa: University of Pennsylvania, 1960); John D. Herbert and Benjamin H. Stevens, "A Model for the Distribution of Residential Activity in Urban Areas," *Journal of Regional Science* 2, No. 2 (Fall 1960); Lowdon Wingo, Jr., *Transportation and Urban Land* (Washington, D.C.: Resources for the Future, 1961); Ira South Lowry, "Residential Location in Urban Areas" (unpublished Ph.D. dissertation, Department of Economics, University of California, 1960).

2. Alonso, *Urban Land Markets*; Wingo, *Transportation and Urban Land*.

II
Human Ecology

4

Human Ecology

Robert Ezra Park

I. THE WEB OF LIFE

Naturalists of the last century were greatly intrigued by their observation of the interrelations and co-ordinations, within the realm of animate nature, of the numerous, divergent, and widely scattered species. Their successors, the botanists, and zoologists of the present day, have turned their attention to more specific inquiries, and the "realm of nature," like the concept of evolution, has come to be for them a notion remote and speculative.

The "web of life," in which all living organisms, plants and animals alike, are bound together in a vast system of interlinked and interdependent lives, is nevertheless, as J. Arthur Thompson puts it, "one of the fundamental biological concepts" and is "as characteristically Darwinian as the struggle for existence."[1]

Darwin's famous instance of the cats and the clover is the classic illustration of this interdependence. He found, he explains, that humblebees were almost indispensable to the fertilization of the heartsease, since other bees do not visit this flower. The same thing is true with some kinds of clover. Humblebees alone visit red clover, as other bees cannot reach the nectar. The inference is that if the humblebees became extinct or very rare in England, the heartsease and red clover would become very rare, or wholly disappear. However, the number of humblebees in any district depends in a great measure on the number of field mice, which destroy their combs and nests. It is estimated that more than two-thirds of them are thus destroyed all over England. Near villages and small towns the nests of humblebees are more numerous than elsewhere and this is attributed to the number of cats that destroy the mice. Thus next year's crop of purple clover in certain parts of England depends on the number of humblebees in the district; the number of humblebees depends upon the number of field mice, the number of field mice upon the number and the enterprise of the cats, and the number of cats—as someone has added—depends on the number of old maids and others in neighboring villages who keep cats.

These large food chains, as they are called, each link of which eats the other, have as their logical prototype the familiar nursery rhyme, "The House that Jack Built." You recall:

> The cow with the crumpled horn,
> That tossed the dog,
> That worried the cat,
> That killed the rat,
> That ate the malt
> That lay in the house that Jack built.

Darwin and the naturalists of his day were particularly interested in observing and recording these curious illustrations of the mutual adaptation and correlation of plants and animals because they seemed to throw light on the origin of the species. Both the species and their mutual interdependence, within a common habitat, seem to be a product of the same Darwinian struggle for existence.

It is interesting to note that it was the application to organic life of a sociological principle—the principle, namely, of "competitive co-operation"—that gave Darwin the first clue to the formulation of his theory of evolution.

"He projected on organic life," says Thompson, "a sociological idea," and "thus vindicated the relevancy and utility of a sociological idea within the biological realm."[2]

The active principle in the ordering and regulating of life within the realm of animate nature is, as Darwin described it, "the struggle for existence." By this means the numbers of living organisms are regulated, their distribution controlled, and the balance of nature maintained. Finally, it is by means of this elementary form of competition that the existing species, the survivors in the struggle, find their niches in the physical environment and in the existing correlation or division of labor between the different species. J. Arthur Thompson makes an impressive statement of the matter in his *System of Animate Nature*. He says:

> The hosts of living organisms are not . . . isolated creatures, for every thread of life is intertwined with others in a complex web . . . Flowers and insects are fitted to one another as hand to glove. Cats have to do with the plague in India as well as with the clover crop at home . . . *Just as there is a correlation of organs in the body, so there is a correlation of organisms in the world of life.* When we learn something of the intricate give and take, supply and demand, action and reaction between plants and animals, between flowers and insects, between herbivores and carnivores, and between other conflicting yet correlated interests, we begin to get a glimpse of a vast self-regulating organization.

These manifestations of a living, changing, but persistent order among competing organisms—organisms embodying "conflicting yet correlated interests"—seem to be the basis for the conception of a social order transcending the individual species, and of a society based on a biotic rather than a cultural basis, a conception later developed by the plant and animal ecologists.

In recent years the plant geographers have been the first to revive something of the earlier field naturalists' interest in the interrelations of species. Haeckel, in 1878, was the first to give to these studies a name, "ecology," and by so doing gave them the character of a distinct and separate science, a science which Thompson describes as "the new natural history."

The interrelation and interdependence of the species are naturally more obvious and more intimate within the common habitat than elsewhere. Furthermore, as correlations have multiplied and competition has decreased, in consequence of mutual adaptations of the competing species, the habitat and habitants have tended to assume the character of a more or less completely closed system.

Within the limits of this system the individual units of the population are involved in a process of competitive co-operation, which has given to their interrelations the character of a natural economy. To such a habitat and its inhabitants—whether plant, animal, or human—the ecologists have applied the term "community."

The essential characteristics of a community, so conceived, are those of: (1) a population, territorially organized, (2) more or less completely rooted in the soil it occupies, (3) its individual units living in a relationship of mutual interdependence that is symbiotic rather than societal, in the sense in which that term applies to human beings.

These symbiotic societies are not merely unorganized assemblages of plants and animals which happen to live together in the same habitat. On the contrary, they are interrelated in the most complex manner. Every community has something of the character of an organic unit. It has a more or less definite structure and it has "a life history in which juvenile, adult and senile phases can be observed."[3] If it is an organism, it is one of the organs which are other organisms. It is, to use Spencer's phrase, a superorganism.

What more than anything else gives the symbiotic community the character of an organism is the fact that it possesses a mechanism (competition) for (1) regulating the numbers, and (2) preserving the balance between the competing species of which it is composed. It is by maintaining this biotic balance that the community preserves its identity and integrity as an individual unit through the changes and the vicissitudes to which it is subject in the course of its progress from the earlier to the later phases of its existence.

II. THE BALANCE OF NATURE

The balance of nature, as plant and animal ecologists have conceived it, seems to be largely a question of numbers. When the pressure of population upon the natural resources of the habitat reaches a certain degree of intensity, something invariably happens. In the one case the population may swarm and relieve the pressure of population by migration. In another, where the disequilibrium between population and natural resources is the result of some change, sudden or gradual, in the conditions of life, the pre-existing correlation of the species may be totally destroyed.

Change may be brought about by a famine, an epidemic, or an invasion of the habitat by some alien species. Such an invasion may result in a rapid increase of the invading population and a sudden decline in the numbers if not the destruction of the original population. Change of some sort is continuous, although the rate and pace of change sometimes vary greatly. Charles Elton says:

> The impression of anyone who has studied animal numbers in the field is that the "balance of nature" hardly exists, except in the minds of scientists. It seems that animal numbers are always tending to settle down into a smooth and harmonious working mechanism, but something always happens before this happy state is reached.[4]

Under ordinary circumstances, such minor fluctuations in the biotic balance as occur are mediated and absorbed without profoundly disturbing the existing equilibrium and routine of life. When, on the other hand, some sudden and catastrophic change occurs—it may be a war, a famine, or pestilence—it upsets the biotic balance, breaks "the cake of custom," and releases energies up to that time held in check. A series of rapid and even violent changes may ensue which profoundly alter the existing organization of communal life and give a new direction to the future course of events.

The advent of the boll weevil in the southern cotton fields is a minor instance but illustrates the principle. The boll weevil crossed the Rio Grande at Brownsville in the summer of 1892. By 1894 the pest had spread to a dozen counties in Texas, bringing destruction to the cotton and great losses to the planters. From that point it advanced, with every recurring season, until by 1928 it had covered practically all the cotton producing area in the United

Human Ecology

States. Its progress took the form of a territorial succession. The consequences to agriculture were catastrophic but not wholly for the worse, since they served to give an impulse to changes in the organization of the industry long overdue. It also hastened the northward migration of the Negro tenant farmer.

The case of the boll weevil is typical. In this mobile modern world, where space and time have been measurably abolished, not men only but all the minor organisms (including the microbes) seem to be, as never before, in motion. Commerce, in progressively destroying the isolation upon which the ancient order of nature rested, has intensified the struggle for existence over an ever widening area of the habitable world. Out of this struggle for a new equilibrium and a new system of animate nature, the new biotic basis of the new world-society is emerging.

It is, as Elton remarks, the "fluctuation of numbers" and "the failure" from time to time "of the regulatory mechanism of animal increase" which ordinarily interrupts the established routine, and in so doing releases a new cycle of change. In regard to these fluctuations in numbers Elton says:

> These failures of the regulating mechanism of animal increase—are they caused by internal changes, after the manner of an alarm clock which suddenly goes off, or the boilers of an engine blowing up, or are they caused by some factors in the outer environment—weather, vegetation, or something like that?

and he adds:

> It appears that they are due to both but that the latter (external factor) is the more important of the two, and usually plays the leading role.

The conditions which affect and control the movements and numbers of populations are more complex in human societies than in plant and animal communities, but they exhibit extraordinary similarities.

The boll weevil, moving out of its ancient habitat in the central Mexican plateau and into the virgin territory of the southern cotton plantations, incidentally multiplying its population to the limit of the territories and resources, is not unlike the Boers of Cape Colony, South Africa, trekking out into the high veldt of the central South African plateau and filling it, within a period of one hundred years, with a population of their own descendants.

Competition operates in the human (as it does in the plant and animal) community to bring about and restore the communal equilibrium, when, either by the advent of some intrusive factor from without or in the normal course of its life-history, that equilibrium is disturbed.

Thus every crisis that initiates a period of rapid change, during which competition is intensified, moves over finally into a period of more or less stable equilibrium and a new division of labor. In this manner competition brings about a condition in which competition is superseded by cooperation.

It is when, and to the extent that, competition declines that the kind of order which we call society may be said to exist. In short, society, from the ecological point of view, and in so far as it is a territorial unit, is just the area within which biotic competition has declined and the struggle for existence has assumed higher and more sublimated forms.

III. COMPETITION, DOMINANCE AND SUCCESSION

There are other and less obvious ways in which competition exercises control over the relations of individuals and species within the communal habitat. The two ecological principles, dominance and succession, which operate to establish and maintain such communal order as here described are functions of, and dependent upon, competition.

In every life-community there is always one or more dominant species. In a plant community this dominance is ordinarily the result of struggle among the different species for light. In a climate which supports a forest the dominant species will invariably be trees. On the prairie and steppes they will be grasses.

> Light being the main necessity of plants, the dominant plant of a community is the tallest member which can spread its green energy-trap above the heads of the others. What marginal exploitation there is to be done is an exploitation of the dimmer light below this canopy. So it comes about in every life-community on land, in the cornfield just as in the forest, that there are layers of vegetation, each adapted to exist in a lesser intensity of light than the one above. Usually there are but two or three such layers; in an oak-wood for example there will be a layer of moss, above this herbs or low bushes, and then nothing more to the leafy roof; in the wheat-field the dominating form is the wheat, with lower weeds among its stalks. But in tropical forests the whole space from floor to roof may be zoned and populated.[5]

But the principle of dominance operates in the human as well as in the plant and animal communities. The so-called natural or functional areas of a metropolitan community—for example, the slum, the rooming-house area, the central shopping section and the banking center—each and all owe their existence directly to the factor of dominance, and indirectly to competition.

The struggle of industries and commercial institutions for a strategic location determines in the long run the main outlines of the urban community. The distribution of population, as well as the location and limits of the residential areas which they occupy, are determined by another similar but subordinate system of forces.

The area of dominance in any community is usually the area of highest land values. Ordinarily there are in every large city two such positions of highest land value—one in the central shopping district, the other in the central banking area. From these points land values decline at first precipitantly and then more gradually toward the periphery of the urban community. It is these land values that determine the location of social institutions and business enterprises. Both the one and the other are bound up in a kind of territorial complex within which they are at once competing and interdependent units.

As the metropolitan community expands into the suburbs the pressure of professions, business enterprises, and social institutions of various sorts destined to serve the whole metropolitan region steadily increases the demand for space at the center. Thus not merely the growth of the suburban area, but any change in the method of transportation which makes the central business area of the city more accessible, tends to increase the pressure at the center. From thence this pressure is transmitted and diffused, as the profile of land values discloses, to every other part of the city.

Thus the principle of dominance, operating within the limits imposed by the terrain and other natural features of the location, tends to determine the general ecological pattern of the city and the functional relation of each of the different areas of the city to all others.

Dominance is, furthermore, in so far as it tends to stabilize either the biotic or the cultural community, indirectly responsible for the phenomenon of succession.

The term "succession" is used by ecologists to describe and designate that orderly sequence of changes through which a biotic community passes in the course of its development from a primary and relatively unstable to a relatively permanent or climax stage. The main point is that not merely do the individual plants and animals within the communal habitat grow but the community itself, i.e., the system of relations between the species, is likewise involved in an orderly process of change and development.

The fact that, in the course of this development, the community moves through a series of more or less clearly defined stages is the fact that gives this development the serial character which the term "succession" suggests.

The explanation of the serial character of the changes involved in succession is the fact that at every stage in the process a more or less stable equilibrium is achieved, which in due course, and as a result of progressive changes in life-conditions, possibly due to growth and decay, the equilibrium achieved in the earlier stages is eventually undermined. In such case the energies previously held in balance will be released, competition will be intensified, and change will continue at a relatively rapid rate until a new equilibrium is achieved.

The climax phase of community development corresponds with the adult phase of an individual's life.

> In the developing single organism, each phase is its own executioner, and itself brings a new phase into existence, as when the tadpole grows the thyroid gland which is destined to make the tadpole state pass away in favour of the miniature frog. And in the developing community of organisms, the same thing happens— each stage alters its own environment, for it changes and almost invariably

enriches the soil in which it lives; and thus it eventually brings itself to an end, by making it possible for new kinds of plants with greater demands in the way of mineral salts or other riches of the soil to flourish there. Accordingly bigger and more exigent plants gradually supplant the early pioneers, until a final balance is reached, the ultimate possibility for that climate.[6]

The cultural community develops in comparable ways to that of the biotic, but the process is more complicated. Inventions, as well as sudden or catastrophic changes, seem to play a more important part in bringing about serial changes in the cultural than in the biotic community. But the principle involved seems to be substantially the same. In any case, all or most of the fundamental processes seem to be functionally related and dependent upon competition.

Competition, which on the biotic level functions to control and regulate the interrelations of organisms, tends to assume on the social level the form of conflict. The intimate relation between competition and conflict is indicated by the fact that wars frequently, if not always, have, or seem to have, their source and origin in economic competition which, in that case, assumes the more sublimated form of a struggle for power and prestige. The social function of war, on the other hand, seems to be to extend the area over which it is possible to maintain peace.

IV. BIOLOGICAL ECONOMICS

If population pressure, on the one hand, cooperates with changes in local and environmental conditions to disturb at once the biotic balance and social equilibrium, it tends at the same time to intensify competition. In so doing it functions, indirectly, to bring about a new, more minute and, at the same time, territorially extensive division of labor.

Under the influence of an intensified competition, and the increased activity which competition involves, every individual and every species, each for itself, tends to discover the particular niche in the physical and living environment where it can survive and flourish with the greatest possible expansiveness consistent with its necessary dependence upon its neighbors.

It is in this way that a territorial organization and a biological division of labor, within the communal habitat, is established and maintained. This explains, in part at least, the fact that the biotic community has been conceived at one time as a kind of superorganism and at another as a kind of economic organization for the exploitation of the natural resources of its habitat.

In their interesting survey, *The Science of Life*, H. G. Wells and his collaborators, Julian Huxley and G. P. Wells, have described ecology as "biological economics," and as such very largely concerned with "the balances and mutual pressures of species living in the same habitat."

"Ecology," as they put it, is "an extension of Economics to the whole of life." On the other hand the science of economics as traditionally conceived, though it is a whole century older, is merely a branch of a more general science of ecology which includes man with all other living creatures. Under the circumstances what has been traditionally described as economics and conceived as restricted to human affairs, might very properly be described as Barrows some years ago described geography, namely as human ecology. It is in this sense that Wells and his collaborators would use the term.

> The science of economics—at first it was called Political Economy—is a whole century older than ecology. It was and is the science of social subsistence, of needs and their satisfactions, of work and wealth. It tries to elucidate the relations of producer, dealer, and consumer in the human community and show how the whole system carries on. Ecology broadens out this inquiry into a general study of the give and take, the effort, accumulation and consumption in every province of life. Economics, therefore, is merely Human Ecology, it is the narrow and special study of the ecology of the very extraordinary community in which we live. It might have been a better and brighter science if it had begun biologically.[7]

Since human ecology cannot be at the same time both geography and economics, one may adopt, as a working hypothesis, the notion that it is neither one nor the other but something independent of both. Even so the motives for identifying ecology with geography on the one hand, and economics on the other, are fairly obvious.

From the point of view of geography, the plant, animal, and human population, including their habitations and other evidence of man's occupation of the soil, are merely part of the landscape, of which the geographer is seeking a detailed description and picture.

On the other hand ecology (biologic economics), even when it involves some sort of unconscious co-operation and a natural, spontaneous, and non-rational division of labor, is something different from the economics of commerce; something quite apart from the bargaining of the market place. Commerce, as Simmel somewhere remarks, is one of the latest and most complicated of all the social relationships into which human beings have entered. Man is the only animal that trades and traffics.

Ecology, and human ecology, if it is not identical with economics on the distinctively human and cultural level is, nevertheless, something more than and different from the static order which the human geographer discovers when he surveys the cultural landscape.

The community of the geographer is not, for one thing, like that of the ecologist, a closed system, and the web of communication which man has spread over the earth is something different from the "web of life" which binds living creatures all over the world in a vital nexus.

V. SYMBIOSIS AND SOCIETY

Human ecology, if it is neither economics on one hand nor geography on the other, but just ecology, differs, nevertheless, in important respects from plant and animal ecology. The interrelations of human beings and interactions of man and his habitat are comparable but not identical with interrelations of other forms of life that live together and carry on a kind of "biological economy" within the limits of a common habitat.

For one thing man is not so immediately dependent upon his physical environment as other animals. As a result of the existing worldwide division of labor, man's relation to his physical environment has been mediated through the intervention of other men. The exchange of goods and services has co-operated to emancipate him from dependence upon his local habitat.

Furthermore man has, by means of inventions and technical devices of the most diverse sorts, enormously increased his capacity for reacting upon and remaking, not only his habitat but his world. Finally, man has erected upon the basis of the biotic community an institutional structure rooted in custom and tradition.

Structure, where it exists, tends to resist change, at lease change coming from without; while it possibly facilitates the cumulation of change within. In plant and animal communities structure is biologically determined, and so far as any division of labor exists at all it has a physiological and instinctive basis. The social insects afford a conspicuous example of this fact, and one interest in studying their habits, as Wheeler points out, is that they show the extent to which social organization can be developed on a purely physiological and instinctive basis, as is the case among human beings in the natural as distinguished from the institutional family.[8]

In a society of human beings, however, this communal structure is reinforced by custom and assumes an institutional character. In human as contrasted with animal societies, competition and the freedom of the individual is limited on every level above the biotic by custom and consensus.

The incidence of this more or less arbitrary control which custom and consensus impose upon the natural social order complicates the social process but does not fundamentally alter it—or, if it does, the effects of biotic competition will still be manifest in the succeeding social order and the subsequent course of events.

The fact seems to be, then, that human society, as distinguished from plant and animal society, is organized on two levels, the biotic and the cultural. There is a symbiotic society based on competition and a cultural society based on communication and consensus. As a matter of fact the two societies are merely different aspects of one society, which, in the vicissitudes and changes to which they are subject remain, nevertheless, in some sort of mutual dependence each upon the other. The cultural superstructure rests on the basis of the symbiotic substructure, and the emergent energies that manifest themselves on the biotic level in movements and actions reveal themselves on the higher social level in more subtle and sublimated forms.

However, the interrelations of human beings are more diverse and complicated than this dichotomy, symbiotic and cultural, indicates. This fact is attested by the divergent systems of human interrelations which have been the subject of the special social sciences. Thus human society, certainly in its mature and more rational expression, exhibits not merely an ecological, but an economic, a political, and a moral order. The social sciences include not merely human geography and ecology, but economics, political science, and cultural anthropology.

It is interesting also that these divergent social orders seem to arrange themselves in a kind of hierarchy. In fact they may be said to form a pyramid of which the ecological order constitutes the base and the moral order the apex. Upon each succeeding one of these levels, the ecological, economic, political, and moral, the individual finds himself more completely incorporated into and subordinated to the social order of which he is a part than upon the preceding.

Society is everywhere a control organization. Its function is to organize, integrate, and direct the energies resident in the individuals of which it is composed. One might, perhaps, say that the function of society was everywhere to restrict competition and by so doing bring about a more effective co-operation of the organic units of which society is composed.

Competition, on the biotic level, as we observe it in the plant and animal communities, seems to be relatively unrestricted. Society, so far as it exists, is anarchic and free. On the cultural level, this freedom of the individual to compete is restricted by conventions, understandings, and law. The individual is more free upon the economic level than upon the political, more free on the political than the moral.

As society matures control is extended and intensified and free commerce of individuals restricted, if not by law then by what Gilbert Murray refers to as "the normal expectation of mankind." The mores are merely what men, in a situation that is defined, have come to expect.

Human ecology, in so far as it is concerned with a social order that is based on competition rather than consensus, is identical, in principle at least, with plant and animal ecology. The problems with which plant and animal ecology have been traditionally concerned are fundamentally population problems. Society, as ecologists have conceived it, is a population settled and limited to its habitat. The ties that unite its individual units are those of a free and natural economy, based on a natural division of labor. Such a society is territorially organized and the ties which hold it together are physical and vital rather than customary and moral.

Human ecology has, however, to reckon with the fact that in human society competition is limited by custom and culture. The cultural superstructure imposes itself as an instrument of direction and control upon the biotic substructure.

Reduced to its elements the human community, so conceived, may be said to consist of a population and a culture, including in the term culture (1) a body of customs and beliefs and (2) a corresponding body of artifacts and technological devices.

To these three elements or factors—(1) population, (2) artifacts (technological culture), (3) custom and beliefs (non-material culture)—into which the social complex resolves itself, one should, perhaps, add a fourth, namely, the natural resources of the habitat.

It is the interaction of these four factors—(1) population, (2) artifacts (technological culture), (3) custom and beliefs (non-material culture), and (4) the natural resources—that maintains at once the biotic balance and the social equilibrium, when and where they exist.

The changes in which ecology is interested are the movements of population and of artifacts (commodities) and changes in location and occupation—any sort of change, in fact, which affects an existing division of labor or the relation of the population to the soil.

Human ecology is, fundamentally, an attempt to investigate the processes by which the biotic balance and the social equilibrium (1) are maintained once they are achieved and (2) the processes by which, when the biotic balance and the social equilibrium are disturbed, the transition is made from one relatively stable order to another.

NOTES

1. *The System of Animate Nature* (Gifford Lectures, 1915-16), II (New York, 1920), 58.
2. J. Arthur Thompson, *Darwinism and Human Life* (New York, 1911), p.72.
3. Edward J. Salisbury, "Plants," *Encyclopedia Britannica* (14th ed.).
4. "Animal Ecology," *ibid.*
5. H.G. Wells, Julian S. Huxley, and G.P. Wells, *The Science of Life* (New York, 1934), pp. 968-69.
6. *Ibid.*, pp. 977-78.
7. H.H. Barrows, "Geography as Human Ecology," *Annals Association American Geographers,* XIII (1923), 1-14. See H.G. Wells, *et al., op. cit.,* pp. 961-62.
8. William Morton Wheeler, *Social Life Among the Insects* (Lowell Institute Lectures, March 1922), pp.3-18.

5

Toward a More Human Human Ecology: An Urban Research Strategy

Harvey L. Molotch

TWO SYSTEMS OF COMPETITION

Influenced by such theorists as Park and Hawley, contemporary ecologists and city planners have tended to view the metropolis and its sub-areas as habitats and the deployment of urban people as the end result of a geographic competition amongst land users.[1] It is generally presumed that certain areas of the landscape are more desirable than are others—a condition which leads to a competition amongst potential land users with "victory" going to that land user who utilizes the contested urban space most intensively. The "victor" becomes the "dominant" area force which determines the conditions to which contiguous "sub-dominants" must adapt if there is to be coexistence in the same larger habitat.

The process is seen as a dynamic one; areas change in the kind of use to which they are put as the struggle for urban space continues. This basic theoretical outlook has been the origin of various explanations of city development—the best known being the Burgess Concentric Zonal Hypothesis.[2] The Burgess theory and similar explanations[3] have led to a description of city areas in terms of shifting land uses caused by an ever-intensifying competition for strategic urban spaces. In light of the elegance of the theories which have been proposed it has been unfortunate that there have been so many cases unveiled of cities and city areas which do not fit the theories.[4]

This paper proposes that the failure of such explanations of urban development are rooted in a very incomplete view of the nature of the association which exists between modern man and specific parcels of urban land. The classical ecology of Park and Hawley is based upon an overdrawn analogy between the natural and the human worlds. By indicating just where the analogy properly ends (at least in terms of relation to habitat) it may be possible to arrive at a more "human" human ecology. In such manner, a more adequate explanation of contemporary metropolitan development and the planning role may be derived.

It is necessary at the outset to confront the basic premise upon which the human ecologist operates: the validity of the analogy between human beings seeking a place to live, shop or invest, and animals (and plants) "seeking" a place to procreate, scavenge and nest. The difficulty is that once people of the metropolis relate themselvs to a certain area, their fortunes and futures become dependent upon the fate of the geographical unit to which they have become attached. In a sense, the same may be true of plant and animal communities. But the significant difference is that plants and animals do not *cognize* the fact that their future and the future of their community habitat are intimately intertwined. Despite the existence of behavior based upon territoriality, animals and plants are in a much poorer position to unite in action to maintain and enhance a shared geographical unit.

Humans have an active and self-conscious interest in the future of certain land areas, perhaps because they own a portion or all of a certain land parcel (and thus their very livelihood depends upon its future) or perhaps because they associate certain land areas with a way of life which they either cherish or despise and thus are anxious that the area undergo a future consonant with their own value systems. An example of both is the identification which occurs with one's own residential community; generally this is a positive identification and residents attempt to enhance their own community in the face of threats which they fear may lead to degrading changes.

When residents perceive a shared interest, the result is often the formation of a voluntary association devoted to the enhancement of a certain land parcel. The result may be a block club, a neighborhood improvement association, or a more comprehensive community development organization. Very often the goal of a community organization, especially one located in the declining "grey areas" of cities, is the maintenance of a white middle-class community through the attraction of whites to the area. Such is the case in the community of South Shore on Chicago's South Side—until recent years an all-white, middle-class area, currently in the process of racial transition, but with a strong community organization explicitly committed to a goal of "racial integration" and preservation of the area as a "high quality" community. Thirty semi-structured interviews with community leaders and twenty-five conducted with other residents during the period of June 1965 through December 1965 by this writer have revealed that what is meant by "high quality" and "integration" amongst South Shore whites is the maintenance of the area as middle-class and the retention of as many whites as possible. The residents of South Shore are joined in this goal by the businessmen who operate in the area, and by planners and civic officials in both public and private pronouncements. Such goals have become ubiquitous amongst neighborhood improvement associations operating in metropolitan America.[5]

What has been said of residential areas can also be applied to business areas. Here the function of maintenance and enhancement is fulfilled by the local chamber of commerce or the shopping street association. Like the residential community, such groups depend for their existence upon a certain communality of interests which are associated with a certain geographical area.

The interest which a group has in maintaining and enhancing a geographical unit becomes manifest in a competition with other areas for certain kinds of land users who are regarded as desirable. Because many areas aim to attract the same kinds of land users and because the potential number of such land users is in scarce supply, the conditions for a competitive situation are present. In the case of an area like South Shore—a "grey area" undergoing an economic decline and a transition from white to Negro occupancy—the scarce resource is white, middle-class (or upper-class) residents. The competitors of South Shore are not only other middle-class "grey areas," but also white (or integrated) areas in the central core as well as in the suburbs and outlying unimproved lands which are ripe for development. Which of these areas will be "victorious" is determined by the relative advantages and disadvantages which each has to offer the scarce middle-class white resident.

This competition system is obviously a very different one than that usually described by the classical ecologists and their followers. In order to explain how humans come to deploy themselves over a geographical area, the ecologist focuses upon the competition amongst land users;[6] here the focus is instead upon the competition amongst land areas. The present attempt has been to bring to light one of the competitive systems which seems to be largely ignored—at least in the literature of ecological theory. True, people and land users continue to compete for scarce, desirable or peculiarly strategic urban spaces. But more and more, urban spaces are competing for certain kinds of people and land users. People compete for areas—and areas compete for people. Thus there are two competitive processes occurring simultaneously and interacting with one another.

THE INCREASING SALIENCE OF COMPETITION FOR LAND-USERS

The two processes are present under almost all conceivable conditions: the opening of newly discovered, uninhabited virgin lands would constitute an exception. But despite this common coexistence of the two systems at certain times and at certain places, the significance of one process may loom larger than the other. It is here contended that the American urban situation is characterized to an increasing degree by the ascendency of the competition amongst land areas in shaping urban growth and change.

Two reasons may be cited for the increase in significance of this second competition system. First, the concept and reality of an active community organization is becoming more prevalent on the urban scene. The rise of such organizations has been a response, in part, to a growing awareness amongst residents and land owners in a community of the very competitive process which has just been described. These organizations are typically devoted to "the maintenance of a stable, high quality neighborhood"—or, as a typical more precise goal—of attracting "high quality people" to the area. These organizations, some of which consult with or hire professional planners, seem aware that they are competing with other areas in creating the kind of environment which will attract such kinds of people. Again, in reference to the study of South Shore, local leaders are very much aware of the necessity of achieving more "clout" with civic officials than is possessed by other communities in order to secure the types of civic services and investments which seem necessary to reach the desired goals. The fact that the most expensive high school ever to be constructed in Chicago is being built in South Shore while the city's slum areas make do with more standard facilities is perceived by South Shore leaders as a consequence of the "connections" which accrue to a community with many sophisticated professionals in residence. The case of the University of Chicago-Hyde Park redevelopment project located just to the north of South Shore serves as an example to local respondents of the importance of achieving the "priority" from governmental agencies which can provide an area with a competitive edge over other areas competing for the same kinds of land users.[7]

There is a second reason why the competition amongst land areas is becoming increasingly significant. Not only are there more community organizations and other "land interest groups" today than in the past but the possibilities for effecting basic changes in the conditions of the competition have been greatly enlarged due to new technologies and the increasing scale of governmental intervention. In the Hyde Park case (not an extraordinary one in this regard), a massive infusion of governmental and institutional dollars into the area permitted a remaking of the environment. New parks, the replacement of obsolete housing, the development of modern, convenient shopping areas and extraordinary efforts at code and law enforcement have revived the community by artificially reversing the "natural" processes of urban decay. The area was able to create a new environment because of an initial advantage it possessed in the competition amongst areas for public funds—due in part to the power and wealth of the University of Chicago and people associated with it. The kind of effort which was expended on behalf of Hyde Park-Kenwood was more or less unprecedented in scope. Since that time there have been numerous projects of similar and larger size which have remade sections of the urban environment by harnessing newly found public resources and technologies to effect an area goal. The future promises even more of the same. But even when efforts are more modest and all that is required is a zoning variance or road improvement, the result is similar: areas are modified with the effect of placing them in a more strategic position vis-a-vis the kinds of land users they are attempting to attract. Thus areas are becoming strategic because of man-made capital and "social" improvements—and not because of certain characteristics relative to natural topology or centrality.

IMPLICATIONS FOR THE PLANNING PROCESS

These kinds of renewal efforts as well as other activities which affect the desirability of certain land areas (e.g., improvements in public transportation systems, park and recreational facilities, highways) require at least the cooperation of governmental authorities even in cases where a commitment of public funds is not required. This being the case, it behooves the public authority and the planner in his employ to face the fact that any such investments which are made in a certain area are likely to affect not only the area in which intervention takes place but also all other areas which are in competition with it. The planner is thus not justified in viewing a single community as though it functioned in a vacuum apart from other areas. Taking neighborhood "quality" (as the term is often used by planners and layman alike) to refer primarily to the "quality" of the neighborhood land-user and not the quality of the land and environment, it becomes apparent that a single area has no "natural process" of quality degeneration or regeneration apart from the occurrences in other areas. The planner is thus obliged to refrain from the habit of "regenerating" one area without taking into account the consequences of his action for other areas which are likely to be "degenerated" as a result. By bringing one area to middle-class status, the planner may be relegating a competing area to working-class status. This then is one more reason for "comprehensive" as opposed to "piecemeal" planning and for the creation of objective rationale for such planning. Otherwise, the distribution of environmental resources is determined by the outcomes of power struggles amongst competing land users at the sacrifice of a "public good" yet to be adequately defined. It is of further significance that the contenders within such a power struggle would not be evenly matched; there would be an inherent tendency for those organized land users already possessing a power advantage—the rich, the articulate, the well-connected—to have most influence upon the deployment of public resources. The tendency would thus be toward a reification of existing land use patterns perhaps to the detriment of minority group members and other "have-nots" who have traditionally depended upon instability and change for the betterment of their lot.

A corollary of this argument is that, while the wishes of indigenous citizens and community leaders may be very relevant to planning decisions, the enthusiasm currently felt in some planning circles for giving the people "what they want" needs to be tempered by the realization that the goals of various community groups may be such that they are mutually exclusive. The problem here is not just the omnipresent one of the limited financial resources of the public coffers but rather involves dilemmas of a more subtle sort.

Again, returning to the South Shore example, requests are frequently made to civic agencies for various amenities — amenities which are not desired because they will enhance the quality of life, *per se*, but amenities which are desired because they are perceived to be important to the goal of attracting certain kinds of persons to the area. Since other communities in Chicago have the same goal as South Shore, they make similar kinds of requests. It is important to note that even if public resources were great enough to permit the granting of all such requests, no one community would be any closer to its goal because the goal of each involves a relative advantage over the others rather than the achievement of an absolute level of environmental quality. The point is that not all communities can be middle-class which wish to be middle-class and which are competing to attract middle-class persons. Some will succeed and some will not. The question becomes, in this example, one of determining by what process the resources are to be distributed which ultimately determine the deployment of economic and social groups within the metropolitan area.

In certain contexts then, planners must assert criteria of their own regarding the distribution of land users in a metropolitan area if they are to play any meaningful role whatever. Again in the South Shore instance, it may indeed be appropriate, according to planning criteria, for South Shore, an outlying area proximate to a job-rich heavy industrial region, to be allowed or even *induced* to serve a Negro working-class population with relocation of its present middle-class residents to a different competing area, perhaps to a close-in community contiguous to the control centers of Chicago's loop. In any event, planners are not justified in compounding the power advantages which a community such as South Shore has by dignifying the community's requests with a seal of objective legitimacy purely on the basis that it is "good" for a community to remain "high quality" (middle-class) and it is "good" to give people what they want. In terms of the goals of the larger metropolis the more rational strategy may be a completely different one.

Perhaps planning decisions will always be influenced by power struggles amongst competing community groups or land interests, and it is naive to assume or even hope for something else. Nevertheless, at least whatever weight the planner has can function as an *independent* component within that power struggle. That is, the competition by areas for certain kinds of people will likely continue—given the exigencies of American democracy—but an awareness of the competition by those who make the planning decisions, and thus of the axes which various lobbying groups have to grind, might function to inject an ingredient of rationality into the resource distribution process. The planner should not be seen as a servant of the neighborhood association; rather a practical goal may be to establish the planner as arbiter of conflicting and often mutually exclusive demands on the basis of a professional expertise which can on occasion be brought to bear.

IMPLICATIONS FOR URBAN RESEARCH

It is for the social scientist to examine in detail the system of competition described in order to more fully explain the present and on-going distribution of public resources and patterns of urban land use and to thus provide the basis for a more informed planning process. More specifically, when an investigator focuses upon any land parcel, there is a series of questions which needs to be asked and answered. They can be summarized under seven possible stages of research—given below as suggestions but not intended as a complete list of all such possibilities:

1. *The Nature of the Association Which Exists Between the Land Parcel and People.* Specifically: Who owns the land? What is the type of use to which the land is put? What are the kinds of non-economic interests which various population groups have in the use and future of the parcel?
2. *Form and Strength of the Organization of Those With Shared Interests.* How well organized and what form is the organization which exists amongst those who share a common interest in a parcel? Is there a series of shared interests in harmony or conflict with one another? Are they represented in voluntary organizations? Are such organizations in harmony or in competition with one another?
3. *Nature of the Scarce Resource.* What is the scarce land use or land user which the shared interest is trying or likely to attempt to attract?
4. *Conditions of Competition for the Scarce Resource.* What other land parcels are competing most directly for the same scarce resource? What kinds of power alternatives do the various competitors have in affecting decisions at the public and quasi-public level?
5. *The Competition Mediators.* How are such competitions ordinarily resolved? Which institutions in the larger arena play a role in affecting the outcome? What is the method by which political and other institutions affect the result of

the struggle? How does the structure of such institutional arrangements influence the success of one type of competitor versus another type of competitor?
6. *Available Resources for Intervention.* What is the form and scope of the kinds of interventions which are available in the political sphere and which are relevant to the parcel's future?
7. *Outcome and Effect.* Who gets what, when, and where and with what effect? How do different forms of intervention have differential effects on land use patterns? How do such distributions of public resources affect the relative power of the various combatants of the "battle" when it is over? That is, what effect is the outcome of the "first round" of competition likely to have upon successive rounds?

Answers to such questions as these would go far in explaining not only the social dynamic of a single land parcel but, when applied to a series of such parcels and then viewed cumulatively, would also provide a more comprehensive view of urban life in general.

NOTES

The research upon which this article is based was originally prepared for and presented at the Annual Institute of the Society for Social Research Spring 1966 meeting, Chicago, Illinois. The author acknowledges the helpful critical readings of an earlier draft of this paper by Brian J. L. Berry, Charles Goldsmid, Andrew Greeley, Jack Meltzer, Robert Stauffer, Paul Williams and R. Joyce Whitley.

1. Amos Hawley, *Human Ecology: A Study of Community Structure* (New York, New York: The Ronald Press, 1950).
2. Ernest W. Burgess, "The Growth of the City: An Introduction to a Research Project" in George W. Theodorson, *Studies in Human Ecology* (Evanston, Illinois: Row, Peterson, 1961), pp. 37-45.
3. For a summary of such explanations see, Chauncey D. Harris and Edward L. Ullman, "The Nature of Cities," Paul K. Hatt and Albert J. Reiss, Jr. (Eds.), *Cities and Society* (New York, New York: The Free Press of Glencoe, 1951).
4. For criticisms of the "classical position," see Theodorson, *op. cit.*, Part I, Section B.
5. Zorita Wise Milva, "The Neighborhood Improvement Association: A Counterforce to the Expansion of Chicago's Negro Population," Unpub. M.A. Dissertation, University of Chicago, June 1951.
6. Amos H. Hawley, *Human Ecology: A Study of Community Structure* (New York, New York: The Ronald Press, 1950).
7. For an analysis of the Hyde Park case see, Peter Rossi and Robert Dentler, *The Politics of Urban Renewal: The Chicago Findings* (New York, New York: The Free Press of Glencoe, 1961).

6

Growth, Politics, and the Stratification of Places

John R. Logan

This is an essay on the process of spatial differentiation of human communities. I argue that the differentiation of places implies sets of advantages and disadvantages for persons who are tied to each place and thus affects the chances for individual upward or downward mobility. A common response to this fact is a continuing collective effort to influence the pattern of development among places through political action. Places with early advantages, by making full political use of their superior resources can potentially reinforce their relative position within the system of places. I hypothesize therefore that spatial differentiation tends to be transformed over time into an increasingly rigid stratification of places.

The study of the development of systems of places found its classical formulation in human ecology. By emphasizing the stratification aspect of spatial differentiation, I am proposing a reorientation toward a more political human ecology with spatial differentiation seen not only as the population's natural selective response to its habitat but also as a means of organizing inequality.

From *American Journal of Sociology,* Vol. 84 (September 1978), pp. 404-416. Copyright (1978) by the University of Chicago. Reprinted by permission of the University of Chicago Press and J. Logan.

I. HUMAN ECOLOGY: A CRITICAL NOTE

In this essay I develop an ecological dimension of stratification taking into account the functional interdependence of systems of places. However, the present perspective contrasts in important ways with human ecology as developed by Park and his associates (see Park, Burgess, and McKenzie 1967) especially in my emphasis on the political determinants of territorial differentiation. Zorbaugh ([1926] 1961) specifically discounted the sociological relevance of what he called administrative areas as distinct from natural areas, and this distinction is carried over in Hawley (1950, pp. 258-59). Ecologists need not necessarily exclude political factors: McKenzie ([1926] 1961) in fact counted "political and administrative measures" among the "ecological factors" which shape the spatial relations among persons. Elsewhere (McKenzie 1933, pp. 158-70) he explicitly considered the competition among cities for favorable positions in an increasingly interdependent system of cities and such phenomena as local boosterism and conflicts over federal tax and expenditure policies. Yet even here McKenzie was primarily interested in the economic forces leading toward system integration, seeing political competition as a passing phenomenon and as a rule human ecologists have ignored geopolitical units as corporate groups.

Whereas I stress the effects of collective action by communities in competition with one another, ecological theories of spatial differentiation have been based upon the analysis of the microeconomic competition of individual land users (Park 1936).

These differences are associated with a more basic divergence in perspective on the nature of community growth. The Chicago School sought explicitly to identify the processes of development at the "biotic level," that is, those processes which manifest the response of the human population to the same constraints faced by all living populations. (On this point see the criticisms made by Alihan [1938], Hollingshead [1947], and Firey [1947]). The community was understood as an adaptive mechanism which maximizes the efficient use of space and other resources under the pressure of population growth (Hawley 1950, pp. 66-68).

Assuming free competition for space, resolved according to the relative marginal utility of particular locations for competing land users, ecologists of the Chicago School could assert that the final highly differentiated ordering of space would be the most effective for the population. Thus, in Park's words, the process "results in the regulation of numbers, the distribution of vocations, putting every individual and every race into the particular niche where it will meet the least competition and contribute most to the life of the community" (Park 1952, p. 161). This perspective is complementary to the functionalist theory of class stratification which is by now better known (Davis and Moore 1945). The similarity is visible in Hawley's discussion of the stratification aspect of spatial differentiation where political inequality among places is seen as a natural, system-maintaining consequence of differentiation:

> A hierarchy of power relations emerges among differentiated units. Two consequences of differentiation contribute to that result. In the first place, inequality is an inevitable accompaniment of functional differentiation. Certain functions are by their nature more influential than others; they are strategically placed in the division of labor and thus impinge directly upon a large number of other functions . . . Secondy, mutual supplementation through functional differentiation necessitates a centralization of control. To insure the regular operation of the system there must be a sufficient governing and coordinating power vested in some one function. [Hawley 1950, p. 221]

The point of my discussion of the competition of places is that persons and organizations constantly seek to affect the growth process in order to maintain or create inequalities among places to their own advantage. The consequent stratification of places is therefore constructed by political action. Political, social, and economic inequality among places should be understood not only as the result of differentiation, but also as a cause of the particular pattern of differentiation which evolves. More precisely, the competition among places normally reinforces the existing stratification, because initial advantages—translated into political power—can be maintained.

The hypothesis of increasing stratification of places resulting from political conflict can be explored in a wide variety of cases. I will present two examples here, one at the level of suburban communities in a metropolitan system, the other at the level of nations in the world system. In both cases there is evidence of increasing inequality in recent years.

The data on suburban inequalities are taken from the case of the 89 suburban communities in the Nassau-Suffolk SMSA (Long Island, N.Y.) which were reported in the census in both 1960 and 1970. The indicator of wealth is median family income, which is relevant to both the social status and the fiscal strength of the community. During the period 1960-70, the standard deviation of median incomes—one indicator of the degree of inequality among suburbs—more than doubled. Even with the 1970 value deflated to control for increases in the mean (due to both inflation and real increases in personal income), the standard deviation increased by 58.9 percent, from $2.121 to $3.370 (adjusted) in the 10-year period. Initial differences among suburbs were consolidated and reinforced as a result of the growth process of the 1960s. Elsewhere (Logan 1976) I have shown how such structural changes in the spatial differentiation of the metropolis can be understood in terms of the interaction between competition among potential land users for desirable locations and collective action by communities to promote favorable growth patterns.

The data on international stratification are based on the 88 countries for which information is provided by Banks's (1971) cross-polity survey for both 1956 and 1966. Here the indicator of wealth is gross domestic product (GDP) per capita, a measure of the total goods and services produced by the national economy. During 1956-66 the standard deviation of GDP per capita increased by 34.2 percent, from $469 to $580 (again controlling for changes in the mean). In the section on international migration below, I apply to systems of countries the same theoretical logic by which I have treated systems of communities. At both geopolitical levels, the flow of goods and people among interdependent places affects the relative position of those places in a stratified order creating the conditions for politicization of the development process.

II. THE BASES AND PROCESSES OF THE POLITICS OF PLACE

I have asserted that patterns of territorial differentiation can be understood as stratified systems reflecting the power relations among places. In the following sections I develop this proposition theoretically considering the relationship between the stratification of places and other dimensions of social stratification, the modes of aggregation and expression of place-based interests and the relationship of the stratification and competition of places to the social system in which they are embedded.

My purpose at this point is not to propose a theory of places, but rather to put forward as a general orienting concept the notion of places as collective actors.

Class, Status, and Place

The uses of spatial relationships to express the class and status differences among individuals are well known. Physical proximity often represents social similarity or intimacy in face-to-face interaction. Even whole cities have been shown to be structured partly according to this principle, as the degree of residential segregation of class and status groups is directly associated with differences in their social position (Duncan and Duncan 1955; Lieberson 1961; Guest and Weed 1976): "The urban neighborhood becomes a highly visible manifestation of the status structure and individual occupational careers come to be mirrored in one's residential movements. A home is not just where you live; it is a location in a well-developed status ecology and, inferentially, a telltale clue to one's location in the occupational hierarchy" (Laumann, Siegel, and Hodge 1970, p. 524; see also Barber 1957, pp. 144-46).

Residential segregation creates a status hierarchy of neighborhoods defined simply by the characteristics of their residents, at the same time as common class or status becomes a symbol through which people identify their physical area as a community. The status hierarchy of places is reinforced by people's individual decisions to translate upward social mobility into change of place of residence.

But the spatial organization of persons is more than a representation of class and status differences acquired by birth, education, etc. Place of residence itself affects the chances for social rewards to the degree that persons are tied to the advantages and disadvantages of places—for example, opportunities of employment and housing, level of income, cost of living, public services and tax rates, and legal rights and obligations. Like class and status groupings, and more substantially than many other kinds of associations, places are "communities of fate" (Stinchcombe 1965). Among others in the study of community, Molotch (1967, pp. 336-37) has emphasized the notion that "once people of the metropolis relate themselves to a certain area, their fortunes and futures become dependent upon the fate of the geographical unit to which they have become attached." More recently, Spilerman and Habib (1976) have shown that the stratification of types of communities reinforces the class stratification between established residents and recent migrants within Israeli society. This is not simply to argue the case for contextual effects (i.e., that one's aspirations and behavior are constrained by interpersonal relations within close, homogeneous communities). There are characteristics definable at the level of a place itself—consequences of the place's economic and political relations with other places—which directly affect the quality of life and life chances of residents. Place is therefore a partially autonomous dimension of stratification in the same sense as the more familiar dimensions of class and status.

Competition of Places

It is because their fortunes are directly affected by the inequalities among places that persons and organizations continuously attempt to influence the development process through political action. Such action takes the form of efforts to determine the goals of local growth policies as well as competition among places to affect decision making at higher geopolitical levels. In either case, interests of place are commonly aggregated according to the territorial boundaries of politically defined places. Such boundaries bind together the many otherwise divergent elements within places. A "place" then is defined as much by its position in a particular web of political institutions (such as boundaries and constitutionally determined legal powers) as by the physical area it occupies. That is, whatever the inherent physical and population characteristics of naturally defined communities, these characteristics become resources and liabilities for residents according in part to the political organization of society.

Illustrations of this point are numerous. The concentration of employment in some suburban communities is a resource if public services are financed through local property taxes and if zoning can be used to externalize service burdens by forcing many local employees to live elsewhere. Ghettoization in the metropolitan core is a liability to central cities if welfare costs are borne by the city: therefore urban-based individuals and groups have pressed hard for federal takeover of these costs. Discovery of oil in Alaska benefits that state if it can tax mineral resources, it benefits Chicago if the federal government can be made to mandate a Trans-Canadian Pipeline to distribute the oil to the Midwest, or it benefits California and Japan if oil companies are free to choose a more profitable Trans-Alaskan route. The physical resources of Angola became a benefit to that territory only after decolonization, and production of commodities for export is being converted from a liability to a resource only to the degree that Third World countries organize effective international cartels.

In conflicts over boundaries, constitutional powers, allocations of public resources, taxation policies, land use controls, etc., places compete for development outcomes which would maintain or improve their relative position in the hierarchy of places. More precisely, coalitions of local interests—recruited and organized along territorial lines determined by political boundaries—compete for outcomes in which coalition partners have a mutual interest, even when at another level their interests may diverge. This is not to say that all internal groups have the same interest in development or that all are equally represented in the definition of local goals. A large research literature on local and national power structures suggests quite the opposite. My point here is that, by providing a communality of interests among internal groups, place accounts for political behavior which cannot be understood in terms of class conflict (e.g., the cooperation of banks, municipal unions, and city government to forestall bankruptcy of New York City). Granted that appeals to national patriotism or local pride are sometimes manipulated as ideological symbols to defuse internal conflict, people and organizations are in fact bound together by the places in which they live or have invested. To this extent it is meaningful to analyze the development process in terms of the competition of places.

Because places tend to be functionally differentiated from one another it may be difficult to distinguish between those common interests of local persons and organizations which derive from place and those which derive from economic sector. "Downtown" and the "ghetto," "Detroit" and "the Farm Belt" are all place designations which carry a clear functional connotation. The fortunes of almost everyone in Detroit, for example, depend upon the fortunes of the automobile industry. Probably the common interests of Detroiters are more powerfully represented by General Motors than by the Detroit city government. Thus the competition of places is closely tied to intersectoral conflicts which are channeled through major business or labor organizations. In principle, however, these are two quite different bases of political action. Intersectoral conflicts correspond to the interest group politics traditionally studied in political science. They become relevant to the competition of places insofar as (1) they affect spatial differentiation, (2) they become understood and acted upon as issues of place, or (3) the definition of local interests is imposed by the organization which controls the local economy, so that local government becomes an instrument of intersectoral conflict.

Social Movements of Place

I have argued that systems of place become ordered partly as a result of competition among places which represents really the search for locational advantages by persons and organizations. That is, the growth process is an interaction of social movements, protecting territory or advancing claims for collective advantage, simultaneously within and among communities (see Molotch [1976, p. 311] and Harvey [1973, pp. 72-73], for statements of a similar position).

The shifting coalitions of political actors referred to here have at least some of the characteristics of social movements even when they do not involve public mobilization. The most important in my view is that the diverse members of these coalitions act to promote the *collective* good in which they share. Sometimes, nonetheless, issues of the competition of place give rise to or reinforce broad popular movements. In these cases the movements are strengthened by the normal overlap of stratification of place with the geographic segregation of persons by class and status. The development process which causes places to be differentiated from one another on the bases of class and status has consequences for the actualization of these classic bases of collective action. Place may so overlap with class and status (race, religion, culture, language) that it may provide an ecological support for organization as well as a symbolic sense of community, at the same time as being itself an objective basis for common action. Berry et al. (1976), noting the common use of place of residence to support the "status claims" of individuals, use this fact to explain the frequency and intensity of solidary action by community residents in opposition to racial integration. Similar reasoning could be applied to movements against busing between white and black neighborhoods, or to apartment construction in single-family areas. Blauner (1969) attributes ghetto revolt to a corresponding protest in the black community against external exploitation and containment in the central city. At another geographic level, the best known recent examples of regional nationalism (as in Northern Ireland, Biafra, and the Basque region of Spain) have resulted from a sense of central government exploitation of places which have a distinct language, culture, religion, and/or economic structure, and much the same may be said for colonial independence movements (see Hechter 1975).

Migration: Individual Mobility in the System of Places

Social movements of place occur to the degree that persons and organizations identify their interests with the future development of the places with which they are associated. There are alternative individual responses to the stratification of places, by which persons seek to manipulate the inequalities among places to their own advantage. Studies of the international system, for example, have long recognized that part of the stability of dependency relationships is due to the cooperation of persons in dependent countries who are able to adapt their interests to continued foreign domination (Baran 1968, pp. 194-96). Perhaps more commonly, residents of disadvantaged places perceive migration as the most effective means of upward mobility.

The phenomenon of migration is especially interesting theoretically because it involves the stratification of both individuals and places and the interaction that occurs on both the individual and the community level in the search for advantages of place. From the perspective of free-market theories of population movement (e.g., Tiebout 1956) migration would minimize the disparities among places as the distribution of persons came to match the distribution of resources. But of course migration is not free. Whether by residential zoning policies or police control of their borders, places regulate migration according to their own interest, and individual efforts to move upward through migration may actually be made to reinforce the system of inequalities among places. Thus the stratification of places can be maintained not only by the outcomes of conflicts among places but also by the ways in which noncollective responses are structured.

Consider the example of migration of workers between the industrial countries of the Common Market and the less-developed Mediterranean countries in the postwar period. First, migrants in this system are assigned social and legal status inferior to that of native workers. Their presence (given full employment) provides a relative class and status advantage to natives, increasing the chances of upward mobility for them and defusing native class militancy (Castles and Kosack 1973). Emigration in turn makes available a nonpolitical response to economic discontent in disadvantaged places (MacDonald 1963). Migration complicates individuals' perceptions of the lines of stratification within and between places and reduces potential opposition to the system as a whole. Second, the division of labor by which some places provide worker reserves for others can be manipulated to the advantage of the latter. Migration can guarantee a sufficient work force to an expanding economy and allow externalization of the political and economic costs of unemployment in periods of contraction; both processes can reinforce the initial division of labor (Castells 1975).

Systems of Places: Levels of Analysis

The notion of competition of places is applicable to systems of places at any geopolitical level—to systems of neighborhoods, cities, regions, and nations. It reflects the fact that within any system (whether the Western world order described by Wallerstein [1974], or the New York metropolis analyzed by Wood [1961]), the growth potential of places is affected by their political-economic position in relation to other places.

Despite their similarities, there are important differences among levels. One is the strength of the political institutions which integrate the systems and the degree of sovereignty of the places within them. The nation-state is clearly the strongest political unit in much of the modern world, determining by law the formal channels of competition of places within the national system, while conflict among nations is only loosely regulated by international structures. The smallest geopolitical units —administrative areas within cities, for example—have the least sovereignty but are the most homogeneous in terms of the interests they must serve.

But beyond comparing these levels as parallel systems of places, it is crucial to discern the ways in which they are interrelated. Systems of neighborhoods are nested within systems of cities within systems of nations. The political process within any system involves not only local places but also interests which are organized at the system level. The latter groups—especially those at the national level—can greatly influence the pattern of interlocal competition by setting the legal framework within which it occurs (see Holden [1964] and Farkas [1971] for discussions of the effects of federal law on interlocal conflict in the United States).

Using a Marxian perspective, some theorists have suggested that the inequalities among places are most relevant, not for their effects on interests based within competing places, but for their consequences for the maintenance of the system as a whole. In his study of migratory labor systems, for example, Burawoy notes that the geographic separation of the sites of renewal and maintenance of the labor force—made possible by the unequal power relations among places—makes possible a reduction in the total costs of reproduction of the labor force. "It is cheaper to educate and bring up a family, and so forth, in a Bantustan or a Mexican shantytown than in Johannesburg or California, where the reproduction of labor power is organized for higher-income groups and where, as a result, lower income groups are penalized" (Burawoy 1976, p. 1082).

Harvey (1973, pp. 261-84) has made a much broader claim for the role of stratification of places in maintaining capitalism. Describing the spatial ordering of Western capitalism as a global structure in which the industrial metropolis rests at the top of a chain of exploitation of places, he argues that such a hierarchical organization of territories has been necessary for the concentration and efficient circulation of surplus value. The particular geographic pattern depends upon both economic and political factors of the type discussed in this essay:

> The exhaustion of a key resource and the opening up of new resources (through technology or the opening up of new trade routes) can bring about rapid shifts in the circulation of surplus and bring powerful and important cities into being, and can just as quickly destroy them... In contemporary times, the shifting allegiance of nations, the interdiction of trade through political action (the partition of Germany, the closure of the Suez Canal) have all affected circulation of surplus. Competition between cities, between sets of cities (such as the Hanse) or between countries, for control over the circulation of surplus will itself alter the geographic pattern of circulation as one side dominates the other... [Harvey 1973, p. 247].

But Harvey is less interested in the particular geographic pattern than in the fact of territorial inequality itself.

Like other recent theorists, he emphasizes the increasing role of the state in preserving this system: by protecting the continued flow of surplus through military and police control, by assuming responsibility for the provision of facilities and services for the maintenance of the population and reproduction of the labor force, and by providing infrastructural support and financing for the profitable expansion of private industry. As others have pointed out, there are potential contradictions in these roles because costs of social control are inherently unproductive expenses and because state revenues cannot keep up with expenditures as long as profit is privately appropriated. O'Connor (1973) and Castells (1972) have suggested that the interrelated fiscal crises and urban political movements which result from these contradictions jeopardize the system itself. On the contrary, I would point to other characteristics of the political organization of the stratification of places which tend to insulate it from such challenges:

1. Governmental fragmentation enables public resources to be concentrated in certain jurisdictions. Thus the fiscal crisis, because it is unequally distributed both within and across metropolitan regions, affects various economic sectors and social classes differentially.
2. Potential opposition to the system tends to become organized within places rather than at the system level. Such action is relatively ineffectual, because disadvantaged places have neither the internal resources nor the power in relation to other places to resolve the problems which generated their political activity.

III. CONCLUSION

At every geographic level the competition of places affects the pattern of development and differentiation of the human community. Spatial differentiation does in practice imply inequalities among places, and thereby advantages and disadvantages to the persons and organizations whose fortunes are linked to specific places. The more powerful of these actors typically established political structures which reinforce the stratification of places to their own advantage. The routine working of such structures insulates the sytem from challenge. It is rare that places disadvantaged by the system can oppose it directly, as the OPEC countries have done temporarily within the world system. And opposition from within advantaged places is muted by the fact that the advantages of place are widely shared by its residents.

I have suggested that place is often an important basis of collective action and that the notion of stratification of places can usefully supplement the more traditional dimensions of class and status. The interactions among these three dimensions provide a rich field for theoretical development.

I have also argued that in order to understand how growth takes place and is socially ordered, one must take into account the conscious efforts of places to influence growth. This approach does not deny the ecological variables of distance and time, but asserts the importance of another political set of variables. It does no more than make positive use of what the Chicago School also recognized (Park 1936; Wirth 1945; Hawley 1950, pp. 55-63; and esp. Hawley 1971, pp. 49-54) but seems too often to have neglected, that the human community itself more than any other life form creates the conditions of its own development.

NOTE

Paper presented in the session "Future of Human Ecology" at the annual meeting of the American Sociological Association, 1977. This essay extends an exchange with Harvey Molotch, some of whose formulations are presented here. For comments on earlier versions of the paper I am indebted to O.A. Collver, Lewis Coser, Paget Henry, and Moshe Semyonov.

REFERENCES

Alihan, Milla A. 1938. *Social Ecology*. New York: Columbia University Press.
Banks, Arthur S. 1971. *Cross-Polity Time Series Data*. Boston: M.I.T. Press.
Baran, Paul. 1968. *The Political Economy of Growth*. New York: Monthly Review Press.
Barber, Bernard. 1957. *Social Stratification*. New York: Harcourt, Brace & World.
Berry, Brian, Carole Goodwin, Robert W. Lake, and Katherine Smith, 1976. "Attitudes Toward Integration: The Role of Status in Community Response to Racial Change." Pp. 221-64 in *The Changing Face of the Suburbs*, edited by Barry Schwartz. Chicago: University of Chicago Press.
Blauner, Robert. 1969. "Internal Colonialism and Ghetto Revolt." *Social Problems* 16, no. 4 (Spring): 393-408.
Burawoy, Michael. 1976. "The Functions and Reproduction of Migrant Labor: Comparative Material from Southern Africa and the United States." *American Journal of Sociology* 81 (March): 1050-87.

Castells, Manuel. 1972. *Luttes urbaines.* Paris: Maspero.
———. 1975. "Immigrant Workers and Class Struggles in Advanced Capitalism: The Western European Experience." *Politics and Society* (1): 33-66.
Castles, S., and G. Kosack. 1973. *Immigrant Workers and Class Structure in Western Europe,* London: Oxford University Press.
Davis, Kingsley, and Wilbert E. Moore. 1945. "Some Principles of Stratification." *American Sociological Review* 10 (April): 242-49.
Duncan, Otis Dudley, and Beverly Duncan. 1955. "Residential Distribution and Occupational Stratification." *American Journal of Sociology* 60 (March): 493-503.
Farkas, Suzanne. 1971. "The Federal Role in Urban Decentralization." *American Behavioral Scientist* 15, no. 1 (September-October): 15-35.
Firey, Walter. 1947. *Land Use in Central Boston.* Cambridge, Mass.: Harvard University Press.
Guest, Avery M., and James Weed. 1976. "Ethnic Residential Segregation: Patterns of Change." *American Journal of Sociology* 81 (March): 1088-1111.
Harvey, David. 1973. *Social Justice and the City.* Baltimore: Johns Hopkins University Press.
Hawley, Amos. 1950. *Human Ecology: A Theory of Community Structure.* New York: Ronald Press.
———. 1971. *Urban Society: An Ecological Approach.* New York: Ronald Press.
Hechter, Michael. 1975. *Internal Colonialism: The Celtic Fringe in British National Development.* Berkeley: University of California Press.
Holden, Matthew. 1964. "The Governance of the Metropolis as a Problem in Dipolomacy." *Journal of Politics* 26 (August): 627-47.
Hollingshead, A.B. 1947. "A Re-examination of Ecological Theory." *Sociology and Social Research* 31 (January-February): 194-204.
Laumann, Edward, Paul Siegel, and Robert Hodge, eds. 1970. *The Logic of Social Hierarchies.* Chicago: Markham.
Lieberson, Stanley. 1961. "The Impact of Residential Segregation on Ethnic Assimilation." *Social Forces* 40 (October): 52-57.
Logan, John R. 1976. "Industrialization and the Stratification of Cities in Suburban Regions." *American Journal of Sociology* 82 (September): 333-48.
MacDonald, J.S. 1963. "Agricultural Organization, Migration, and Labour Militancy in Rural Italy." *Economic History Review* (August): 61-75.
McKenzie, R.D. (1926) 1961. "The Scope of Human Ecology." Pp. 30-36 in *Studies in Human Ecology,* edited by George A. Theodorson. Evanston, Ill.: Harper & Row.
———. 1933. *The Metropolitan Community.* New York: McGraw-Hill.
Molotch, Harvey. 1967. "Toward a More Human Human Ecology: An Urban Research Strategy." *Land Economics* 43 (August): 336-41.
———. 1976. "The City as a Growth Machine: Toward a Political Economy of Place." *American Journal of Sociology* 82 (September): 309-32.
O'Connor, James. 1973. *The Fiscal Crisis of the State.* New York: St. Martin's.
Park, Robert E. 1936. "Human Ecology." *American Journal of Sociology* 42 (July): 1-15.
———. 1952. *Human Communities: The City and Human Ecology.* New York: Free Press.
Park, Robert E., Ernest Burgess, and Roderick McKenzie. 1967. *The City.* Chicago: University of Chicago Press.
Spilerman, Seymour, and Jack Habib. 1976. "Development Towns in Israel: The Role of Community in Creating Ethnic Disparities in Labor Force Characteristics." *American Journal of Sociology* 81 (January): 781-812.
Stinchcombe, Arthur. 1965. "Social Structure and Organizations." Pp. 142-93 in *Handbook of Organizations,* edited by James G. March. New York: Rand McNally.
Tiebout, Charles, 1956. "A Pure Theory of Local Expenditure." *Journal of Political Economy* 64 (October): 416-24.

Wallerstein, Immanuel. 1974. *The Modern World-System--Capitalist Agriculture and the Origins of the European World-Economy in the Sixteenth Century*. New York: Academic Press.
Wirth, Louis. 1945. "Human Ecology." *American Journal of Sociology* 50 (May): 483-88.
Wood, Robert, 1961. *1400 Governments*. Cambridge, Mass.: Harvard University Press.
Zorbaugh, Harvey. (1926) 1961. "The Natural Areas of the City." Pp. 45-49 in *Studies in Human Ecology*, edited by George A. Theodorson. Evanston, Ill: Harper & Row.

7

Men Without Property: The Tramp's Classification and Use of Urban Space

James S. Duncan

There is a steadily growing interest among social geographers and others in individual and group cognition of areas within the city.[2] Considering this as well as the long term interest geographers maintain in developing models by which to regionalize the city, we can expect to see an alternative to these overviews in the form of regionalizations from the perspective of one group.[3] These "folk geographies" are the basis of much spatial decision making and as such ought to be of great interest to geographers.

In this essay, I will be concerned with the perspective of one group, the tramps, and will try to show how the perspective of other groups shapes it.[4] I will concentrate on the tramps' classification of various areas only as it pertains to their spatial movements and not necessarily as it reflects their full and complex set of attitudes toward these areas. The interdependent perspectives on the city which I will be discussing, it must be remembered relate to action, to spatial movements and to attempts to secure rights to space or to restrict others' rights to space. These rights, both legally and informally defined, are the product of and thus reveal the central ideology of the particular form of social organization which I will term "the market society."

From *Antipode*, Vol. 10 (March 1978), pp. 24-34. Reprinted by permission of *Antipode* and J. Duncan.

Differential mobility, access to space and inequalities in power to influence others' use of space reflect the interrelationships between social groups in the city. In fact, land is divided up and access to space is limited in such ways that land can be said to constitute a relationship between men.[5] Power and other social relationships between men are in various ways enacted in the use of land and in restrictions of others' use of land.

This paper is about the difficulty that tramps, being members of an extremely marginal group, encounter when they try to carve out a niche for themselves in the American city whose moral orders have little place for them.[6] It concerns the strategies they employ to exist in the nooks and crannies of the urban world whose moral order denies the legitimacy of their nomadic existence. The tramp roams from city to city by freight train, on foot, or by broken down car. He attempts to adapt as best he can to the hostile urban environment. He wanders the skid rows, hides in alleyways, sleeps under bridges, on the sidewalks, in garbage dumps and in parks. He is perpetually on the move to avoid arrest, to look for a job or a handout, and to find a place to sleep.

In the first half of this essay I will discuss the relationship between the two groups under consideration, the tramp and the host population, the latter being those who have control over the various areas of the city through which the tramp wanders. Also mentioned will be the dominant ideology which provides a framework within which the host group operates. Next I consider the strategies the tramp employs to make a place for himself in the spatial order of the city. In particular, I will discuss the way the tramp takes the role of the host group in order to derive a classification of the city pertinent to his attempts to survive there.

THE MORAL ORDER OF THE LANDSCAPE

The city is composed of more or less well defined social areas each of which is controlled by one or more groups who sustain a moral order there. The moral order of an area is the public order.[7] I use the term moral order here to capture the feeling of a group that the way it organizes its world is inherently correct. It is defined here as the set of customary relations in an area and the etiquette governing its landscape; it constitutes what is believed by the dominant group to be the proper arrangement and use of artifacts and the proper form that interaction in that landscape should take. It stipulates what people under what circumstances are allowed to engage in what activity in what places.[8]

This moral order is not arrived at, however, without some negotiation on the part of the participants. The negotiation process is not only of a formal political nature but also arises out of routine social interaction. Superimposed upon local moral orders is the largely middle class moral order of the city as a whole. This is codified in laws and enforced by the police and other official agencies. Indirect attempts at control are also made by architects and planners who design buildings and outdoor spaces to keep order.[9] The local moral orders also have their guardians in the form of residents (peer pressure), shopkeepers, gangs, and others who enforce the local etiquette. There is a certain tension between the local and city-wide moral orders that arises from the differences between them.

The police are expected to keep this tension under control. They accept the fact that local moral orders do exist and often take precedence over the city-wide order as long as they do not grossly contradict it or spill over into other areas. Rubenstein found that the policeman:

> ... develops notions about what is the "normal" character of behavior in different parts (of the city) . . . behavior tolerated in one place is disallowed in another because it violates his notion of what is right in that place.[10]

The police tolerate certain deviant behavior as normal on skid row, which is one of the few areas the tramp may occupy with a minimum of risk. In this sense they respect the moral order of the row; they find, however, that other behavior there so flagrantly violates the larger moral order that they must intervene.

THE MARKET PLACE IDEOLOGY OF THE HOST GROUP

In a society such as ours, whose organization is based on individual property rights, a poor person will be viewed as a problem for the group controlling the area in which he lives.[11] He possesses little property and hence has little stake in the existing order which functions primarily to protect property and ensure that orderly market relations take place. The tramp poses all of the same problems for the controlling group that the poor local person does but these problems are magnified as he, being an itinerant, has even less stake in the area. Not only does he lack property but he rarely has any ties with local residents. Thus the tramp feels no obligation to maintain the moral order and furthermore his mobility makes it difficult to force him to comply with it.[12] The locals view the tramp as a threat and do their best to drive him away.

Social value in our society is based primarily upon property, real property or labor which one is willing and able to sell.[13] While the tramp occasionally has a few possessions, a watch, a ring, a little money made on a temporary job or panhandled, perhaps a radio purchased in good times to be sold when the times get rough, these possessions come and go. The only property a tramp has on a fairly regular basis is his labor power which he can sell if he is willing, though often he is not because the wages offered are often less than can be made panhandling. Furthermore, his lack of skill or his frequent inability to hold a job because of alcoholism makes his labor worth very little to society.

Bahr, in a recent summary of the literature on tramps, states that he cannot understand why the tramp is so loathed.[14] He thinks that his poverty is not sufficient to explain the virulence of this reaction. Bahr, however, fails to view the tramp within the context of the marketplace morality. Once seen within this context the able-bodied tramp becomes a person who willfully negates the established order.[15] It should be noted, however, that a certain tension is produced by the conflict between Stoic and Christian natural law on the one hand, which suggests that all men are equal, and the law of the marketplace which suggests that they are not. Nevertheless, the tramp offends the larger society when he consciously reduces his value to virtually zero. Furthermore, by panhandling, he forces the host group to engage in non-market relations.

According to the dominant ideology in society one must have sufficient property to be able to own or rent a place to sleep if he is not to be charged with vagrancy. Vagrancy laws, which restrict the movement of individuals from place to place, have been in effect in England since the fourteenth century and were adopted by the colonies and subsequently the United States. The social problem that they were originally intended to alleviate has long since disappeared while other totally unrelated problems have become their target.[16] Vagrancy laws should be of special interest to geographers because they reflect the prevailing ideology concerning private places and freedom of movement. For example, it is illegal not to own the right of access to some private place. Every person who wanders about without access to a private place to sleep, who can show no means of support ". . . shall be deemed a tramp, and shall be subject to imprisonment . . . "[17] It is such access that provides ". . . evidence that a man has a legitimate relationship to the social structure."[18] The vagrancy laws are selectively applied to contain tramps within skid row or to banish them entirely from the city.[19] Thus, those who are penniless or without normal occupation in the broad sense of the term may be severely restricted in their spatial mobility and even declared criminal.

STRATEGIES FOR GETTING BY

Let us now turn to a consideration of the strategies that are adopted by the tramp who finds that the moral order of the host group has no place for him. There are a variety of possible strategies, e.g., mobility, and eschewing cumbersome possessions and attachments to members of the local population. I will restrict myself here to a discussion of those strategies that make use of the landscape.

In order to avoid the guardians of the host landscape, the tramp must adopt a low profile.[20] Often this is not easy to accomplish because the tramp wears old, worn clothes that are easily recognizable. It is not easy to change this because it involves an outlay of resources that are usually not available. He would also severely diminish his chances of being able to panhandle successfully because his clothes are a sign, often the only visible one, that he needs a handout.

> I believe that the dirtier the man is the better for the street make. If I am dirty, a man will give me a coin rather than have me walk down the street and have people think that I might be one of his friends.[21]

Since passing as a member of the established moral order is not a viable method of adopting a low profile, the tramp must resort to another tactic, that of using the landscape as a cover. This method requires a large amount of environmental knowledge. He must know for example where he can find a warm place to spend a winter's night unobserved.

> You've got to have ingenuity. You've got to know New York, its people, how to get around. I sleep in the subways nowadays. It works out fine ... You can't sleep there when an officer's on duty. That's from eight p.m. to four a.m. So I go there about ten minutes till four; sleep to noon, usually ... I like the Eighth Avenue line. Less stops. I sleep on one of the front or back cars; never the middle. Too many disturbances.[22]

At times he must out of necessity sleep on the street and is therefore potentially open to harassment from the police and jackrollers (muggers). He finds ingenious ways to hide himself in this kind of exposed landscape. "There's garbage cans back there . . . I'd lay there with half my body in a garbage can and the upper half in a pasteboard box . . . that way no one knows."[23] Once a tramp finds a place that provides good cover he may wish to protect it from others. Often some ingenious tactics are employed to attempt to claim a bit of public space.

> Snead, a dope addict, slightly past middle age, has been living for some time in the doorway of an unoccupied building. This doorway consists of a sort of vestibule and has plenty of room for a person to lie down. His only furniture is a broom and a box of broken glass. When he leaves he scatters the broken glass over the floor to keep others away. And when he returns he uses the broom to sweep up the glass.[24]

Most of this environmental knowledge is very specialized. It is of interest to the tramp alone although certain members of the local population, notably the police, may also be tangentially interested. He knows certain ethnic streets where begging is especially good, specific street corners where truckers stop to pick up cheap labor, and that public libraries are good places to sleep during the day.[25] He knows many different spots where he can sleep and keep warm on a cold winter night, such as in bus depot toilet stalls, near city steam pipes, in heated sandboxes in railroad yards, in warm stacks of bricks in brickyards, and in open churches. In fact Spradley discovered that tramps could name over one hundred categories of sleeping places.[26]

Whereas most tramps are aware of these relatively stable elements of the urban environment, the more astute quickly capitalize on changes in the environment. For example, shortly after a chapter of Alcoholics Anonymous started holding meetings in a church near the Bowery in New York, a number of tramps congregated about the church during meetings taking advantage of the fact that members of A.A. are a "soft touch" for a handout.[27]

Earlier I stated that a certain tension was produced between Christian natural law and the law of the marketplace. Both ideologies are of course present throughout the city, although the law of the marketplace predominates. There are however, certain temporal-spatial pockets of Christian natural law. Astute tramps have learned that it is profitable to seek out such areas.

> I had a friend come into Minneapolis and we didn't have no money so I said to him lets go up to one of those churches and see if we can get some money. Now the people were just coming out and so I said to my friend, they can't refuse you when they still got Jesus in them—you let them get a few blocks away and they haven't got that "Jesus" feeling... I got two dollars and he got a little over a buck... and my friend never quite got over that new pitch. He said he's gonna try that again in Denver.[28]

The predominance of the market ideology is suggested by the fact that these pockets of Christian natural law cover an area with a radius of a mere two blocks and last for approximately fifteen minutes on Sundays.

Alongside the marketplace ideology which guides relations between most strangers within the city struggles the tramp's non-market ideology which is based on reciprocity and is termed "brotherhood of the road" by its adherents.[29] The maintenance of this alternative ideology may be considered a strategy for survival. A tramp shares with others whether he knows them or not, knowing that he may be taken care of when he is in need. He will share his bottle, flop (any of a wide variety of places to sleep), clothes, food, and information about local police practices and availability of spot jobs, etc. A tramp may give his jacket to another inmate when he leaves jail and then go out into the street to "cut in" on someone's bottle. According to informal rules one must never refuse to share his bottle.[30]

A tramp's environmental knowledge must include all the intricacies of how the host group classifies space and specifically the social value that it attaches to different landscapes. Gaining such knowledge is the most important of all his strategies.

PRIME AND MARGINAL SPACE

Most citizens find public versus private the primary constraining classification in their use of space: one ought to be able to use any public space by virtue of his being a citizen provided he behaves in a fairly "normal" and legal fashion for the time and place. Private spaces, of course, are far more exclusive. The distinction between public and private is usually clear although it can be a little fuzzy around the edges.[31] The propertyless are generally excluded from private places (they can sometimes stay in flop-houses or go into bars or missions but not on a regular basis). What is more, they are also driven out of public places, for full citizenship rights are apparently not extended to the propertyless, a notion which has survived from the eighteenth century when citizenship was legally extended only to those who had property.[32] Public property apparently, then, belongs to the citizenry as a whole, which has the right to exclude the tramp. As Spradley states

> what they do is much less significant than who they are. They are not seen as citizens; in fact they are not even perceived as criminals, but, rather they are identified as bums. The concept of equal justice in American society applies to those who are considered equal and ... it is difficult for the police not to consider the tramps inferior. "Decent people" and "bums" are not equal, except in some ultimate and, at the moment, irrelevant sense.[33]

Elsewhere, Spradley mentions the case of a tramp who was walking to a job but because he looked like a bum was arrested.

> And do you know what kind of a charge they had there? Idling! Yes—idling, that was a form of vagrancy. I got up before the judge and told him, I says, kind of funny anymore you can't even walk down the streets of Seattle.[34]

In contrast to the propertied population and the relatively simple public versus private distinction which reflects its spatial movements, tramps are forced to use a different system of determining usable space within the city. This system is based on an unstated scale of social value which the host groups apply to different areas. The scale ranges from what I would term prime to marginal space. This implies no inherent value in the space itself; on the contrary the value is assigned to the space by a given group on the basis of how it uses the space. The social value of space, furthermore, is an ever-evolving phenomenon which is based upon varying degrees of consensus. Thus the tramp must learn the social value that the host group assigns to different types of urban space and to the regular temporal variations in these values; he must then resign himself to spending as much time as possible in marginal space.

Marginal space includes alleys, dumps, space under bridges, behind hedgerows, on the roofs of buildings, and in other no man's lands such as around railroad yards, which are not considered worth the cost of patrolling. As one tramp put it,

> If you are under the bridge down below Pike Street Market you are safe—the police don't walk down there, just too lazy.[35]

Skid row and a few other very poor residential or commercial areas are also considered marginal. Here the tramp can achieve a low profile because the shabbiness of his dress does not stand out as it does elsewhere. Skid row is ceded to the tramps because the authorities realize that tramps must stay somewhere and there are definite advantages from the point of view of social control to keeping them together in one place.[36] Dunham sums up the police's attitude nicely when he states

> The law enforcement officer in general, sees the skid row problem as one of achieving that minimum of enforcement of the law which will keep the row from the consciousness of the rest of the community.[37]

The terms prime and marginal refer not to a dichotomy but a continuum. It must also be noted that they are relative terms. By looking at the city as a whole and grossly dividing it into space which is prime and marginal in the eyes of the host group I have in effect lumped all the citizens of the city except the tramps into one group, which is an obvious oversimplification. Whether a place is prime or marginal depends upon the perspective from which one views the situation. The tramp is aware of the diversity of perspectives within the host population. In day-to-day decisions he must see things from their perspective. He must take into consideration the fact that what one person considers prime space another considers marginal. He takes the perspective of some into account more than others because he realizes the relative inequalities of power among these groups to enforce their perspective. It must be remembered, however, that there is some general agreement as to prime and marginal in the gross sense for the lower class citizen is forced to a certain extent to accept the perspective of the middle class citizen and to realize that effectively his area is considered marginal even if it is of prime importance to him.

Likewise the tramp must "take the role of" the police officers in their subdivision of marginal space into more or less marginal. For example, the police categorize abandoned buildings as extremely marginal space.

> The patrolman knows these buildings are in use, for he constantly sees evidence ... (but) he does not examine these places on his route . . . They are no longer buildings in the formal sense. They are like the alleys the patrolman does not go into because he does not see them as being either public or private places . . . [38]

These places, which are neither public nor private, have been classified by the patrolman as places with no property value and hence as jurisdictional voids.[39] The tramp is quick to see the personal benefits to be derived from the patrolman's classification of marginal space. He also learns to divide marginal space on the basis of accessibility and inaccessibility to the police, who, for matters of safety and convenience like to patrol their beat in cars. In effect, the police have given up jurisdiction over certain areas in which they cannot drive a car. Rubinstein notes that alleys that are too narrow for a squad car to enter are ignored. The policeman

> . . . even acknowledges the tactical superiority of teenagers, whose skill in exploiting local topography frequently allows them to escape capture.[40]

Similarly tramps take advantage of the policeman's classification of alleys as inaccessible space and use them for drinking and other illicit activities.

THE USE OF PRIME SPACE

The tramp is faced with a problem that really has no solution. In order to survive without being arrested he must occupy marginal areas, while in order to secure the wherewithal to survive he must often venture into high risk, prime areas. The vast majority of the city is prime space and therefore space which the tramp finds dangerous. Prime space, however, does not have a uniformly high social value. The tramp, knowing the relative value assigned to different spaces by the host group, minimizes his risk by using prime space which has moderate social value.

> ... the central business district, and certain main thoroughfares, are the only places in the metropolis (with the exception of skid row) where the bum can successfully ply his trade. If he tries door-to-door begging... householders call the police.[41]

It is extremely difficult to adopt a low profile in any prime area while one is trying to panhandle. On most city streets there are few if any places that provide cover. Furthermore, interaction with strangers violates the norms of conduct on such public streets, and panhandling is therefore easily noticed. "Normal" and hence acceptable conduct on such a street consists of walking purposefully and not interacting with others unless they are walking with you.

> In Chicago, an individual in the uniform of a hobo can loll on "the stem," but once off this preserve he is required to look as if he were intent on getting to some business destination.[42]

The practice of picking up cigarette butts from the street, "snipe shooting," illustrates some of the problems inherent in using various types of prime space. To compete for these snipes one must have a detailed knowledge of the good snipe hunting areas.

> He told me the best place for snipes was outside a church—the Sunday folk always left long ones before they entered. On a good day you could pick up enough to make a pack of almost new ready-rolls.[43]

However, although one can find good snipes on the Loop one must be careful of the police there.

> I wouldn't advise you to hunt snipes in the Loop, for while the butts are as long as this (measuring with his hands the length of a lead pencil), you are almost sure to get picked up by the police.[44]

The advantages to be gained from using prime space, therefore, must be weighed against the risks.

There are certain other prime spaces that the tramp uses upon occasion in order to keep warm or to catch some sleep where he may not be noticed by the police. Two such places are public libraries, and train stations.

> Thus in some urban libraries, the staff and the local bums may reach a tacit understanding that dozing is permissible as long as the dozer first draws out a book and props it up in front of his head.[45]

Likewise it appears that

> ... newspaper readers never seem to attract the attention (of the station guards) and even the seediest vagrant can sit in Grand Central all night without being molested if he continues to read a newspaper.[46]

In both cases the tramp adopts the strategy of using a prop, in this case reading material, in order to legitimize his presence in this prime space. These props appear to submerge his stigmatized identity sufficiently to stop it from spreading to others in the place. This can only be accomplished in impersonal, low interaction places where the stigmatized person can easily be disattended by others. These are places and props which isolate individuals, "remove them" as it were from others.[47] It is as if they were required to build a wall around themselves in order that their presence might be tolerated in prime space.

For matters of convenience I have been speaking of the host group as if it were a single monolithic group which of course it is not. Within it there are many social worlds and factions with more or less conflicting interests. Some are reasonably friendly to tramps and occasionally will form temporary alliances and make deals with them against other segments of the host population. For example, tramps have a certain working relationship with homosexuals who exchange food, shelter, a chance to get cleaned up, clothes and occasionally money, for sexual relations. A third party to this relationship is often the police who tolerate such activity if it remains reasonably unobtrusive. Tramps whistle to get the attention of homosexuals who are "cruising" the park.

> They whistle low. They cannot whistle loud. The coppers will hear them. The coppers will let you whistle low, but not loud.[48]

Such agreements are the product of implicit bargaining, or negotiation, between the police and tramps. The tramps continually try to make gains in freedom to use certain prime space to make contact with members of the host population while the police attempt to hold them in check without expending too much extra effort.

The fact that the tramp is forced to enter prime space on occasion should not obscure the fact that his principal strategy is to occupy marginal space. Excursions into prime space constitute a small but dangerous part of the tramp's existence.

ON THE SEPARATION OF NORMAL AND SPOILED IDENTITIES

There is a belief in our society that the social value of an individual must be roughly commensurate with the social value of the place he frequents. In a society which is socially mobile the objects and settings that one surrounds oneself with are an inseparable part of one's self.[49] This argument logically leads to the notion that if one shares a setting with another then, to a degree, he shares his identity thus allowing stigma to spread by spatial association. A tramp does not have a "normal," that is propertied, identity but to put it in Goffman's terms, one that is "spoiled."[50] Such people must be separated out for their spoiled identities can spoil the setting and by extension the "normal" people who are a part of it.[51] Hence the hierarchical division of space according to social value is of critical importance to the host population.

Private spaces are the most closely associated with an individual's identity. The home in particular is an important part of one's self.[52] Impersonal, highly public places do not usually constitute an integral aspect of an individual's identity. Sharing such a place does not entail sharing a part of one's social identity to the extent it does in a private place. Thus the separation of spoiled and normal identities is more easily accomplished. If the tramp walks briskly and purposefully through such an area he runs a fairly low risk of being arrested. By his rapid movement he makes little claim on space, thereby reducing the stigma he might otherwise spread. Sitting or standing, however, constitute much more of an involvement of one's identity with a place, i.e., it is an implicit claim that one somehow "belongs" there. The tramp therefore is rarely allowed to remain stationary in such an area for very long unless, as I have mentioned, he restricts himself to a few places such as the library and uses a prop to disassociate himself from others, so as to minimize the spread of stigma.

One could say that the prime areas with the highest social value are those residential sections with which middle to upper class individuals associate their identity. These areas convey positive information about such people. Other prime space includes the highly public places which are fairly neutral in terms of association with individuals' identities. In contrast, marginal areas are negative in the sense that they convey stigmatizing information about their inhabitants.

It is interesting to note that not all highly public areas are neutral in the above sense. There appears to be a generalized association of the identity of many propertied citizens with certain key places which are thought to represent the city. This association is generally termed civic pride. These key places are thought to be an important part of the city's presentation of self to outsiders. This is especially true when large numbers of tourists come to the city for special events or during the tourist season. At these times the city is on display and must be cleared of its unesthetic elements.

Drunks are also arrested in significant numbers before any large conventions, celebrations, or fairs. This is done primarily to "clean up" the area so it will not be unnecessarily offensive to visitors.[53]

Thus the social value of prime space ebbs and flows at different times. The tramp cannot afford to be unaware of the temporal nature of the value of space.

Certain areas of the central business district of large cities, such as the Loop in Chicago, are thought to be continuously on display and therefore tramps are discouraged from ever going there.

The main emphasis of the court is stay out of the Loop. That statement was made again and again, in fact in some instances a judge even stated, if you have to beg do it anywhere but in the Loop.[54]

Skid row is thought of as an area which is morally bankrupt. The characterization of its inhabitants as morally defective leads to the conception of the row as an open asylum. People with "normal" propertied identities therefore should be kept out. The police have little sympathy for tourists who want to see the row or locals who want to take a "moral holiday" thereby engaging in illicit activity.[55] These people cause trouble for the police and as such are discouraged from entering this marginal space.

CONCLUSION

Classification and use of space are intimately tied. One can describe the tramp's use of urban space; one can map it; however, one cannot begin to explain it without reference to the tramp's classification of various areas within the city. To understand his classification, one must examine the process by which he derives it. His classification of areas represents a plan of action, a plan which takes into account the action of others. Reconciling these lines of action requires negotiation which must be viewed in the context of power relationships and the ideology or concept of society held by the more powerful parties to the relationship. Occupying a very marginal place in the prevailing concept of society, tramps are in a very poor position from which to negotiate for rights to use space. Their classification of areas within the city is largely shaped by the prime/marginal distinction of the host group. Similarly their strategy of occupying marginal space is a direct result of the host's strategy of containment. The tramp, however, pays a price for using what is defined by the host group as marginal space. To quote sociologist Erving Goffman:

A status, a position, a social place is not a material thing, to be possessed, and then displayed, it is a pattern of appropriate conduct, coherent, embellished, and well articulated ... it is ... something that must be enacted and portrayed.[56]

By occupying marginal space, the tramp acts out and reconfirms his social marginality in the eyes of the host group. His strategy merely reaffirms the host's perspective and causes only minimal adjustments to be made in the host's moral order.

The division of the city into prime and marginal space as I have outlined it here is not in itself as important as the idea that the classification and use of urban areas by any group must be viewed in the context of that group's relation to other groups. Any group, including the most powerful, must negotiate with others, and this inevitably leads to compromise in their perspective. Thus the classification of prime and marginal, or relatively unsafe and safe, to look at the same distinction from the perspective of the tramp, should serve to indicate the relative or interactional nature of any regionalization of the city by any individual or social group.

NOTES

1. I am grateful to Nancy G. Duncan, Justin C. Friberg, Elihu M. Gerson, M. Sue Gerson, and David E. Sopher for advice, criticism and suggestions.

2. D. Dejong, "Images of Urban Areas: Their Structure and Psychological Foundations," *Journal of The American Institute of Planners*, Vol. 28 (1962), pp. 266-276; R. M. Downs and D. Stea, *Image and Environment: Cognitive Mapping and Spatial Behavior*. (Chicago: Aldine, 1973); F.C. Ladd, "Black Youths View Their Environment: Neighbourhood Maps," *Environment and Behavior*, Vol. 2 (1970), pp. 74-99; J.D. Harrison and W.A. Howard, "The Role of Meaning in the Urban Image," *Environment and Behavior*, Vol. 4 (1972), pp. 389-411; B. Goodey, "City Scene: An Exploration into the Image of Central Birmingham as Seen by the Area Residents," *Research Memorandum No. 10* (Birmingham: Center for Urban and Regional Studies, 1971); J. Gulick, "Images of the Arab City," *Journal of the American Institute of Planners*, Vol. 29 (1963), pp. 179-197; W.H. Ittleson (ed.), *Environment and Cognition* (New York: Seminar Press, 1973); D. Ley, *The Black Inner City as a Frontier Outpost*, Monograph Series, No. 7 (Washington, D.C.: Association of American Geographers, 1974); D. Lowenthal and M. Riel, *Publications in Environmental Perception*, 8 Volumes (New York: American Geographical Society, (1972); K. Lynch, *The Image of the City* (Cambridge: M.I.T. Press, 1960); G.T. Moore and R. Golledge, *Environmental Knowing: Theories, Research, and Methods* (Pennsylvania: Dowden, Hutchinson and Ross, 1976); A.L. Strauss, *Images of the American City* (New York: Free Press, 1961); A.L. Strauss, *The American City: A Sourcebook of Urban Imagery* (Chicago: Aldine, 1968).

3. Examples of models developed either by geographers or others who have had an influence on geographers are to be found in: E. Shevsky and W. Bell, *Social Area Analysis: Theory, Illustrative Applications and Computative Procedures* (Stanford: Stanford University Press, 1955); P.H. Rees, "Concepts of Social Space: Toward an Urban Social Geography," in B.J.L. Berry and F.E. Horton (eds.), *Geographic Perspectives on Urban Systems* (Englewood Cliffs: Prentice Hall, 1970), pp. 306-394; H. Hoyt, *The Structure and Growth of Residential Neighborhoods in American Cities* (Washington: Federal Housing Administration, 1939); W. Firey, "Sentiment and Symbolism as Ecological Variables," *American Sociological Review*, Vol. 10 (1945), pp. 140-148; W. Firey, *Land Use in Central Boston* (Cambridge: Harvard University Press, 1947); C.D. Harris and E.L. Ullman, "The Nature of Cities," *Annals of the American Academy of Science*, Vol. 142 (1945), pp. 7-17; E.W. Burgess, "The Growth of the City," in R.E. Park, E.W. Burgess and R.D. McKenzie (eds.), *The City* (Chicago: University of Chicago Press, 1925); B.J.L. Berry (ed.), "Comparative Factorial Ecology," *Economic Geography*, Vol. 47, Supplement (1971); R.C. Tryon "Comparative Cluster Analysis of Social Areas," *Multivariate Behavior Research*, Vol. 3 (1968), pp. 213-232.

4. An excellent discussion of how perspectives on places are shaped is to be found in E.M. Gerson and M.S. Gerson, "The Social Framework of Place Perspectives," in G.T. Moore and R. Golledge (eds.), *Environmental Knowing: Theories, Research and Methods* (Pennsylvania: Dowden, Hutchinson and Ross, 1976).

5. I draw here on Marx's relational concept of society. For an elaboration of this position see, B. Ollman, *Alienation: Marx's Conception of Man in Capitalist Society* (Cambridge: Cambridge University Press, 1971).

6. On the concept of marginality see: R.E. Park, "Human Migration and the Marginal Man," *American Journal of Sociology,* Vol. 33 (1923), pp. 881-893; E.V. Stonequist, *The Marginal Man: A Study in Personality and Culture* (New York: Scribners, 1937); There was a continuing decline in the economic need for unattached men " . . . until in the public view they were considered unnecessary for the maintenance of the economy . . . The unattached men of skid row effectively set apart from the rest of the community, ecologically isolated, and labeled deviant. Defined as inferior, alien or malicious, the skid row men were placed outside the network of contractual obligations and emotional controls of the community. Despite the retention of economic roles by many of them, their predominant status changed from worker to outcast." J.F. Rooney, "Societal Forces and the Unattached Male: An Historical Review," in H. M. Bahr (ed.), *Disaffiliated Man: Essays and Bibliography on Skid Row, Vagrancy and Outsiders* (Toronto: University of Toronto Press, 1970), p. 21.

7. The term "moral order" was originally used by Park although he was vague as to its definition. R. E. Park, "The Urban Community as a Spatial and a Moral Order," in E.W. Burgess (ed.), *The Urban Community* (Chicago: University of Chicago Press, 1926).

8. The located nature of "correct" activity is discussed at length in: E. Goffman, *Behavior in Public Places: Notes on the Social Organization of Gatherings* (New York: Free Press, 1963); Goffman (1971), *op. cit.*; L. Lofland, *A World of Strangers: Order and Action in Urban Public Space* (New York: Basic Books, 1973).

9. O. Newman, *Defensible Space* (New York: Macmillan, 1972); R. Sommer, *Tight Spaces: Hard Architecture and How to Humanize It* (Englewood Cliffs: Prentice Hall, 1974); C. Ward (ed.), *Vandalism* (New York: Van Nostrand, Reinhold, 1973).

10. J. Rubinstein, *City Police* (New York: Farrar, Straus, Giroux, 1973), pp. 150-151.

11. Macpherson, in his analysis of liberal democracies, states that "Political society is a contrivance for the protection of the individual's property in his person and his goods, and therefore for the maintenance of orderly relations of exchange between individuals regarded as proprietors of themselves." C.B. Macpherson, *The Political Theory of Possessive Individualism: Hobbes to Locke* (London: Oxford University Press, 1964), p. 264.

12. The problems that the stranger poses the host group and vice versa are developed in: G. Simmel, "The Stranger," in K. Wolff (ed.), *The Sociology of Georg Simmel* (New York: Free Press, 1964), pp. 402-408; A. Schutz, "The Stranger: An Essay in Social Psychology," *American Journal of Sociology*, Vol. 49 (1944), pp. 499-507; M.M. Wood, *The Stranger: A Study in Social Relationships* (New York: A.M.S., 1969).

13. Macpherson stresses the fact that property does not consist only of goods but of one's labor power as well. "If a single criterion of the possessive market society is wanted it is that man's labor is a commodity, i.e., that a man's energy and skill are his own, yet are regarded not as integral parts of his personality but as possessions, the use and disposal of which he is free to hand over to others for a price." Macpherson (1964), *op. cit.*, p. 48; This notion is also discussed at length in K. Marx, *Economic and Philosophical Manuscripts of 1844* (New York: International Publishers, 1964).

14. H.M. Bahr, *Skid Row: An Introduction to Disaffiliation* (New York: Oxford University Press, 1973), p. 119.

15. Macpherson claims that in liberal democratic societies one of the principal ontologies or views of the essence of man is the " . . . liberal, individualist concept of man as essentially a

consumer of utilities, an infinite desirer and infinite appropriator." C.B. Macpherson, *Democratic Theory: Essays in Retrieval* (London: Oxford University Press, 1973), p. 24. It is unnatural to reduce one's property value to nothing; one who does so is thought to lack a part of man's essence (i.e., he is not an infinite desirer and appropriator). He cannot by definition, therefore, be fully human and hence is not entitled to those "natural rights" due those who are.

16. W.J. Chambliss, "A Sociological Analysis of the Law of Vagrancy," *Social Problems*, Vol. 12 (1964), pp. 66-77; F.F. Piven and R.A. Cloward, *Regulating the Poor: The Functions of Public Welfare* (New York: Random House, 1971); It is interesting to note that the fourteenth century law represented an attempt on the part of landowners to expropriate labor at a time when it was in short supply and its value was high. Its twentieth century counterpart is used as a catch-all device for controlling people who are viewed as having virtually no labor value.

17. H.E. Flack, *The Annotated Code...of Maryland*, Art. 27, Sec. 666 (1951).

18. A.L. Stinchcombe, "The Behavior of Police in Public and Private Places," in E. Rubington and M.S. Weinberg (eds.), *Deviance: The Interactionist Perspective* (New York: Macmillan, 1968), p. 147.

19. "Philadelphia magistrates ... expressed the policies which guided their administration of vagrancy-type law. They viewed their function as a deterrent one to banish bums from Philadelphia and keep them out ("after this you stay where you belong") or as a form of civic sanitation ("I'll clean up this district if I have to stay here until five o'clock every afternoon"). C. Foote, "Vagrancy-Type Law and its Administration," in W.J. Chambliss (ed.), *Crime and the Legal Process* (New York: McGraw Hill, 1969), p. 303.

20. Failure to avoid the guardians of the landscape usually results in a stiff jail sentence. The normal sentence for vagrancy related charges is three months in the house of correction. See Foote, *op. cit.*

21. E.H. Sutherland and H.J. Locke, *Twenty Thousand Homeless Men: A Study of Unemployed Men in Chicago Shelters* (Chicago: Lippincott, 1936), p. 140.

22. Bahr (1973), *op. cit.*, p. 216.

23. J.P. Spradley, *You Owe Yourself a Drunk: An Ethnography of Urban Nomads* (Boston: Little, Brown, 1970), p. 122.

24. H.W. Gilmore, *The Beggar* (Chapel Hill: University of North Carolina Press, 1940), pp. 145-146.

25. Sutherland and Locke, *op. cit.*, p. 139; Sutherland and Locke, *op. cit.*, p. 102; Goffman (1963), *op. cit.*, p. 55.

26. Spradley, *op. cit.*, p. 99.

27. G. Nash, *The Habitats of Homeless Men in Manhattan* (New York: Columbia University Bureau of Applied Social Research, 1964), p. E65.

28. W.H. Eckland, "Participant Observation Journal" (Minneapolis: Unpublished Research Report, University of Minnesota, Department of Sociology, 1958), quoted in S.E. Wallace, *Skid Row as a Way of Life* (New York: Harper and Row, 1968), pp. 196-197.

29. D.J. Bogue, *Skid Row in American Cities* (Chicago: University of Chicago Press, 1963), p. 63; J.F. Rooney, "Group Processes Among Skid Row Winos: A Reevaluation of the Undersocialization Hypothesis," *Quarterly Journal of Studies on Alcohol*, Vol. 22 (1961), pp. 444-460; S.E. Wallace, *Skid Row as a Way of Life* (New York: Harper and Row, 1968), pp. 156-158.

30. Bahr (1973), *op. cit.*, p. 157.

31. Outsiders are often not welcomed in certain "public" places such as well "guarded" residential areas dominated by a single ethnic group or a powerful upper class group. G.D. Suttles, *The Social Construction of Communities* (Chicago: University of Chicago Press, 1972); Newman, *op. cit.*; Y. Ginsburg, *Jews in a Changing Neighborhood* (New York: Free Press, 1975); D. Ley and R. Cybriwsky, "Urban Graffiti as Territorial Markers," *Annals, Association of American Geographers*, Vol. 64 (1974), pp. 491-505.

Men Without Property

32. Macpherson (1964), *op. cit.*, p. 273.
33. Spradley, *op. cit.*, p. 128.
34. Spradley, *op. cit.*, p. 118.
35. Spradley, *op. cit.*, p. 119.
36. Bogue, *op. cit.*, pp. 61-62; Tenants Relocation Bureau, *The Homeless Man on Skid Row* (Chicago: Tenants Relocation Bureau, 1961), p. 8.
37. H.W. Dunham, *Homeless Men and Their Habitats: A Research Planning Report* (Detroit: Wayne State University Press, 1953), p. 30.
38. Rubinstein, *op. cit.*, pp. 147-148.
39. For a discussion of an ecological approach to the notion of jurisdiction see, P.D. Roos, "Jurisdiction: An Ecological Concept," *Human Relations*, Vol. 21 (1968), pp. 75-84; A discussion of the use of jurisdictional voids for illicit activity is found in, D. Ley and R. Cybriwsky, "The Spatial Ecology of Stripped Cars," *Environment and Behavior*, Vol. 6 (1974), pp. 53-68.
40. Rubinstein, *op. cit.*, p. 139.
41. Bogue, *op. cit.*, p. 61.
42. Goffman (1963), *op. cit.*, p. 57.
43. M. Mathers, *Riding the Rails* (Boston: Houghton Mifflin, 1974), p. 78.
44. Sutherland and Locke, *op. cit.*, p. 99.
45. Goffman (1963), *op. cit.*, p. 55.
46. E.G. Love, *Subways are for Sleeping* (New York: Harcourt Brace, 1957), p. 28.
47. Similar isolation postures and props are discussed by E.T. Hall, *The Hidden Dimension* (New York: Doubleday, 1966); R. Sommer, *Personal Space: The Behavioral Basis of Design* (Englewood Cliffs: Prentice Hall, 1969); E. Goffman, *Stigma: Notes on the Management of Spoiled Identity* (Englewood Cliffs: Prentice Hall, 1963b); M.R. Henderson, "Acquiring Privacy in Public," *Urban Life and Culture*, Vol. 3, (1975), pp. 446-455.
48. T. Kromer, *Waiting for Nothing* (New York: Knopf, 1935), p. 66.
49. The classic work on the self in the sense used here is G.H. Mead, *Mind, Self and Society* (ed.), C.W. Morris (Chicago: University of Chicago Press, 1934); Some geographical implications of this notion are developed in J.S. Duncan, "Environmental Components of the Self: Socio-Psychological Aspects of the Man-Land Relationship in Hyderabad, India," in D.E. Sopher (ed.), *Explorations in Indian Social Geography* (in preparation).
50. Goffman (1963b), *op. cit.*; See footnote 21 for an explanation of the relationship between property and a normal identity.
51. A good example of this is found in, G.D. Suttles, *The Social Order of the Slum: Territory and Ethnicity in the Inner City* (Chicago: University of Chicago Press, 1968), p. 119.
52. C. Cooper, *The House as Symbol of Self* (Berkeley: Institute of Urban and Regional Planning, University of California, Berkeley, 1971); J.S. Duncan, "Landscape Taste as a Symbol of Group Identity: A Westchester County Village," *The Geographical Review*, Vol. 63 (1973), pp. 334-355; J.S. Duncan and N.G. Duncan, "Social Worlds, Status Passage, and Environmental Perspectives: A Case Study in Hyderabad, India," in G.T. Moore and R. Golledge (eds.) *Environmental Knowing: Theories, Research and Methods* (Stroudsburg, Pennsylvania: Dowden, Hutchinson and Ross, 1976); J.S. Duncan and N. G. Duncan, "Housing as Presentation of Self and the Structure of Social Networks: The Old Elite of Hyderabad and the West Enders of Boston," in G.T. Moore and R. Golledge (eds.), *Environmental Knowing: Theories, Research and Methods* (Stroudsburg, Pennsylvania: Dowden, Hutchinson and Ross, 1976); M. Fried, "Grieving for a Lost Home," in L. Duhl (ed.), *The Urban Condition* (New York: Basic Books, 1963); M. Fried and P. Gleicher, "Some Sources of Residential Satisfaction in an Urban Slum," *Journal of The American Institute of Planners*, Vol. 27 (1961), pp. 305-315; L. Rainwater, "Fear and the House as Haven in the Lower Class," *Journal of the American Institute of Planners*, Vol. 32 (1966), pp. 23-30.
53. Wallace, *op. cit.*, p. 95.

54. Sutherland and Locke, *op. cit.*, p. 139.

55. Such touristry is reminiscent of the days when aristocrats used to be taken on tours of the back wards of asylums for their amusement. The attitude of police towards tourists and locals who come to the row is discussed in E. Bittner, "The Police on Skid Row: A Study of Police Keeping," in W.J. Chambliss (ed.) *Crime and the Legal Process* (New York: McGraw Hill, 1969), p. 145.

56. Goffman (1959), *op. cit.*, p. 75.

III
Conflict and Institutional Constraints

8

Local Interests and Urban Political Processes In Market Societies

Kevin R. Cox

In general terms, this paper is concerned with the relationships between market processes and local political processes in urban areas. In particular, the objective is to specify the conditions under which, in market societies, local interests are likely to be reflected in spatially decentralized, localistic political processes.

More specifically, the paper addresses itself to a curious Anglo-American contrast. American cities are characterized by a vigorous competition between local groups and their political agents solicitous of the future of respective turfs. In British cities this structure of relationships does not emerge with equal clarity.

The paper has two major sections. In the first the contrasting structures of local political processes in American and British cities are identified. In the second major section an attempt is made to arrive at a specification of: first, the general conditions under which these contrasting structures are likely to emerge; and, secondly, of those particular attributes of American and British societies which contribute, to a differential degree, towards the satisfaction of these conditions.

Copyright (1979) by Kevin R. Cox. Reprinted from *Urbanization and Conflict in Market Societies* by permission of the publisher, Methuen, Inc. and K. Cox.

THE STRUCTURE OF LOCAL POLITICAL PROCESSES

In American metropolitan areas, distinctively localized political processes can be identified at two geographical scales: that of the jurisdiction and that of the neighborhood. At the jurisdictional level one can document a variety of attempts by respective local governments to manipulate locational relationships to the advantage of their constituents and, presumably, to their own advantage as well. Broadly speaking, a local government attempts, on the one hand, to attract into its jurisdiction that which is utility enhancing and, on the other hand, to keep out that which is utility detracting. "Utility" at this jurisdictional level is defined largely in fiscal terms.[1] A major policy objective of local governments in American metropolitan areas is to minimize the tax rate. Achievement of this goal depends on maximizing the tax base relative to expenditures and, therefore: (1) attracting into the jurisdiction those individuals and associated land uses which provide positive fiscal externalities and (2) keeping out those imposing negative fiscal externalities.[2] Somewhat less important goals are behavioral in nature: attracting those residents who will provide positive behavioral externalities in the educational, public safety, and property maintenance areas and keeping out those unable to do so.[3]

The fiscally desirable are attracted by low tax rates which, however, are achieved by keeping out the fiscally undesirable. Achievement of fiscal goals, therefore, depends largely on a variety of exclusionary policies. The most publicized of these are the minimum lot size and single-family residential zoning policies that go under the blanket term "exclusionary zoning."[4] There are other exclusionary policies, however. These include building codes calling for expensive construction, and "gold-plated" subdivision regulations.[5] These can add costs to new homes and, hence, exclude those poorer families likely to generate more in terms of need for public service spending than they would contribute to the local tax base. Failure to implement a program of public housing is an additional exclusionary strategy.[6]

These policies are particularly appropriate for those jurisdictions large areas of which are yet undeveloped. Those inner suburbs and central cities which are entirely built over have focused on a different set of strategies designed to counter the policies of outer suburbs. It is no exaggeration to state, for example, that one of the attractions of urban renewal and highway construction programs in central cities has been physical removal of the fiscally burdensome poor.[7] Other approaches have included housing code enforcement policies designed to monitor incoming families and attempts to secure rights of extraterritorial taxation.[8]

Policies of this nature, intended primarily to achieve fiscal goals, also facilitate achievement of certain behavioral objectives. Provision of desirable fiscal externalities by households tends to be a concomitant of the behaviorally more desirable. Households consuming relatively large amounts of housing and land and generating little in terms of need for public safety expenditures or other poverty-linked services also tend to be more middle class. Behaviorally, middle-class households are regarded as more desirable by local governments and the constituents they represent: they are publicly safe, their children provide desirable peer groups, and they are more likely to maintain their property.

At the neighborhood level an analogous structuring of the political process is apparent. In this case, however, the counterpart of the local government is the neighborhood organization; and instead of a jurisdictional turf, concern is with geographically more restricted neighborhood turfs. Nevertheless, broad objectives are similar: attract into the neighborhood that which is utility enhancing and keep out that which is utility detracting. More specific expressions of utility, however, do not extend to the fiscal. Rather, major concerns are confined to neighborhood schools, public safety problems, and property values.[9] These three issues, moreover, are clearly interrelated. Public school problems in terms of pupil composition are likely to be reflected in increased delinquency and vandalism in the neighborhood and, possibly, in more mature forms of criminality. Property values represent competitive bids for residential property; these bids, in turn, will be partly based on evaluations of public safety and school problems in the neighborhood.[10]

As at the jurisdictional level, attracting those who provide the positive externalities at issue depends on keeping out those who do not. Exclusion, however, is achieved by policy acts designed to enhance demand for local housing and place it beyond the financial means of families regarded as less desirable. Rezonings, alterations of school pupil composition, alterations in school catchment areas, the location of public housing—all are seen as affecting the demand for neighborhood real estate and, hence, through the price filter, the social composition of the neighborhood. Given the public source of these effects, it is logical to expect neighborhood organizations to attempt to manipulate them in favor of their neighborhood: to lobby, therefore, for those policies thought to enhance the residential quality of the neighborhood and, hence, demand for housing there; and to lobby against those public policies and administrative decisions regarded as having adverse effects on such demand.

In fact, in very general terms, it seems reasonable to characterize these locally based policies, at both neighborhood and jurisdictional levels, as attempts to control housing market processes to local advantage. Housing markets in American cities have welfare impacts of a highly localized character. The view of the metropolitan area held by those directly involved in the production and exchange of housing is as an investment surface. Certain areas are seen as ripe for development, while other areas are regarded as less profitable. Banks regard some neighborhoods as good for mortgage loans, while others are red-lined and starved of credit.[11] Alternatively, banks may merely follow the red-lining activities of insurance companies.[12] Realtors, on the other hand, may regard certain neighborhoods as ripe for social change and attempt to instigate it by blockbusting. The result is a geographical structure of housing opportunities which goes far to explain residential shifts and investment flows among neighborhoods and among jurisdictions.

Residential shifts, however, have important welfare consequences for the residential populations left behind and for those into the midst of whom the newcomers move. Suburban local governments, for example, may find themselves having to raise tax rates in order to cope with an influx of residents moving into properties which detract from, rather than enhance, the jurisdiction's per capita tax base. Older city neighborhoods find themselves having to compete for middle-class residents with newer suburban developments or fashionable prestige rehabilitation projects in the central city. Failure to attract new middle-class residents into existing vacancies results in a deterioration in local school quality, public safety problems, and a general decline in property values.[13]

The function of attempts to manipulate public policy in favor of the neighborhood or to protect the fiscal position of a jurisdiction is to alter the geography of housing investment opportunity. Neighborhood-based action, for instance, serves to maintain the attractiveness of the neighborhood for middle-class buyers and, hence, to preserve a flow of mortgage money into the area. Exclusionary policies on the part of suburban local governments serve to enhance the attractiveness of the jurisdiction for investment in properties, the ultimate owners of which will provide positive, rather than negative, fiscal externalities.

In brief, in American cities households are increasingly forced to participate in the operations of the residential property market. This they do either indirectly, by attempting to make the neighborhood attractive to the housing investor, or directly, by participation in the real estate market itself. With respect to the latter, the degree to which neighborhood organizations form their own real estate operations to bypass private realtors is impressive.[14]

This structuring of urban political processes in America is in substantial contrast to that existing in Britain. Fiscal mercantilism of the sort engaged in by American local governments is—with a few exceptions—virtually unknown.[15] Neighborhood activity is also less apparent. On those occasions when it does emerge, the issues are quite different. Issues of public safety and local schools are notable for their absence. Much more common are, for example: concerns over obnoxious land uses, such as polluting activities, taverns, or nightclubs; and concerns over the destruction of historically meritorious physical fabric. Symptomatic is the contrast in disputes over the location of public housing: these seem endemic to the American urban scene, while in Britain dispute is much more exceptional.[16]

In addition, it seems fair to claim that in the British case the interest of local groups and local governments in manipulating housing market flows to local advantage is considerably less apparent.[17] Moreover, in the view of this writer, the housing market focus of local political processes in the U.S. is critical for understanding the conditions under which they emerge. In brief, it has been argued that the competitive involvements of local groups in the urban political process are a response to the localized welfare impacts of urban housing markets. By structuring flows of funds and of residents between jurisdictions and neighborhoods, the welfare of local groups may be placed at risk. Local political involvement is an attempt to manage these housing market flows to local advantage.

This, however, begs two critical questions: First, under what conditions does the housing market have localized welfare impacts? If it is true that local political processes are a response to welfare impacts, then additional clarification should be provided by an understanding of the forces underlying their emergence. Moreover, if this is a correct viewpoint, conditions promoting localized welfare impacts should be more apparent in the American case and less evident in the British one.

The second question focusses on the form taken by the response to local welfare impacts. While it frequently assumes a political form, there has been no obvious reason why this should be so. Given localized welfare impacts, some areas are likely to gain and some to lose, so that the welfare of those in areas which have tended to be adversely impacted could be maintained by relocating to areas favorably affected. In fact, this second question can be handled rather more briefly than the first and is addressed initially in the following section.

UNDERSTANDING LOCAL POLITICAL PROCESSES

Political Response

Critical significance attaches to the role of homeownership. For many households in advanced market societies, the house they own and occupy represents their biggest investment, far exceeding in value other assets, such as savings deposits, securities, and durable consumer goods. Like other investments, moreover, it is one from which they expect a rate of return in the form of a capital gain. Relatively favorable tax treatment of capital gains increases the attractions of the house as an investment so that, for example, a dollar invested in housing is worth considerably more than a dollar invested in a savings account.[18]

Capital gains in the housing market, however, are very dependent on what goes on in the vicinity. The nature of the neighborhood and, in particular, the social character of residents, exercise a serious effect on demand for residential property there and, hence, upon housing values. Housing, moreover, has the important quality of immobility. Relocation of the housing unit and the lot on which it stands to a neighborhood where values are appreciating is precluded by the nature of things.

Protection and enhancement of the value of the house as an investment, therefore, shifts the balance from solutions to localized welfare impacts of a relocational character to in situ political solutions. Consequently, where there are threats to the residential desirability of a neighborhood, one should expect the homeowners to be the ones to become most involved in local political activity. Renters, on the other hand, would be more likely to relocate. There is, in fact, some empirical evidence consistent with this interpretation. Homeowners are substantially more likely to belong to neighborhood-based voluntary organizations, even when holding household income constant.[19] In addition, the fact that renters are almost twice as likely to move as homeowners is well known.[20]

Localized Welfare Impacts

Nevertheless, homeownership only assumes this significance for local political action where there is some stimulus in the form of a threat to the value of housing, i.e., a localized welfare impact. In explaining these localized welfare impacts, moreover, substantial significance is attached to the nature of residential preferences.

Localized welfare impacts presuppose some locational structuring of the housing market which, in turn, sets in motion flows of housing market money and residents having welfare impacts on local populations. Basic to both this locational structuring and resultant welfare impacts are residential preferences. In market societies, three aspects of residential preferences are regarded as important to the argument presented here: In the first place, it is suggested that residential preferences converge more and more on preferences for co-residents; alternative residential locations are increasingly evaluated in terms of the social composition of existing residents.[21] This may be related, for example, to the desirable behavioral externalities provided by middle-class families—desirable peer groups for children, low crime rates, etc.—and to the fiscal externalities provided via their substantially greater per capita consumption of real property.

Second, preferences for co-residents are of a remarkably homogeneous character. In particular, it is assumed that both lower-class and middle-class households prefer to live in middle-class neighborhoods.[22] This is not to say that the preferences of lower-class households are of the same intensity as those of middle-class households[23] or that middle-class neighbors are attractive to lower-class households for the same reasons that they are attractive to middle-class households.[24] Rather, it is to argue that there is some basis, rooted in preference functions, for the attempts of developers, for example, to introduce lower-income housing developments into more middle-class ambiences.

Third, and finally, preferences for co-residents have an asymmetric character about them. While all prefer to live in middle-class neighborhoods, not all are able to contribute to the maintenance and enhancement of that "middle classness." While a lower-class household may satisfy its desire to live in a middle-class neighborhood, its presence there reduces the "middle classness" of the neighborhood for existing residents. This is in contrast to a situation in which preferences for co-residents are symmetric, so that those desiring certain co-residents are able to contribute mutually the social attributes regarded as desirable.[25]

While these statements are applicable to residential preferences in market societies everywhere, the *intensity* of preferences for co-residents could conceivably exhibit considerable variability: it is perfectly possible, for example, that households would be more indifferent about co-residents in some national contexts than in others. This has important consequences for the emergence of localized welfare impacts.

Consider, for example, the implications of the following set of circumstances: A town is divided into two areas, one of which is more middle class in its residential composition than the other; preferences for middle-class co-residents are especially intense. Two results follow: On the one hand, there will be a demand to relocate residentially from the more lower-class area to the more middle-class area. This demand will be exhibited by both middle-class and lower-class households. To the extent that money can be made from facilitating the relocation of lower-class households into the middle-class area, one can anticipate that this will take place. The real world phenomena of blockbusting, partition into apartments for lower-class use of large houses in erstwhile middle-class areas, and the like suggest that this is not an unreasonable expectation. As a general consequence, the housing market will exhibit considerable order of a locational character, investment occurring in the more middle-class area and disinvestment occurring in the more lower-class area.[26]

The result of this locational structuring of the housing market, however, will be serious welfare impacts for some residents of the more middle-class area. As some neighborhoods become socially more mixed, so schools will be seen to deteriorate and problems of public safety, to be aggravated.[27] If the initial partition into middle-class and lower-class areas happens to coincide with a jurisdictional division, then fiscal concerns will be added to these behavioral ones.

On the other hand, consider the consequences of a situation where preferences for co-residents are characterized by a greater degree of indifference.

The housing market will exhibit less geographic structuring in terms of social class as other facets of residential desirability become relatively more significant. At the same time the welfare impacts of lower-class residents in middle-class neighborhoods will be substantially reduced. Residential preferences, therefore, provide the nexus linking up the geographic structuring of the housing market on the one side and its localized welfare impacts on the other.

To clothe these speculations with some predictive power, however, it is necessary to ask why, in some societies, preferences for co-residents might be more intense than in others. Critical in this respect, it is suggested, are the interactions between the social differentiations induced by market processes on the one hand, and nation-specific aspects of culture and jurisdictional organization on the other.

Socially, for example, market relationships tend to differentiate people in manners critical for their acceptability as co-residents. The income inequality typical of market societies, therefore, has implications for variations in the consumption of real property and, hence, for differences in fiscal desirability. It may also be apparent in variations in those public behaviors which distinguish the residentially less desirable from the more desirable. As Smolensky and Gomery have written:

> Reductions in income inequality are good in our view because within obvious limits, it is desirable to get individuals in an urban setting to restrict the range of differences in their consumption bundles. For those activities which we assign to the private sector, some chosen consumption bundles lead to significant negative externalities for everyone, but particularly (at least over significant time intervals) middle-income groups.[28]

How residentially undesirable lower-class people are seen to be, however, depends on the specific nature of the national cultural legacy. The interaction of market processes with aspects of history and culture in the U.S., for example, serves to make the lower class considerably more crime-prone than, say, the lower class in Japan.[29]

Similar interactions can be observed between the socially differentiating effects of market societies and jurisdictional organization. A variety of jurisdictional organizations, for example, appear compatible with market societies. As an important consequence, the degree of local home rule in funding and public provision can vary considerably from one national context to another. This has implications for the desirability of socially differentiated co-residents; the poor, evidently, are seen as considerably more undesirable fiscally where home rule applies than in those cases where local governments receive the bulk of their revenue from the central government.

The U.S.-British Contrast

Consider, in review, the argument thus far: In the first section of the paper the locationally decentralized character of political processes in American metropolitan areas was contrasted to urban political processes in Britain; it was then related to attempts to manage, to local advantage, the localized welfare impacts of the housing market. Subsequent arguments presented an abstract explanation for emergence of localized welfare impacts. These were related to particularly intense preferences for co-residents which result in a locational structuring of the housing market and serious welfare impacts for residents in the areas regarded as desirable. The intensity of preferences for co-residents was, in turn, related to interactions between the socially differentiating effects of the market on the one hand, and aspects of national culture and jurisdictional organization on the other.

Consider now the relevance of this argument for the U.S.-British contrast. Since this has been related to variations in the localized welfare impact of the housing market, it should be indirectly traceable to variations in the intensity of preferences for co-residents; i.e., these preferences for co-residents should be substantially more intense in the U.S. than in Britain. Unfortunately, there is no direct, cross-national evidence bearing on this question.[30] Intensity of preferences for co-residents, however, was also related to variations in national culture and jurisdictional organization. On these variations there is evidence, and it is to this that attention now turns.

To the extent that these differences can be documented, one can make out a case for preferences for co-residents being considerably more intense in the U.S.; this should allow one to make contact with those localized welfare impacts held to be basic to the emergence of decentralized political processes in urban areas.

In terms of jurisdictional organization, a major contrast is the extent of local government home rule. Where central government grants account for large proportions of local revenue and, furthermore, where those grants are redistributional in character, then fiscal externalities will be markedly attenuated. Consider in this context sources of money in the U.S. and Britain, respectively, for the critical local function of education. Local spending on education amounts to fifty-five percent of total spending in American cities[31] and to fifty-two percent of total spending in the British case.[32] In the American case, over half (fifty-five percent) of the money for education must be found locally.[33] In the British case, the appropriate figure is closer to twenty percent.[34]

In fact, local spending, as a whole, is much more subsidized by central government grants in the United Kingdom. Approximately two-thirds of local spending comes ultimately from central government taxation.[35] In the U.S., state and federal financing of local government amounts to about forty-five percent of total revenue needs.[36] In addition, British government grants to local government have a strong redistributive element: for those local governments with an assessed valuation of property per capita less than the national average, the central government intervenes with a grant to provide the per capita revenue that would have been derived locally if assessed valuation per capita had been the same as the national average. There is in the United Kingdom, therefore, an institutionally mandated lower limit below which negative fiscal externalities will not be experienced. This is a considerable deterrent to the local government fiscal mercantilism common in the U.S.

Indeed, interstate variations in funding arrangements in the U.S. lend additional credence to this viewpoint. A recent study suggests that local government exclusionary policies are of substantially reduced significance where state grants make up a large proportion of local government spending. Further, where state grants are redistributional in character, the exclusionary incentive is even further attenuated.[37]

A second pertinent aspect of jurisdictional organization concerns arrangements for education. A crucial, historical difference between the U.S. and Britain has been the role of the neighborhood school. As a result of the structure of the British educational system up until the late 1960s, residential location had limited significance for school peer group. This was the result of a two-tier educational system which, at the age of eleven, segregated the brighter, usually more middle-class, pupils from the less bright. Those passing the "eleven-plus" examination went on to the so-called grammar schools, while those failing proceeded to quite separate secondary modern schools. In the mid-1960s the proportion proceeding to grammar school was about twenty-nine percent.[38] This stream, moreover, was evidently more middle class than the secondary modern stream. In London in the early 1950s the middle-class/lower-class ratio was 20:80 in secondary modern schools and 48:52 in grammar schools.[39] And the lower-class children attending grammar schools were the brighter representatives of their class, anyway, and therefore more acceptable to middle-class parents. In addition, a vigorous private school system segregated large numbers of middle-class children from the lower class.[40]

As a consequence, in the British case it has historically been possible for middle-class and lower-class households to live in the same neighborhood and for the children to attend different schools. This is in sharp contrast to the American situation, where application of the neighborhood school concept in the absence of academic segregation among schools has served to increase the intensity of preferences for co-residents.

In Britain the two-tier educational system is now being phased out and replaced with a system of comprehensive schools akin to the American high school. As a consequence parents have become more dependent on those living around them for the type of peer groups their children have in school. On the basis of American experience, one would expect this to generate residential shifts between school catchment areas based on the reputation of different schools and the social class composition of their pupils. It will be important to see if this change in institutional arrangements is also reflected in an increased local involvement in the political process aimed at enhancing neighborhood social class composition.

A third, and final, contrast significant for the intensity of preferences for co-residents resides in aspects of culture. More specifically, this involves the public safety problem. This has been well publicized and requires little additional comment here. Suffice it to say that in Britain, public safety is rarely a basis either for residential choice or for locally based political action. This contrast to the U.S. would appear, however, to be of major importance, for in addition to its additive effects on intensity of preference, it also interacts with aspects of jurisdictional organization. In particular, the neighborhood school concept intensifies the impact of school vandalism and delinquency on resident welfare in predominantly middle-class areas.[41]

There are good reasons, of a broadly cultural and institutional character, therefore, for expecting preferences for co-residents in the U.S. to be markedly more intense than in the British case. These preferences provide the precondition, first, for a housing market structured by considerations of social class geography; and, second, for the localized welfare impacts resulting from investment flows and residential relocations set in motion by this housing market. In their turn these localized welfare impacts create the conditions necessary for the emergence of locationally decentralized political processes. The absence of those same conditions in the British case, where local interests are substantially less apparent in urban political processes, lends support to this view.

CONCLUDING COMMENTS

Broadly speaking, this analysis has attempted to explain the differential form assumed by urban political processes in different countries in terms of the conditioning of the housing market by aspects of cultural and jurisdictional organization peculiar to those countries. One might summarize our findings regarding that conditioning by postulating that the housing market in American cities has historically been much more sensitive to social class geography than has the housing market in British cities.

This is pertinent to certain other observations one might make about housing markets in American and British cities. In general, major American cities have been characterized by rapid rates of suburbanization and by a general deterioration in the viability of inner-city housing markets: in the extreme case, of course, this loss of viability is expressed in the abandonment of whole neighborhoods.[42] In British cities, on the other hand, not only has suburbanization been less rapid, but inner-city abandonment in the American style is virtually unknown.[43] Rather, rehabilitation of deteriorating neighborhoods for middle-class use is much more common. This also appears to be the pattern in Canadian cities.[44]

Of course, the link between suburbanization and decline in the viability of inner-city housing markets could be forged in a number of ways. According to one theory, for example, it could be related to the filtering down of older, less fashionable housing to lower-income families in a city in which the desirability of housing stock increases with increasing distance from the city center. More recently, however, attacks on conventional filtering theory have underlined the significance of neighborhood desirability, particularly in terms of neighborhood social class composition; change in neighborhood occupancy, it is hypothesized, stimulates the demand for suburban housing and distance from "them."[45] The image conveyed, therefore, is one in which pressure to live in socially more desirable neighborhoods results in a continual outward pressure on the spatial form of the city, resulting in the collapse of inner-city housing markets.

The desirability of middle-class neighborhoods, it could be argued, is due precisely to those considerations of public safety and public schools which loom so large in American urban consciousness — and which seem to play so small a role in British residential preferences. Of course, this line of reasoning does raise difficulties of its own. Recent work in Britain and the U.S., for example, has drawn attention to the effects of urban containment policies in Britain: reduced rates of suburbanization and low vacancy rates in inner-city housing markets.[46] To what extent, however, could one justify the view that these institutional considerations are exogenous to the system? In the American context it may well be that the payoffs to suburban development are such as to preclude the type of rigid land-use control characteristic of the British rural fringe and appropriate to a less buoyant suburban housing and land market.

NOTES

1. Discussion and documentation of this viewpoint is provided by Mason Gaffney, "Tax Reform to Release Land," in *Modernizing Urban Land Policy*, ed. Marion Clawson (Washington, D.C.: Resources for the Future, 1973) pp. 115-51.

2. The concept of fiscal externality refers to the fiscal implications of a land use or individual for a local government. If the individual or land use generates a greater demand (in dollar terms) for public services than its contribution to local revenue, then negative fiscal externalities are said to be imposed. Those individuals or land uses contributing more to local revenue than the value of the public services provided as a result of their presence are said to provide positive fiscal externalities.

3. The significance of these concerns at the neighborhood level in American cities is discussed in Anthony Downs, *Opening Up the Suburbs* (New Haven, Conn.: Yale University Press, 1973), chap. 7

4. For an exhaustive discussion of exclusionary zoning and its welfare implications, see Lynne B. Sagalyn and George Sternlieb, *Zoning and Housing Costs* (New Brunswick, N.J.: Rutgers University, Center for Urban Policy Research, 1972).

5. See Gaffney, "Tax Reform to Release Land," pp. 126-27.

6. Municipalities are under no obligation to provide federally subsidized public housing, they merely have the right if they so desire. See Kevin R. Cox and John A. Agnew, "The Location of Public Housing: Towards a Comparative Analysis," Ohio State University Department of Geography Discussion Paper no. 45 (Columbus, 1974), p. 12.

7. This has been documented in U.S. Commission on Civil Rights, *Above Property Rights* (Washington, D.C.: Government Printing Office, 1972), pp. 21-22.

8. An excellent example of code-enforcement strategy was implemented by University City in the St. Louis metropolitan area. See U.S. Commission on Civil Rights, *Hearing Before the United States Commission on Civil Rights: St. Louis, Missouri, January 14-17, 1970* (Washington, D.C.: Government Printing Office, 1971), pp. 314-21.

9. The salience of local school and public safety issues is clearly apparent in a recent study of the St. Louis housing market: James Little et al., *The Contemporary Neighborhood Succession Process* (St. Louis, Mo.: Washington University Institute for Urban and Regional Studies, 1975), p. 133. The same emphases are apparent in a recent survey of changing neighborhoods in Chicago. See Brian J. L. Berry et al., "Attitudes Towards Integration: The Role of Status in Community Response to Racial Change," in *The Changing Face of the Suburbs*, ed. Barry Schwartz (Chicago: University of Chicago Press, 1976), chap. 9.

10. There is a wide variety of studies of the determinants of residential property values. A useful review of these studies can be found in Michael Ball, "Recent Empirical Work on the Determinants of Relative House Prices," *Urban Studies* 10, no. 2 (June 1973): 213-33.

11. U.S. National Commission on Urban Problems (The Douglas Commission), *Building the American City* (Washington, D.C.: Government Printing Office, 1968), p. 101. See also: Calvin P. Bradford and Leonard S. Rubinowitz, "The Urban-Suburban Investment-Disinvestment Process: Consequences for Older Neighborhoods," *Annals of the American Academy of Political and Social Science* 422 (1975): 77-86; and Arthur J. Naparstek and Gale Cincotta, *Urban Disinvestment: New Implications for Community Organization, Research, and Public Policy* (Washington, D.C.: National Center for Urban Ethnic Affairs, 1976).

12. On the spatial choices of insurance companies, see Richard F. Syron, "The Hard Economics of Ghetto Fire Insurance," *New England Economic Review* (March/April 1972), pp. 2-11.

13. See, for instance, Eleanor P. Wolf and Charles N. Lebeaux, eds., *Change and Renewal in an Urban Community* (New York: Praeger, 1969), pt. 1.

14. For instance, see Harvey Molotch's study of the South Shore area of Chicago: Harvey Molotch, *Managed Integration: Dilemmas of Doing Good in the City* (Berkeley and Los Angeles: University of California Press, 1972): see also a study of the Bagley neighborhood in Detroit: Wolf and Lebeaux, *Urban Community.*

15. Some of the few instances include: David E.C. Eversley, "Rising Costs and Static Incomes: Some Economic Consequences of Regional Planning in London," *Urban Studies* 9, no. 3 (October 1972): 347-68; and G. McDonald, "Metropolitan Policy and the Stress Areas," *Urban Studies* 11, no. 1 (February 1974): 27-37.

16. Cox and Agnew, "*Location and Public Housing*," pp. 42-43.

17. For example, there are no instances, to the author's knowledge, of attempts by neighborhood groups to intervene directly in the real estate market such as those referred to in note 14 (above).

18. In particular, taxation of capital gains in the U.S. is deferred if a new house is bought for more than the old house was sold. In Britain there is no capital gains tax on the sale of first homes.

19. According to one study carried out in the late 1960s, membership of renters in community organizations was about 10 percent, irrespective of income; for homeowners, membership rates increased from 11 percent (for those with annual incomes below $5,000) to 25 percent (for those with incomes over $10,000). See Irving A. Spergel, ed., *Community Organization* (Beverly Hills, Calif.: Sage Publications, 1972).

20. Peter A. Morrison, "Population Movements and the Shape of Urban Growth: Implications for Public Policy," in *Population Distribution and Policy*, ed. Sara Mills Maizie (Washington, D.C.: Government Printing Office, 1972), p. 301.

21. There is no firm empirical evidence on this point, though providing such evidence would not seem beyond the ingenuity of historical property value studies. Moreover, there are good reasons for experiencing such a shift in emphasis. With improved mobility, for example, access to the work place should decline in significance and permit greater discretion in residential choice.

22. On the basis of the findings of numerous studies of residential choice and neighborhood change, this proposition seems obvious. Studies of neighborhood deterioration, for example, have shown how incoming lower-income populations are attracted by the good schools and low crime rates of middle-class neighborhoods; since incoming populations, of course, tend to detract from these qualities, the existing middle-class populations move out in search of more homogeneous middle-class neighborhoods. See, in particular: Molotch, *Managed Integration*; Wolf and Lebeaux, *Urban Community*; and Gary A. Tobin, "An Analysis of Attitudinal Responses of Movers in Transition Neighborhoods," Washington University Institute for Urban and Regional Studies Working Paper HMS 7 (St. Louis, Mo., n.d).

Despite its obviousness, however, there is little direct evidence on residential preferences themselves. The most direct evidence I have been able to identify comes from my sample survey of 110 households in Columbus, Ohio, in 1973. Respondents were asked to rank three neighborhoods in terms of their desirability as places in which to live (assuming no budgetary obstacles): a relatively upper-class suburb, a lower middle-class, older neighborhood, and a respectable working-class neighborhood. Irrespective of respondent social class, the rankings were of a highly repetitive character: Almost invariably the upper-class suburb was preferred to the lower middle-class neighborhood, and the lower middle-class neighborhood was preferred to the respectable working-class district. In addition, respondents were asked to rate their own neighborhood as a place in which to live; this showed a reasonably strong and significant relationship (Pearsonian r = .53) with a measure of census tract social class.

23. A number of existing statements, for example, tend to support the idea that lower-class households have less intense preferences for middle-class neighborhoods than do middle-class households. Martin Bailey, for example, has written: "It is generally true that people consider it unpleasant to live near groups of people with lower incomes and with tastes and habits 'inferior' to their own, while the reverse is sometimes and perhaps generally not the case." See Martin Bailey, "Note on the Economics of Residential Zoning and Urban Renewal," *Land Economics* 35, no. 3 (August 1959), 288. More recently, Alan Evans has suggested that both high-income and low-income households are prepared to pay more to live in upper-income neighborhoods; the intensity of the preferences of lower-income households, however, is considered less than that of upper-income households. See Alan Evans, "Economic Influences on Social Mix," *Urban Studies* 13, no. 3 (October 1976): 257.

24. Recent evidence from St. Louis, for example, suggests that public safety considerations are of major significance in the attractions of middle-income neighborhoods for those of lower income. For those of higher income, on the other hand, the major attractions of the middle-class neighborhood derive from the quality of local schools. See Gary Tobin, "Moves in Transition Neighborhoods," pp. 13-20.

25. A clear instance of this symmetry is that which relates Protestants and Roman Catholics to their coreligionists in the Belfast context. See F. W. Boal, "Territoriality on the Shankill-Falls Divide, Belfast," *Irish Geography* 6, no. 1 (1969): 30-50.

26. If we carry this logic a little further, it is clear that ultimately the housing market will result in convergence in the social composition of the two areas and consequent elimination of differentials in residential desirability.

27. Wolf and Lebeaux, *Urban Community*; and Molotch, *Managed Integration*.

28. Eugene Smolensky and J. Douglas Gomery, "The Urban Problem as an Exercise in the Theory of Efficient Transfers," University of Wisconsin Institute for Research on Poverty Discussion Papers 100-171 (Madison: n.d.), p. 8.

29. David H. Bayley, "Learning About Crime--The Japanese Experience," *Public Interest*, no. 44 (Summer 1976): 55-68.

30. Inter-nation comparison of levels of residential segregation, though difficult, might provide some indirect evidence on this point.

31. Dick Netzer, *Economics and Urban Problems* (New York: Basic Books, 1970), p. 172.

32. John Pratt et al., *Your Local Education* (Harmondsworth, Middlesex: Penguin Books, 1973), p. 82.

33. Netzer, *Economics and Urban Problems*, p. 173.

34. Pratt, *Your Local Education*.

35. Sir Harry Page, "Local Government — The Final Phase?" *Three Banks Review*, no. 106 (June 1975): 13.

36. Netzer, *Economics and Urban Problems*, p. 172.

37. Bruce Hamilton, Edwin Mills, and David Puryear, "Benefits and Costs of Metropolitan Area-wide Goverment," in *Fiscal Zoning and Land Use Controls*, ed. Edwin S. Mills and Wallace E. Oates (Lexington, Mass.: Lexington Books, 1975).

38. John Vaizey and John Sheehan, *Resources for Education* (London: Allen and Unwin, 1968), p. 60.

39. H. T. Himmelweit, "Social Status and Secondary Education Since the 1944 Act: Some Data for London," in *Equal Opportunity in Education*, ed. Harold Silver (London, Methuen, 1973), p. 123.

40. In 1965, somewhere between seven and eight percent of all pupils aged eleven and over were in private schools: this estimate is based on information supplied in Vaizey and Sheehan, *Resources for Education*: a figure of 2,921,713 for all school pupils aged eleven and over (p. 61); and a figure of 217,823 for all pupils aged eleven and over in private schools (p. 109).

41. For instance, see Wolf and Lebeaux, *Urban Community*, p. 80.

42. A good survey of this problem is provided in U. S. Department of Housing and Urban Development, *Abandoned Housing Research: A Compendium* (Washington, D.C.: Government Printing Office, 1973).

43. Marion Clawson and Peter Hall, *Planning and Urban Growth* (Baltimore: The Johns Hopkins University Press, 1973), chap. 4.

44. S. T. Roweis and A. J. Scott, "The Urban Land Question," in *Urbanization and Conflict in Market Societies*, ed. Kevin R. Cox (Chicago: Maaroufa Press, 1978), chap. 2.

45. Little, *Neighborhood Succession Process*.

46. Clawson and Hall, *Planning and Urban Growth*.

9

Locational Conflict and the Politics of Consumption

David Ley
John Mercer

The overdependence of land use theory upon neoclassical economics has recently come under criticism from both liberal and radical sources. Liberal writers have provided an internal critique of such assumptions of land use models as the dominant employment source in the central business district, equal transportation access throughout the city, the development of concentric residential zones, and reliance upon pure market conditions of supply and demand [21]. The radical critique has challenged the political naivety of land use models, arguing that the concept of market equilibrium implies a consensus which conceals the reality of power relations (defined not simply by market power) as these direct the course of urban development and the distribution of external costs and benefits [12]. In a radical political economy, in contrast, analysis would be concerned with "the deep structure of urban property relations in relation to which the competitive bidding for land is only the faintest and most superficial pulsation" [22].

The now sizable literature on conflict over locational decision making represents a first step toward a more critical approach to land use theory [4].

Locational Conflict and the Politics of Consumption 119

The concept of locational conflict challenges politically mute interpretations of market equilibrium as it emphasizes the disharmonious and asymmetric costs and benefits resulting from a land use decision. These relations have been exposed in a number of detailed case studies which have documented the unequal impact of new developments and the tactics employed by different participants in the decision process according to the power they hold [15; 33]. But there remains something of a conceptual and theoretical gap between this empirical work and more general discourses on power, conflict, and crisis in contemporary society [6]. There have been, for example, no significant attempts in geography to link the case studies which have identified the role of critical managers and gatekeepers in locational decision making (the "manipulated city" thesis) with such theoretical traditions as *elite theory* or *theory of bureaucracy*, where some potentially fruitful connections might be made. An isolated and ambitious attempt to apply Dahrendorf's *conflict theory* to locational conflict ended by criticizing the theory itself as too rigid to incorporate the flux and complexities of land use controversies [23]. Most recently, it has been claimed that land use conflict is simply an urban manifestation of a more fundamental class conflict, "mere reflections of the underlying tension between capital and labor" to be brought to light by a Marxian political economy [13]. At present, the potential absorption of locational conflict into Marxian theory is an assertion which remains to be tested.

Moreover, even the emergence of a political economy incorporating the social distribution of power would remain too narrow a theoretical formulation if it failed to treat as problematic the diverse and constitutive values of social groups. It has become evident in the past decade that social goals transcend not only such market objectives as efficiency and maximization but also state goals of welfare and equity, to include aspirations such as the safeguarding of the ecological realm, the celebration of the aesthetic, the maintenance of consumption lifestyles, or even the challenging of growth. But the realm of values and beliefs is not treated as problematic in political economy as currently developed. In neoclassical formulations, tastes and preferences, though granted some importance, are regarded as simple and unproblematic. Land value theory begins by suppressing the plural world of human values and meaning as human subjectivity is "reduced to that uninteresting individual, economic man..."[1]. Such reductionism is carried over into Marxian formulations, where attitudes and preferences are regarded as wholly derivative, as "purely epiphenomenal" [22].

But intellectual traditions outside political economy identify the symbolic realm of social and cultural values as far more volatile and theoretically central in an understanding of human action [2; 18]. From such a perspective Marxian political economy retains too many of the shortcomings it seeks to correct, as "the social sphere is filtered, inexorably, through the concepts of production and labor which become the unquestioned metaphysical reference points of social reality" [20]. In contrast, a broader theoretical framework would admit the role of symbolic factors alongside economic categories, recognizing that consumption lifestyles might steer the pattern of urban land use down one of several alternative and perhaps competing paths.[1] There is, in short, a plurality of value positions intersecting in the urban arena, and a one-dimensional reduction to economic categories alone brings about an inappropriate theoretical foreclosure. As Adorno once put it, "to conceptualize problems only in the categories of political economy is to make the world over into a giant workhouse."

The present study will illustrate the role of guiding ideologies by examining the divergent values of participants in a number of land use conflicts which occurred in Vancouver, British Columbia, between 1973 and 1975. We will note the ascendancy of a social and aesthetic ideology under circumstances of rising real wealth, an ideology which prescribed that urban development should follow what Thorstein Veblen called the canons of good taste [31].

During this period a new elite of professional and senior white collar workers, espousing humane values and a "livable city," rose into local prominence and attained political office at city hall. This middle-class and upper middle-class echelon of state employees and self-employed professionals, divorced from significant land or commercial ownership, prized apart any simple definition of a dichotomous class division. A longitudinal study of land use conflicts over a three-year period will show the conjunction of socio-cultural life-style values with political and economic factors in directing the course of urban development. A longitudinal study of a number of locational controversies, which examines both interest groups and their values, might well be more contextually grounded than research which examines only a single case study or else is abstracted away from real geographical conditions. However, the aggregation of conflicts does introduce a limitation, precluding a discussion of individual cases with their often informative idiosyncrasies.

This research will also provide an illustration of a more general principle, namely, the *political* (rather than the economic) implications of consumer sanctions within a mixed economy. In contemporary North American society the forces of consumption are fundamentally political in that they confer legitimacy to existing political authority. Withdrawal of legitimacy and consequent loss of support may accompany the failure of political leadership to meet citizen aspirations in the maintenance or advancement of consumption. In Vancouver, as will be shown, the failure of city council after 1968 to satisfy the consumption styles in urban development of a newly emergent professional and liberal elite led to a loss of legitimacy by council and the

Locational Conflict and the Politics of Consumption 121

successful launching of a new urban reform party to promote the liberal platform of the livable city. A decade later in North America, beginning in California, countervailing conservative social movements have prompted a second change in allocation procedures and a shift in the political rules of the game. In each instance, the withdrawal of support by politicized groups of consumers has led to a change in policies and/or political leadership and to a redirection of government programs in a range of areas including those with direct consequences for the built environment.

So, too, land use controversies during the 1970s have focussed upon questions like freeway construction, redevelopment, and the provision of public goods such as open space—questions which have frequently been resolved through political initiative or through the courts. In this manner, locational decision making (and locational conflict) is increasingly being mediated through *political processes* and not simply through the operation of the marketplace. In this transfer toward the political level, the realm of consumption, as a result of interest group lobbying, may again assume a significant political identity. In short, partly through consumer mobilization for political action, the culture of consumption emerges as a significant component for a coherent theory of urban land use.

THE CONTEXT

In 1976 Vancouver was a city of 410,000 people, whose suburban municipalities contributed to a metropolitan area of over one million. The city had developed as a port and western terminus of two trans-Canada railroads, with an employment base dominated by the lumber industry [11]. But, during the 1950s and more rapidly in the 1960s there was a shift toward a white collar, service-dominated economy. The proportion of the city's labor force employed in services and public administration rose by more than 50 percent between 1951 and 1971, and by 1976 white collar occupations accounted for more than 70 percent of the city's jobs. The service oriented economy was expanding rapidly, as 8,000 new jobs were generated each year from 1971 to 1975 [26]. Seventy-five percent of new jobs were accommodated in new offices, so that accompanying employment expansion was a downtown construction boom of remarkable extent for the city's size. In the decade from 1967 to 1977 downtown office space doubled to 14 million square feet; it was estimated that every million square feet added generated about 5,000 office jobs.

Rapid population growth was associated with Vancouver's new stature as a center of managerial and service employment. The population of the metropolitan area increased by 13 percent, 21 percent, and 8 percent in the three, successive, five-year periods from 1961 to 1976. Within the city itself, immigration was highly biased in nature. Among the different age cohorts there was a net in-migration of about 22,000 persons from 1966 to 1971; 60

percent of these were in the 20-24 age groups. In contrast, half the net out-migration by cohort consisted of 6,000 children under five years of age [29]. These trends have carried into the 1970s with the loss of a further 5,600 young children (23 percent) and the gain of 9,000-10,000 adults in the 25-34 age group between 1971 and 1976 [27]. As this latter cohort is of potential child-raising age, the clear inference is that the city is losing families with children and gaining adult households without children. No other cohorts under 60 years of age increased in numbers from 1971 to 1976; the more limited gains in the elderly population would inevitably be of small childless households.

These demographic shifts have had an obvious impact on housing needs. While the city's population was at approximately the same level in 1976 as in 1966 the smaller size of families has been accompanied by an increase of five percent in the number of households. Not only are there more households and smaller households, but in the absence of child-raising costs, these households have greater discretionary income. There has been a dramatic increase in the purchasing power of Vancouver residents, as almost a quarter of households earned more than $20,000 in 1976; in constant dollars this represented a gain of over 12,000 households in this top category between 1972 and 1976 [28]. To accommodate this population there has been extensive redevelopment of the apartment-zoned inner city neighborhoods. During the 1960s there was significant development of rental units, both high and low rise, but since 1970 this trend has been overtaken by the construction, up to 1976, of 5,000 inner city condominiums, many catering to the wealthier recent arrivals.

These economic and demographic transformations have not been independent of Vancouver's reputation as a high amenity city with the immediacy of mountains, ski-slopes, forests, parks, beaches, and the ocean providing an unusually favored natural setting. This milieu has aided the development of an aesthetic lifestyle, of consumption with taste, among the professionals and senior white collar workers who have emerged as a new elite; this association between high levels of amenity and quaternary occupations is not of course unique to Vancouver [9;24]. In the late 1960s this subculture merged with other social movements of the day advocating more open and responsive government, greater attention to the environment, and a more humane, livable city. These popular movements were institutionalized in the formation of a new civic reform party in 1968, The Electors Action Movement (TEAM), which was headed not by businessmen but by professionals; in 1973 when more than 700 households held TEAM membership, 25 percent of the members were teachers, university professors, architects, or in the legal profession. A profile of TEAM leadership in 1969 showed that almost 60 percent were professionals or semi-professionals, while a little over 20 percent were businessmen [5]. In contrast, the Non-Partisan Association (NPA), which dominated Vancouver politics unopposed from 1937 to 1968, had always been a free enterprise party, and in 1969 almost three-quarters of its leaders were businessmen. Vancouver civic politics had always been controlled by business interests, and it was not until the late 1960s and 1970s that "business" was surpassed as the occupation of a majority of newly elected council members; the newly ascendant group have been the professionals, with a liberal ideology frequently placing them in opposition to NPA development and social policy. Consequently, the early and mid-1970s represented a period of repeated conflict between TEAM and the NPA, and the plural elites of which they were an expression. On the one hand, there were interests favoring the livable city, the quality of urban life; on the other, there was growth boosterism with its attendant freeway and high rise landscape as the objective (16).

The first successful TEAM aldermen were elected in 1968, and by 1972 TEAM had won control of City Hall. With Vancouver's at-large system of municipal representation, a residential clustering of aldermen is always possible, and in 1972 seven of the eight members of TEAM's majority on council lived in professional, westside neighborhoods (the eighth lived outside the city in the highest status suburb). A major campaign issue in the 1972 election was the nature of urban development, especially in the downtown area, as TEAM adopted a livable city platform, critical of unregulated change and of a system which gave altogether too much freedom to an entrepreneurial ethic and the business lobby. In a city where a marked degree of growth and change was occurring, such an ideology held by a council majority was a prescription for widespread controversy over land use issues. This, then, was the socio-political context within which land use change was proposed and flashpoints of land use controversy erupted.

THE PATTERN OF LAND USE CHANGE

Since conflict is usually associated with a change or potential change in use, an inventory was made to assess the pattern of land use changes during the three calendar years 1973-1975. The most complete indicator, if one tedious to collect, was development permit applications made to City Hall. These permits covered all structural changes or proposed changes to the built environment and also changes in function to an existing property. The permits have the advantage of specifying an exact address and including various other details about the proposed use. In their raw form they were too comprehensive for our purpose, for even a minor change like the installation of an air conditioning unit required a permit. Guidelines were established to separate small alterations, and the number of permits was reduced from 12,000 to 2,000, covering only substantial structural and land use developments. Next, a 25

FIGURE 1
Permits Issued for Major Developments in Vancouver, 1973-1975

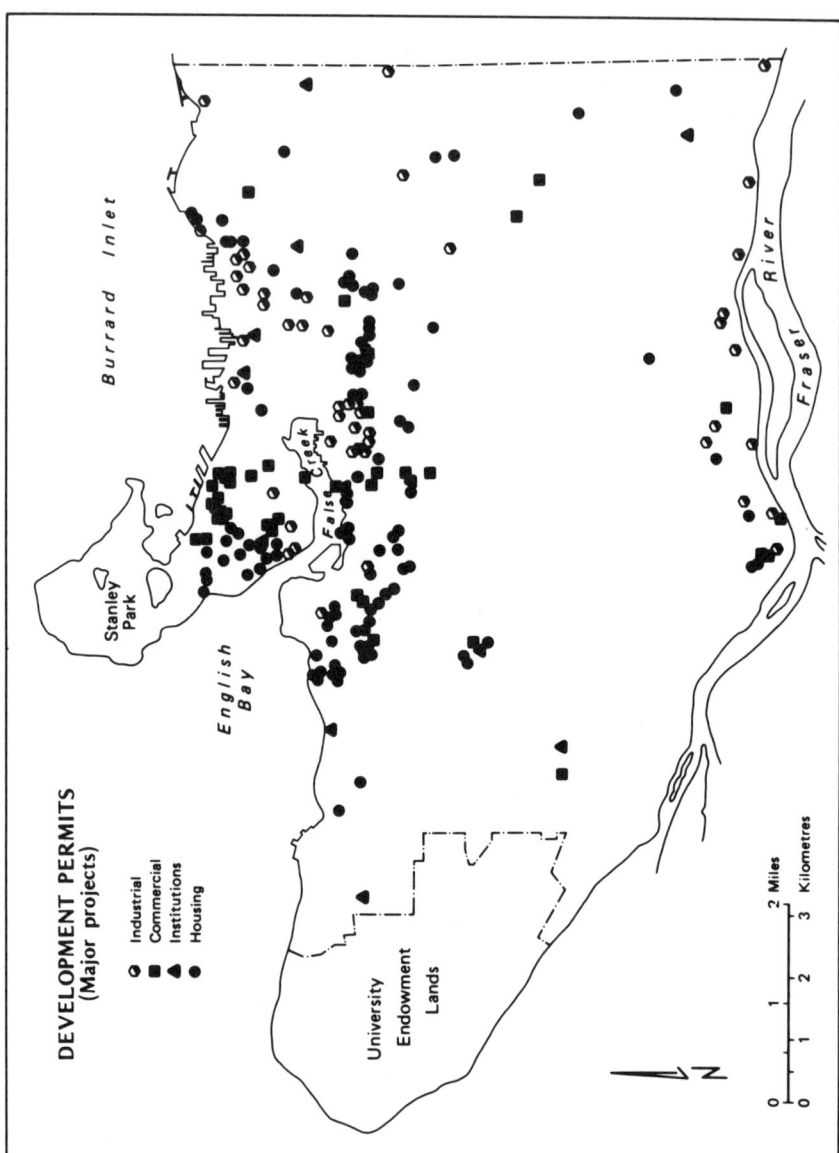

percent systematic sample was taken, which, disregarding applications that were refused, left a final sample of 495 permits which form the basis of our computations of land use change. The permits were grouped into five categories: industrial uses (which accounted for 11 percent of the permits), commercial uses (42 percent), institutional uses (15 percent), multiple family dwellings (26 percent), and single family dwellings (6 percent). The land use categories were classified further to identify the largest developments, and these were mapped (Figure 1).

The geography of development from 1973 to 1975 forms a highly ordered pattern with the distribution of proposed uses guided by existing zoning. Commercial proposals are concentrated in the downtown core, with a small cluster in an emerging secondary core south of False Creek. Industrial development applications are grouped in two well-defined areas in the northeast of the city and in the extreme south along the Fraser River, following the established zoning map for industry. They are notably absent from the west side of Vancouver. Residential applications form three major clusters, the west side of the downtown peninsula (the West End), the southwest (Kitsilano, Fairview), and southeast (Mount Pleasant) of False Creek. Applications of institutional uses are the most widely scattered of the four major categories.

The pattern of development applications bears some similarities with Bourne's analysis of land use change in Toronto [3]. The trends are symptomatic of a managerial and service dominated economy with the consolidation of a high rise office and commercial core and the redevelopment of the inner city ring in multiple family dwellings. Against the dominance of these categories (68 percent of development permits) other uses are secondary. Industrial expansion near the core is more limited and is increasingly occurring in fringe areas; in Vancouver, for example, lumber related industries have been displaced from False Creek to their present site along the Fraser River. Outside the turbulent construction activity in the inner city ring, very little major development is occurring in the inner suburbs, particularly those on the west side of Vancouver. The development pressures on the central neighborhoods have occasioned an institutional response with major rezoning policies accomplished in the central business district and the inner, westside, residential neighborhoods of the West End, Kitsilano, and Fairview. No such blanket rezoning occurred in any other neighborhood between 1973 and 1975. The rezoning, limiting densities in the West End and Kitsilano, and permitting housing and green space redevelopment of an industrial area in Fairview, was related to the new ideology held by city council and its newly appointed planning staff.

To what extent does this refurbishing of Vancouver's central neighborhoods represent a redistribution of costs and benefits which are perceived and contested by residents? How closely does conflict accompany change? At a temporal level, there was a steady reduction in development permit applications through the three-year study period, with 1975 applications more than

25 percent lower than the 1973 figure. This trend matched the reduction of land use conflicts over the same period, though here the decline was more rapid, with the number of new controversies in 1975 over 80 percent below the level for 1973.[2] In turning to the spatial coincidence between land use change and locational conflict we will see the same relationship of a correspondence of major trends, though these disguise significant regional variations within the city.

THE DIMENSIONS OF LOCATIONAL CONFLICT

The incidence of conflict was assessed from newspaper coverage, following the method adopted by Janelle in his analysis of locational controversy in London, Ontario [14]. In this study, each daily issue of the *Vancouver Sun* published between January 1, 1973 and December 31, 1975 was subjected to a detailed content analysis. As the *Sun* has the widest daily circulation of any newspaper in the metropolitan area, its coverage of development issues might be expected to be the most complete, particularly within the city of Vancouver itself, to which this analysis is limited. Nevertheless, there are legitimate grounds for doubt as to the representativeness of any newspaper coverage; systematic biases, both conscious and unconscious, may well exist. Ultimately, such criticisms are unanswerable, though one might observe, firstly, that any other source would probably be equally biased and probably less complete, and secondly, that potential bias has not prevented newspapers from being a major data source in other areas of social science and historical research. It is also reassuring to note that in London, Janelle found a significant positive correlation to exist between the distribution of conflicts uncovered from newspapers and those retrieved by an analysis of the minutes of council committee meetings.

Two other difficulties with the data should be noted. Firstly, as the analysis of each conflict becomes more detailed, so there is a greater likelihood of missing data from incomplete news reporting. Secondly, there are the normal coding problems inherent in content analysis and, indeed, in any structured research technique which imposes a fixed set of categories upon events which are not only complex but also in flux. For example, double counting was necessary when the definition of conflicts and protagonists could not be limited to a single item, or else shifted in the course of the controversy. Inevitably with such qualifications, the analysis can only be expected to reveal major trends; nuances of interpretation fall beyond its range.

A locational event was recorded as a conflict if it involved a reported disagreement between interest groups over the use of a site. A disagreement was defined as ranging from verbal dissent to a demonstration where arrests were made (in fact, though there were demonstrations, no arrests were made in any land use conflict in the period examined). The use of a site was defined

FIGURE 2
The Pattern of Locational Conflict in Vancouver, 1973-1975

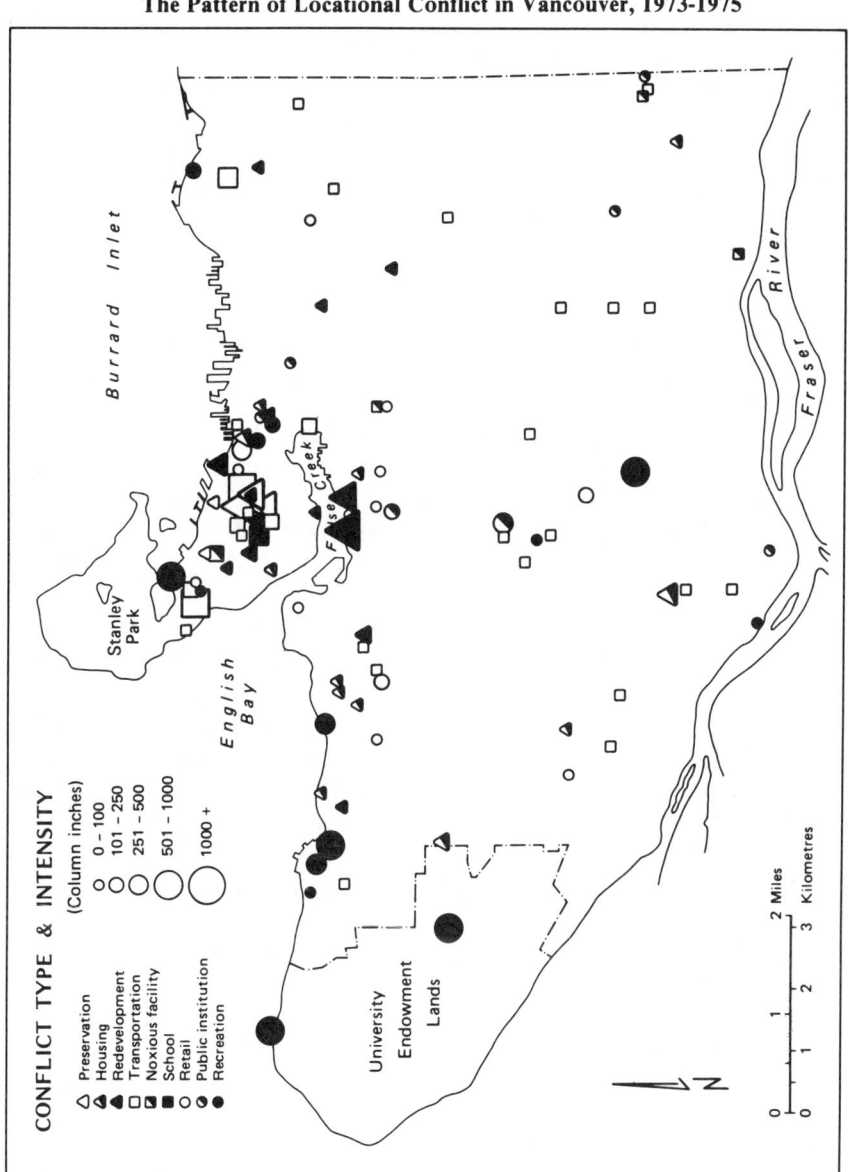

broadly to include both form and function, so that conflicts ranged from a conventional redevelopment proposal, to a zoning controversy, to lobbying for a pedestrian traffic light. Under this definition of a locational conflict, 98 incidents took place between January 1973 and December 1975 within the City of Vancouver. Each incident was coded by location, date, and amount and type of news coverage. Present and proposed land uses were noted, and the conflict was assigned to one of nine land use types; the degree of conflict and eventual resolution were also recorded. Participants and their expressed grounds for involvement in the controversy were assessed; a note was made of which participants were successful in the outcome and which were not. Space and clarity permit only some of the detailed set of tabulations and cross-tabulations to be introduced into the discussion here.

An indication of the magnitude of a conflict could be judged from either the number of stories newspapers devoted to the incident, or else from the total number of column inches of space it received. It was found that these two measures of intensity were highly correlated and therefore interchangeable; in the analysis, column inches was preferred.

The map of locational conflict shows both the type and also the intensity of each controversy (Figure 2). There was a predictably high concentration of major conflicts of varied types in the central business district and inner city ring, particularly to the west and southwest of the business core. Far fewer conflicts were recorded in the eastern inner city ring, or indeed on the east side of the city generally. On the west side, several major flashpoints were indicated beyond the inner city ring, most of them connected with recreational issues. Over the entire city there was a scattering of local transportation problems, most of them concerned with the installation of pedestrian traffic lights.

A discussion of some of the simple tabulations will identify a conflict framework within which we may then examine more carefully the relations indicated by cross-tabulation (Table 1). The recurrent conflict types fell in the categories of transportation, recreation, redevelopment, housing, and commerce (Table 1A). The somewhat different classification by proposed land use

TABLE 1
Major Characteristics of Locational Conflicts

A. CONFLICT TYPE	No. Issues	B. PROPOSED LAND USE	Percent*
Transportation	27	Transportation	32
Recreation	15	Housing	32
Redevelopment	14	Commerce	28
Commerce	12	Parks/open space	19
Housing	12	Public services	14
Public institution	7	Industry	3
Preservation	5	Unknown	2
Noxious facility	4		
School	2		
Total	98		

TABLE 1 (Continued)

C. PARTICIPANTS

	Initiators Percent of Issues	Advocates Percent of Issues*	Opponents Percent of Issues*
Households	11	33	54
Neighborhood groups	6	19	31
Civic organizations	3	15	32
Land developers	28	32	5
Other entrepreneurs	5	9	10
Elected officials	26	56	48
Administrative officials	18	31	33
Unknown	3	0	0

D. CONFLICT INTENSITY

	Percent of Issues*
Verbal disagreement (face-to-face)	77
Verbal disagreement (indirect)	72
Appeal to government	53
Group organizing	48
Petition	29
Brief presented	21
Demonstration	20
Injunction served	6
Arrests	0

E. GROUNDS FOR INVOLVEMENT

	Advocates	Opponents
	(Percent of Issues*)	
I. *Economic factors*	13	19
Cost of change	5	7
Impact on property values	1	6
Other economic factors	7	6
II. *Social factors*	38	67
Need for improved services	11	9
Compatibility with neighborhood	2	12
Impact on traffic	3	12
Safety	15	3
Availability of housing	3	9
Other social factors	4	22
III. *Aesthetic factors*	14	22
Visual attractiveness	8	14
Other aesthetic factors	6	8

TABLE 1 (Continued)

IV. Procedural factors	6	15
V. Miscellaneous factors	2	13

*Multiple counting prevents percent from summing to 100.

implicated transportation, residential, and commercial uses and parks and open space (Table 1B). Public services were less commonly identified with conflict and industrial use scarcely at all. Significantly, the major metropolitan issues concerning industry and noxious facilities occurred in the suburbs, where such uses have increasingly been displaced. Interest groups involved in the controversy played a different role at various stages of the process (Table 1C). Initiators of the issue were most usually land developers or elected officials, or, less commonly, administrative officials. An advocacy role was most often adopted by the elected officials, but also by households, developers, and the city hall staff. In contrast, developers scarcely appeared as issue opponents, though households and elected politicans provided an opposition in half the issues contested. The overall picture is one where city hall politicians were active at all stages of policy, considerably more active than their own bureaucracy, while entrepreneurial interests were the proponents of potential change and community groups acted as an opposition. But around this typical situation there were numerous departures. Half the conflicts involved group mobilization, almost one-third involved petitions, and in one-fifth of them a demonstration was staged (Table 1D).

To complete this preliminary discussion we might note the grounds of involvement expressed by the various lobbyists (Table 1E). This information should be treated cautiously, for not only are the figures most likely compromised by incomplete reporting, but there is also the possibility of either deliberate distortion or else sympathetic rationalization by protagonists concerning their reasons for entering a conflict. Nevertheless, the dominant status of social factors is notable. So too is the relative standing of aesthetic factors; indeed the leading single argument raised against a land use proposal was its failure to satisfy a required level of visual attractiveness. While the various factors are not of course unrelated, during this period of urban growth, livability arguments were uppermost. In light of the much publicized fiscal crisis of certain American cities, the silence over the economic costs and benefits of proposals is remarkable. Of the 98 conflicts, on only *one* occasion was an allusion to potential tax revenues made; in Vancouver it seemed as if the assurance of growth allowed the values of a leisure society to be pursued, at least during this period.

THE RELATIONS OF LOCATIONAL CONFLICT

From the range of possible questions that might be asked of the conflict data, we shall confine ourselves to four: what were the neighborhood characteristics of conflict areas? Who were the participants? What were their grounds for involvement? And how were the issues resolved?

Neighborhood Characteristics

The general similarity between the distribution of flashpoints and the pattern of permit applications is strongly suggestive of a relationship between change and conflict (Figures 1 and 2). At an aggregate level this proposition holds, for both permit applications and conflict decrease from a peak in the central business district to a moderate level in the inner city and to a minimum in the stable inner suburbs within the city boundaries. But as the patterns are

TABLE 2
Land Use Change and Conflict by Zone and Sector

	Mean Permits Per District		Mean Conflict Inches Per District	
	West	*East*	*West*	*East*
Inner city	51	44	1799	127
Inner suburbs	7	12	505	150

disaggregated, some important variations on this theme appear. While land use change follows a *concentric* surface, the conflict surface is more accurately described as *sectoral*. A division of the planning districts into west and east, a standard regional classification in Vancouver [11], demonstrates this pattern. Although development applications were made fairly evenly in both sectors, conflicts were strongly concentrated in the west (Table 2). While eastside conflicts were uniformly limited, westside controversies were greater in number and more likely to be prolonged, particularly in the inner city districts. But this does not tell us *why* the westside districts were so conflict prone. If controversy was not a function of a disproportionate share of externally induced change, then it must have originated in the characteristics of the neighborhoods themselves, in a neighborhood effect which inflated the probability of conflict in westside districts while depressing it on the eastside.

A number of variables were examined for their ability to differentiate between sectors and zones. With one exception they were taken from the 1971 census, which is available at the level of the city's 22 planning districts. The districts were classified zonally as inner city or inner suburban on the basis of local planning definitions, and into sectors according to whether they fell west or east of the Cambie-Main Street area, universally regarded in Vancouver as the division between the two sectors.[3] The classification thereby gave rise to four residential regions. As the analysis was concerned with residential contrasts, the central business district was not included in this part of the analysis.

TABLE 3
Neighborhood Correlates of Locational Conflict

	INNER CITY		INNER SUBURB	
	Westside Mean	Eastside Mean	Westside Mean	Eastside Mean
1. Percent owned	12	26	65	75
2. Percent apartments	82	55	27	10
3. Percent resident over 10 years	14	20	35	40
4. Percent earning over $10,000	26	19	57	40
5. Percent rent over $150	25	8	48	27
6. Percent owner-occupied over $42,500	23	7	31	3
7. Percent Anglo-Canadian	61	34	66	47
8. Percent white collar	84	59	82	57
9. Percent professional, managerial	28	8	33	10
10. Percent university education	23	8	30	9
11. Percent TEAM vote, 1972	44	33	50	40

It might be expected that community resistance to change would be associated with ownership of a single detached house, as owner-occupancy in a single family home is often thought to be linked with conservative, parochial, and defensive responses. But the data do not support such an interpretation, for ownership levels are higher in eastside districts while the proportion of apartments is greater on the westside (Table 3, variables 1 and 2). Moreover, in aggregate terms, westside residents have lived in their homes for a somewhat shorter period than their neighbors on the eastside (variable 3). We, therefore, find the paradox that controversies appear more likely to erupt in districts where ownership rates are lower, the apartment proportion is higher, and the length of residence is shorter.

Economic data begin to suggest an explanation for this paradox. Income levels are higher on the westside, though not by a large amount, particularly in a comparison of the inner city districts (variable 4). However, it is possible that the economic differential is much broader in the proportion of disposable income spent on housing, for both rental and ownership costs are very much higher on the westside (variables 5 and 6), where amenity and status levels are most pronounced. If this interpretation is correct, then westside residents are choosing to allocate a greater share of their income to housing, whether owned or rental. For them the meaning of the home and neighborhood is a leading consumption priority, reflected in allocation decisions. If this hypothesis stands, it would provide one explanation for the predisposition of westside residents to protect their economic and symbolic investment against proposed changes. Certainly, the 1972-1974 council with its TEAM majority had been returned in a campaign where the electorate had identified the major issues as development and transportation policy and the need to challenge the power of real estate interests through political reform [19]. These issues were voiced more emphatically in westside than in eastside polling districts. Westside vigilance to development policy for the built environment coincided with TEAM's development platform, so it is no surprise that 80 percent of TEAM members lived in the westside districts and provided the party with its regional base of electoral support.

This interpretation is reinforced by several other census variables. The westside districts are overrepresented in their numbers of Anglo-Canadian residents, Canada's dominant ethnic group, and in the size of their white collar labor force (variables 7 and 8). The concentration is even more marked in terms of the presence of the white collar, professional, and managerial workers with the highest level of educational achievement (variables 9 and 10). We are encountering here the components of the subculture of the highly educated professional elite, a subculture oriented to the symbolic values of consumption with style, the pursuit of the canons of good taste [16]. It was from this subculture that TEAM, with its view of the livable city, was formed in 1968, and it has continued to provide the core of TEAM electoral strength (variable 11). In the TEAM-dominated council of 1972, four of the party's eight aldermen were university professors and the remaining four were university-qualified professionals; on a measure of occupational prestige, the 1972 council stood at the 94th percentile. Seven TEAM aldermen lived in the professional, westside neighborhoods. The TEAM platform, derived from westside cultural beliefs, made landscape aesthetics and the quality of urban development a major political issue. In his nomination speech in 1972, the successful TEAM mayoralty candidate had declared his view of the humane city: "I want to make Vancouver a place to live in and enjoy" [30]. A preoccupation with the quality of life, urban aesthetics, and leisure time found one expression in the prevalence of conflicts over recreational land use in the westside districts. There were eleven such issues accounting for over 3700 column inches; on the eastside there was only one recreational conflict, where the expansion of port facilities took much of the land that residents had planned for the site of a neighborhood park.

Conflict Participants

The lobbyists involved in locational controversies were assigned to seven categories, covering private, public and entrepreneurial interests. There was a clear indication of geographical bias to their entry into conflicts (Table 4). In the central business district, conflicts typically included land developers as advocates and city council, which assumed the stance of both advocate and opponent. Both of these clusters, together with citywide civic organizations were very active in downtown controversies. Where previous councils had given the land development industry a free hand in the CBD, the TEAM council as the political expression of westside consumption styles, pressed policies stressing aesthetics and livability, which culminated in a number of conflicts with entrepreneurial groups.

In contrast, citizens' groups (both private households and neighborhood associations) were most vigilant in the residential districts. But there was a striking difference in the activity levels of westside and eastside residents' groups, particularly in the inner city districts where eastside groups were inactive in contrast to the energetic intervention of westside groups both as advocates and opponents to change. The same sectoral variation appeared in the inner suburbs, though here the differences were not as marked. However, other groups were more active in the westside suburbs, including civic organizations and city council. This is a significant finding, which is reinforced if we examine the group initiating the proposal leading to controversy. City council was the initiator of fifteen issues in westside planning districts but of only three issues on the eastside. Reinforcing the evidence of permit applications, land developers were the interest group with the most uniform level of involvement across all five regions.

In summary, the data show that community interests, civic organizations, and city council and its departments were energetically involved in downtown and westside disputes in several capacities—as initiators, advocates, and opponents to an intended change. In contrast, all of these parties were more passive in eastside disputes. The evidence strongly supports the existence of an articulate and politicized citizenry in the higher income, white collar westside districts who could engage issues and enlist the involvement of city council, while on the eastside there was far less political activity directing the course of change. The westside professionals mobilized as an urban reform movement in opposition to the NPA, whose development policies at city hall were an extension of the goals of the city's commercial elite. The movement, expressing the urban development values of a second elite, quickly received popular support in the westside districts and, institutionalized in TEAM, actively pursued its development policies in downtown and westside districts, leading to frequent conflict with entrepreneurial interests.

Participants were also unequally involved in the various types of conflict.

TABLE 4
The Geographical Involvement of Conflict Groups

	CBD		INNER CITY				INNER SUBURBS			
			Westside		Eastside		Westside		Eastside	
	Conflicts		Conflicts		Conflicts		Conflicts		Conflicts	
	Pro	Con	Pro	Con	Pro	Con	Pro	Con	Pro	Con
Households	4	9	11	13	1	2	7	18	9	8
Neighborhood Groups	2	3	8	11	0	3	4	9	3	3
Civic Organizations	4	9	3	11	1	1	5	7	1	3
Land Developers	10	1	7	3	4	1	6	0	4	0
Other Entrepreneurs	3	5	4	6	1	0	2	1	0	2
Elected Officials	14	17	12	9	5	3	15	12	8	5
Administrative Officials	5	6	12	7	1	4	7	7	3	8

Community interests initiated mainly transportation conflicts, most of them concerned with pedestrian crossings. Developers initiated proposals leading to conflicts associated with redevelopment, housing, commercial uses, and preservation. City council initiated a range of issues, but half of them were related to recreational uses. This relationship is sustained when we consider the overall pattern of advocacy and opposition, as the entry of the varied groups continued to be unequal. Community groups were more usually opponents than advocates of an issue; land developers scarcely ever presented a formal posture of opposition; while a majority of city council was as likely to be in favor as they were to be opposed to a proposal.

The relations of advocacy and opposition suggested that a repetitive network of alliances might have existed. Among proponents, the greatest consensus occurred between households and city council; the most isolated group was the land developers. In opposition, the consensus between aldermen and residents' groups was even more marked, while it was the city hall bureaucrats who found themselves most often isolated. The dissenting department was usually the city engineer's office, whose vision of the city efficient in its transportation policy was rarely shared either by city council or by residents with their frequently skeptical view of schemes for road improvement.

The Grounds for Involvement

We have seen that the expressed grounds for involvement in a land use dispute were ascribed primarily to social factors and secondarily to aesthetic and economic factors (Table lE). Economic arguments were raised most frequently in proportional terms in the CBD, and it was also over downtown conflicts that aesthetic concerns were most often voiced. But in each of Vancouver's five regions social factors were predominant, accounting for more than half of the expressed reasons for involvement in the residential areas. Economic arguments took second position in these four residential regions, except in the westside suburbs where they were replaced by aesthetic arguments. An impression of which of the motives were held most deeply may be gained by examining disputes which escalated to the highest levels of intensity—the collection of a petition, a demonstration, or the issuing of a restraining injunction. Of the 24 reasons for conflict participation those most commonly expressed in the most intense conflicts were safety (mainly concerning pedestrian crossings) and the visual appearance of a proposed development, an aesthetic judgement made particularly of major developments in the downtown core.

The reasons for participation expressed by the various interest groups add another dimension to the conflict structure (Table 5). The community groups are all heavily inclined toward broadly conceived social motivations, and the entrepreneurial groups predictably favored economic factors. Most interesting is the record of the elected officials which differs little from the response of the residents. For both residents and aldermen, aesthetic arguments were slightly more prominent than economic factors, a remarkable posture for a city council to take.

TABLE 5
Grounds for Involvement Among Conflict Participants

	Economic (Percent)	*Social* (Percent)	*Aesthetic* (Percent)	*Procedural* (Percent)	*Other* (Percent)
Households	10	55	17	13	5
Neighborhood Groups	11	57	11	15	5
Civic Organizations	20	44	19	10	7
Land Developers	40	12	20	20	8
Other Entrepreneurs	39	29	19	3	10
Elected Officials	16	47	20	13	5
Administrative Officials	16	59	11	5	10

The Pattern of Conflict Resolution

The proposals of advocates were successful in 58 of the 98 conflicts; in a further 30 cases implementation was denied, and in the final 10 conflicts proposals were either withdrawn voluntarily or else no resolution occurred during the study period. No systematic bias in the rate of implementation occurred by planning district, although the central business district was the only region where there was a slight tendency for the implementation to be denied.

More revealing was the success of proposals according to their conflict type, arguments for and against implementation, and the interest groups contesting the issue. Of the major conflict types, implementation invariably occurred in housing issues (92 percent of the time), and less frequently followed arguments over retail uses (75 percent), redevelopment (64 percent), recreation (60 percent), and public services (57 percent). In conflicts involving transportation and preservation, development was checked more often than not. There was no simple formula for the success of proposals according to the type of argument that was raised in support or opposition to their implementation, although arguments based on social criteria tended to be more successful than those predicated on aesthetic or economic grounds.

The equivocal status of primarily economic arguments is reflected in the relative success of the various interest groups in the implementation decision. This relationship was stable whether the actors took the role of initiator, advocate, or opponent in the conflict. While advocates were able to realize their objectives in almost two out of three conflicts, there was considerable variation in this proportion among different lobbyists. Entrepreneurs and administrative officials failed to secure their objectives in over 40 percent of conflicts, whereas elected officials and the array of citizens' interests were successful in seven out of ten conflicts with a definite resolution. In the role of opposition in a controversy, council members and citizens' groups were victorious better than 40 percent of the time. Entrepreneurs were found in an adversary role in relatively few conflicts, though in these issues they were invariably unsuccessful.

The overall performance of the interest groups may be summarized by assessing the proportion of successes in conflicts in which they were engaged. Neighborhood groups were victorious in two out of three conflicts (66 percent) in which they were involved, and elected officials did almost as well (62 percent). They were followed by households (58 percent), civic organizations (54 percent), administrative officials (53 percent), other entrepreneurs (47 percent), and land development interests (46 percent). Outcomes also varied according to the conflict type. Citizens' groupings enjoyed their best results in conflicts over transportation but fared far more poorly in housing controversies. In contrast, entrepreneurial lobbyists consistently won housing related issues but had mixed results in most other categories including redevelopment and commercial proposals. Elected officials were successful in redevelopment conflicts, and in recreation related issues, the other major area in which they were active protagonists, although here there was an internal conflict on a number of occasions between council members and the elected parks board officials.

Finally, the geographic distribution of outcomes by planning district was examined. In the CBD, entrepreneurs fared less well in conflicts than council or citizens' groups. In the inner city districts, outcomes were more equally shared, but in the inner suburbs residents were again the most successful interest group. Somewhat surprisingly there were no important east-west differences in the *proportion* of successes in the residential sectors outside the downtown core. But in absolute terms, the much greater participation by both residents and council members in westside land use questions meant a closer social control of space than in eastside districts, where change, as we have seen, was far less frequently contested and control thereby far more loosely exercised.

CONCLUSION: SOME THEORETICAL IMPLICATIONS

In conclusion, we will draw back from the detailed empirical characteristics of land use conflict in Vancouver to consider some of the broader implications of the case study. But before doing so, it is important to treat the results with some caution, for they cannot present other than a general representation of the politics of land use in Vancouver. As with all behavioral methodology, behind the formal classes, fixed categories, and firm numbers lies a realm of events and relationships which are fluid and evolving, often ambiguous and partly hidden, and which a classificatory template can only represent as precise at the cost of its own accuracy. The certainty of numbers and categories does not always coincide with the contingency of the world they describe. A development permit for housing may erupt into a controversy over the open space that is to be lost, as a redevelopment proposal may stimulate a conflict over preservation. Moreover, as a conflict evolves, both the actors and the arguments may shift. It is important to note too that the interest groups themselves are not homogeneous, and in a number of incidents were divided over an issue; elected aldermen disagreed both with elected parks board members and with each other; the planning department was at odds with the city engineer; developers were challenged by store owners; and conservative and progressive community groups opposed each other over a development in the neighborhood they both claimed to represent. Nor are conflicts necessarily zero sum games with easily defined outcomes. Compromise, postponement, and a mismatch between short-term and long-term effects confound any simple notation of losers and winners. In addition, outcomes frequently fragment an interest group, favoring one neighborhood but not another, supporting one entrepreneur but penalizing a second. In this manner, once in its geographical context, an apparently discrete conflict shatters into a web of evolving and contingent relationships.

Such dynamic and complex circumstances refute the imposition of simple categories or the posing of simple relationships, and here empirical events challenge the precise abstractions of theoretical formulations. We noted earlier the inability of Dahrendorf's theory of social conflict to engage the subtleties of locational controversies. So, too, critics of both neoclassical and recent radical perspectives have identified the large gap that exists between theoretical formalism and the world of real events and the real people that it seeks to illuminate. But at the same time, empirical study has its own limitations in laying bare the distribution of power. We have already suggested that expressed motives in a locational conflict may not be the same as real motives. So, too, an analysis of overt conflicts need not reveal covert conflict, the ability of an interest group to suppress conflict in the pursuit of its own interests [17].

Nevertheless, even if the analysis is partial, the empirical examination of locational conflicts generates some useful conclusions for the development of a theory which is both more grounded in geographical events and also broader in its conceptualization than positions based on a narrow reading of political economy. We have seen, initially, the imperfect geographic response to urban change as expressed in the map of land use conflict in Vancouver. While the spatial pattern of change was concentric, the pattern of conflict was sectoral. In westside Vancouver, land use change was often an explicitly political event involving negotiation among alert neighborhood groups and private households, city hall politicians and officials, and entrepreneurial interests. In this politicized setting there was opportunity for success, defeat, and compromise. However, on the eastside, conflict was irregular, and both community groups and city hall representatives were less effective gatekeepers of neighborhood development. It is noteworthy that in the three inner planning districts on the eastside, 53 percent of the city's successful development permits for industrial use were filed. If we accept that industry and residential areas are incompatible (or at least undesirable) neighbors, then it might be argued that a loss occurred in the amenity value of eastside districts. Equally suggestive is the localized reduction of industrial land in westside districts over the same period and the substantial extension of park acreage. There is then a relationship between the discretionary power of community interests and the changing pattern of urban amenity. Moreover, in the past five years these amenity benefits have been associated with a significant acceleration of house prices in westside districts. A second important finding is the differential ranking of interest groups and their arguments in the conduct and outcome of conflicts. Broadly social criteria were cited both by community interests and city hall officials in half the controversies that they joined. For these groups, economic grounds were mentioned in only 10-20 percent of issues, no more frequently than aesthetic criteria. This demotion of the primacy of economic arguments is surprising and perhaps rare among politicians. The same trend was evident in the outcome to conflicts, where entrepreneurial lobbyists with their economic arguments were the least successful of the competing groups. The decision making climate of land use controversies in Vancouver was characterized by plural values, and the positing of a one-dimensional value structure would be seriously incomplete. The city might well be more unusual in the extent to which its council downgraded economic factors in the pursuit of "a place to live and enjoy." The TEAM council was a diligent guardian of quality of life arguments. It was the major (indeed, almost the only) initiator of conflicts over recreational use, and was the group which raised most often the aesthetic argument of the visual attractiveness of a proposed development as a criterion for responding to it.

But TEAM was itself a product of a distinctive urban subculture. The geographic incidence of conflicts over the city was related less to patterns of home-ownership, length of residence, or even income and market power than to a set of educational and occupational variables which identified in westside districts a cohort of politically articulate professional and managerial workers, a group sensitive to the style of urban development. This commitment to the quality of the built environment expressed itself in active neighborhood associations which resisted incompatible land use change and ultimately spawned TEAM as an urban reform party which would challenge the power of the NPA council and its allies in the development industry and give substance in the landscape to its own vision of the livable city, both in residential districts and in the CBD. Inasmuch as these values were concerned with the canons of good taste in urban development, the symbolic values of the built environment, their arguments were concerned with choice in consumption patterns, lifestyle, and status relations.

In a semi-managed society, decisions are increasingly referred to the political arena where public opinion influences both urban and national politicians. As recent conservative populist movements have proved, political leadership may be swayed, redirected, or rejected through powerful grassroots arguments, particularly when (as with Proposition 13 in California) these movements are reinforced by endorsement in a referendum. The art of government by opinion poll is a growing feature of the western democracies. But, at the same time, the popular legitimization of government rests largely on the continued maintenance of consumption styles, so that political crisis may accompany an erosion or threat to these standards [10]. In the late 1960s in Vancouver, the articulation among an emergent elite of a new style for urban development, summarized as a quest for the "livable city," led to a political crisis and the birth of a new civic reform party which assumed control at city hall in 1972. During the mid 1970s, land use conflict in the city then turned upon the attempt by the new city council and neighborhood interests to introduce their ideology to land use decision making. By the late 1970s, lower middle-class and free enterprise interests saw their own consumption standards threatened in a period of slow growth and initiated a renewed phase of support for a fiscally conservative ideology at city hall, a shift which is likely to work its way into new patterns of urban development and new configurations of land use conflict.

Demand pressures, which have conventionally figured as an element in market decisions, need also to be emphasized in their political context. This expansion would cast demand in the form of consumption expectations which have legitimizing implications for political authority and its attendent urban policies. Failure to meet the consumption expectations of a mobilized group may lead to a renegotiation of allocation procedures at the political level. In this manner, consumption styles may be constitutive of political change and crisis, so that the politics of consumption become an important reference point in an understanding of locational conflict and in the formulation of an integrated theory of land use decision making.

NOTES

The authors are grateful to the Social Science and Humanities Research Council of Canada and the Ministry of Labour of the province of British Columbia for grants in support of this research, and to Joy Jenkins who acted as research assistant.

1. While this emphasis was presented in an earlier literature on urban land use [7;8;32], its potentialities have not been seriously pursued. In part, this may well be due to the weaker theoretical content often ascribed to such cultural explanation [25]. But such a conclusion indicates a limited knowledge of contemporary social theory and casts a revealing light on the sociology of human geography itself.

2. This figure tends to exaggerate the rate of decline of new conflicts, as the 1973 entries included a number which carried over from 1972. Nevertheless, there was an undoubted reduction of conflicts through the period of analysis; the mean monthly number of newspaper features on conflicts declined from 45 in 1973, to 33 in 1974, to 13 in 1975. One interpretation of the reduction in conflict would point to a downturn in the provincial economy, which slowed the pressures for growth and land use change.

3. The east-west residential distinction in Vancouver is a prominent feature of factorial ecologies using 1961 and 1971 data, and is discussed in the standard urban geography text on the city [11]. As table 3 indicates, westside districts are characterized by higher status professional and managerial occupations and Anglo-Canadian ethnicity. Eastside districts are characterized by low levels of higher education, substantial blue-collar employment, and minorities with non-English mother tongues.

REFERENCES

1. Alonso, W. *Location and Land Use.* Cambridge, Mass.: Harvard University Press, 1965.
2. Bell, D. *The Coming of Post-Industrial Society.* New York: Basic Books, 1976.
3. Bourne, L. "Urban Structure and Land Use Decisions," *Annals, Association of American Geographers,* 66 (1976), pp. 531-47.
4. Cox, K. *Conflict, Power and Politics in the City: A Geographic View.* New York: McGraw-Hill, 1973.
5. Easton, R. and P. Tennant. "Vancouver Civic Party Leadership: Backgrounds, Attitudes, and Non-Civic Party Affiliations," *B.C. Studies,* 2 (1969), pp. 19-29.

6. Evans, D. *A Critique of Locational Conflict.* University of Toronto, Department of Geography Discussion Paper No. 20, 1976.
7. Firey, W. *Land Use in Central Boston.* Cambridge, Mass.: Harvard University Press, 1947.
8. Form W. "The Place of Social Structure in the Determination of Land Use," *Social Forces,* 32 (1954), pp. 317-23.
9. Gottman, J. "The Rising Demand for Urban Amenities," *Planning for a Nation of Cities.* Edited by S.B. Warner, Cambridge, Mass.: MIT Press, 1966.
10. Habermas, J. *Legitimation Crisis.* Boston: Beacon Press, 1975.
11. Hardwick, W. *Vancouver,* Toronto: Collier Macmillan, 1974.
12. Harvey, D. *Social Justice and the City.* London: Arnold, 1973.
13. Harvey D. "Labor, Capital, and Class Struggle around the Built Environment in Advanced Capitalist Societies," *Urbanization and Conflict in Market Societies.* Edited by K. Cox, Chicago: Maaroufa Press, 1978.
14. Janelle, D. "Structural Dimensions in the Geography of Locational Conflicts," *Canadian Geographer,* 21 (1977), pp. 311-28.
15. Ley, D. (ed.) *Community Participation and the Spatial Order of the City.* Vancouver: Tantalus Publications, B.C. Geographical Series No. 17, 1974.
16. Ley, D. "Liberal Ideology and the Postindustrial City," *Annals, Association of American Geographers,* 70 (June 1980).
17. Lukes, S. *Power, A Radical View.* London: Macmillan, 1974.
18. McCarthy, T. *The Critical Theory of Jurgen Habermas.* London: Hutchinson, 1978.
19. Minghi, J. and D. Rumley. "The Vancouver Civic Elections of 1970 and 1972: A Comparative Analysis," *The Kootenay Collection of Research Studies in Geography.* Edited by B. Barr. Vancouver: Tantalus Publications, B.C. Geographical Series No. 18, 1974.
20. Poster, M. "Translator's Introduction," in Jean Baudrillard, *The Mirror of Production.* St. Louis: Telos Press, 1975.
21. Richardson, H. "The Relevance of Mathematical Land Use Theory to Applications," *Mathematical Land Use Theory.* Edited by G. Papageorgiou. Lexington, Mass.: D.C. Heath, 1976.
22. Roweis, S. and A. Scott. "The Urban Land Question," *Urbanization and Conflict in Market Societies.* Edited by K. Cox. Chicago: Maaroufa, 1978.
23. Seley, J. "Towards a Paradigm of Community Based Planning," *Community Participation and the Spatial Order of the City.* Edited by D. Ley. Vancouver: Tantalus Publications, B.C. Geographical Series No. 17, 1974.
24. Svart, L. "Environmental Preference Migration: A Review," *Geographical Review,* 66 (1976), pp. 314-30.
25. Timms, D. *The Urban Mosaic.* Cambridge: The University Press, 1971.
26. Vancouver City Planning Department. *Employment Growth in Vancouver,* Vancouver, B.C., 1975.
27. Vancouver City Planning Department. *Quarterly Review,* 5 (April 1978), p. 16.
28. Vancouver City Planning Department. *Quarterly Review,* 4 (October 1977), p. 19.
29. Vancouver City Planning Department. *Understanding Vancouver.* Vancouver, B.C., 1977.
30. *Vancouver Province,* October 5, 1972.
31. Veblen, T. *The Theory of the Leisure Class.* New York: New American Library, 1953.
32. Willhelm, S. *Urban Zoning and Land Use Theory.* New York: Free Press, 1962.
33. Wolpert, J., A. Mumphrey, and J. Seley. *Metropolitan Neighborhoods: Participation and Conflict over Change.* Washington, D.C.: Association of American Geographers, Resource Paper No. 16, 1972.

10

Urban Social Theory and Research

Ray E. Pahl

In 1958 Martindale remarked "No subtlety of perception is required to determine that the contemporary American theory of the city is in crisis" (Weber, 1960, p. 9). He felt that students were so bored by the textbooks that were available, that they would sooner fail their courses than read them. Over the last decade teachers have wearily tramped a path through the literature, boring the student and convincing themselves that previous research is conceptually confused, outdated, or trivial. In an urbanized society, 'urban' is everywhere and nowhere; the city cannot be defined and neither, therefore, can urban sociology.

It seemed that urban sociology might cease to be a special type of inquiry: Manheim (1960) noted that urban society was rapidly becoming American society; Ruth Glass (1962) felt that in a highly urbanized country like Great Britain the label 'urban' could be applied to any branch of current sociological study and so it seemed pointless to apply it at all. As sociologists a decade ago dismissed the city as a distinctive focus of interest, courses for undergraduates became either unpopular, non-existent, or soft options, based on the kaleidoscope-of-life aspect of community studies. Some sociologists in the American Mid-West continued to use the most recent census volumes as a source of promotion, by providing commentaries and tabulations of the available statistical information on areas administratively designated as urban.

Looking back, one can have sympathy with Martindale, who, writing from his heart, asked "Surely in this valley of dry bones one may ask with Ezekial, 'Can these bones live?'" Faced with the possible elimination of their subject, other urban sociologists remembered that in the 1920's, when there really was an urban sociology and Park and his colleagues concentrated on the zone of transition in Chicago, it was the integration of the 'rural' population with 'the city' that provided the central focus (Park *et al.*, 1925). If urban sociology did not exist, urbanization in the Third World certainly did—that is, urbanization as acculturation. And so, one after the other, urban sociologists cheered each other on to India, Africa, or Latin America in the hope of what Manheim called 'theoretical yield.' Sjoberg urged that urban sociologists should amass data on *the* preindustrial city and on comparative urban studies. In his contribution to *Sociology Today* (Sjoberg, 1959) he particularly deplored the lack of knowledge about cities in Japan and Eastern Europe which resulted from language difficulties; knowledge about American cities was taken for granted. Ruth Glass (1955) certainly had no false complacency but still urged an interest in world urbanization or urban diffusion instead of the current vogue for "sporadic, detailed evidence about personal relationships within individual small communities", which, she claimed, did little more than provide opportunity for 'vicarious neighbouring'. British urban sociology, she implied, was distinctly *parochial* and British sociologists too much preoccupied with "the bric-a-brac of our own parlours." Finally, Reissman (1962, p. 236), in his book on *The Urban Process*, provided a brilliantly destructive critique of urban social theory of the first half of the twentieth century and concluded that all previous theories of the city were oversimplified. "The path to urban analysis must run through a broader societal analysis" he claimed, and following the new fashion, he brought the developing societies into his typology of urbanization. His advice on future research was to use his own typology and "describe and compare cities drawn from the range of societies at different stages in their development."

Thus it was that, leaving their own cities behind them, those who called themselves urban sociologists packed their bags for the tropics. And this was reflected in teaching. The widely-used Prentice Hall series, edited by Professor Inkeles, *The Foundations of Modern Sociology* has no title on urban sociology, although the companion series on the *Modernization of Traditional Societies* has a title on urbanization. Similarly, the Centre for Urban Studies, University of London, has a post graduate course in 'Urbanization in Developing Countries' but not one on urban sociology *per se*. Undergraduates elsewhere are still being taught the sociology of integration, the ecological fallacy, and a rag-bag of studies, which happen to have been done in urban areas.

It is somewhat bizarre that at the time when urban sociologists were discovering the delights of what they defined as real, urban problems in Third World cities, the anthropologists, who had been working there, were returning to introduce urban anthropology to the natives of Europe and America. Centres like the Rhodes-Livingstone Institute, Lusaka, were a product of the colonial power's enlightened self-interest. Research on 'the natives' could have all sorts of practical implications for administrators and bureaucrats. It is greatly to the credit of British social anthropologists that they never allowed themselves to become tools of their masters. Careful analysis of actual social relationships by scholars such as Epstein and Mitchell provided important insights into the mechanisms which relate the formal to the informal patterns of relationships. Work on distinct *types* of relationships, *types* of urban situations, and *types* of social networks provided a distinctive focus for the study of the African townsman (Mitchell, 1966). One of the main problems of the urban situation was the linking of different levels: the social anthropologists provided a valuable organizing framework. However, they too became worried about what constituted 'urban': Mitchell (1956) in Central Africa, Mayer (1961) in South Africa, and Gugler (1966) in East Africa tried to operationalize urban, with only modest success. How 'urban' are migrants with strong rural reference groups: are the Red Xhosa, described by Mayer, more or less urban than the Mambwe described by Watson (1958), and so on. Gluckman (1961) was certainly making an important point when he categorically stated "an African townsman is a townsman", but as Epstein (1967) has shown, there are townsmen and townsmen.

However, to return to our theme, newly independent nations were less enthusiastic to support research on 'how the natives live,' and the ex-colonial powers had other problems on their hands. The anthropologists came home and looked around in New York and Manchester: urban jungles and urban villages lay waiting to be explored. Armed with some sharp concepts for dealing with patterns of social relationships, social anthropologists wait for the dramatic events of urban life to create situations to analyze. Unfortunately they are less well-equipped to anticipate the emergence of dramatic events arising out of the structural situation.

Another strand in this sociology of urban sociology is of course the solid British empirical tradition. Life in blocks of flats or new housing estates is described in great detail and 'urban' is taken to mean simply physically constrained, *informal*, social relationships. Undergraduates in a variety of institutions doing a variety of courses wrote essays on 'Neighbourhood and Community', 'The Ideology of the Garden City Movement', and the 'Social Composition of Voluntary Associations'. Such issues did not seem very important to some sociologists in comparison with real sociological issues such as *embourgeoisement* (which does not exist) or the work situation of miners (who are rapidly declining in numbers).

Thus, we have a situation in Britain today where students read in the newspapers of the urban crisis, the urban programme, and the need for urban research, but are told in the lecture hall that urban sociology does not exist. "Certainly there are problems of racial discrimination, poverty, bad housing, and educational deprivation but these are not *urban* problems" runs a well-known argument. "The label 'urban' is simply a ploy of the elite to distract attention away from the basic inequalities of our stratification system. We 'know' all about that and so there is no need for research." Alternately, others argue that it is simply a matter of redistribution and 'policies'. 'Policies' are left to those who study social administration to think up on an *ad hoc* basis. Social administration is often seen as a kind of poor relation for those without the strength of mind to tackle the meat of sociological 'theory'. Some, who are interested in the uses of sociology, may feel obliged to apologize to their colleagues who are weaving their spells of conceptual purity or advancing the frontiers of the discipline in a more professionally acceptable way.

Most of the work which has been done in the name of urban sociology is about urbanization—that is change, disorganization, and adaptation. It is as if sociologists cannot define urban without a rural contrast: when they lose the peasant they lose the city too. The response to the discovery that 'sociological urban' is everywhere is, as I have suggested, to go somewhere where still it is not everywhere, rather than to construct a truly *urban* sociology. Instead of asking the sort of questions to which urban sociology should provide an answer, urban sociologists have simply looked at what the field has produced in the past and, seeing its irrelevance, lack of cumulative development, and feeble ability to explain or predict what they have defined as 'important' problems, have discarded the field, instead of asking new questions. The dissatisfaction with urban sociology relates more to what has been done in its name than what might be its potential. Certainly a subject with no problems is not worth having. Some sociologists would say that the study of stratification, the family, political and religious institutions and so on, provides an understanding of society. The fact that this all takes place in an urban context is said to add nothing more than the fact that it also takes place in a certain climatic context. They would argue that organizational analysis or the sociology of industry is more acceptable because the enterprise has a unity:

> "The industrial system imposes its own structure of relationships on managers and workpeople. To maintain and expand the system requires the widespread acceptance of an ordered array of values by which persons in different positions in the system set their aims in life and guide their day-to-day actions, and these values have to be inculcated by a variety of means. For industrial concerns to operate at all there has to be specified a range of roles, each with a set of

constraints: there have to be also disciplinary codes or social controls in order to confine admissible conduct within these constraints. In all these senses, the industrial system marks the host society with its own special imprint"(Burns, 1962, p.186).

Yet even the industrial sociologists have difficulty in closing their system. The studies by Goldthorpe and his colleagues on the affluent worker minimized the importance of the primary work group, supervisory styles, or the technological constraints structuring work-roles and role relationships. Rather they emphasize the attitudes towards work which workers *bring to* their employment arising from the workers' out-plant roles and patterns of association (Goldthorpe *et al.*, 1967).

I have been arguing in this short ethnography of urban sociology that the field exists, if only because a number of individuals style themselves urban sociologists and have a common language and culture. Much of the best work in the field, has, however, been accomplished by those who simply call themselves sociologists, and who have applied the concepts developed by the discipline as a whole in this particular field. No one doubts that sociologists can do useful work in problem areas which, for one reason or another, have been defined as urban. However, the flow of ideas appears to have been from sociologists working in other fields rather than from urban sociology to the discipline as a whole. Even Whyte's *Street Corner Society* is more a contribution to small group studies than any cumulative urban sociology (Whyte, 1943). Of course, some would argue there is no reason why this should not continue: the particular body of concepts, approaches, and methodology which makes up sociology can be applied in any field.

One danger of few sociologists willingly accepting the adjective urban as part of their title would be that areas of investigation are likely to be suggested from outside rather than from within the discipline. Whilst sociologists are quick to point out that expectations of the field of urban sociology are overrated, few would deny that teams designing new cities would be better equipped by having sociologists amongst them. There are still only a few hundred sociologists in Britain and urban problems are too big to leave to traffic engineers, economists, and what have you.

Thus, some sociologists should be obliged to make themselves aware of urban problems—and here we move from the ethnography to the sociology of urban sociology. What are or should be the *values* of urban sociologists? What problems should they choose and which groups should they advise? Why have they chosen to specialize in the urban situation—is it that they have moved in sociology from a spatially-oriented discipline and/or do they enjoy the status to be gained from the, perhaps, less discriminating audience of planners and architects? If they are working at the periphery of the profession do they suffer from status anxiety, relative deprivation, or any other symptom of stress or marginality?

THE DISTRIBUTION OF RESOURCES AND FACILITIES

It is my view that the most useful contribution of sociologists to urban problems will, in the long run, depend on their contribution to sociology. This paper represents some preliminary thinking towards a redefinition of the field, which might provide a distinctive approach to urban problems and may have possibilities of enlarging our basic understanding of the social structure of an advanced industrial society. The main propositions in my argument may be stated as follows:

1. There are fundamental *spatial* constraints on access to scarce urban resources and facilities. Such constraints are generally expressed in time/cost distance.
2. There are fundamental *social* constraints on access to scarce urban facilities. These reflect the distribution of power in society and are illustrated by:
   — bureaucratic rules and procedures;
   — social gatekeepers who help to distribute and control urban resources.
3. Populations in different localities differ in their access and opportunities to gain the scarce resources and facilities holding their economic position or their position in the occupational structure constant. The situation which is structured out of 1 and 2 may be called a socio-spatial or socio-ecological system. Populations limited in this access to scarce urban resources and facilities are the *dependent* variables; those controlling access, the managers of the system, would be the *independent* variable.
4. Conflict in the urban system is inevitable. The more the resource or facility is valued by the *total* population in a given locality, or the higher the value and the scarcer the supply in relation to demand, the greater the conflict.

By way of example let us consider the non-random distribution of a facility, which differs in its quality even though it is distributed to all the population within a given age range: education provision is known to vary considerably between Local Education Authorities.

Variation in expenditure by L.E.A.'s can be shown by comparing annual expenditure per pupil on books and stationery: this gives some measure of the importance education holds in the overall budgetary planning. It is of course extremely difficult to get good quantitative indicators for such things as the quality of education, but size of class, turnover of teaching staff, age of building, and so on might be combined to provide an index of educational quality for a given school or area. Hence, for those *at the same position in the occupational structure* different localities will offer different degrees of educational opportunity.

The same variation of opportunity relates to housing. However unreliable local authority waiting lists, or statistics relating to multi-occupation or to the numbers of families in temporary accommodation, no one would seriously dispute that Glasgow is in a worse situation than Bristol. Housing clearly operates on a local, or at the most a city-regional level, since housing is clearly related to employment market areas. Furthermore, as Donnison (1967),

Elizabeth Burney (1967), and others have shown, access to housing is tightly controlled in some areas by various bureaucratic rules and procedures and by gatekeepers from various public and private agencies. These opportunities of access to housing are structured: "among those who share the same relation to the means of production there may be considerable differences in ease of access to housing. This is part of the superstructure which manifestly takes on a life of its own. A class struggle between groups differently placed with regard to the means of housing develops, which may *at a local level* be as acute as the class struggle in industry. Moreover, the independence of this process is emphasized the more home and industry become separated" (Rex, 1968, present author's italics). The housing market and the job market need not be congruent: there may be availability of houses but jobs may be declining locally, or there may be approximate parity between the total number of jobs and dwellings but the dwellings may be too expensive in relation to local wages or may not fit the household structure of the given population. Similarly, the job market may not fit the skills and capabilities of those entering the labour market or those obliged by structural unemployment or other reasons to seek re-employment; there may, for example, be a strong demand for female workers in offices and shops, whilst opportunities for male school leavers are negligible or, again, technologically advanced industries may put their factories in areas of un- or under-employment and then may be obliged to import nearly all their skilled workers.

Undoubtedly each of these examples of educational opportunity, housing market, and job market are well understood by specialists in each of these fields. However, *the implications of their interrelationships* may not be so well understood. Education, jobs, and housing as scarce resources are all potential sources of conflict: access to such resources is systematically structured in a *local* context. Such contexts may be physically "urban", "rural", or a mixture of the two: the urban or spatial sociologist is interested in the areas in which decisions crucially affecting the life chances of those living there are made. The units for urban sociology are bureaucratically defined.

There are, of course, other facilities and resources, which are not randomly distributed, which affect the life chances of those in specific localities to a greater or lesser degree. Some people, for example, have easy access to cut-price stores; others would have to travel, at the cost of considerable time and money, to reach these facilities. The larger the concentration of population the wider the range of choice and the less danger of monopolistic price fixing. Hence, other things being equal, and they rarely are, as I am arguing, the poor would be at less disadvantage in larger settlements than in smaller ones. There is, of course, a wide range of potential local authority provision, from swimming baths to specialist social services such as clinics for physically and mentally handicapped children, and these can be systematically quantified to get compound indices of opportunity.

It is obvious that the mere summation of public expenditure on basic infrastructure and facilities in given areas will not provide any kind of guide to the overall quality of opportunity in such areas. There are basic conflicts over the most appropriate form of expenditure. Hence, it is not possible to devise an immensely complicated functional model to show the "perfect" urban system in operation, providing the maximum social benefit at least cost to everyone. This would imply a static distribution of power in some kind of political concensus—we have not reached the end of ideology yet! Nor, of course, are we in a situation of war of all against all. Conflicts are structured both socially and spatially. Analysts of the urban system cannot do without the sociologist and political scientist, but they in turn cannot do without the geographer and economist, who help to determine the spatial distribution of economic welfare and diswelfare in urban areas.

The basic framework for urban sociology is then *the pattern of constraints which operates differentially in given decision-making contexts.* Fundamental life chances are affected by the type and nature of access to facilities and resources and this situation is likely to create conflict in a variety of forms and contexts: the definition of the area of the locality is itself a matter of great political importance and conflict, as the coming battle over the Report of the Royal Commission on Local Government in England (1969) will illustrate.

THE INTERVENTION BY THE COMMUNITY IN THE DISTRIBUTIVE PROCESSES

Intervention into the market takes place in all societies to a greater or lesser degree, but the mixture of both a market and a plan rationality in Britain is peculiarly delicate. Intervention can either underline the differential rewarding system already operating or it can moderate it. In the case of some forms of intervention it is not clear how the "punishments" and "rewards" are distributed. A common political debate is implicit in such intervention: that is, is it "better" to discriminate in favour of those already advantaged, so that economic efficiency may be promoted to the ultimate advantage of those presently disadvantaged, or is it "better" positively to discriminate in favour of those presently disadvantaged and thus to engage total support and effort for societal goals? The type and nature of intervention into the market in a given locality will depend on a number of factors, which will include:

1. The political history of the area.
2. The present distribution of political, social and economic power.
3. The values and ideologies of local technocrats.
4. Awareness of relative deprivation in respect of other localities.

It is well known, for example, that payment of capital grants by the

Department of Education and Science depends partly on the amount of pressure coming from the area making the request. Outside the Educational Priority Areas new schools will depend more on this and the above factors than on any objective analysis based on the appropriate social indicators. There are, of course, some decisions which may be taken more as a result of technocratic calculations than political opportunism. These are more likely to be long-term budgeting decisions, such as a motorway programme, which preempts funds that might otherwise have gone on short term political fundgiving such as family allowances or education. However, once taken these long-term budgetary decisions are a very strong determining factor, stronger I suspect than most political groups at a lower scale appreciate. This closing of options outside the political arena may be only temporarily politically neutral: it should be part of the task of a vigorous urban sociology to explore and expose these fundamental limiting constraints on life chances. Perhaps by making explicit the conflicts at a "regional" level the involvement of the sociologist may help to open up a new political dimension.

Much of the argument up to now implies a somewhat static situation. What are the potentialities for *mobility* within the urban system? If position in the housing market is, in certain respects and areas, *independent* of position in the occupational structure, what are the possibilities for an individual of movement into a less disadvantaged situation with regard to the scarce resources and facilities I have been discussing? How much will geographical mobility of individuals and familites to localities where the punitive measures and diswelfares are less, *of itself* lead to social mobility? That is, can an individual's life chances be improved *independently of his position in the job market?* There are certainly indications that middle class people are concerned about the *areas* to which their careers take them, and are also concerned about the facilities in those areas, and it is at least possible that this concern will spread. In the same way that sociologists drew attention to the inequalities of educational opportunity (for example Douglas, 1964), which made the middle class more "*Where*"—conscious[1] in their choice of school, so that the work of urban sociologists is likely to make the population more "where-conscious" generally. Instead of "nice" areas being considered a luxury, they may be seen as a necessity or a right.

It is evident that I have taken as my starting point the fact that *the whole society is urban*, but that, since peoples' life chances are constrained to a greater or lesser degree by the non-random distribution of resources and facilities, urban sociology is concerned with *the understanding of the causes and consequences of such distributions for relevant populations.* The values and ideologies of the distributing, organizing, and caretaking professions, or the relations between the formal and informal patterns of social relationships, are of central importance to urban sociology.

Strauss (1967) has recently urged that we need to know more about the social worlds of urban types—by these he is more likely to mean abortionist physicians, garbage collectors, or radio announcers.[2] The argument of this paper is that the *crucial* urban types are those who control or manipulate scarce resources and facilities such as housing managers, estate agents, local government officers, property developers, representatives of building societies and insurance companies, youth employment officers, social workers, magistrates, councillors, and so on. These occupations and professions should be the subject of a comparative study to discover how far their ideologies are consistent, how far they conflict with each other, and how far they help to confirm a stratification order in urban situations. These managers of the urban system provide the independent variables of the subject. It may be, for example, that the further one is down the social hierarchy, the more the lack of resources and facilities compound together and create an urban underclass out of which it is extremely difficult to escape.

Some sources and measures of intervention, intended to alleviate cumulative diswelfare or punitive measures on those least able to defend themselves, may often fail. People do not always take or get what they are entitled to; certain sections of the population—apparently for a variety of reasons—fail to enmesh with more generally-held goals and values of the wider society. Under these circumstances the ego-centered approach of the social anthropologist, which uses social network analysis, may help to elucidate patterns of social control and to explore the defensive mechanisms based on kin or patron-client relationships as means of coming to terms with the wider society.

Some recent studies do give indications of a renewed vigour in the subject—Foster (1968) in his study of nineteenth century towns, Rex and Moore (1976) in their study of Sparkbrook, and the work on housing by Ruth Glass and her colleagues in London (Centre for Urban Studies, 1964), and by Dennis (forthcoming) in Sunderland. Little else has been done. Research has proceeded on a very *ad hoc* basis—loneliness on new estates, images of the city, a bit of social area analysis, and so on: the literature is patchy, unsystematic, and certainly not cumulative. A similar conclusion was arrived at by Castells (1968) who asked "*y-a-t-il une sociologie urbaine?*". He felt that urban sociology should concentrate on interaction between different levels—local and national, formal and informal—especially where social and physical space coincide, and secondly should relate social processes to the ecological system. His approach is very similar to that outlined here and it seems evident that so long as important life chances are determined locally there will be degrees of coincidence between spatial and social structure which I have elsewhere described as a socio-ecological system (Pahl, 1968a).

Thus, there can be a sociology of the organization of urban resources and facilities: the controllers, be they planners or social workers, architects or education officers, estate agents or property developers, representing the market or the plan, private enterprise or the state, all *impose* their goals and values on the lower participants in the urban system. We need to know not only the rates of access to scarce resources and facilities for given populations but also the *determinants* of the moral and political values of those who control these rates. We need to know how the basic decisions affecting life chances in urban areas are made. The application of organization theory to urban contexts might well reveal authority/compliance structures analogous to those studied in other fields. This is particularly likely to be the case where the operational fields of various bureaucratic structures overlap and the same clients suffer the same subordinate position in each structure.

There are, however, two very important differences between organization theory and urban sociology. Firstly, in industrial concerns and other organizations lower participants can escape "outside" to some degree of autonomy; secondly, such organizations have some commonly accepted goals, such as making a profit, turning out a given number of students, or converting peasants to new forms of agricultural production. Of course, these goals are never clear cut and most organizations have conflict over goals.

In the case of the urban system (if there be such) it is less clear where "outside" is: to where can the lower participant escape? Even the most intimate aspects of family life may be open to the activity of some social caretaker or other. The controllers of the urban system seem to control more completely than the controllers of the industrial system. Defensive mechanisms or informal stratagems such as Goffman describes in *Asylums* (Goffman, 1961) may operate for the underclass in the urban system, who are in some ways trapped in a total institution. The dehumanizing effect of the urban managers on the urban poor is worth further investigation.

Similarly, we are not clear what are the goals of the urban system, or rather the goals of those who manipulate it. We agree that certain urban resources will always be scarce and that social and spatial constraints will mutually reinforce one another, whatever the distribution of power in society may be. However, given that certain managers are in a position to determine goals, what are these goals and on what values are they based? Should facilities be shared around more equally, or more equitably, or more efficiently? How do the managers measure the effectiveness of the goal-oriented action, or policies, which they devise? Is positive discrimination in favour of those disadvantaged in one sphere a necessary concern of all planning or of only some planning, and how does this relate to other managers, whose goal is to make a profit?

In this discussion of an analogy between industrial or organizational analysis and urban sociology it is implicit that the urban system has both a spatial *and* a non-spatial character. This provides its distinctiveness. Thus, groups of the population can be both spatially and socially defined, as can the resources and facilities which are in demand. Social "problems" may or may not have "spatial" solutions: decisions by the manipulators of the spatial structure may have unintended consequences on the social structure and *vice versa*. The current fashion among physical planners for "diversity and choice" implies an acceptance that differential access to scarce resources and facilities is an *independent* variable. The whole theme of this paper, which certainly deserves much more extended discussion, is that such patterns of access are *dependent* upon the allocation by the system managers. Lower participants can be classified both spatially and socially and suffer different degrees of constraint in different socio-spatial systems.

I see that I am open to criticism by those who would use the sociology of sociology on me. Non-sociologists are wishing an "urban problem" on the discipline and obligingly the discipline responds with an emphasis on constraints and opportunities for the underprivileged. Surely, some may argue, this is simply academic opportunism once again, this time stealing the clothes of those studying social administration. I should like to conclude by considering such potential criticisms. Firstly, most scientific activity is social; problems may seem to arise of themselves but I think they follow rather from the economic and social situation of a society at a given point of time. The levelling out of our national rate of growth, the rising expectations for facilities and resources, the decline and decay of the basic physical infrastructure of our cities, built or established a century ago, the "discovery" that work is not a central life interest for large sections of the working population, and the increasing concern with consumption and style—all these and many other factors, such as expanding levels of education or the increase in ownership of private cars, are leading to a concern about the access to, or quality of, urban resources and facilities. No one doubts that they are urban: indeed it is this common urbanity which makes for the conflict for scarce resources.

No one disputes the multiplicity of life styles argument: this was put most vigorously by Burns (1968) who based his argument on the flexibility/ diversity/variety/choice/styles of life theme. I would not deny that there is much in the case for viewing "post-industrial man", responding to the whim of fashion, cavorting around in mobile homes or vertical take-off bubble planes. There is much comfort in describing the non-community of fellow architects and sociologists as being the style for the future. There is a sort of meritocratic ideology of social capillarity which suggests that what professionals in the South East (or California) do today, the rest of the society will do in the year 2000. I have argued elsewhere against the ideology of a mobile society and also against the idea that all urban-industrial societies are converging in certain important respects (such as the pattern of access to facilities and resources for certain sections of society) (Pahl, 1968b). The important point I want to emphasize is that urban sociology may indeed encompass different ideologies: I have crudely contrasted my 'constraint'-oriented approach with the 'choice'-oriented approach and I am fully aware of the ambiguities and dangers in making such a distinction.

Far from being opportunists I think urban sociologists must stand firm against the strong pressure by planners to turn them into futuristically-oriented market research consultants; by system and model building colleagues, who demand sociological unreality to make their models more tidy; by those who disregard underlying social conflicts in favour of *ad hoc* amelioration; and by social anthropologists, who may be more interested in the mechanisms of social interaction than in the source of inequalities in the wider system. A truly *urban* sociology should be concerned with the social and spatial constraints on access to scarce urban resources and facilities as dependent variables, and with the managers or controllers of the urban system, seen as the independent variable. Whether this provides 'theoretical yield' at a general level is not dependent on subject material but on quality of scholarship. A new approach[3] to the subject along these lines might be cumulative, might systematically aid our understanding of a complex urban society, and could have great practical value. It is time that we stopped confusing our students by explaining away the urban society in which they live.

NOTES

This paper was presented at a seminar, together with papers by H. Gracey and J. Musil. For a full report of the seminar and discussion see Centre for Environmental Studies Information Paper 9, London. The author wishes to state that any critical comments from readers on the paper will be welcomed.

The author would like to acknowledge the very valuable critical comments made on an earlier draft of this paper by P. Stirling, D. Morgan, and R. Haddon.

1. 'Where' is the journal of the Advisory Centre for Education. Much of the trend towards increased consumer-consciousness has been generated by the work of this and similar groups.

2. "Rather than studying the usual occupations, or those that seem important to the city's functioning, why not study those that are little noted, even in popular magazines" (p.92). Also why not look at "some category of economic activity or some business, which is not likely to be studied for its importance to the city e.g. antique auctions or the sale of second-hand yachts" (p.93).

3. This so-called 'new' approach is by no means as clear and unambiguous as I would like. I am leaving the paper as I wrote it in March 1969 but its inadequacies in certain respects are more clear to me now (September 1969).

REFERENCES

Burney, E., 1967, *Housing on Trial* (Oxford University Press, Oxford).
Burns, T., 1962, "Industrial Sociology," in *Society*, Eds. A.T. Welford, M. Argyle, D.V. Glass, and J.N. Morris (Routledge and Kegan Paul, London), p. 186.

Burns, T., 1968, "Urban Life Styles," Working Paper 5, Centre for Environmental Studies, London.
Castells, M., 1968, "*Y-a-t-il une sociologie urbaine?*," *Sociologie du Travail*, 10, 72-90.
Centre for Urban Studies, 1964, *London Aspects of Change* (MacGibbon and Kee, London).
Dennis, N. (forthcoming), *People and Planning* (Faber and Faber, London).
Donnison, D.V., 1967, *The Government of Housing* (Penguin Books, London).
Douglas, J.W.B., 1964, *The Home and the School* (MacGibbon and Kee, London).
Epstein, A.L., 1967, "Urbanization and Social Change in Africa," *Current Anthropology*, 8, number 4, 275-296.
Foster, J., 1968, "Nineteenth-century Towns—A Class Dimension," in *The Study of Urban History*, Ed. H.J. Dyos (Edward Arnold, London).
Glass, R., 1955, "Urban Sociology in Great Britain," *Current Sociology*, IV, 5-19.
Glass, R., 1962, "Urban Sociology," in *Society*, Eds. A.T. Welford, M. Argyle, D.V. Glass, and J.N. Morris (Routledge and Kegan Paul, London), pp. 481-497.
Gluckman, M., 1961, "Anthropological Problems Arising from the African Industrial Revolution," in *Social Change in Modern Africa*, Ed. A. Southall (Oxford University Press, Cape Town).
Goffman, E., 1961, *Asylums* (Anchor Books, New York).
Goldthorpe, J.H., Lockwood, D., Bechhofer, F., and Platt, J., 1967, "The Affluent Worker and the Thesis of *Embourgeoisement*," *Sociology*, 1, number 1, 11-31.
Gugler, J., 1966, *Measuring Urbanization*, Paper presented to the Sixth World Congress of Sociology (Evian), mimeo.
Manheim, E., 1960, "Theoretical Prospects of Urban Sociology in an Urbanized Society," *American Journal of Sociology*, 66, 226-229.
Mayer, P., 1961, *Townsmen or Tribesmen* (Oxford University Press, Cape Town).
Mitchell, J.C., 1956, *The Kalela Dance*, Rhodes-Livingstone Papers number 27 (Manchester University Press, Manchester).
Mitchell, J.C., 1966, "Theoretical Orientations in African Urban Studies," in *The Social Anthropology of Complex Societies*, Ed. M. Banton (Tavistock Publications, London), pp. 37-51.
Pahl, R.E. 1968, *Readings in Urban Sociology*, Ed. R.E. Pahl (Pergamon Press, Oxford), pp. 10-20.
Pahl, R.E. 1968, "Spatial Structure and Social Structure," Working Paper 10, Centre for Environmental Studies, London.
Park, R.E., 1925, *The City*, Eds. R.E. Park, E.W. Burgess, and R.D. McKenzie (reprinted 1967 by University of Chicago Press, Chicago).
Reissman, L., 1962, *The Urban Process* (Free Press, Glencoe).
Rex, J.A., 1968, "The Sociology of a Zone of Transition," in *Readings in Urban Sociology*, Ed. R.E. Pahl (Pergamon Press, Oxford), p. 215.
Rex, J.A., and Moore, R., 1967, *Race, Community and Conflict* (Oxford University Press, Oxford).
Royal Commission on Local Government in England, 1969, Cmnd. 4040 (H.M.S.O., London).
Sjoberg, G., 1959, "Comparative Urban Sociology," in *Sociology Today*, Eds. R.K. Merton, L. Broom, and L.S. Cottrell, Jr. (Basic Books, New York), pp. 334-359.
Strauss, A., 1967, in *Urban Research and Policy Planning*, Eds. L.F. Schnore and H. Fagin (Sage Publications, Beverly Hills, California).
Watson, W., 1958, *Tribal Cohesion in a Money Economy* (Manchester University Press, Manchester).
Weber, M., 1960, *The City*, translated by D. Martindale and Gertrud Neuwirth with Introduction by D. Martindale (Heinemann Educational Books, London).
Whyte, W.F., Jr., 1943, *Street Corner Society* (University of Chicago Press, Chicago).

11

The Role of Institutions in the Inner London Housing Market: The Case of Islington

Peter R. Williams

The purpose of this paper[1] is to examine mechanisms of population change in an urban area by a study of the role of institutions functioning in the private sector of its housing market. Specifically, it concentrates upon the relationship between the process of gentrification[2] and the role of institutions in the London Borough of Islington. A study of the gentrification process is a useful way to illustrate how the private housing market operates and the intention is to provide a counter to the viewpoint which sees consumer choice as being the fundamental mechanism of the housing market and of being the sole cause of gentrification.[3] Although choice, which can be equated with demand, is clearly an important component, in both the market and in gentrification, factors of supply, of control and of constraint are of equal if not greater importance, particularly with regard to certain groups of the population.[4] The housing market is structured by local and central government, the construction industry, financial instititions and the finance market, the land and property industry and the nature of the economy at large. A process such as gentrification must be related to these. The institutions considered here are building societies and other financial agencies, estate agents and, to a limited

---

From *Transactions, Institute of British Geographers*, Vol. 1, No. 1 (1976), pp. 72-82. Reprinted by permission of the Institute of British Geographers.

degree, local and central government. The period under consideration is from the mid-1950s to 1973. Much of the information presented is drawn from a sample survey of estate agents and building societies conducted during the summer of 1974.

Important changes have taken place in Islington during the last two decades. Set against a background of substantial population decline and the rapid diminution of the private-rented sector, there have been significant shifts within the population and tenure types present. The proportion of persons in socio-economic grouping I[5] has increased from 1.35 percent in 1951 to 11.46 percent in 1971; households in the private-rented sector have declined from 71 percent in 1961 to 56 percent of all households in 1971, while owner occupation has increased from 11 to 13 percent[6] and households in the public sector from 17 to 29 percent. These statistics give some small indication of the degree to which "gentrification" has occurred, but since they apply to the borough they are without doubt misleading in that this type of change has been concentrated in certain areas.[7]

It is now appropriate to consider the mechanisms that have produced such changes. As already noted, although demand is obviously one causal element in gentrification it is not treated here and attention is given entirely to the role of institutions in this process. Furthermore, demand can only be understood in the context of the situation in which it arose and was able to be expressed and this requires a consideration of the factors of supply. The analysis proceeds by examination of the changes that have occurred within the private housing market and then considers the role of building societies, estate agents and, briefly, central and local government. Each of these institutions or agencies is examined to determine how they have contributed to the gentrification of Islington.

THE HOUSING MARKET IN ISLINGTON

Within the context of the London housing market, Islington had functioned since the late nineteenth century as an area providing housing for the working classes. Most of the housing was privately rented. Before the 1950s property sales in the borough largely comprised the transfer of rented houses from one landlord to another.[8] Prices for these properties were generally quite low —often based upon a calculation of ten times the annual rent giving a price of approximately £400. Although many properties were still controlled, the return appeared to have remained attractive (often at the expense of maintenance). Furthermore, rented property, despite all the legislation, was considered a secure investment since it was "bricks and mortar". Thus one finds that transactions continued even though a better return on capital might have been had elsewhere. Sales involving owner occupation were less frequent and this was a reflection of the limited number of suitable properties available, the problems of finance and limited expressed demand. One agent estimated that his house sales (excluding investment sales, i.e. sales between landlords) were about 70 properties a year in the borough of Islington. Most of the agents were primarily involved in the management of rented property.

Towards the end of the 1950s and in the early 1960s elements of change had appeared in the market. The decontrol of rented properties was proceeding quite rapidly, partly as a result of Rent Acts and perhaps more importantly through the movement of controlled tenants.[9] A housing stock that had been "frozen" was steadily reverting to the market and landlords, agents, consumers and others were poised to exploit the situation.

It was also during this period that immigration to Britain from the West Indies and other parts of the New Commonwealth took place on a large scale. Many of these people settled in inner London. They experienced great difficulty in obtaining decent rented accommodation and many were forced to buy their own property. Others moved into leasehold property and, following the Leasehold Reform Act 1967, were able to buy their homes at advantageous prices. Agents in Islington sold many properties to immigrants in the late 1950s and early 1960s — many of them being the large Victorian rented houses. Immigrants were noticeably more able to raise the capital to do this than other social groups.[10] They often then rented them out to fellow immigrants.

During this period middle-class interest in Georgian Islington began to be apparent — a development perhaps best supported by anecdotal evidence such as that of the agent who recalled a television producer buying a property in Duncan Terrace (the heart of a gentrified area near the *Angel*) for £1700 in 1958 and that this person's intention was to "get things moving". Properties in this street now sell for £60,000. *The London Property Letter* (a privately circulated journal) stated in 1967, "About five years ago when the 'Chelseafication' of property was little more than a twinkle in most middle-class Londoners' eyes, Islington was fast gaining a reputation as the up and coming young thing around town." In 1965 the Milner Holland Inquiry took evidence from a property company which since the late 1950s had been restoring the Northampton estate in Canonbury to its former architectural and social standing.

As the return on rented property steadily fell behind comparable investment opportunities, landlords by their own volition or by the prompting of their agents sought to gain vacant possession and sell.[11] The survey revealed that up to 90 percent of the properties sold by estate agents in the early 1960s to owner-occupiers was formerly rented property. Larger, more commercial, property companies bought up tenancies in the realization that an active market for owner occupation was emerging. Much of this property would only be released on to the market after it had been converted into self-contained flats — thereby increasing the capital gain enormously. Similarly, new and more "active" estate agents began operations in the Borough with every intention of exploiting the new situation. Furthermore, as this new situation emerged, the problems of obtaining mortgage finance steadily diminished.

By the late 1960s vacant-possession and part-possession properties were widely available for purchase by owner-occupiers; the demand from young professionals (often working in the City) continued to grow. Prices which for long had been low compared with similar properties in other boroughs began

TABLE 1
Sales by Year

1965	1966	1967	1968	1969	1970	1971	1972
45	68	62	83	114	123	216	323

Source: Author's survey

to rise sharply. Average prices calculated from the sales data of one agent give the following: 1959, £2750; 1963, £4000; 1966, £5000; 1967, £4196; 1969, £7154; 1970, £8743; 1971, £10,241 and 1972, £17,392. Clearly the rise in 1971 was very rapid in comparison with the steady rise during the 1960s. House sales also increased, with almost all agents reporting a steady growth through the decade. Figures given by one agent would support this (Table 1).

As sales and prices increased it would appear that the Islington market came more into line with other boroughs. The Department of the Environment survey of house prices revealed that areas such as Islington experienced disproportionate increases in their house prices: a reflection, presumably, of the catching-up after a long period of depression.[12] The proportion of rented property to owner-occupied property being sold on the owner-occupied market had changed from 90 percent rented to 50 percent rented — though, of course, more property was being purchased.

BUILDING SOCIETIES AND OTHER FINANCIAL AGENCIES IN ISLINGTON

Until the late 1950s and early 1960s there existed a financial void in Islington. Although the Local Authority could grant mortgages[13] and a number of small building societies existed which would make loans, the larger building societies, banks and insurance companies were very reluctant to make any loans at all in this area. Indeed they would appear to have been operating policies somewhat similar to that outlined in the publication *Building Society Work Explained*[14] which states: "The Society's general lending policy will also have a bearing on the decision (to make a loan). It may have been decided for example to restrict lending in a certain area because of certain disadvantages attached to that area."[15]

Of the 22 societies interviewed, twelve said that they would not have lent money in Islington in the 1950s. All of these were large societies. Of the ten that had made loans, nine were small London-based societies (four being in Islington or North London). The remaining society was a large national society, but the number of mortgages it had granted was well below that of the smaller societies (whose advances ranged from twenty to over 100). The reasons behind the collective policy of refusal adopted by the larger societies can be explained as follows.

(1) A building society's first concern is with the security of its investors' money. Given that societies have reversed the normal process of borrowing and lending (since they borrow short and lend long), they have adopted extremely strict and conservative procedures to ensure that the confidence of their investors can remain unshaken. On any advance therefore their first concern is with the liquidity of the asset; i.e., if the borrower defaults and the society is forced to foreclose, the sale of the property will produce sufficient return to cover at least the sum advanced. In assessing this "liquidity" the society appraises the likely demand for the property in terms of size, price, area, etc. Many of Islington's houses had poor facilities, were large three-to-four-storey houses commanding relatively low prices and were set in areas rather unlike the suburban alternatives for mortgage funds. Large houses represent to building societies a threat of subletting and all the consequent problems which would ensue in the event of foreclosure.

(2) The persons most likely to apply for a mortgage on an Islington property during this period, the skilled worker, would often fail to meet the stringent financial requirements of the larger societies. Because of their lack of confidence in both purchaser and property these stipulations would include a shortened term (thus higher monthly payments), a limited advance (thus bigger down payments) and the withholding of part of the loan until essential repairs had been carried out. All of these factors would combine to make it impossible for any but the wealthiest applicants to proceed. Furthermore, a person who applied without large savings would have been treated with great suspicion, even though he may have been paying rents large enough to exclude the possibility of saving.

(3) These societies lacked detailed knowledge of the Islington area. Almost without exception, none of them had branch offices in the borough. Several

had agency arrangements with local professionals, but in most cases these were for the channelling of investment funds to the society rather than outlets for mortgage. Indeed, as one society's London manager said, to open an office in an area such as Islington "would be equivalent to putting one's head in a noose". Thus their agency arrangements were with solicitors and accountants, persons handling trust funds, legacies and so forth. In one or two cases the societies appointed estate agents, but evidence obtained from those agents would support the view that the societies did not expect to grant mortgages. In view of their absence from the area and their consequent lack of knowledge, it is no surprise to learn of their reluctance to grant mortgages there.

(4) Much of Islington was scheduled for clearance, although most of this property is still standing and likely to remain so. Thus large areas were and are blighted and conditions therefore were not appropriate to a secure investment.

(5) There were far better investment opportunities elsewhere, particularly in the suburbs. Except for 1972 and one short period in the 1960s, building societies have never been in the position of having surplus funds. They have always been able to choose between applicants. Under these conditions it is clear that a middle-income applicant for a mortgage on a modern semi-detached property in Barnet would have been preferred to a low-income or even a middle-income applicant and an unimproved four-storey nineteenth-century terraced villa in Islington.

Given the above, it is no wonder that the larger societies did not, except under special circumstances, give mortgages in Islington. The policy of the smaller London-based societies has clearly been more liberal, but that too is a reflection of their position. The smaller societies generally offer a higher rate to investors than the large national societies. Similarly they charge a higher rate on their mortgages.[16] As a result of this and the fact that they are less well known to the public, they tend to receive fewer applications from persons who can obtain cheaper mortgages elsewhere and proportionately far more applications from persons who have either been refused or know that they would be refused by the larger societies. Thus, although applicants from Islington may achieve greater success with the small society, it is at a cost. Furthermore, though the small London-based society would consider an application for property in Islington (and that included part-possession property) the loan term was often quite short (10-15 years) and the advance limited to 75 percent of the valuation (or lower if part-possession).

Substantial downpayments were often required, though frequently the applicant had been a saver with the society for years and was well known. Also the local society knew the area and even the house under consideration and was therefore in a good position to evaluate the risks involved. Given their dependence upon the local community for funds, they could not afford to refuse applicants from the local area. In the late 1950s the applications were often by local blue-collar workers for property in the area. By the mid 1960s these applicants were frequently seeking mortgages for properties in the suburbs of London and beyond. Applicants for Islington mortgages tended to be middle-class and because of the greater security they could offer, it was a welcome development for the smaller societies.[17]

In Islington the alternatives to a building society mortgage were as follows: the local authority, banks, insurance companies, finance houses and private mortgages. The relative importance of these sources indicate that building societies and the local authority are the most important. This is supported by the evidence given in the report *The Housing Situation in 1960*[18] and the 1964 *Housing Survey of England and Wales*.[19] According to the 1964 survey, the evidence for Greater London was as follows: 60 percent of all owner-occupiers with a current mortgage obtained their funds from building societies; 15 percent from local authorities; and 10 percent from insurance companies. The remainder were banks 3 percent, private loans 2 percent, mainly cash 5 percent, employer 2 percent, other 3 percent.

In Islington, local authority mortgages were obtainable both from the Borough itself and from the Greater London Council. Since 1965, the Borough has granted an average of approximately 300 mortgages a year, though it has fallen below this recently. Of the mortgages granted since 1971, 58 percent were for properties within the Borough (out of a total of 292), and it has been suggested that on average the loans were to persons in the higher socio-economic groupings.[20] Investigation of the Borough's role is continuing although the evidence presented here suggests that it has operated at a level marginally below the smaller societies in terms of the number of mortgages granted, but has tended to lend to a wider spectrum of the community. The Greater London Council's contribution appears to be minimal. Very poor records are kept, but in April 1974 only 23 mortgages were outstanding on properties in Islington.[21]

Insurance companies lend principally on highly priced property and, in Islington, survey evidence suggests they have been an important source of finance for extremely expensive properties. The costs of such finance tend to be higher and, as a consequence, use of such sources is more exclusive.[22] Similar or even higher costs pertain to finance-house usage, but the extent to which this sector is used is not known.[23]

Banks generally do not consider loans on housing—the term of lending being too long. It appears, however, that many immigrants, particularly those from the West Indies, obtained finance from Barclays Bank. Whether this is a reflection of the savings such persons had with the Barclays D.C.O. branches in the West Indies or a calculated policy by the bank in order not to cause offence in the West Indies by refusal is not known. But in general very special circumstances must pertain to obtain funds from a bank. The other source of funds, the private mortgage, was not known. The money would be advanced either by a local solicitor administering a trust fund, or by the vendor actually allowing the purchaser to pay by installments, or some other localized arrangement. With such local knowledge and control this was probably a fairly risk-free arrangement. The frequency with which either the bank or a private mortgage was used is not known. The evidence from the 1964 housing survey would suggest that they are rare.

The general conclusion to be drawn from this assessment and from interviews with the major estate agents in the Borough is that it was extremely difficult to obtain funds during the 1950s and 1960s and that, for house purchase, success in obtaining them was largely a reflection of personal connections. For instance, in one case the solicitor who acted for an estate agent was also director of a small London society. In another case, the estate agent himself was director of such a society. It was by means of these webs of personal contacts that finance was obtained.[24]

As the 1960s progressed, a gradual change became apparent in the financing of Islington's housing market. Almost imperceptibly building society policy changed so that by 1972 all but one of the 22 societies interviewed had granted between 30 and 50 mortgages. Their policy had changed from virtual refusal to extreme caution and it is valuable to consider how this came about.

As part of the overall context in which this change in attitude occurred, one must consider the role of government. Throughout the period in question, increase of owner occupation remained a central thread of housing policy and several attempts were made to expand this sector. Under the 1959 House Purchase and Housing Act, £100 million was made available to building societies to increase the amount of owner occupation in older properties (pre-1919). The policy was double edged in as much as it encouraged building societies to give loans on older property and at the same time it liberated what funds they had committed to this for use in the higher-price brackets. The £100 million was taken up and the proportion of older properties purchased certainly increased, though no evaluation of this scheme is known to the author. In 1967, the Leasehold Reform Act was passed to enable tenants of houses held on long leases at low rents to acquire the freehold at advantageous prices thus increasing the levels of owner occupation. Similarly the Option Mortgage Scheme, introduced in 1967, was intended to increase the opportunities of low-income persons for house purchase. Since this involved cheaper property it was also likely to be older property. Furthermore, policy shifted from the development of areas to rehabilitation, and government grants to assist in the improvement of older houses became widely available. Again for building societies this meant that the purchaser of older property would gain assistance in bringing his property up to a good standard (and a safe standard in terms of the security of building society investment). The policies introduced clearly reduced the risks to building societies and at the

The Role of Institutions

same time brought matters, such as older areas, into their consideration.

Other pressures were important. Local agents, be they solicitors or estate agents, are in a position to encourage policy changes within individual societies, either by way of the regular meetings of agents with the society or by acts of individual enterprise. For instance, an agent might take a mortgage manager on a tour of an area with the express purpose of encouraging him to lend there. On visiting an area such as Islington, the building society's representative would be shown houses which demonstrated the potential of such areas.

These external pressures aside, there was the direct experience gained from granting a loan. In a number of cases the larger societies have found themselves in a position where it was impossible to refuse a mortgage applicant (the person being a large investor). In these situations the society in question had to proceed with good grace while attempting to make their commitment as small as possible. By only lending a few thousand pounds and with the borrower's clear intention of spending several thousand pounds on the property their investment was secure. Having experienced one such loan, the next would be approached with greater enthusiasm. In one instance a society was persuaded to make a loan on a property in Islington and later the whole board of directors visited the house in order to see the effects. They were impressed (the house in question, bought by an architect in the late 1950s, had been fully renovated). Experiences such as these bred confidence and the ability of building societies to judge applications for mortgages in Islington was consequently increased. The situation for the other financial agencies would have been similar in some cases and different in others. Insurance companies and banks would probably have undergone similar pressures, but the Local Authority, although influenced to some degree by the change in attitude of the building societies, would always have had some responsibility to grant loans in the Borough.

It is appropriate at this point to briefly chronicle the way the finance market progressed in Islington. In the 1950s and early 1960s houses were bought using finance from small societies, the local authority, private mortgages and cash. In the case of the middle-class purchaser (and by and large that is with whom we are concerned) their purchases would have been concentrated in areas such as the Angel and Canonbury—these being areas of Georgian and early Victorian housing. The effects of their purchases would be an "improving" environment and an increasingly buoyant local housing market. In total it represented a clear expression of a demand, backed by means sufficient to overcome institutional barriers, for living in such an area. Local agents became aware of this demand and in turn so did the larger societies. Rather than "no" it became "possible". Thus, as confidence increased so did the means by which change was enabled. The beneficiaries of this change in attitude were the affluent newcomers, the landlords, estate agents and property companies rather than the local populace, because, even though finance became steadily easier, terms were still stringent and substantial amounts of cash were necessary for both downpayment and improvement. By the late 1960s successful applicants for mortgages on properties in Islington were no longer exceptional. To apportion responsibility for filling the financial void is difficult. Clearly many factors were at work at the same time. The Local Authority itself may have done much to begin the trend to grant mortgages which it now regrets (i.e. gentrification). The void had been filled for those who had substantial means; for the low-income purchaser it remains and the pressures generated by the former bear directly upon the latter. The new attitude adopted by the building societies and the financial institutions can be seen as a direct outcome of the activities of estate agents, government policy and the "invading" middle-class.

ESTATE AGENTS AND PROPERTY DEVELOPMENT

This final section draws together elements from the preceding two sections in considering the role of estate agents and property development companies. The conclusion to be drawn is that estate agents are not the passive intermediary seen by Lean,[25] but can and do act as agents of change.

There has been an interesting transformation in the role and nature of estate agents in the Borough of Islington. Until the early 1960s the agents could be classified as being mainly concerned with property management, with active sales, valuation and survey departments. Most of them were operated by professionally qualified chartered surveyors or had such persons on their staff. Management provided the main income and though sales were of importance, it was management that provided the "bread and butter" of their business. Because of all the difficulties in arranging housing finance and in the lack of properties considered suitable for owner occupation, the level of sales was held down, though in part it depended upon the area in which the agent operated. For instance, house sales in an area of two-storey properties were more buoyant than in areas of larger properties. Management has remained a major function of these agencies even though some have expanded their house sales activities.

Since the early 1960s, a number of new agencies have opened in the Borough, two of which have risen to be amongst the most important estate agencies (by number of properties sold). Significantly, one of these agencies is a branch office of agents operating in the Borough of Camden where a similar process of change is apparent and the other was founded by a former employee of that Camden agency. Several other agents in the Borough are also "graduates" of that agency. Whether the movement of offices and personnel from Camden to Islington indicates a recognition of the 'potential' of Islington is not known, but the timing is suggestive.

The Role of Institutions

The new agents can be distinguished from the old in being concerned primarily with house sales with a limited management role. The profit from house sales is far more immediate and the procedure is less complex. To develop a management portfolio that produces a good return takes a considerable period of time and reflects a fairly long-term view. However, several of these new agencies have a management function partly as a result of the large property companies who, being interested only in the long-term capital appreciation, have handed over the management of the tenancies that they buy to them. Given that most of these newly established businesses are committed largely, if not entirely, to house sales, it is no wonder that they employ methods to ensure that house sales continually increase. Thus they utilize circulars soliciting properties for sale and advertise extensively. Such practices are often in conflict with the codes of practices laid down by the Royal Institute of Chartered Surveyors (R.I.C.S.) and other estate agent organizations.[26] As a consequence, although some of the agents are themselves members of R.I.C.S. they do not advertise this. Indeed these new agencies see their role as "house salesmen" offering a thoroughly businesslike service. This includes operating from smart modern premises (in contrast to the brown stain varnish of the older agents) and the adoption of a variety of selling techniques. Given that a market for property in Islington has been identified within the middle class, advertising is concentrated in papers such as *The Times*, *Sunday Times* and *Observer*. The *Observer*, in particular, was felt to be a good way of reaching the "liberal" intellectual type, who apparently favoured Islington. In addition to these agents who specialize in the middle-class market, a number of agencies have been established who specifically cater to the immigrant market. For many reasons it was found to be difficult to interview such agents and as a consequence no details of their activities are provided here.

In the case of an estate agent who is mainly dependent upon house sales, it is clear that he has a direct interest in the price of any particular sale (thus the higher the prices the better; and higher prices mean higher class) and in the general market conditions in the area in which he operates. Thus it is good business and good for business for him to do his utmost to promote such an area. A number of the estate agents interviewed agreed that it was possible for an agent to do this, particularly if he had close links with a property company. Any doubt about estate agents' awareness of these possibilities is dispelled by a reading of the *London Property Letter* (L.P.L.) which is a journal devoted to such matters and written by cells of estate agents.[27] A selection of statements will perhaps suffice:

> L.P.L. No. 166 comments on the Archway area: But nestling down at the bottom is a distinctly working-class area which presents possibilities for reclamation.

> L.P.L. No. 201: The fascinating thing about London is that it throws up an endless supply of new possibilities for the property pioneer and Brixton is about as near to the Klondike as you can get without actually digging.
>
> L.P.L. No. 189: Grubby Kennington has been providing rich killings for sharp hunters. But the best parts of the Kennington carcass are disappearing fast leaving late comers only the bones to pick over. Where next will the South Bank hunt turn? Our money goes on the Stockwell Vauxhall sector where prices are at last starting to skip in anticipation of the Victoria line's arrival in the second part of this year.

Finally and perhaps most threateningly under the title 'London, a dying swan', the writers of L.P.L. 192 discuss the social geography of London and suggest that it will be stood on its head in years to come.

Agents managing property are of course in a good position to advise owners to sell and in a number of cases this has been done. By doing so they can encourage the trend to owner occupation. Similarly, an agent in recognizing the potential sales value of a particular area can do much to organize change there. He might circulate owners of properties seeking property to sell; he can also purchase dwellings himself, renovate and resell them in an attempt to generate activity. Numerous possibilities exist. It is only a logical extension of good business practice which moves an estate agent from a totally advisory role to active involvement in a local housing market. Recently publicity has been given to this in *The Times, Evening Standard* and *The Guardian*.[28] It is obvious that an estate agent has a well-developed sense of what property is worth and having acted as an intermediary for property sales and purchases which have bought substantial capital gains for others it was an inevitable step to take. As *The Economist*[29] stated:

> Since estate agents now know much about finance, about what other people are doing and about the arithmetic of investment (many run the property portfolios of the institutions) the temptation to become entrepreneurs as well is very strong.

The Royal Institute of Chartered Surveyors has always been troubled by this, but is virtually powerless to do anything. In the Institute's official history it says of estate agency[30] "plainly a commercial more than a professional activity."

In a number of cases, therefore, agents in Islington were linked with property development companies who were buying, renovating and reselling property. The profit was high and results significant. In one case known to the author an estate agent has direct control over a building society, a property company and a second mortgage company—all operating from the same premises—a well-integrated business. Through their role as advisors to landlords, building societies and property companies, estate agents are in an important position with regard to the generation of change. As Whitehouse states[31] "Property development is an extension of the function of an estate agent".

LOCAL AND CENTRAL GOVERNMENT

Brief consideration is now given to the role of public authorities in the private sector. Mention has already been made of the effects that changes in policy have had upon the attitude of financial agencies, such as building societies, to Islington. The introduction of these various policies has also had direct consequences for the processes of change. For instance, the Leasehold Reform Act enabled a substantial number of tenants to purchase their accommodation. As prices rose, the pressure upon them to sell and capitalize their gain increased and some did so. Thus one now fashionable square was in the mid-sixties occupied by immigrant tenants who by way of the Act acquired properties which they then sold to the incoming middle class.

It has been argued that improvement grants are an important factor in the process of change in inner areas such as Islington.[32] However, while it is accepted that the availability of such grants was an added incentive, it is suggested that it cannot be held to explain the process.[33] It is likely that its effect was to heighten demand rather than cause it. Other interventions such as the improvement of transport and the development of traffic schemes also had an impact upon changes in Islington. Similarly, it has been suggested that the activities of the Rent Office will induce changes in the housing market,[34] as will the provision of local authority mortgages. These and other factors are of importance, but cannot be considered here. It is an unfortunate fact that all policy has unintended consequences, and the evidence is that Islington's housing market is no exception.

CONCLUSION

The evidence presented is that there has been a slow but steady growth in the owner-occupied sector of the Islington housing market and in the proportions of persons in socio-economic group I. It is suggested that these changes result in part from the ways in which the housing market of an inner London borough is controlled and manipulated. The policies of central government with regard to rent control maintained a stock of vulnerable housing in a central location and did little to reduce the vulnerability of both the housing stock itself and of its occupants. The policies of financial agencies similarly worked to prevent many of the occupants gaining control of their own accommodation. When, for a variety of reasons not discussed here, a demand by relatively affluent persons for accommodation within the Borough began to emerge, a situation primed for change existed. Estate agents and property companies were able to exploit the new situation. Financial agencies approached the position cautiously thus adding to the exclusiveness of the process. Their policies only really altered when the price of large portions of inner-area property had risen sufficiently to exclude the less affluent from the possibility of purchase, and at the same time reach desired levels of security. The policies applied by central and local government probably exacerbated the position. The effects of these changes upon the "original" community vary with their ability to capitalize upon the situation. For many it has meant worsening housing conditions in an ever-diminishing stock of property and only of late has the local authority intervened on a substantial scale.

The purpose of this paper is to demonstrate that changes in urban areas are not simply a reflection of choice but also of control. Indeed, although accepting that choice and control are two opposites that exist within each other the element of control is rarely considered and thus it was felt necessary to emphasize its function in the processes of change. Certainly discussions of patterns of urban land use are dominated by studies of individual behaviour and ecological processes, while control and constraint are dismissed in a few lines. By considering aspects of control and thus of supply rather than demand, a clearer understanding of change and of the mechanisms producing it emerge. In practical terms whether such changes can or will be controlled is not known. Certainly if unchecked the implications of such changes for Islington and London as a whole are considerable. If control is exercised then the implications for our present land and housing market are also substantial.

NOTES

I am very grateful to Dr. Sophia Bowlby for her excellent advice and supervision and to fellow postgraduates in the Department of Geography, University of Reading, for their valuable comments.

1. This paper is a report of some of the findings and conclusions reached in a wider research project titled 'Change in an urban area, the role of institutions in the process of gentrification in inner London.' This study, conducted by the author, is still in progress.

2. Gentrification is the term used to describe the process by which areas of working-class residence become increasingly occupied by the middle classes. This process is widespread in inner London and elsewhere. For a general discussion of gentrification see Counter Information Services (1973) *The Recurrent Crisis of London* (London) pp. 40-4.

3. For other literature which considers the control and manipulation of land use and housing see the following: Counter Information Services (1973) *The Recurrent Crisis of London*; Edwards, J. (1973) 'The other housing problem; access and accountability,' unpubl. paper. Cent. Urban Reg. Stud.; Form, W.H. (1954) 'The place of social structure in the determination of land use: some implications for a theory of urban ecology', *Soc. Forces* 32, 255-66; Harvey, D. and Chatterjee, L. (1974) 'Absolute rent and the structuring of space by governmental and financial institutions', *Antipode* 6, 22-36.

4. Be they groups defined in terms of race, income, employment, class or education.

5. Based on males, economically active: Socio-Economic grouping 1 comprises Socio-Economic groups, 1,2,3,4, and 13. These figures are not strictly comparable. They are intended as a guide.

6. It will be noted that the owner-occupied sector has expanded by only 2 percent. However, this figure disguises certain trends. First, it would appear that considerable quantities of owner-occupied accommodation have been demolished in clearance schemes, and therefore the growth

of the sector has been maintained only by the addition of newly purchased properties. Second, the original owner-occupiers themselves have been replaced.

7. A detailed study of enumeration district data has identified specific parts of Islington where gentrification is occurring.

8. Even if a property became vacant, only rarely could an individual raise the finance to buy it for personal use. Thus properties tended to stay in the rented sector.

9. The 1957 Rent Act secured the decontrol of rented dwellings of over £40 rateable value in London and over the period 1957-59, 12 percent of these became owner-occupied. However, 300,000 houses were decontrolled by movement in the first year following the Act. Cullingworth suggests that this was the more important factor; see Cullingworth, J.B. (1965) *English Housing Trends* (London).

10. See Davies, J. (1972) *The Evangelistic Bureaucrat* (London) and Burney, E. (1967) *Housing on Trial* (Oxford).

11. Alternative investments were by then considerable and the costs of maintenance and repairs were increasing rapidly.

12. This survey, based upon Inland Revenue data, was produced by the Housing Statistics section of the Department of the Environment. The report was titled, *The Movement of House Prices in the Greater London Area, 1961-1970*.

13. Under the Small Dwelling Acquisitions Act, Islington has granted mortgages from at least 1928 though the number was very small due to the very limited amount of funds the Council had available.

14. Ashworth, H. (1970) *Building Society Work Explained*, Building Societies Institute.

15. Such policies exist today. A number of societies mentioned Brixton as an area where they would not lend and one society had a policy of labelling areas 'stop', 'go', and 'caution' as descriptions of the action they would take on receiving an application from any of the areas concerned.

16. Rates are from 1 to 1½ percent higher depending on the type of property.

17. Survey evidence.

18. Gray, P. and Russel, R. (1962) *The Housing Situation in 1960*. The Social Survey, (London).

19. Woolf, M. (1967) *The Housing Survey of England and Wales*. The Social Survey, H.M.S.O.

20. Islington Planning Department (1974) personal communication.

21. Ibid.

22. See *Housing Survey of England and Wales*, 1964, p. 28.

23. It is believed to be of particular importance for immigrant owner-occupiers.

24. Surveys of finance for owner occupation are rare. The report *The Housing Situation in 1960* and the 1964 *Housing Survey of England and Wales* provide information on this. According to the 1964 survey, 49 percent of all owner-occupiers interviewed in Greater London obtained their funds from building societies (60 percent of those with a current mortgage) 10 percent had local authority loans (15 percent with current mortgage) and 7 percent used insurance companies (10 percent with current mortgage). Insurance companies lend on high-priced property. In Islington they are known to be an important source of finance for the exremely expensive properties. Building society lending by borough over the last five years is presently being analyzed by the author.

25. Lean, W. (1965) 'Some aspects of the real estate market', unpub. M.Sc. thesis, Univ. of London.

26. Monopolies Commission (1969) *Estate Agents: A Report on the Supply of Certain Services by Estate Agents*, H.M.S.O.

27. One has the feeling when studying the L.P.L. that the persons writing and reading this journal have the ability to ensure that the changes predicted will occur.

28. *The Times*, 12 March 1974; *Evening Standard*, 12 March 1974; *The Guardian*, 13 March 1974.
29. *The Economist*, 18 March 1972.
30. Thompson, F. (1968) *Chartered Surveyors: The Growth of a Profession* (London).
31. Whitehouse, B.P. (1964) *Partners in Property* (London).
32. Hamnett, C. (1973) 'Improvement Grants as an Indicator of Gentrification in Inner London', *Area* 5, 252-61.
33. Dugmore, K. and Williams, P. (1974) 'Improvement Grants', *Area* 6, 159-60.
34. Harloe, M. et al. (1974) *The Organization of Housing: Public and Private Enterprise in London* (London).

12

Large Builders, Federal Housing Programmes, and Postwar Suburbanization

Barry Checkoway

I

It is customary in the literature on postwar American suburbanization to neglect the decision process and institutional context by which suburban places were established and developed. In one popular image, for example, postwar residential suburbs 'exploded' on the American landscape or appeared as the sudden product of unspecified or invisible hands. Once there were rural farmlands and small villages at the edge of the city, then suddenly there were Levittown, Park Forest, and even Los Angeles, all the overnight work of get-rich-quick developers or families in flight (Editors of *Fortune*, 1958). In another image, postwar suburbs resulted from a virtual 'tidal wave of metropolitan expansion'. Suburbanization was no overnight explosion at all, but only the latest episode in a secular shift of metropolitan population from centre to periphery and an *ad hoc* decision process fragmented and diffused among a large number of separate decision-makers (Blumenfeld, 1954; an earlier example is given in Warner, 1962). In yet another image, postwar

---

From *International Journal of Urban and Regional Research,* Vol. 4 (March 1980), pp. 21-44. Reprinted by permission of Edward Arnold (Publishers) Ltd., London, and B. Checkoway.

suburbs resulted from the shifting preferences of consumers. Suburban development prevailed bcause the public demanded it, directed government to provide incentives for suburban production and consumption and fueled a revolution in the residential construction industry (Dobriner, 1958; Donaldson, 1969; Masotti and Hadden, 1973). Suburbanization appears as a product of 'forces' originating elsewhere. It has an uncanny, dramaturgical quality. It appears irreversible.

In all this, there has been little effort to conceptualize postwar suburbanization as a product of decisions and institutional interactions. Yet there was no magic in the appearance of postwar suburbs. On the contrary, at any moment metropolitan form is the product of understandable processes put in motion and perpetuated by its key decision-makers. But there are few accounts that approach suburbanization as a process rather than as something to be taken for granted, and little is known about its principal postwar participants, their interests and aims, their partners and handmaidens. There *are* studies of the decision behaviour of home-buying consumers, but few which examine the prior, precipitating decisions in this period (an exception is Clawson, 1971; see also Harvey, 1973).

This paper reports a search for the historical background of the decisions and institutions that together 'built the suburbs'. Who were the key actors? What factors influenced their decisions? What interests and values were involved? Who participated in—and who was excluded from—the process? And what are the lessons of this history? The focus is on large residential builders and the federal government. They do not comprise all those who participated in postwar suburban development, but they are among the most important. They have been selected for their importance in postwar suburban *residential* development.[1]

My own belief is that the key decisions in postwar suburbanization were made by large operators and powerful economic institutions supported by federal government programmes and that ordinary consumers had little real choice in the basic pattern that resulted. My hope is that the pattern may be altered and improved by an analysis of problems and policy alternatives from this view.

II

The growth of many postwar suburbs was precipitated by decisions by large residential builders to select and develop suburban locations. There was nothing new about suburban development in America. What was new in this period was the developed capacity of large builders to take raw suburban land, divide it into parcels and streets, install needed services, apply mass production methods to residential construction, and sell the finished product to unprecedented numbers of consumers. These decisions are best explained in terms of the changing market conditions of housing and developed technological capacity of housebuilding itself.

There was a shortage of adequate housing in postwar America. In 1947 it was estimated that between 2,750,000 and 4,400,000 families were living with other families and 500,000 more were occupying transient or non-family quarters. Although estimates of the quantity of housing required to replace deteriorated structures and stay abreast of population and family increases ranged between 1,000,000 and 1,500,000 units per year, the building industry was unable to construct more than 500,000 units per year. Housing surveys in 1947 found more than 6,000,000 low-income urban families either searching for better housing or planning to do so (Rosenman, 1946; Newcomb and Kyle, 1947; Hauser and Jaffe, 1947; Bauer, 1948).

Several factors were cited to explain the housing shortage. Some analysts attributed it to wartime conditions and military priorities which had virtually stopped civilian residential construction and created shortages among postwar consumers (Abrams, 1948). Others attributed it to increases in family formation and birth rates which had resulted in a population that was eager for better housing (Glick, 1957; Taeuber and Taeuber, 1958). Others attributed it to postwar prosperity and a rising standard of living which had resulted in a growing demand for more products and consumers with purchasing power to back up demand (Saulnier *et al.*, 1958; Haar, 1960; Miller, 1965). Yet others attributed it to the shortcomings of the residential construction industry. Housebuilding was dominated by small and local firms lacking the capacity to reduce shortages and reach demand. The typical small builder could not employ a permanent labour force, develop a research staff, bargain for materials in volume at lower cost, or buy a substantial area of land for large-scale development.[2] Housebuilding was, in a popular contemporary image, the 'industry capitalism forgot' (*Fortune* 36, August 1947, 61-7).

TABLE 1

New Housing Units Started in the U.S., by Decade, 1930-1959

Decade	New Housing Units Started
1950-59	15,068,000
1940-49	7,443,000
1930-39	2,734,000

Source: U.S. Bureau of the Census, 1966, 18.

The national production of housing increased significantly in the period that followed. In the decade after 1950 more than 15,000,000 new housing units were started. The rate of new residential construction in 1950-59 was approximately twice that in 1940-49, six times that in 1930-39. The number of new housing units started was 515,000 in 1939, 1,466,000 in 1949, and 1,554,000 in 1959. In 1946, housing production almost quadrupled; in 1950 the housebuilding industry produced more houses than in any one year in history. Although the shortage remained, production advances were nonetheless significant (Maisel, 1953, 11ff).

Important in postwar production advances were basic changes in the residential construction industry. What distinguished the period was an increase in the number, size, and importance of large residential builders. Postwar studies by Sherman Maisel in the San Francisco Bay Area documented the primacy of these builders. Maisel examined all Bay Area residential builders in 1949-50 and identified four basic types by size. A builder was classified as large if he annually completed 100 or more houses, had a volume of more than $1,000,000 and more than $600,000 in total assets, and employed 100 or more workers and a large overhead staff. Maisel found that although small builders were the most numerous type, they were of less overall importance than the small number of larger builders that built most of the houses and dominated the market. In 1949, large and medium builders comprised only 2 percent of the local total but accounted for 55 percent of the houses produced. Follow-up studies showed that between 1950 and 1960 large builders increased their share to 74 percent of all houses produced. By 1960 large builders built three out of every four houses in this area (Maisel, 1953; follow-up studies include Herzog, 1963, 19-32).

The Bay Area findings typified the national pattern. Several builders had developed gradually and grown before 1940, and others were born of the defence programmes that followed. In 1939, it was estimated that there were 480 large and medium builders that together accounted for less than 20 percent of the houses produced nationally. In 1949, there were 3750 builders of this size and they accounted for 45 percent of the total. The total number of units built by these builders was more than six times greater in 1949 than in 1939 (Maisel, 1953, chapter 2). Fully 70 percent of the houses built in 1949 were built by only 10 percent of the builders. Large builders alone accounted for 5 percent of all houses built in 1938, 24 percent in 1949, and 64 percent in 1959. This period thus saw a significant increase both in the number of large builders and in the number of houses built by them.

The large builder was distinguished by his size, scale, and operating structure. These were not small and local craftsmen but large, often national operators identified more with automobile industrialists than with small operators of their own field. The typical large builder reduced costs through

TABLE 2

Number of New Housing Units Started and Percentage Built by Large Builders, 1938-1959

Year	New Housing Units Started	Percentage of Houses Built by Large Builders
1959	1,554,000	64%
1949	1,466,000	24%
1938	406,000	5%

Sources: 1938 data from U.S. Bureau of Labor Statistics (1940); 1949 data from U.S. Department of Labor (1954); 1959 data from National Association of Homebuilders (1960, 17). Data on the housebuilding industry in this period is generally unavailable. On this point, see Maisel (1953, 3-9).

direct buying of materials, purchased in carload lots, maintained large inventories, developed new and more efficient subcontractual relationships, and specialized his labour force. He applied government financial aids and housing research to his work. Government research laboratories cooperated with large builders to make advances in materials and equipment (Anon, 1954, 42-56; Dietz, 1959 *et al.*, 1959), in land development and site planning (Spring, 1959), and in faster and less costly methods (Sasaki, 1959; Whyte, 1958). Mass production and prefabrication promised factory engineering, standardized dimensions, preassembled units and prefitted systems.[3] It also promised more rapid construction and higher production.

The large builder also was distinguished by his reduced costs and higher profits. In 1949, the cost of building the composite house was $9500 for a small builder, $9250 for a medium builder, and $8750 for a large builder. The consequent selling price of the house was $12,400 for a small builder, $10,500 for a medium builder, and $9,250 for a large builder. The consequent net profit before taxes was equivalent to 5.7 percent of sales volume for a small builder, between 6.7 and 8.5 percent for a medium builder, and 10 percent for a large builder (Maisel, 1953, especially chapter 8). Profits thus increased with size and volume.

The large builder also was distinguished by his suburban orientation. Mass production required large, less expensive tracts of land typically found near the city limits or in suburban areas beyond. In the suburbs was open and available land at the right price and without restriction and the promise of excellent transportation by automobile and expressways. Retail, manufacturing, wholesale, office, and service establishments all sought suburban locations in the postwar period. Given the orthodox market assumptions and locational principles, postwar suburbanization was a logical alternative to investment in the central city.[4]

The overall result was a significant increase in postwar American suburban development. In 1950 the growth rate of suburbs was more than ten times that of central cities. Between 1950 and 1955 the total metropolitan population increased by 11.6 million people, 9.2 million of whom were suburban. Between 1950 and 1956, 64 percent of the net national increase in housing was in metropolitan areas. Of this, 19.4 percent was in central cities, 80.6 percent was in suburbs. New residential construction was by far the most important single factor of change: the total volume of new construction in suburbs was almost three times that in central cities in this period (US Bureau of the Census, 1958; 1966; US Department of Labor, 1959). It was among the great population migrations in American history.

Large-scale residential development spearheaded and symbolized the movement. Orange County, California, increased in population by 65 percent between 1940 and 1950. The increments outside Los Angeles alone were phenomenal. Torrance increased by 124 percent, Lynwood by 133 percent, Monterey Park by 140 percent, Arcadia by 154 percent, Montebello by 171 percent, Manhattan Beach by 175 percent, Compton by 198 percent, and Hawthorne Covina by 350 percent. Levittown, New York, had more than 51,000 people living in 15,000 identical houses by 1950. Park Forest, Illinois, housed 30,000 on 2400 acres 30 miles south of Chicago by 1956. In 1957 the editors of *Fortune* estimated that suburban land was being bulldozed at a rate of 3000 acres per day. It was a triumph for the suburbs and the large builders who built them.

III

Levitt and Sons exemplified the growing potential of large residential builders in postwar suburbanization. The firm had been founded in 1929 by Abraham Levitt, whose early background in real estate helped him to recognize the profitability of large-scale housebuilding operations, and by his two sons, Abraham and William. In the 1930s, Levitt had built custom homes for affluent families in suburban Long Island and Westchester County, New York, and the company continued to build by conventional methods until the second world war. A wartime ban on most civilian construction forced Levitt to build low-cost housing in government defence areas. This experience gave Levitt an opportunity to experiment with prefabrication, to grasp the principles of mass production, and to imagine a housebuilding scheme of unprecedented scale. By the end of the war, Levitt had grown in size, developed in capital, and was ready to expand (Gans, 1967; Larrabee, 1948; Levitt, 1951; Liell, 1952; Levitt, 1968).

In 1947 Levitt acquired 1400 acres of Long Island farmland about 30 miles from New York City and proceeded to revolutionize the housebuilding industry. By 1948 Levitt was completing more than 35 houses per day and 150 houses per week and rapidly selling the low-cost product. More than 17,000 identical houses for over 70,000 people were finally built side-by-side in uniform rows and sold for the same price of $7990. By 1950 'Levittown' was praised as 'an accomplishment of heroic proportions' and the Levitt house was known as 'the best house for the money in the United States.' [5]

How did Levitt do it? Levitt adapted assembly line techniques to the mass production of housing. An army of trucks speeding along new-laid roads stopped and delivered neatly packaged bundles of materials at exact 100 foot intervals. Giant machines followed the trucks, digging rectangular foundations in which heating pipes were embedded. Each site then became an assembly line on which houses were built. Men, materials and machines moved past each site in teams, each performing one of 26 operations over and over again from site to site according to standards derived from systematic studies of time and motion. Every possible part and system was preassembled, prefabricated or precut to specification and size in the factory, and then brought to the site ready to assemble with machinery developed just for the purpose. As operations were shifted from site to shop, scheduling and delivery grew in importance. Materials reached the site only minutes before a team would arrive to perform its particular operation. Mechanization and labour-saving machinery, forbidden or prohibitive in traditional operations, were everywhere evident in Levittown. Levitt was less a builder, more a manufacturer of houses.[6]

Each Levittown house was controlled by Levitt from start to finish. Over several years Levitt had recruited executives with specialized competence in all aspects of housebuilding. Levitt also had developed a construction crew which was thoroughly familiar with company techniques and capable of any construction task. Construction workers were non-unionized and assured of steady employment. Such stability and permanence were atypical of the housebuilding industry.

Levitt applied vertical organization and rationalization as rigorously as housebuilding would allow. He altered traditional distribution channels and reduced costs. Lumber, for example, came from Levitt's own company and was cut from his own timber on his own equipment to the exact specification and size at which it later was used in assembling the house, enabling further savings in handling and freight. Nails and concrete blocks were made in Levitt's own factory by contractors working only for him. Those few materials not produced by Levitt were bought in carload quantities directly from manufacturers by Levitt's own wholesaler, eliminating middle-men and markups. The typical builder was entangled in a costly distribution web.

Levitt in comparison eliminated charges and even influenced product design to suit his own needs.[7]

Levitt also had an enviable capital position and a profitable partnership with government. In addition to personal resources, he boasted the largest line of credit ever offered a privately owned American housebuilding firm. This proved an important competitive advantage at every stage. He had easy access to government credit and financial aids. For large builders like Levitt, the federal government offered billions of dollars of credit and insured loans up to 95 percent of the value of the house. Such builders easily received FHA 'production advances' before purchases were made. Levitt was able to get FHA commitments to finance 4000 houses before clearing the land. Veterans using the GI Bill of Rights could buy in Levittown with no down payment and installments of only $56 a month.

The completed Levitt house was attractive to consumers. Levitt spent more money on consumer research than any builder of small houses in history. The Levitt house—and Levittown itself—was meticulously designed to match consumer preferences. Each house was small, detached, single family, Cape Cod in style, and centrally located on a small lot in a development in the suburbs. To ensure the sale, each house came complete with radiant heating, fireplace, electric range and refrigerator, washer, built-in television, and landscaped grounds. All were included at no added cost. For middle-income consumers, Levittown offered a virtual dream house, and Levitt was the dream's entrepreneur.[8]

Levitt also rationalized and simplified his marketing and merchandising. Full-page advertisements directed customers to a display building adjacent to Levittown. Inside were carefully decorated model rooms and all the appliances, design innovations and gadgets for which Levitt was known; a scale model of the completed development; and several salespeople to answer questions, offer advice, and take deposits. The entire financing and titling transaction was reduced to two half-hour steps, one to purchase and another to clear title. Contract forms already stamped with fixed title enabled clerks to sign up to 350 buyers per day. In minutes customers could be assured of a completed transaction. Levitt could get three banks, a mortgage broker, and the construction superintendent on a single telephone to arrange several thousand FHA and VA mortgages for veterans. Levitt handled all legal and real estate details and charged $10 flat for closing costs. For an inexperienced buyer entering the market for the first time and looking for investment security, Levitt offered a creditable commodity and proven reliability. In 1947 Levitt undersold his nearest competitor by $1500 and still earned $1000 profit on each $7990 house.[9]

In 1950 Levitt sought to expand further and to create an entire community somewhere on the eastern seaboard. Levittown, New York, was the largest housing development ever built by a single builder, but now he wanted to build more than houses alone. The scheme was detailed by Alfred Levitt in the *Journal of the American Institute of Planners* in 1951. The proposed community could incorporate past Levitt experiences and 'principles of good planning laid down by leaders in the field'. It would include neighbourhood residential areas divided by parks, playgrounds and schools; an industrial area separated by a green wooded shelter belt; and an interior expressway connecting the neighbourhoods and on which commercial facilities would be located. Because all land would be owned in advance, it would be possible 'to plan right down to the last tree and shrub' (Levitt, 1968).

Construction originally was intended for Long Island and several hundred New Yorkers had made cash deposits before examining the proposed plans or the model house. But the Korean national emergency forced postponent of construction, and Levitt instead proposed to adapt the plan to one of several critical defence areas around the country. He sought a large area of land requiring little modification and easily converted to large-scale use. He also sought an active housing market, assurances of consumer demand, and access to government financial aids aimed at large builders. Several sites were considered: all were suburbs.

Levitt decided to locate outside Philadelphia in Lower Bucks County, Pennsylvania. This area offered agricultural land on the suburban fringe of a large city which shared strongly in the postwar housing shortages. It also offered assurances of government financial aids. A prior decision by United States Steel to construct a major defence-related steel plant had made the area eligible for designation as a critical defence area. But the particular location was not key. It is fair to assume that any of several similar suburban sites also would have been acceptable. (These decisions are described in detail in Checkoway, 1977a, chapter 2.)

Levitt was the largest but not the only builder of his kind. Large builders were increasing in number and production outside every major city. Among them was John Mowbray outside Baltimore, Waverly Taylor outside Washington, D.C., Don Scholz outside Toledo, Maurice Fishman outside Cleveland, Irvin Blietz outside Chicago, J.D. Nichols outside Kansas City, Del Webb outside Phoenix, Carl Gellert and Ellie Stoneson outside San Francisco, and Dave Bohannon, Fritz Burns, and James Price outside several cities. They symbolized a revolution in housebuilding and were instrumental in postwar suburbanization. Maisel said of them:

> These are the new giants in an industry once populated by pygmies. Here, at the very peak of their housebuilding pyramid, are the leaders of construction who are not content merely to build homes. They construct communities (Maisel, 1953, 95).

IV

State support of large residential builders by federal government programmes was crucial in postwar suburban development. For, in addition to the changing market conditions of housing and the developed technological capacity of large builders, some measures were required to guarantee the mortgage money, share the risk, and ensure the profitability of the suburban enterprise. Although there was nothing new about government aids to private industry in America, postwar conditions combined to enlarge the federal role in the housing field.

The shortage of housing was viewed by some as a problem of industrial production. Wartime conditions had resulted in record rates of production; had depleted supplies of many materials; and had reduced the capacity of industry. Wartime production had virtually exhausted America's plants, and facilities were too small, strained and inadequate to meet the growing demands of a heavily consuming economy. Production backlogs in excess of six months were common. Shortages of some non-military goods had accumulated to alarming proportions. Postwar supply fell short of demand. Postwar industry thus found itself searching to install capacity and increase production. (The postwar industrial production problem is described in Checkoway, 1977a, chapter 3).

Residential construction was only one of several industries with postwar production problems, but it was considered among the most important. The housing shortage was commmonly identified as a failure of residential construction. Legislators and analysts generally agreed that federal intervention would benefit both the housebuilding industry and the entire economy. Residential construction is considered a bellwether of the economy, an effective pump-primer in an economic slump (Abrams, 1950; Meyerson et al., 1962, 18-31). They also agreed on the importance of suburbanization as a 'built form' for residential construction in particular and production in general.[10] Several housing bills were prepared and introduced.

The federal housing policy that followed was mostly suburban in its orientation.[11] It is customary to believe otherwise. The customary view focuses on the stated aims and more controversial programmes of the Housing Acts of 1949 and 1954. It begins with an image of postwar urban decline and housing shortages and contends that these acts were the principal federal response to these conditions. It contends that the stated aims of these acts were their real aims. Thus, the famous Title I of the Housing Act of 1949 set forth policies 'to eliminate substandard and other inadequate housing through clearance of slums and blighted areas . . . , [to] stimulate sufficient housing production and community development to remedy the housing shortage . . . , [and to] realize the goal of a decent home and a suitable living environment for every American family . . . ' Thus the legislative debate indicated a belief that the cycle of urban obsolescence would be interrupted, that the stated aims of better homes, improved neighborhoods, and the elimination of slums were within reach, and that low-income housing was an important priority. Urban renewal and public housing were among the most widely discussed programmes established or revitalized by the Act. Other federal housing programmes were less often the object of general discussion.[12]

Consequent legislators and analysts focused on the inconsistencies and contradictions that developed. Early evaluations of urban renewal, for example, found that between 1950 and 1960 more homes were destroyed than were built; that those homes destroyed were predominantly low-rent homes and those homes built were predominantly high-rent homes; that housing conditions were made worse for those whose conditions originally had been bad; that forced relocation often resulted in serious psychological grief and depression among those forced to relocate; and that small businesses which were relocated either had lower average monthly sales in their new locations or disappeared altogether. As poor people were forcibly relocated to other areas also substandard or mapped for future renewal, their original neighbourhoods were replaced with high-rise luxury apartments, commercial facilities, and plazas and pedestrian malls. The programme destroyed homes, cleared slums, and constructed corporate offices, but its focus was never 'predominantly residential' or for the poor (Anderson, 1964, quoted in *Harvard Business Review* 43, 21). Early evaluations of public housing also found inconsistencies and contradictions between stated aims and actual practice (Dean, 1949; Wurster, 1957).

These inconsistencies and contradictions were reported in the consequent literature on federal practice. So widespread were the reports that an effort was made to explain and correct the deficiencies. Thus the customary belief is that the Housing Act of 1954 shared the stated aims of the earlier act and was designed in part to correct its temporary deficiencies (Abrams, 1946, 232; Checkoway, 1977b, 31-2). There also resulted an image that urban renewal and other city-oriented efforts were the principal programmes in the federal housing policy of which they were only a part. The literature on the federal urban renewal and public housing programmes is massive (see, for example, Wilson, 1966; Real Estate Research Corporation, 1974).

But the real aims of postwar federal programmes are revealed by the irrefutable facts of federal practice. The Housing Act of 1949 authorized $1 billion in loans and $500 million in capital grants for slum clearance and urban redevelopment over a five-year period. In 1949 Congress also increased the amount that could be insured under the FHA home mortgage programme to $6 billion. In 1950 Congress increased the FHA mortgage insurance authorization by $2.25 billion, amended FHA sales housing programmes to provide incentives for production of three- and four-bedroom houses, liberalized FHA terms on loans for manufactured houses and large-scale residential construction, established a new FHA programme for homes in suburban and outlying areas, and reduced the low-rent public housing authorization to 75,000 units for the year. In 1951 Congress increased the FHA mortgage insurance authorization by $1.5 billion, authorized loans to facilitate the production of prefabricated houses and major components for new houses, authorized $60 million for loans and grants for facilities and services in critical defence areas, and further reduced the public housing authorization to 50,000 units for the year. In 1953 Congress increased the FHA mortgage insurance authorization by $1.5 billion, liberalized FHA terms on loans for new owner-occupied homes and in suburban areas, and further reduced the public housing authorization to 35,000 units for the year and subsequent years. Early in 1954 Congress again reduced the public housing authorization to 20,000 units and added the condition that unwanted public housing under construction could be stopped by the locality. The Housing Act of 1954 increased all FHA mortgage insurance authorizations by another $1.5 billion, liberalized the amounts and terms of FHA sales housing mortgages, and established another FHA mortgage insurance programme for single-family dwellings in suburban and outlying areas (US Congress Subcommittee on Housing and Urban Development, 1975; see also the various works of Charles Abrams). The 1954 act was hailed by large builders as 'an aid to private enterprise'. Public policy is not what is stated or intended but what is actually done. Federal housing policy was mostly suburban in its orientation.

Federal housing programmes operated as an economic instrument to stimulate production in the housing field and the entire economy. One focus was on homeownership. FHA was only one of several programmes designed to make homeownership possible for more people by bringing carrying charges within reach of a mass market through long-term indebtedness. FHA joined with chambers of commerce, real estate operators, and large builders to actively promote homeownership, putting hundreds of government salesmen in the field to organize local drives, circulate promotional literature, and sponsor 'better selling meetings' and expositions. Local realtors and builders advertised the virtues of homeownership by using the FHA seal as a symbol of government approval. Ownership and sales were central to federal housing programmes (Dean, 1945, chapters 3 and 4).

Another focus was on new construction. A class of consumers was ready to purchase new houses, and the federal government sought to effectuate their demands through special incentives and financial aids to large suburban builders. A Veteran's Emergency Housing Program was enacted in 1946 to facilitate the financing of priority housing for returning veterans. The prefabrication industry got an important boost under this programme, as government contracts were offered to all prefabrication firms and several hundred thousand dwellings were finally built. The Housing and Home

Finance Agency was established in 1947 and soon began cooperating with government laboratories, universities, and the largest builders to develop products, methods, and ideas for housing. The emphasis was on new single-family suburban houses. New construction was by far the most important factor of change in the national housing inventory in this period (US Bureau of the Census, 1958, 14).

Another focus was on large builders. The federal government encouraged small builders to grow large and large builders to further grow to a size that would be economically more meaningful. To the builder ignored by past federal programmes, noted Charles Abrams, 'FHA brought a rare prize'. And the larger the builder, the larger the prize. Large builders more easily received credit advances and more easily negotiated with the FHA. Large operators and powerful economic institutions were among the principal beneficiaries of federal programmes. Small operators were either excluded, penalized, or driven from the market. Any builder who could promise a large quantity of mortgages was eagerly sought after by a federal programme (Abrams, 1946, 232; Stone, 1973; Eichler and Kaplan, 1967).

Another focus was on suburban residential construction. FHA, a profit-making enterprise based upon bankers' standards, encouraged new building in the suburbs and discouraged development in the central city. Its overall concern for 'economic soundness' shaped a belief that poor and minority neighbourhoods were bad credit risks and placed further emphasis on homeownership, new construction, and large builders. Mark Gelfand documents how builders and buyers generally could take advantage of FHA home mortgage insurance programmes only if they located themselves beyond the inner city.[13] The result was that the vast majority of FHA houses were built in the suburbs and the suburbs could not have expanded as they did in the postwar years without FHA.[14]

The suburban orientation had far-reaching consequences for central cities and suburbs alike. FHA 'redlined' large areas of central cities beyond the business districts, refusing to insure mortgages there and practically guaranteeing further decline. FHA also intensified racial segregation in cities, accepting the belief that racial homogeneity was essential to maintain neighbourhood stability and property values. Its *Underwriting Manual* indicated the need to 'prevent the infiltration of adverse influences' and 'inharmonious racial groups' and gave official approval to racial segregation through restrictive covenants (Gelfand, 1975, 220; National Commission on Urban Problems, 1968, 101; Warner, 1972, chapter 2). Large builders typically required restrictive covenants and FHA was handmaiden to the large builders. And the federal focus on the new single-family house was at the expense of planned suburban neighbourhoods. FHA placed restrictions on the design of new houses and even on their placement on individual lots. But it lacked the necessary comprehensive planning or citizen participation, and the resulting 'FHA town' is easily identified by its failure of design (Gelfand, 1975, 218-19; Warner, 1972, 37-52; among the strongest critics was Allen, 1954a; 1954b).

Other federal programmes also promoted suburbanization. The federal highway programme made possible the roads that made large tracts of suburban land more accessible for development. The roads and highways that resulted laced metropolitan areas and transformed farmlands and old villages into real estate for suburban developers (Gelfand, 1975, 222-35; Howard, 1957, 38-9; 1959; Mumford, 1968; Leavitt, 1970; Rae, 1971; Muller, 1976). Federal tax policies also promoted suburban construction. Federal income tax deductions on owner-occupied houses made government contribute a fifth or more of costs of homeownership and virtually subsidized the new suburban houses (Meyerson *et al.*, 1962, 236-37; other federal suburban programmes are described in Arnold, 1971).

The suburban orientation was the direct result of the effort to stimulate production in the housing field and the national economy. The focus on homeownership and new construction stimulated the production and consumption of house-related goods in the marketplace and the flow of capital in the entire economy. It allowed for capital outlays in public works, physical facilities, social services, transportation systems and more. It offered incentives to realtors, large builders, bankers, lumber dealers, highway contractors, automobile manufacturers and others. Postwar suburbanization was a 'built form' and an economic instrument for production, and federal legislators were predisposed to facilitate the process.

V

Large builders also organized to determine the direction of the programmes which benefited them. There was nothing new about their efforts. The National Association of Real Estate Boards (NAREB) from its inception had a standing committee concerned with federal legislation and was instrumental in the housing acts of the 1930s. (The standard work on NAREB is Davis, 1958. On NAREB influence in the 1930s, see McDonnell, 1957). The National Associaton of Home Builders (NAHB) originated in NAREB and then developed as an independent organization concerned primarily with large builders and new suburban houses (Mason, n.d.; Lilley, 1973). Postwar shortages and the promise of federal intervention necessitated more active involvement in legislation. In 1942, the Realtor's Washington Committee was formed to represent, promote, and protect the industry's position in Congress. This committee was led by NAREB and NAHB and was backed by the US Savings and Loan League, the US Chamber of Commerce, the American Bankers Association, the Mortgage Bankers Association of America, the

Building Products Institute, the National Retail Lumber Dealers Association of America, the Associated General Contractors, the National Association of Retail Lumber Dealers Association, the National Clay Products Association, the Producers Council, and other trade associations representing apartment house owners, building materials manufacturers, lumber industrialists, subcontractors, prefabricators and others. (The formation of the Washington Realtor's Committee is described in Davies, 1966, chapter 2.)

The housebuilding lobby became one of the most powerful political groups in Congress. It operated from a well-defined although not singular position. It sought to facilitate the production and sales of new suburban houses. It favoured FHA, VA, and other programmes to remove risks and ensure profits of residential construction, and opposed public housing as a 'socialistic' threat to private enterprise. It employed pressure tactics which were fundamentally grass roots in nature. NAREB alone reported 44,000 members in 1100 communities, NAHB 16,000 members in 130 local chapters. Local affiliates placed Congressmen on boards of directors, thus contributing to congressional understanding of, and responsiveness to, their position. On any given day the lobby could flood Congress with letters, telegrams, and telephone calls from influential constituents in every part of the country. Local leaders were also major advertisers in local media, thus contributing to media willingness to report their position and lend editorial support. A full-time, well-paid Washington staff prepared leaders for participation in hearings and meetings, produced form letters for constituents to mail, conducted active public information programmes, sponsored homeownership fairs and displays, maintained a constant flow of press releases and news feature stories, and wrote model curricula for school teachers. Large sums of money were spent on advertising to persuade consumers to prefer homeownership and new construction and to direct government to provide programmes to facilitate these preferences.[15]

The housebuilding lobby influenced the legislation and programmes that developed. It effectively delayed the Taft-Ellender-Wagner housing act for four years mainly out of opposition to the proposed public housing. When the bill finally reached the congressional floor as the Housing Act of 1949, the lobby worked to limit the number of public housing units authorized, to further aids to private housebuilding through expanded FHA and VA programmes, and to assure inclusion as a national housing goal 'that private enterprise shall be encouraged to serve as large a part of the total need as it can'. It was estimated that more than $5,000,000 was spent by homebuilders in the struggle over this act. So aggressive were their tactics that a full-scale congressional investigation was conducted.[16]

The housebuilding lobby also influenced policy through administrative action. Homebuilders gave sustained support to administrative agencies such as the FHA and VA, which in return tended to respond to the policy suggestions of their support groups. Homebuilders also worked to supply agencies with most of their personnel and guidelines.[17] At the national scale, Harry Truman appointed as head of the FHA Raymond Foley, who referred to himself as 'a champion of free enterprise in housing' and said 'the chief activity of government in housing should be to aid and stimulate private enterprise'. Dwight Eisenhower replaced Foley with Albert Cole, a long-term opponent of public housing who labelled federal housing legislation as socialistic and voted against the Housing Act of 1949. Cole was later replaced by Norman Mason, who came to government after a career as a building supply and lumber retailer (Keith, 1973, chapter 6). It was no surprise that the FHA adopted guidelines consistent with the building and real estate industry and fully accepted the racial practices of the private society.

The homebuilders' lobby also influenced policy through local implementation. The FHA was relatively decentralized in its administration, permitting closer connections between field directors and local real estate operators, financial institutions, and homebuilders. When the Housing Act of 1949 was finally enacted and authorized public housing, the lobby immediately worked to amend the legislation and to defeat its implementation through local opposition and referenda. As a result, only 283,400 of 810,000 authorized units were actually produced in the scheduled period, and the number of authorized units was reduced in each successive legislative year after 1949 (Davies, 1966, 123-32). At the same time, programmes benefiting home-ownership, new construction, and large builders increased greatly.

The production of new single-family suburban houses was not the only focus of postwar federal housing practice, but others were minor in comparison. Urban renewal and public housing, for all of their clamour and controversy, were secondary to the houses whose mortgages were financed and guaranteed by federal housing programmes. These programmes operated as an economic instrument to stimulate production and large builders were influential in developing the programmes which benefited them.

VI

Most suburban studies attribute postwar suburbanization to the shifting preferences of consumers. Indeed, so common is the focus on suburban consumers that they are pictured as independent actors in a process in which they chose to participate. In this image, postwar suburbanization followed from the selective migration of individuals with unprecedented preferences for social homogeneity and conformity, compulsory neighbouring and membership in voluntary associations, a return to religion and a Republican Party switch, and other attributes of 'the new suburbia' (Marshall, 1973). It was 'a new way of life', 'a new state of mind', and 'one of the major social changes of the twentieth century'. There was shaped a virtual 'image of suburbia' in the American public mind, and so frequently have its attributes been addressed that when we think of suburbs we typically think of these attributes.

Later analysis argued instead that suburbanization resulted not from selective migration but from other more independent factors. In this image, postwar suburbanization was explained as an effort to achieve middle-class status and upward social mobility (Dobriner, 1963), or a 'new bourgeois style' (Dobriner, 1963, chapter 1) or the homeownership ideal (Gans, 1967; Berger, 1960). Leo Schnore, for example, rejected the 'social psychological approach' and argued 'that differential housing opportunities are the major determinants of growth differentials between sub-areas of the metropolitan community' (Schnore, 1968, 162). Herbert Gans (1962, 625-48) argued that there was little to distinguish the way of life in suburbs from cities, that those who sought suburbs mainly sought the best available house for the money (Gans 1967, chapter 2), and that the nature of suburban community derived more from the consequent population mix than from selective migration (Gans, 1967, chapter 7). Postwar suburbanization was, in the revisionist image at least, 'new homes for old values' (Ktsanes and Reissmann, 1959).

The problem in this analytic exchange is the assumption on which it is based. It is assumed by both the selective migration analysts and their revisionists alike that consumers were free to choose among several residential alternatives, that their choices reflected real preferences, and that their preferences were the independent factor in suburbanization. The only real point of dispute is whether the preferences resulted from 'a new state of mind', or from middle-class mobility, or from some other factor. Not in dispute is the assumption that consumers were the independent factor in the suburban pattern that evolved. This paper breaks with this assumption.

The customary view of the postwar consumer residential choice derives from a history that is well known and widely accepted (Checkoway, 1977b, chapter 4). It contends that the consumer decision and consequent federal programmes were a response to urban decline and housing shortages. Central cities were surrounded by seas of deterioration in which housing quality and municipal facilities were allowed to decline. Studies of Philadelphia, for example, found central areas so blighted that they were wholly undesirable for business or residence; the majority of houses were grossly deficient and dilapidated; fully one-third of all dwelling units were labelled unfit for human habitation and nothing short of demolition was recommended. Declining conditions were commonly identified with racially changing neighbourhoods, lower property values, and an unsafe financial investment.

Suburban homeownership was believed more attractive. Consumers were turned away from conditions in the central city and toward the 'suburban ideal'. The suburbs offered a new, free-standing, well-equipped, carefully designed and attractively landscaped house, with ample yard space to play and garden. They also offered an escape from the city, a more wholesome environment, and a more neighbourly community. The American predisposition to 'suburbia' was confirmed by contemporary surveys of the subject.

The suburbs also offered the best available financial investment. The growing demand for suburban housing steadily increased its relative value. A slightly higher initial price seemed little to pay for a better product and investment security. Indeed, it probably confirmed the quality of the product and security of the investment in the minds of those purchasing their first house. And given the suburban orientation of FHA and other federal housing programmes, suburban homeownership offered virtually the only sensible investment location.

Postwar consumers easily recognized the significance of any announced decision by a large builder to locate in a metropolitan suburb. For those turned away from central Philadelphia, for example, Levittown promised a planned alternative, a suburban oasis at a distance from the city, and a pioneering opportunity in a wholly new environment. It also promised a known commodity, a national reputation, and proven reliability. The advertised image—of a detached house with flower-filled windowboxes surrounded by grass, trees, shrubs, high clouds, and no other houses in sight—was hardly resistible. When the first model houses were opened for inspection in December 1951, more than 50,000 people filed through during the very first weekend. As salesmen on loudspeakers urged buyers to return on another day, police were needed to keep crowds in line. Several families squatted for days outside the salesroom waiting for the chance to put a deposit on a house which had not yet been built. On the first two days alone, more than $2,000,000 worth of houses were sold. It was, as the national media reported, 'the most spectacular buyers' stampede in the history of American housebuilding'.[18] This is the customary view of the postwar consumer choice.

This paper suggests something different about the postwar consumer residential choice. It does not question that growing families were justifiably turned away from conditions in the central city; or that suburban housing was more attractive and a better investment; or that residential suburbs did offer an escape from the city and a wholesome arena for family and child rearing; or that increased consumer demand did affect federal housing programmes and residential construction decisions. Houses in suburbs like Levittown were a bargain and did offer a version of the suburban ideal to consumers who had never before been able to achieve it. All of these images are easily confirmed in the literature.

This paper does question those studies which fail to explain the impossibility of inferring the spatial dynamics and decision behaviour of large operators and government partners from the residential aspirations and satisfactions of the eventual suburban consumers, or which fail to specify the narrow range of alternatives actually available, or which fail to emphasize the fact that consumers were important but not decisive actors in the decisions which produced the choices they made. Consumers made a logical choice among alternatives developed elsewhere. The evidence that consumers aspired to, bought in, or expressed satisfaction with suburbs is not proof enough that they would have chosen to do so if a different set of alternatives had been available to them. The assumptions that consumers were free to choose among several residential alternatives, that their choices reflected real preferences, and that their preferences were the independent factor in postwar suburbanization, all ignore the fact that final decisions do not always reflect real preferences and that prior decisions may predetermine a narrow range of alternatives from which consumers can choose. (A general perspective on the fallacy of consumer sovereignty is given in Galbraith, 1971.)

It is wrong to believe that postwar American suburbanization prevailed because the public chose it and will continue to prevail until the public changes its preferences. Suburbanization prevailed because of the decisions of large operators and powerful economic institutions supported by federal government programmes, and ordinary consumers had little real choice in the basic pattern that resulted. Postwar suburbanization resulted from a decision process and institutional context and the consequences and policy problems flow from the nature of the process. To alter the consequences, it is first necessary to alter the process.

NOTES

This paper was presented at the 1978 annual meeting of the American Political Science Association. Among those who commented on earlier versions are Bernard Frieden, Herbert Gans, Mark Gelfand, Chester Hartman, Seymour Mandelbaum, Roger Montgomery, Heywood Sanders, Allen Wakstein, Frederick Wirt, Michael Zuckerman, and colleagues at the Childhood and Government Project at the University of California at Berkeley.

1. This is not to suggest that large residential builders were the only large operators in postwar suburban development. Other important actors—mortgage lending institutions and local suburban governments, for example—have not been selected for examination here but have been or will be treated elsewhere. I treat the role of large transportation and industrial operators in Checkoway, 1977a, and of local suburban government in Checkoway, 1977b. Michael Stone (1973) examines the role of mortgage lenders. The literature on suburban economic development is massive.

2. Among the general studies are Abrams, 1950; Maisel, 1953; Foote *et al.*, 1960; Beyer, 1965. On housebuilding operations and constraints see Grebler, 1950; Kelly *et al.*, 1959; and Meyerson *et al.*, 1962. On local building practices see Killingsworth, 1950, 538-80. On obstacles to production advances see US Congress House Subcommittee of the Joint Committee of Housing, 1946, especially pp. 144-64.

3. Between 1948 and 1954, the number of manufactured homes produced in the United States increased from 30,000 to 77,000 (Beyer, 1965, 244). The development of prefabrication is explored in Bemis, 1936; Bruce and Sandbach, 1945; and Kelly, 1951. Prefabrication principles are

described in Chapman, 1954; "Where is prefabrication?" *Fortune* 33 (April, 1946), 127-32; 'More houses for less money', *Better Homes and Gardens* 28 (October, 1949), 189-92; 'Prefabrication', *Architectural Forum* 92 (April, 1950), 160-64; 'Prefabs fill special needs', *House and Home* 2 (November, 1952), 89-114.

4. It could be argued that economies of scale would have made large-scale development desirable in any given location. In this period, however, government programmes developed to bear the public costs of new residential construction, encourage homebuilders to grow larger, and give development a suburban orientation. This is discussed in section V of this paper.

5. The construction of Levittown, New York, is described in Larrabee, 1948; Liell, 1952; and in 'Up from the potato fields', *Time* 56 (3 July 1950), 67-72.

6. See Larrabee, 1948; Liell, 1952; '4000 houses a year', *Architectural Forum* 90 (April 1949), 84-93; 'The most popular builder's house', *Architectural Forum* 92 (April, 1950), 20-22; 'Levittown on the assembly line', *Business Week* 1172 (16 February 1952), 26-27; 'Biggest new city in the US', *House and Home* 2 (December, 1952), 80-91.

7. 'A large company, in short, by its very size and prestige and integrity, can accomplish, can achieve, can perform, where individuals are helpless and disunited', wrote William J. Levitt (1948, 253-56).

8. The Levitt house and consumer research are described in Lader: 'The most popular builder's house'; and 'Levitt keeps experimenting with . . . ', *House and Home* 5 (February 1954), 118-23.

9. Lader; 'Levittown on the assembly line'. It is revealing to contrast Levitt practices with the more common practices described in Dean, 1945.

10. The image of suburbanization as 'built form' for production is introduced by Harvey, 1973, 261-74. See also Downie, 1974; Sawyers, 1975.

11. The evolution of federal housing policy is described in Wheaton, 1953: McKelvey, 1966; Gelfand, 1975. See also Friedman, 1968; National Commission on Urban Problems, 1968; Frieden, 1968, 170-225; Hartman, 1975; and Checkoway, 1977c.

12. Levin, 1952; National Association of Housing Officials, 1950; Public Law 171, 81st Congress, 1st Session (15 July 1949), Housing Act of 1949, Section 2.

13. My debt to the work and prose of Gelfand (1975, especially pp. 216-22) is obvious.

14. La Guardia, 1935, 13-14; Bartholomew, 1939; 1940; 'Rebuilding the cities', *Business Week* (6 July 1940), 38-39; *FHA Homes in Metropolitan Districts* (Washington: Government Printing Office, 1942; 'FHA policies said to hinder urban rebuilding', *American City* 63 (March 1948), 120; Bauer, 1956; 'FHA in suburbia', *Architectural Forum* 57 (September, 1957), 160-61; National Commission on Urban Problems, 1968, 99. See also Chatterjee *et al.*, 1976.

15. The position of the housebuilding lobby is well described in testimony in US Congress House Committee on Banking and Currency, 1954; and US Congress Senate Committee on Banking and Currency, 1954. Lobbying activities and tactics are described in US Congress House Select Committee on Lobbying Activities, 1949.

16. The influence and delaying tactics of the housebuilding lobby are described in Schriftgiesser, 1951, chapter 14. The political history of the Housing Act of 1949 is described in Davies, 1966, chapter 8; Keith, 1973, chapters 2-5; Meyerson *et al.*, 1962, 272-89; and *Congressional Quarterly Almanac* 4, 137-43, 339-44.

17. Herbert V. Nelson, executive director of the Washington Realtors' Committee, told a US Senate Committee in 1950: 'We put several hundred of our people, whom we found and persuaded to go into goverment service, into positions where they could give their services' (quoted in Abrams, 1965, 61). But Nelson is probably best known for his statement after passage of the Housing Act of 1949: 'I do not believe in democracy. I think it stinks. I don't think women should be allowed to vote at all. Ever since they started, our public affairs have been in a worse mess than ever before' (US Congress House Select Committee on Lobbying Activities, 1949, 5).

18. On public affairs in Levittown in the 1950s, see Checkoway, 1977a, chapters 4 and 5. On Levittown 20 years later, see Popenoe, 1977, chapters 5 and 6.

REFERENCES

Abrams, C. 1946: The Future of Housing. New York: Harper and Brothers.
— 1948: Housing—The Ever-Recurring Crisis: In Harris, S.E., editor, *Saving American Capitalism*, New York: Alfred A. Knopf, 183-92.
— 1950: The Residential Construction Industry. In Adams, W., editor, *The Structure of American Industry*, New York: Macmillan.
— 1965: *The City is the Frontier*. New York: Harper and Row.
Allen, F.L. 1954a: The Big Change in Suburbia, Part I. *Harper's Magazine* 208, 21-8.
— 1954b: Crisis in the Suburbs, Part 2. *Harper's Magazine* 209, 47-53.
Anderson, M. 1964: *The Federal Bulldozer*. Cambridge, Massachusetts: MIT Press.
Anon, 1954: *Housing...USA*. New York: Simmons-Boardman Publishing Corporation.
Arnold, J.L. 1971: *The New Deal in the Suburbs: A History of the Greenbelt Town Program 1935-54*. Columbus: Ohio State University Press.
Bartholemew, H. 1939: The Case for Downtown Locations. *Planners Journal* 4, 32-3.
— 1940: Present and Ultimate Effects of Decentralization upon American Cities. In *Mortgage Bankers Association of America Yearbook, 1940*, Chicago: Mortgage Bankers Association of America.
Bauer, C., editor, 1948: *A Housing Program for Now and Later*. Washington: National Public Housing Conference.
— 1956: First Job: Control New City Sprawl. *Architectural Forum* 55, 105-12.
Bemis, A.F. 1936: *The Evolving House*. Cambridge, Massachusetts: MIT Press.
Berger, B.M. 1960: *Working-Class Suburb: A Study of Auto Workers in Suburbia*. Berkeley: University of California Press.
Beyer, G.H. 1965: *Housing and Society*. New York: Macmillan.
Blumenfeld, H. 1954: The Tidal Wave of Metropolitan Expansion. *Journal of the American Institute of Planners* 20, 3-14.
Bruce, A. and Sandbach, H. 1945: *A History of Prefabrication*. Raritan, New Jersey: John B. Pierce Foundation.
Chapman, G. 1954: Public Acceptance of Prefabrication. *Appraisal Journal* 22, 57-68.
Chatterjee, L., Harvey, D. and Klugman, L. 1976: *FHA Policies and the Baltimore City Housing Market*. Washington: National League of Cities.
Checkoway, B. 1977a: *Suburbanization and Community: Growth and Planning in Postwar Lower Bucks County, Pennsylvania*. University of Pennsylvania, unpublished Ph.D. thesis.
— 1977b: *The Politics of Postwar Suburban Development*. University of California, Berkeley: Childhood and Government Project.
— 1977c: The Failure of Citizen Participation in Federal Housing Programs. *Planning and Public Policy* 3, 1-4.
Clawson, M. 1971: *Suburban Land Conversion in the United States: An Economic and Governmental Process*. Baltimore: Johns Hopkins University Press.
Davies, R.O. 1966: *Housing Reform During the Truman Administration*. Columbia: University of Missouri Press.
Davis, P.J. 1958: *Real Estate in America*. Washington: Public Affairs Press.
Dean, J.P. 1945: *Homeownership: Is it Sound?* New York: Harper and Brothers.
— 1949: The Myths of Housing Reform. *American Sociological Review* 14, 281-88.
Dietz, A.G.H. 1959: Housing Industry Research. In Kelly, 1959.
Dietz, A.G.H., Murray, J.A., Koch, C. and Kelly, B. 1959: Construction Advances. In Kelly, 1959.
Dobriner, W.M., editor, 1958: *The Suburban Community*. New York: G.P. Putnam.
— 1963: *Class in Suburbia*. Englewood Cliffs: Prentice Hall.

Donaldson, S. 1969: *The Suburban Myth*. New York: Columbia University Press.
Downie, L. Jr. 1974: *Mortgage on America*. New York: Praeger.
Editors of *Fortune* 1958: *The Exploding Metropolis*. New York: Doubleday.
Eichler, E.P. and Kaplan, M. 1967: *The Community Builders*. Berkeley: University of California Press.
Foote, N.N., Abu-Lughod, J., Foley, M.M. and Winnick, L. 1960: *Housing Choices and Housing Constraints*. New York: McGraw Hill.
Frieden, B.J. 1968: Housing and National Urban Goals: Old Policies and New Realities. In Wilson, J.Q., editor, *The Metropolitan Enigma*, Cambridge, Massachusetts: Harvard University Press.
Friedman, L.M. 1968: *Government and Slum Housing*. Chicago: Rand McNally.
Galbraith, J.K. 1971: *The New Industrial State*, revised edition. New York: New American Library.
Gans, H.J. 1962: Urbanism and Suburbanism as Ways of Life: A Re-evaluation of Definitions. In Rose, A., editor, *Human Behavior and Social Processes*, Boston: Houghton-Mifflin.
    1967: *The Levittowners*. New York: Vintage Books.
Gelfand, M.J. 1975: *A Nation of Cities: The Federal Government and Urban America 1933-1965*. New York: Oxford University Press.
Glick, P.C. 1957: *American Families*. New York: John Wiley.
Grebler, L. 1950: *Production of New Housing*. New York: Social Science Research Council.
Haar, C.M. 1960: *Federal Credit Aid and Private Housing: The Mass Financing Dilemma*. New York: McGraw Hill.
Hartman, C.W. 1975: *Housing and Social Policy*. Englewood Cliffs: Prentice Hall.
Harvey, D. 1973: *Social Justice and the City*. London: Edward Arnold; Baltimore: Johns Hopkins University Press.
Hauser, P.M. and Jaffe, A.J. 1947: The Extent of the Housing Shortage. *Law and Contemporary Problems* 12, 3-15.
Herzog, J.P. 1963: Structural Changes in the Housebuilding Industry. In Real Estate Research Program, *The Dynamics of Large-scale Housebuilding*. Berkeley: University of California Press.
Howard, J.T. 1957: Impact of the Federal Highway Program. In *Planning 1957*, Chicago: American Society of Planning Officials.
    1959: Arresting the Highwaymen. *Architectural Forum* 60, 93.
Keith, N.S. 1973: *Politics and the Housing Crisis Since 1930*. New York: Universe Books.
Kelly, B. 1951: *The Prefabrication of Houses*. New York: John Wiley.
Kelly, B. *et al.* 1959: *Design and Production of Housing*. New York: McGraw Hill.
Killingsworth, C. 1950: Organized Labour in a Free Enterprise Economy. In Adams, W., editor, *The Structure of American Industry*, New York: Macmillan.
Ktsanes, T. and Reissmann, L. 1959: Suburbia: New Homes for Old Values. *Social Problems* 7, 187-94.
La Guardia, F.H. 1935: The Federal Work Program and the Cities. In *City Problems of 1935*, Washington: US Conference of Mayors.
Larrabee, E. 1948: The Six Thousand Houses that Levitt Built. *Harper's Magazine* 197, 79-88.
Leavitt H. 1970: *Superhighway—Superhoax*. Garden City: Doubleday.
Levin J. 1952: *Your Congress and American Housing—the Actions of Congress from 1892 to 1951*. H. Doc. 532, 82nd Congress.
Levitt, A.S. 1951: A Community Builder Looks at Community Planning. *Journal of the American Institute of Planners* 17, 80-88.
Levitt, W.J. 1948: More Houses and Better Values. *Journal of the American Institute of Planners* 9, 253-56;

1968: Revolutionizing an Industry. In Editors of *Nations Business, Lessons of Leadership: 21 Top Executives Speak Out on Creating, Developing and Managing Success*, Garden City: Doubleday.
Liell, J.T. 1952: *Levittown: A Study in Community Development and Planning.* Yale University, unpublished Ph.D. thesis.
Lilley, W.III 1973: The Homebuilders' Lobby. In Pynoos, J., Schafer, R. and Hartman, C.W., editors, *Housing Urban America*, Chicago: Aldine, 30-48.
Maisel, S.J. 1953: *Housebuilding in Transition.* Berkeley: University of California Press.
Marshall, H. 1973: Suburban Life-Styles: A Contribution to the Debate. In Masotti and Hadden, 1973, 123-48.
Mason, J.B. n.d.: *A Brief History of Housing, 1940-1949: Decade of War and Progress.* National Association of Home Builders Library, unpublished manuscript.
Masotti, L.H. and Hadden, J.K., editors, 1973: *The Urbanization of the Suburbs.* Beverly Hills: Sage.
McDonnell, T. 1957: *The Wagner Housing Act: A Case Study of the Legislative Process.* Chicago: Loyola University Press.
McKelvey, B. 1966: *The Emergence of Metropolitan America, 1915-1968.* New Brunswick: Rutgers University Press.
Meyerson, M., Terrett, B. and Wheaton, W.L.C. 1962: *Housing, People and Cities.* New York: McGraw Hill.
Miller, H.P. 1965: *Income of the American People.* New York: John Wiley.
Muller, P.O. 1976: *The Outer City: Geographical Consequences of the Urbanization of Suburbs.* Washington: Association of American Geographers.
Mumford, L. 1968: *The Urban Prospect.* New York: Harcourt, Brace and World.
National Association of Homebuilders 1960: The Homebuilder—What Does He Build? *Journal of Homebuilding* 14 (March).
National Association of Housing Officials 1950: *Legislative History of Certain Aspects of the Housing Act of 1949.* Publication no. N278.
National Commission on Urban Problems 1968: *Building the American City.* Washington: Government Printing Office.
Newcomb, R. and Kyle, H.C. 1947: The Housing Crisis in a Free Economy. *Law and Contemporary Problems* 12, 186-205.
Popenoe, D. 1977: *The Suburban Environment: Sweden and the United States.* Chicago: University of Chicago Press.
Rae, J. 1971: *The Road and the Car in American Life.* Cambridge, Massachusetts: MIT Press.
Real Estate Research Corporation 1974: *Urban Renewal Land Disposition Study: Literature Search.* Chicago: Real Estate Research Corporation.
Rosenman, D. 1946: *A Million Homes a Year.* New York: Harper and Row.
Sasaki, H. 1959: Land Development and Design. In Kelly, 1959, 112-36.
Saulnier, R.J., Halcrow, H.G. and Jacoby, N.H. 1958: *Federal Lending and Loan Insurance.* New Jersey: Princeton University Press.
Sawyers, L. 1975: Urban Form and the Mode of Production. *Review of Radical Political Economics* 7, 52-68.
Schnore, L. 1968: *The Urban Scene.* New York: Free Press.
Schriftgiesser, K. 1951: *The Lobbyists: The Art and Business of Influencing Lawmakers.* Boston: Little, Brown and Co.
Scott, M. 1971: *American City Planning Since 1890.* Berkeley: University of California Press.
Spring, B.P. 1959: Advances in House Design. In Kelly, 1959, 57-82.
Stone, M. 1973: Federal Housing Policy: A Political-Economic Analysis. In Pynoos, J., Schafer, R. and Hartman, C.W., editors, *Housing Urban American*, Chicago: Aldine, 423-33.

Taeuber, C. and Taeuber, I.B. 1958: *The Changing Population of the United States*. New York: John Wiley.

U.S. Bureau of Labor Statistics 1940: *Builders of One-family Homes in 72 Cities*, serial no. R-1151. Washington: Government Printing Office.

U.S. Bureau of the Census 1958: *1956 National Housing Inventory: Components of Change, 1950 to 1956, United States and Regions*, volume 1, part 1. Washington: Government Printing Office, 14-15.

1966: *Housing Construction Statistics, 1889 to 1964*. Washington: Government Printing Office.

U.S. Congress House Committee on Banking and Currency 1954: *Hearings*, HR 7839, 83rd Congress.

U.S. Congress House Select Committee on Lobbying Activities 1949: *Hearings—The Role of Lobbying in Representative Self-Government, 81st Congress*.

U.S. Congress House Subcommittee of the Joint Committee on Housing 1946: *High Cost of Housing*. Washington: Government Printing Office.

U.S. Congress Senate Committee on Banking and Currency 1954: *Hearings*, S 2889, S 2949, S 2938, 83rd Congress.

U.S. Congress Subcommittee on Housing and Urban Development 1975: *Evolution of Role of the Federal Government in Housing and Community Development*. Washington: Government Printing Office.

U.S. Department of Labor 1954: *Structure of the Residential Building Industry*, Bulletin no. 1170. Washington: Government Printing Office.

1959: *Nonfarm Housing Starts, 1889 to 1958*. Bulletin no. 1260. Washington: Government Printing Office, 15 and 24.

Warner, S.B. Jr. 1962: *Streetcar Suburbs: The Process of Growth in Boston 1870-1900*. Cambridge, Massachusetts: Harvard University Press.

1972: *The Urban Wilderness: A History of the American City*. New York: Harper and Row.

Wheaton, W.L.C. 1953: *The Evolution of Federal Housing Programs*. University of Chicago, unpublished Ph.D. thesis.

Whyte, W.H. 1958: Urban Sprawl. In Editors of *Fortune*, 1958, 138-58.

Wilson, J.Q., editor, 1966: *Urban Renewal: The Record and the Controversy*. Cambridge, Massachusetts: MIT Press.

Wurster, C.B. 1957: The Dreary Deadlock of Public Housing. *Architectural Forum* 106, 140-42, 219, 221.

IV
Marxist Approaches

13

The Urban Process Under Capitalism: A Framework for Analysis

David Harvey

My objective is to understand the urban process under capitalism. I confine myself to the capitalist forms of urbanization because I accept the idea that the "urban" has a specific meaning under the capitalist mode of production which cannot be carried over without a radical transformation of meaning (and of reality) into other social contexts.

Within the framework of capitalism, I hang my interpretation of the urban process on the twin themes of *accumulation* and *class struggle*. The two themes are integral to each other and have to be regarded as different sides of the same coin—different windows from which to view the totality of capitalist activity. The class character of capitalist society means the domination of labour by capital. Put more concretely, a class of capitalists is in command of the work process and organizes that process for the purposes of producing profit. The labourer, on the other hand, has command only over his or her labour power which must be sold as a commodity on the market. The domination arises because the labourer must yield the capitalist a profit (surplus value) in return for a living wage. All of this is extremely simplistic, of course, and actual class relations (and relations between factions of classes) within an actual system of production (comprising production, services, necessary costs of circulation, distribution, exchange, etc.) are highly complex. The essential marxian insight, however, is that profit arises out of the domination of labour by capital and that the capitalists as a class must, if they are to reproduce themselves, continuously expand the basis for profit. We thus arrive at a conception of a society founded on the principle of "accumulation for accumulation's sake, production for production's sake". The theory of accumulation which Marx constructs in *Capital* amounts to a careful enquiry into the dynamics of accumulation and an exploration of its contradictory character. This may sound rather "economistic" as a framework for analysis, but we have to recall that accumulation is the means whereby the capitalist class reproduces both itself and its domination over labour. Accumulation cannot, therefore, be isolated from class struggle.

I. THE CONTRADICTIONS OF CAPITALISM

We can spin a whole web of arguments concerning the urban process out of an analysis of the contradictions of capitalism. Let me set out the principal forms these contradictions take.

Consider, first, the contradiction which lies within the capitalist class itself. In the realm of exchange each capitalist operates in a world of individualism, freedom and equality and can and must act spontaneously and creatively. Through competition, however, the inherent laws of capitalist production are asserted as "external coercive laws having power over every individual capitalist". A world of individuality and freedom on the surface conceals a world of conformity and coercion underneath. But the translation from individual action to behaviour according to class norms is neither complete nor perfect—it never can be because the *process* of exchange under capitalist rules always presumes individuality while the law of value always asserts itself in social terms. As a consequence, individual capitalists, each acting in their own immediate self-interest, can produce an aggregative result which is wholly antagonistic to their collective class interest. To take a rather dramatic example, competition may force each capitalist to so lengthen and intensify the work process that the capacity of the labour force to produce surplus value is seriously impaired. The collective effects of individual entrepreneurial activity can seriously endanger the social basis for future accumulation.

Consider, secondly, the implications of accumulation for the labourers. We know from the theory of surplus value that the exploitation of labour power is the source of capitalist profit. The capitalist form of accumulation therefore rests upon a certain violence which the capitalist class inflicts upon labour. Marx showed, however, that this appropriation could be worked out in such a way that it did not offend the rules of equality, individuality and freedom as they must prevail in the realms of exchange. Labourers, like the capitalists, "freely" trade the commodity they have for sale in the market place. But labourers are also in competition with each other for employment while the work process is under the command of the capitalist. Under conditions of unbridled competition, the capitalists are forced willy-nilly into inflicting greater and greater violence upon those whom they employ. The individual labourer is powerless to resist this onslaught. The only solution is for the labourers to constitute themselves as a class and find collective means to resist the depredations of capital. The capitalist form of accumulation consequently calls into being overt and explicit class struggle between labour and capital. This contradiction between the classes explains much of the dynamic of capitalist history and is in many respects quite fundamental to understanding the accumulation process.

The two forms of contradiction are integral to each other. They express an underlying unity and are to be construed as different aspects of the same reality. Yet we can usefully separate them in certain respects. The internal contradiction within the capitalist class is rather different from the class confrontation between capital and labour, no matter how closely the two may be linked. In what follows I will focus on the accumulation process in the absence of any overt response on the part of the working class to the violence which the capitalist class must necessarily inflict upon it. I will then broaden the perspective and consider how the organization of the working class and its capacity to mount an overt class response affects the urban process under capitalism.

Various other forms of contradiction could enter in to supplement the analysis. For example, the capitalist production system often exists in an antagonistic relationship to non- or pre-capitalist sectors which may exist within (the domestic economy, peasant and artisan production sectors, etc.) or without it (pre-capitalist societies, socialist countries, etc.). We should also note the contradiction with "nature" which inevitably arises out of the relation between the dynamics of accumulation and the "natural" resource base as it is defined in capitalist terms. Lack of space precludes any examination of these matters here. But they would obviously have to be taken into account in any analysis of the history of urbanization under capitalism.

II. THE LAWS OF ACCUMULATION

We will begin by sketching the structure of flows of capital within a system of production and realization of value. This I will do with the aid of a series of diagrams which will appear highly "functionalist" and perhaps unduly simple in structure, but which nevertheless help us to understand the basic logic of the accumulation process. We will also see how problems arise because individual capitalists produce a result inconsistent with their class interest and consider some of the means whereby solutions to these problems might be found. We will, in short, attempt a summary of Marx's argument in *Capital* in the ridiculously short space of three or four pages.

1. The Primary Circuit of Capital

In volume one of *Capital*, Marx presents an analysis of the capitalist production process. The drive to create surplus value rests either on an increase in the length of the working day (absolute surplus value) or on the gains to be made from continuous revolutions in the "productive forces" through reorganizations of the work process which raise the productivity of labour power (relative surplus value). The capitalist captures relative surplus value from the organization of cooperation and division of labour within the work process or by the application of fixed capital (machinery). The motor for these continuous revolutions in the work process, for the rising productivity of labour, lies in capitalist competition as each capitalist seeks an excess profit by adopting a superior production technique to the social average.

The implications of all of this for labour are explored in a chapter entitled "the general law of capitalist accumulation". Marx here examines alterations in the rate of exploitation and in the temporal rhythm of changes in the work

FIGURE 1
The Relations Considered in "The General Law of Accumulation"
(Volume I of *Capital*)

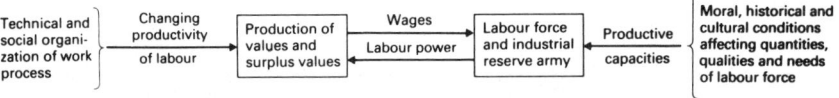

process in relation to the supply conditions of labour power (in particular, the formation of an industrial reserve army), assuming all the while, that a positive rate of accumulation must be sustained if the capitalist class is to reproduce itself. The analysis proceeds around a strictly circumscribed set of interactions with all other problems assumed away or held constant. Figure 1 portrays the relations examined.

The second volume of *Capital* closes with a "model" of accumulation on an expanded scale. The problems of proportionality involved in the aggregative production of means of production and means of consumption are examined with all other problems held constant (including technological change, investment in fixed capital, etc.). The objective here is to show the potential for crises of disproportionality within the production process. But Marx has now broadened the structure of relationships put under the microscope (see Figure 2). We note, however, that in both cases Marx assumes, tacitly, that all commodities are produced and consumed within one time period. The structure of relations examined in Figure 2 can be characterized as the *primary circuit of capital*.

FIGURE 2
The Relations Considered for "Reproduction on an Expanded Scale"
(Volume 2 of *Capital*)

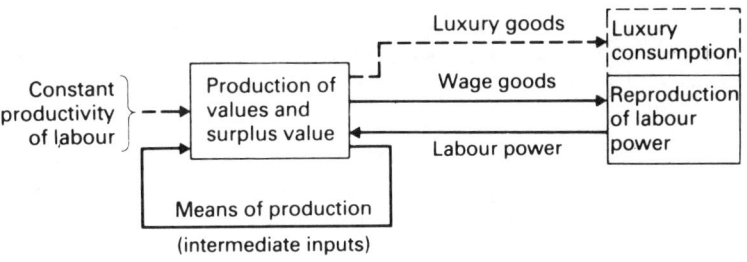

Much of the analysis of the falling rate of profit and its countervailing tendencies in volume 3 similarly presupposes production and consumption within one time period although there is some evidence that Marx intended to broaden the scope of this if he had lived to complete the work. But it is useful to consider the volume 3 analysis as a synthesis of the arguments presented in the first two volumes and as at the very least a cogent statement of the internal contradictions which exist within the primary circuit. Here we can clearly see the contradictions which arise out of the tendency for individual capitalists to act in a way which, when aggregated, runs counter to their own class interest. This contradiction produces a tendency towards *overaccumulation*—too much capital is produced in aggregate relative to the opportunities to employ that capital. This tendency is manifest in a variety of guises. We have:

1. Overproduction of commodities—a glut on the market.
2. Falling rates of profit (in pricing terms, to be distinguished from the falling rate of profit in value terms which is a theoretical construct).
3. Surplus capital which can be manifest either as idle productive capacity or as money capital lacking opportunities for profitable employment.
4. Surplus labour and/or rising rate of exploitation of labour power. One or a combination of these manifestations may be present at the same time. We have here a preliminary framework for the analysis of capitalist crises.

2. The Secondary Circuit of Capital

We now drop the tacit assumption of production and consumption within one time period and consider the problems posed by production and use of commodities requiring different working periods, circulation periods, and the like. This is an extraordinarily complex problem which Marx addresses to some degree in volume 2 of *Capital* and in the *Grundrisse*. I cannot do justice to it here so I will confine myself to some remarks regarding the formation of *fixed capital* and the *consumption fund*. Fixed capital, Marx argues, requires special analysis because of certain peculiarities which attach to its mode of production and realization. These peculiarities arise because fixed capital items can be produced in the normal course of capitalist commodity production but they are used as aids to the production process rather than as direct raw material inputs. They are also used over a relatively long time period. We can also usefully distinguish between fixed capital enclosed within the production process and fixed capital which functions as a physical framework for production. The latter I will call the *built environment for production*.

On the consumption side, we have a parallel structure. A *consumption fund* is formed out of commodities which function as aids rather than as direct inputs to consumption. Some items are directly enclosed within the consumption process (consumer durables, such as cookers, washing machines, etc.) while others act as a physical framework for consumption (houses, sidewalks, etc.)—the latter I will call the *built environment for consumption*.

We should note that some items in the built environment function jointly for both production and consumption—the transport network, for example—and that items can be transferred from one category to another by changes in use. Also, fixed capital in the built environment is immobile in space in the sense that the value incorporated in it cannot be moved without being destroyed. Investment in the built environment therefore entails the creation of a whole physical landscape for purposes of production, circulation, exchange and consumption.

We will call the capital flows into fixed asset and consumption fund formation the *secondary circuit of capital*. Consider, now, the manner in which such flows can occur. There must obviously be a "surplus" of both capital and labour in relation to current production and consumption needs in order to facilitate the movement of capital into the formation of long-term assets, particularly those comprising the built environment. The tendency towards overaccumulation produces such conditions within the primary circuit on a periodic basis. One feasible if *temporary* solution to this overaccumulation problem would therefore be to switch capital flows into the secondary circuit.

Individual capitalists will often find it difficult to bring about such a switch in flows for a variety of reasons. The barriers to individual switching of capital are particularly acute with respect to the built environment where investments tend to be large-scale and long-lasting, often difficult to price in the ordinary way and in many cases open to collective use by all individual capitalists. Indeed, individual capitalists left to themselves will tend to under-supply their own collective needs for production precisely because of such barriers. Individual capitalists tend to overaccumulate in the primary circuit and to under-invest in the secondary circuit; they have considerable difficulty in organizing a balanced flow of capital between the primary and secondary circuits.

A general condition for the flow of capital into the secondary circuit is, therefore, the existence of a functioning capital market and, perhaps, a state willing to finance and guarantee long-term, large-scale projects with respect to the creation of the built environment. At times of overaccumulation, a switch of flows from the primary to the secondary circuit can be accomplished only if the various manifestations of overaccumulation can be transformed into money capital which can move freely and unhindered into these forms of investment. This switch of resources cannot be accomplished without a money supply and credit system which creates "fictional capital" *in advance* of actual production and consumption. This applies as much to the consumption fund (hence the importance of consumer credit, housing mortgages, municipal debt) as it does to fixed capital. Since the production of money and credit are relatively autonomous processes, we have to conceive of the financial and state institutions controlling them as a kind of collective nerve centre governing and *mediating* the relations between the primary and secondary circuits of capital. The nature and form of these financial and state institutions and the policies they adopt can play an important role in checking or enhancing flows of capital into the secondary circuit of capital or into certain specific aspects of it (such as transportation, housing, public facilities, and so on). An alteration in these mediating structures can therefore affect both the volume and direction of the capital flows by constricting movement down some channels and opening up new conduits elsewhere.

3. The Tertiary Circuit of Capital

In order to complete the picture of the circulation of capital in general, we have to conceive of a *tertiary circuit of capital* which comprises, first, investment in science and technology (the purpose of which is to harness science to production and thereby to contribute to the processes which continuously revolutionize the productive forces in society) and second, a wide range of social expenditures which relate primarily to the processes of reproduction of labour power. The latter can usefully be divided into investments directed towards the qualitative improvement of labour power from the standpoint of capital (investment in education and health by means of which the capacity of the labourers to engage in the work process will be enhanced) and investment in cooptation, integration and repression of the labour force by ideological, military and other means.

Individual capitalists find it hard to make such investments as individuals, no matter how desirable they may regard them. Once again, the capitalists are forced to some degree to constitute themselves as a class—usually through the agency of the state—and thereby to find ways to channel investment into research and development and into the quantitative and qualitative improvement of labour power. We should recognize that capitalists often *need* to make such investments in order to fashion an adequate social basis for further accumulation. But with regard to social expenditures, the investment flows are very strongly affected by the state of class struggle. The amount of investment in repression and in ideological control is directly related to the threat of organized working-class resistance to the depredations of capital. And the need to coopt labour arises only when the working class has accumulated sufficient power to require cooptation. Since the state can become a field of active class struggle, the mediations which are accomplished by no means fit exactly with the requirements of the capitalist class. The role of the state requires careful theoretical and historical elaboration in relation to the organization of capital flows into the tertiary circuit.

III. THE CIRCULATION OF CAPITAL AS A WHOLE AND ITS CONTRADICTIONS

Figure 3 portrays the overall structure of relations comprising the circulation of capital amongst the three circuits. The diagram looks very "structuralist-functionalist" because of the method of presentation. I can conceive of no other way to communicate clearly the various dimensions of capital flow. We now have to consider the contradictions embodied within these relations. I shall do so initially as if there were no overt class struggle between capital and labour. In this way we will be able to see that the contradiction between the

FIGURE 3
The Structure of Relations Between the Primary, Secondary and Tertiary Circuits of Capital

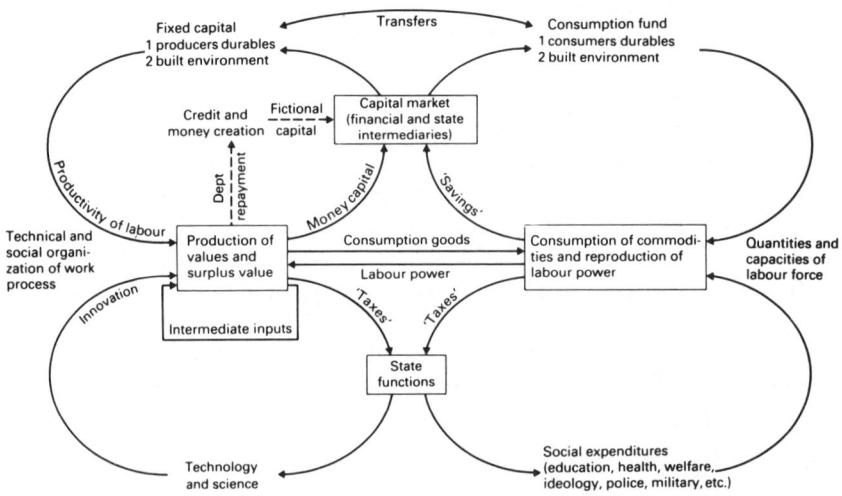

individual capitalist and capital in general is itself a source of major instability within the accumulation process.

We have already seen how the contradictions internal to the capitalist class generate a tendency towards overaccumulation within the primary circuit of capital. And we have argued that this tendency can be overcome temporarily at least by switching capital into the secondary or tertiary circuits. Capital has, therefore, a variety of investment options open to it—fixed capital or consumption fund formation, investment in science and technology, investment in "human capital" or outright repression. At particular historical conjunctures capitalists may not be capable of taking up all of these options with equal vigour, depending upon the degree of their own organization, the institutions which they have created and the objective possibilities dictated by the state of production and the state of class struggle. I shall assume away such problems for the moment in order to concentrate on how the tendency towards overaccumulation, which we have identified so far only with respect to the primary circuit, manifests itself within the overall structure of circulation of capital. To do this we first need to specify a concept of productivity of investment.

1. On the Productivity of Investments in the Secondary and Tertiary Circuits

I choose the concept of "productivity" rather than "profitability" for a variety of reasons. First of all, the rate of profit as Marx treats of it in volume 3 of *Capital* is measured in value rather than pricing terms and takes no account of the distribution of the surplus value into its component parts of interest on money capital, profit on productive capital, rent on land, profit on merchant's capital, etc. The rate of profit is regarded as a social average earned by individual capitalists in all sectors and it is assumed that competition effectively ensures its equalization. This is hardly a suitable conception for examining the flows between the three circuits of capital. To begin with, the formation of fixed capital in the built environment—particularly the collective means of production—cannot be understood without understanding the formation of a capital market and the distribution of part of the surplus in the form of interest. Second, many of the commodities produced in relation to the secondary and tertiary circuits cannot be priced in the ordinary way, while collective action by way of the state cannot be examined in terms of the normal criteria of profitability. Third, the rate of profit which holds is perfectly appropriate for understanding the behaviours of individual capitalists in competition, but cannot be translated into a concept suitable for examining the behaviour of capitalists as a class without some major assumptions (treating the total profit as equal to the total surplus value, for example).

The concept of productivity helps to by-pass some of these problems if we specify it carefully enough. For the fact is that capitalists as a class—often through the agency of the state—do invest in the production of conditions which they hope will be favourable to accumulation, to their own reproduction as a class and to their continuing domination over labour. This leads us immediately to a definition of a productive investment as one which directly or indirectly expands the basis for the production of surplus value. Plainly, investments in the secondary and tertiary circuits have the *potential* under certain conditions to do this. The problem—which besets the capitalists as much as it confuses us—is to identify the conditions and means which will allow this potential to be realized.

Investment in new machinery is the easiest case to consider. The new machinery is directly productive if it expands the basis for producing surplus value and unproductive if these benefits fail to materialize. Similarly, investment in science and technology may or may not produce new forms of scientific knowledge which can be applied to expand accumulation. But what of investment in roads, housing, health care and education, police forces and the military, and so on? If workers are being recalcitrant in the work place, then judicious investment by the capitalist class in a police force to intimidate the workers and to break their collective power, may indeed be productive indirectly of surplus value for the capitalists. If, on the other hand, the police are employed to protect the bourgeoisie in the conspicuous consumption of their revenues in callous disregard of the poverty and misery which surrounds them, then the police are not acting to facilitate accumulation. The distinction may be fine but it demonstrates the dilemma. How can the capitalist class identify, with reasonable precision, the opportunities for indirectly and directly productive investment in the secondary and tertiary circuits of capital?

The main thrust of the modern commitment to planning (whether at the state or corporate level) rests on the idea that certain forms of investment in the secondary and tertiary circuits are potentially productive. The whole apparatus of cost-benefit analysis and of programming and budgeting, of analysis of social benefits, as well as notions regarding investment in human capital, express this commitment and testify to the complexity of the problem. And at the back of all of this is the difficulty of determining an appropriate basis for decision-making in the absence of clear and unequivocal profit signals. Yet the cost of bad investment decisions—investments which do not contribute directly or indirectly to accumulation of capital—must emerge somewhere. They must, as Marx would put it, come to the surface and thereby indicate the errors which lie beneath. We can begin to grapple with this question by considering the origins of crises within the capitalist mode of production.

2. On the Forms of Crisis Under Capitalism

Crises are the real manifestation of the underlying contradictions within the capitalist process of accumulation. The argument which Marx puts forward throughout much of *Capital* is that there is always the potential within capitalism to achieve "balanced growth" but that this potentiality can never be realized because of the structure of the social relations prevailing in a capitalist society. This structure leads individual capitalists to produce results collectively which are antagonistic to their own class interest and leads them also to inflict an insupportable violence upon the working class which is bound to elicit its own response in the field of overt class struggle.

We have already seen how the capitalists tend to generate states of overaccumulation within the primary circuit of capital and considered the various manifestations which result. As the pressure builds, either the accumulation process grinds to a halt or new investment opportunities are found as capital flows down various channels into the secondary and tertiary circuits. This movement may start as a trickle and become a flood as the potential for expanding the production of surplus value by such means becomes apparent. But the tendency towards overaccumulation is not eliminated. It is transformed, rather, into a pervasive tendency towards over-investment in the secondary and tertiary circuits. This over-investment, we should stress, is in relation solely to the needs of capital and has nothing to do with the real needs of people which inevitably remain unfulfilled. Manifestations of crisis thus appear in both the secondary and tertiary circuits of capital.

As regards fixed capital and the consumption fund, the crisis takes the form of a crisis in the valuation of assets. Chronic overproduction results in the devaluation of fixed capital and consumption fund items—a process which affects the built environment as well as producer and consumer durables. We can likewise point to crisis formation at other points within our diagram of capital flows—crises in social expenditures (health, education, military repression, and the like), in consumption-fund formation (housing) and in technology and science. In each case the crisis occurs because the potentiality for productive investment within each of these spheres is exhausted. Further flows of capital do not expand the basis for the production of surplus value. We should also note that a crisis of any magnitude in any of these spheres is automatically registered as a crisis within the financial and state structures while the latter, because of the relative autonomy which attaches to them, can be an independent source of crisis (we can thus speak of financial, credit and monetary crises, the fiscal crises of the state, and so on).

Crises are the "irrational rationalizers" within the capitalist mode of production. They are indicators of imbalance and force a rationalization (which may be painful for certain sectors of the capitalist class as well as for labour) of the processes of production, exchange, distribution and consumption. They may also force a rationalization of institutional structures (financial and state institutions in particular). From the standpoint of the total structure of relationships we have portrayed, we can distinguish different kinds of crises:

a. *Partial crises* which affect a particular sector, geographical region or set of mediating institutions. These can arise for any number of reasons but are potentially capable of being resolved within that sector, region or set of institutions. We can witness autonomously forming monetary crises, for example, which can be resolved by institutional reforms, crises in the formation of the built environment which can be resolved by reorganization of production for that sector, etc.

b. *Switching crises* which involve a major reorganization and restructuring of capital flows and/or a major restructuring of mediating institutions in order to open up new channels for productive investments. It is useful to distinguish between two kinds of switching crises:

1. *Sectoral switching crises* which entail switching the allocation of capital from one sphere (e.g. fixed capital formation) to another (e.g. education);
2. *Geographical switching crises* which involve switching the flows of capital from one place to another. We note here that this form of crisis is particularly important in relation to investment in the built environment because the latter is immobile in space and requires interregional or international flows of money capital to facilitate its production.

c. *Global crises* which affect, to greater or lesser degree all sectors, spheres and regions within the capitalist production system. We will thus see devaluations of fixed capital and the consumption fund, a crisis in science and technology, a fiscal crisis in state expenditures, a crisis in the productivity of labour, all manifest at the same time across all or most regions within the capitalist system. I note, in passing, that there have been only two global crises within the totality of the capitalist system—the first during the 1930s and its Second World War aftermath; the second, that which became most evident after 1973 but which had been steadily building throughout the 1960s.

A complete theory of capitalist crises should show how these various forms and manifestations relate in both space and time. Such a task is beyond the scope of a short article, but we can shed some light by returning to our fundamental theme—that of understanding the urban process under capitalism.

IV. ACCUMULATION AND THE URBAN PROCESS

The understanding I have to offer of the urban process under capitalism comes from seeing it in relation to the theory of accumulation. We must first establish the general points of contact between what seem, at first sight, two rather different ways of looking at the world.

Whatever else it may entail, the urban process implies the creation of a material physical infrastructure for production, circulation, exchange and consumption. The first point of contact, then, is to consider the manner in which this built environment is produced and the way it serves as a resource system—a complex of use values—for the production of value and surplus value. We have, secondly, to consider the consumption aspect. Here we can usefully distinguish between the consumption of revenues by the bourgeoisie and the need to reproduce labour power. The former has a considerable impact upon the urban process, but I shall exclude it from the analysis because consideration of it would lead us into a lengthy discourse on the question of bourgeois culture and its complex significations without revealing very much directly about the specifically capitalist form of the urban process. Bourgeois consumption is, as it were, the icing on top of a cake which has as its prime ingredients capital and labour in dynamic relation to each other. The reproduction of labour power is essential and requires certain kinds of social expenditures and the creation of a consumption fund. The flows we have sketched, in so far as they portray capital movements into the built environment (for both production and consumption) and the laying out of social expenditures for the reproduction of labour power, provide us, then, with the structural links we need to understand the urban process under capitalism.

It may be objected, quite correctly, that these points of integration ignore the "rural-urban dialectic" and that the reduction of the "urban process" as we usually conceive of it to questions of built environment formation and reproduction of labour power is misleading if not downright erroneous. I would defend the reduction on a number of counts. First, as a practical matter, the mass of the capital flowing into the built environment and a large proportion of certain kinds of social expenditures are absorbed in areas which we usually classify as "urban." From this standpoint the reduction is a useful approximation. Second, I can discuss most of the questions which normally arise in urban research in terms of the categories of the built environment and social expenditures related to the reproduction of labour power with the added advantage that the links with the theory of accumulation can be clearly seen. Third, there are serious grounds for challenging the adequacy of the urban-rural dichotomy even when expressed as a dialectical unit, as a primary form of contradiction within the capitalist mode of production. In other words, and put quite bluntly, if the usual conception of the urban process appears to be violated by the reduction I am here proposing then it is the usual conception of the urban process which is at fault.

The urban-rural dichotomy, for example, is regarded by Marx as an expression of the division of labour in society. In this, the division of labour is the fundamental concept and not the rural-urban dichotomy which is just a particular form of its expression. Focusing on this dichotomy may be useful in seeking to understand social formations which arise in the transition to capitalism—such as those in which we find an urban industrial sector opposed to a rural peasant sector which is only formally subsumed within a system of commodity production and exchange. But in a purely capitalist mode of production—in which industrial and agricultural workers are all under the real domination of capital—this form of expression of the division of labour loses much of its particular significance. It disappears within a general concern for geographical specialization in the division of labour. And the other aspect to the urban process—the geographical concentration of labour power and use values for production and reproduction—also disappears quite naturally within an analysis of the "rational spatial organization" of physical and social infrastructures. In the context of advanced capitalist countries as well as in the analysis of the capitalist mode of production, the urban-rural distinction has lost its real economic basis although it lingers, of course, within the realms of ideology with some important results. But to regard it as a fundamental conceptual tool for analysis is in fact to dwell upon a lost distinction which was in any case but a surface manifestation of the division of labour.

1. Overaccumulation and Long Waves in Investment in the Built Environment

The acid test of any set of theoretical propositions comes when we seek to relate them to the experience of history and to the practices of politics. In a short paper of this kind I cannot hope to demonstrate the relations between the theory of accumulation and its contradictions on the one hand, and the urban process on the other in the kind of detail which would be convincing. I shall therefore confine myself to illustrating some of the more important themes which can be identified. I will focus, first, exclusively on the process governing investment in the built environment.

The system of production which capital established was founded on a physical separation between a place of work and a place of residence. The growth of the factory system, which created this separation, rested on the organization of cooperation, division of labour and economies of scale in the work process as well as upon the application of machinery. The system also promoted an increasing division of labour between enterprises, and collective economies of scale through the agglomeration of activities in large urban centres. All of this meant the creation of a built environment to serve as a physical infrastructure for production, including an appropriate system for the transport of commodities. There are abundant opportunities for the

The Urban Process under Capitalism 211

productive employment of capital through the creation of a built environment for production. The same conclusion applies to investment in the built environment for consumption. The problem, is, then, to discover how capital flows into the construction of this built environment and to establish the contradictions in this process.

We should first say something about the concept of the built environment and consider some of its salient attributes. It is a complex composite commodity comprising innumerable different elements—roads, canals, docks and harbours, factories, warehouses, sewers, public offices, schools and hospitals, houses, offices, shops, etc.—each of which is produced under different conditions and according to quite different rules. The "built environment" is, then, a gross simplification, a concept which requires disaggregation as soon as we probe deeply into the processes of its production and use. Yet we also know that these components have to function together as an ensemble in relation to the aggregative processes of production, exchange and consumption. For purposes of exposition we can afford to remain at this level of generality. We also know that the built environment is long-lived, difficult to alter, spatially immobile and often absorbent of large lumpy investments. A proportion of it will be used in common by capitalists and consumers alike and even those elements which can be privately appropriated (houses, factories, shops, etc.) are used in a context in which the externality effects of private uses are pervasive and often quite strong. All of these characteristics have implications for the investment process.

The analysis of fixed capital formation and the consumption fund in the context of accumulation suggests that investment in the built environment is likely to proceed according to a certain logic. We presume, for the moment, that the state does not take a leading role in promoting vast public works programmes ahead of the demand for them. Individual capitalists, when left to their own devices, tend to under-invest in the built environment relative to their own individual and collective needs at the same time as they tend to overaccumulate. The theory then suggests that the overaccumulation can be syphoned off—via financial and state institutions and the creation of fictional capital within the credit system—and put to work to make up the slack in investment in the built environment. This switch from the primary to the secondary circuit may occur in the course of a crisis or be accomplished relatively smoothly depending upon the efficiency of the mediating institutions. But the theory indicates that there is a limit to such a process and that at some point investments will become unproductive. At such a time the exchange value being put into the built environment has to be written down, diminished, or even totally lost. The fictional capital contained within the credit system is seen to be just that and financial and state institutions may find themselves in serious financial difficulty. The devaluation of capital in the built environment does not necessarily destroy the use value—the physical resource—which the built environment comprises. This physical resource can be used as "devalued capital" and as such it functions as a free good which can help to reestablish the basis for renewed accumulation. From this we can see the logic of Marx's statement that periodical devaluations of fixed capital provide "one of the means immanent in capitalist production to check the fall of the rate of profit and hasten accumulation of capital-value through formation of new capital".

Since the impulses deriving from the tendency to overaccumulate and to under-invest are rhythmic rather than constant, we can construct a cyclical "model" of investment in the built environment. The rhythm is dictated in part by the rhythms of capital accumulation and in part by the physical and economic lifetime of the elements within the built environment—the latter means that change is bound to be relatively slow. The most useful thing we can do at this juncture is to point to the historical evidence for "long waves" in

FIGURE 4

Investment in Selected Components of the Built Environment in Britain (Million £ at Current Prices)

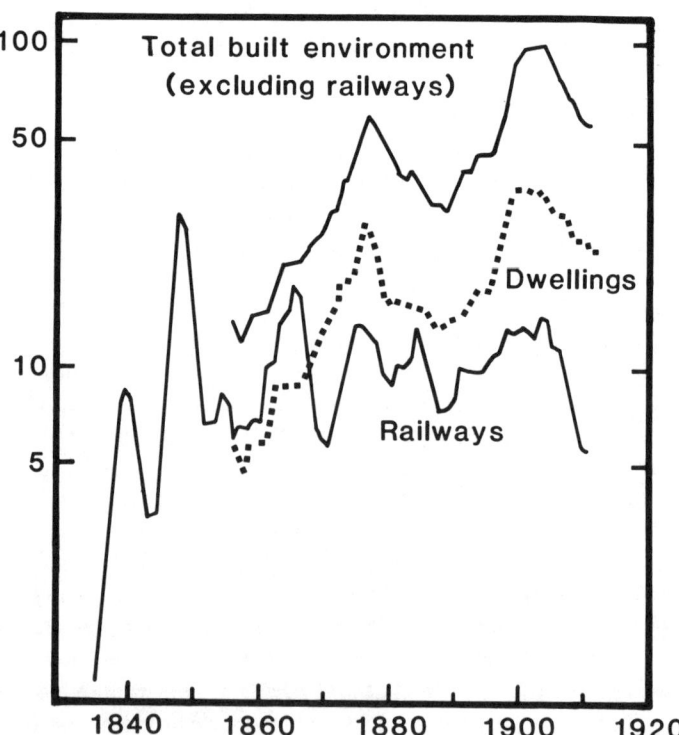

FIGURE 5

Construction Activity in Paris—Entries of Construction Materials into the City (Millions of Cubic Metres). After *Rougerie*

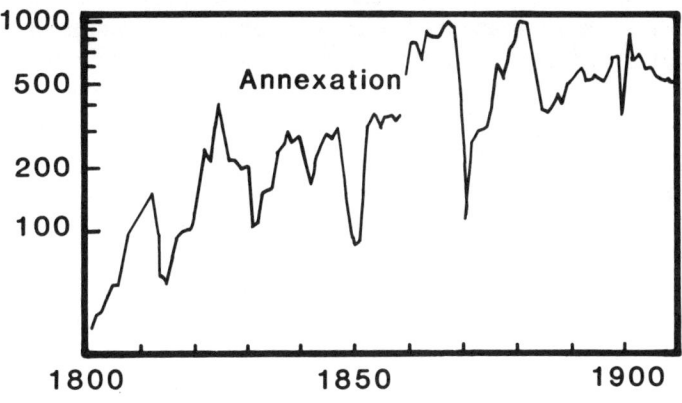

FIGURE 6

"Long-waves" in Investment in the Built Environment of the United States

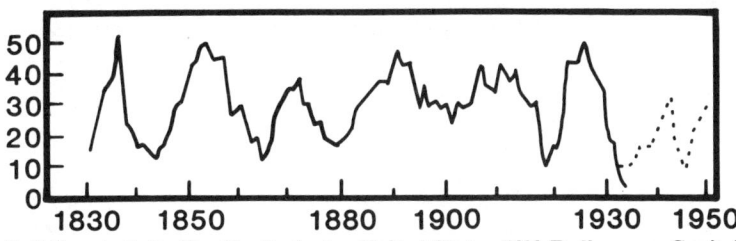

Building Activity Per Capita in the United States (1913 Dollars per Capita). After *Brinley Thomas*

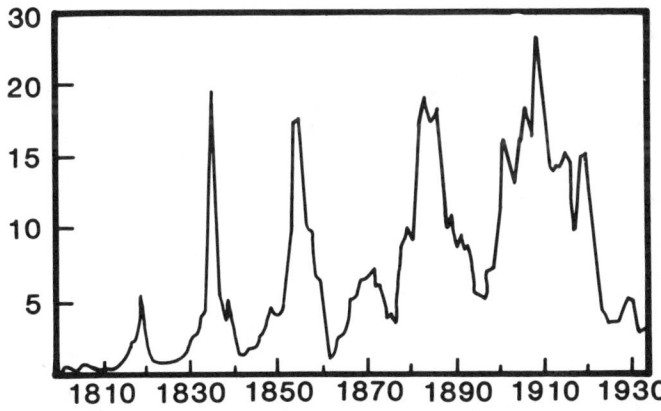

Sales of the Public Lands in the United States (Millions of Acres of Original Land Entries: U.S. Dept. of Agriculture Figures)

investment in the built environment. Somewhere in between the shortrun movements of the business cycle—the "Juglar cycles" of approximately ten-year length—and the very long "Kondratieff's", we can identify movements of an intermediate length (sometimes called Kuznets cycles) which are strongly associated with waves of investment in the built environment. Gottlieb's recent investigation[1] of building cycles in 30 urban areas located in eight countries showed a periodicity clustering between 15 and 25 years. While his methods and framework for analysis leave much to be desired, there is enough evidence accumulated by a variety of researchers to indicate that this is a reasonable sort of first-shot generalization. Figures 4, 5 and 6 illustrate the phenomenon. The historical evidence is at least consistent with our argument, taking into account, of course, the material characteristics of the built environment itself and in particular its long life which means that "instant throw-away cities" are hardly feasible no matter how hard the folk in Los Angeles try.

The immobility in space also poses its own problematic with, again, its own appropriate mode of response. The historical evidence is, once more, illuminating. In the "Atlantic economy" of the nineteenth century, for example, the long waves in investment in the built environment moved inversely to each other in Britain and the United States (see Figures 7 and 8). The two movements were not independent of each other but tied via

FIGURE 7

Different Rhythms of Investment in the Built Environment—Britain and the United States (Per Cent of GNP [USA] and GDP [Britain] Going to Investment in the Built Environment—5-Year Moving Averages)

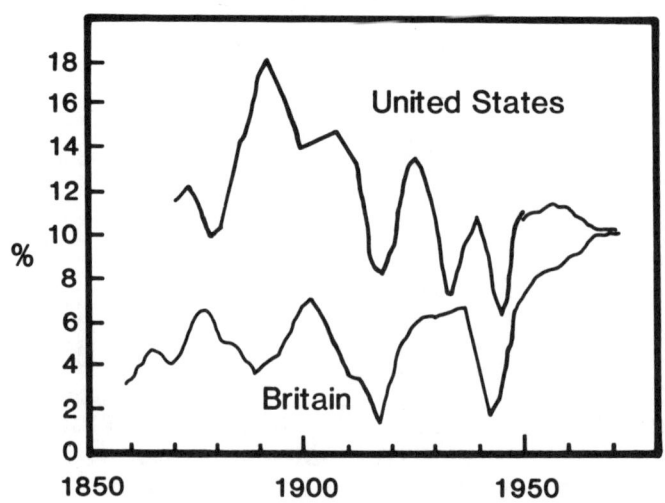

FIGURE 8

Uneven Development in the Atlantic Economy--Britain and the United States After *Brinley Thomas*

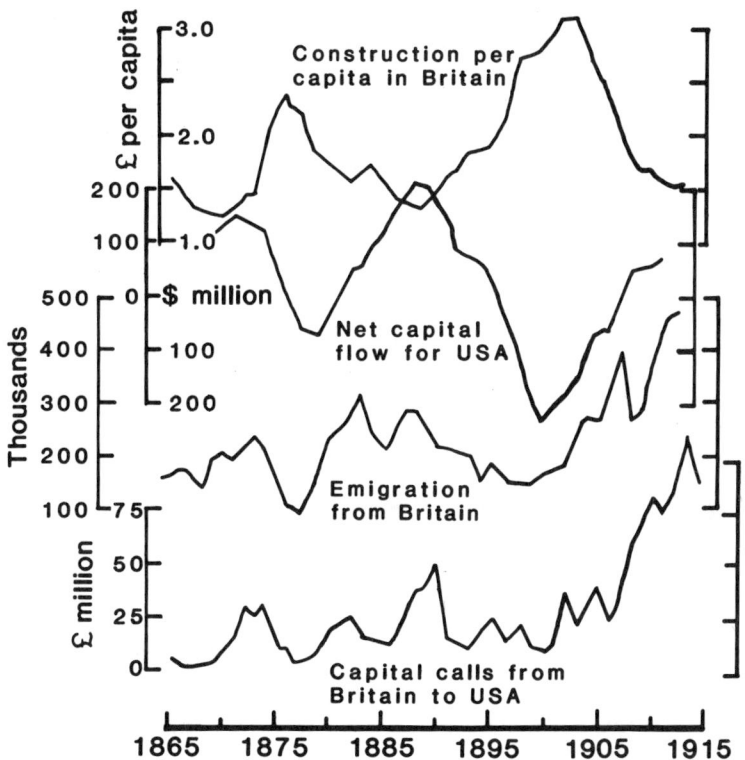

migrations of capital and labour within the framework of the international economy at that time. The commercial crises of the nineteenth century switched British capital from home investment to overseas investment or vice versa. The capitalist "whole" managed, thereby, to achieve a roughly balanced growth through counterbalancing oscillations of the parts all encompassed within a global process of geographical expansion.[2] Uneven spatial development of the built environment was a crucial element to the achievement of relative global stability under the aegis of the *Pax Britannica* of the nineteenth century. The crises of this period were either of the partial or switching variety and we can spot both forms of the latter—geographical and sectoral—if we look carefully enough.

The global crises of the 1930s and the 1970s can in part be explained by the breakdown of the mechanisms for exploiting uneven development in this way. Investment in the built environment takes on a different meaning at such

FIGURE 9

Some Indices of the Property Boom—Britain and United States

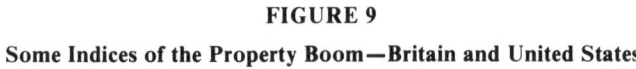

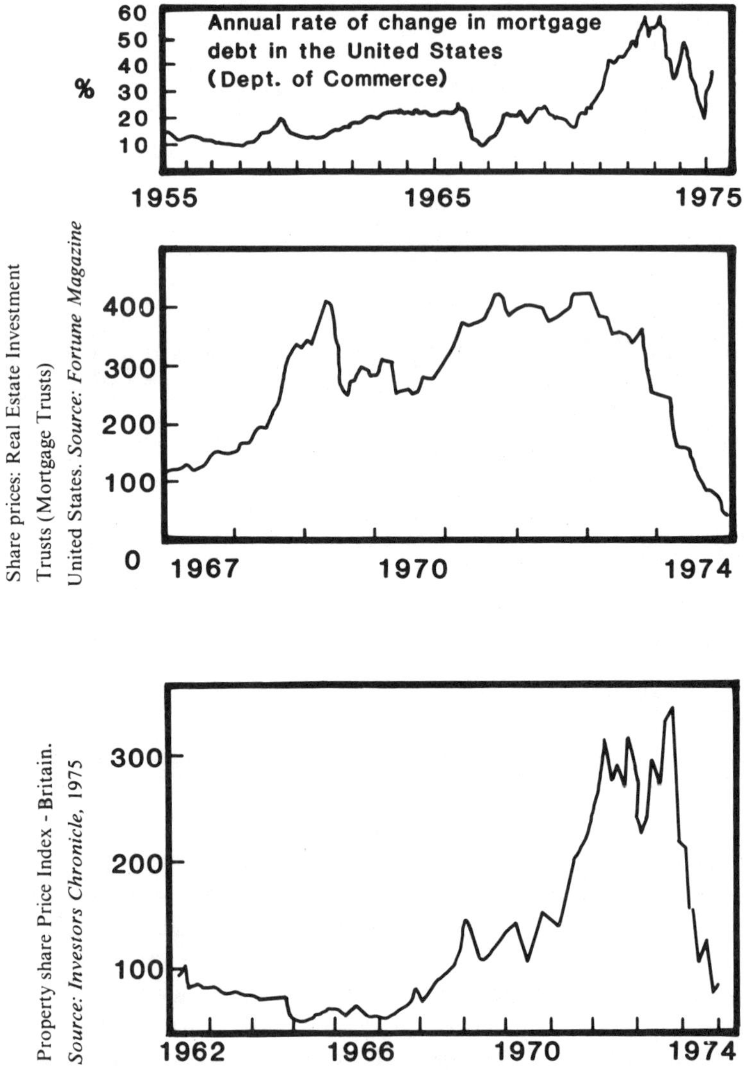

conjunctures. Each of the global crises of capitalism was in fact preceded by the massive movement of capital into long-term investment in the built environment as a kind of last-ditch hope for finding productive uses for rapidly overaccumulating capital. The extraordinary property boom in many advanced capitalist countries from 1969-73, the collapse of which at the end of 1973 triggered (but did not *cause*) the onset of the current crisis, is a splendid example. I append some illustrative materials in Figure 9.

While I am not attempting in any strict sense to "verify" the theory by appeal to the historical record, the latter most certainly is not incompatible with the broad outlines of the theory we have sketched in. Bringing the theory to bear on the history is in fact an extraordinarily difficult task far beyond the scope of a short paper. But rather than make no argument at all I will seek to illustrate how the connections can be made. I will therefore look a little more closely at the two aspects of the theory which are crucial—overaccumulation and devaluation.

The flow of investment into the built environment depends upon the existence of surpluses of capital and labour and upon mechanisms for pooling the former and putting it to use. The history of this process is extremely interesting. The eighteenth century in Britain was characterized, for example, by a capital surplus much of which went into the built environment because it had nowhere else to go. Investment in the built environment took place primarily for financial rather than use-value reasons—investors were looking for a steady and secure rate of return on their capital. Investment in property (much of it for conspicuous consumption by the bourgeoisie), in turnpikes, canals and rents (agricultural improvement) as well as in state obligations were about the only options open to rentiers. The various speculative crises which beset investment in the turnpikes and canals as well as urban property markets, indicated very early on that returns were by no means certain and that investments had to be productive if they were to succeed.[3]

It would be difficult to argue that during this period the surplus of capital arose out of the tendency to overaccumulate as we have specified it. The latter is, strictly speaking, a phenomenon which arises only in the context of the capitalist mode of production or in capitalist social formations which are relatively well-developed. The "long waves" of investment in the built environment pre-date the emergence of industrial capitalism and can be clearly identified throughout the transition from feudalism.[4] We can see, however, a strong relationship between these "long waves" and fluctuations in the money supply and in the structure of capital markets. Perhaps the most spectacular example is that of the United States (Figure 6)—when Andrew Jackson curbed land deals in paper currency and insisted on *specie* payment in 1836, the whole land development process came to a halt and the financial reverberations were felt everywhere, particularly by those investing in the built environment. The role of "fictional capital" and the credit and money supply system has always been fundamental in relationship to the various waves of speculative investment in the built environment.

When, precisely, the tendency towards overaccumulation became the main agent producing surplus capital and when the "long waves" became explicitly tied to overaccumulation is a moot point. The evidence suggests that by the 1840s the connections had been strongly forged in Britain at least. By then, the functioning of the capital market was strongly bound to the rhythms imposed by the development of industrial capitalism. The "nerve centre" which controls and mediates the relations between the primary and secondary circuits of capital increasingly functioned after 1830 or so according to a pure capitalist logic which affected both government and private activity alike. It is perhaps symptomatic that the fall of the July monarchy in France in 1847 was directly related to the indebtedness of that regime incurred in the course of promoting a vast programme of public works (many of which were not very productive). When the financial crisis, which had its origins in England and the extraordinary speculation in railroad construction, struck home in late 1846 and 1847, even the state debt of France could not withstand the shock.[5] For good reason, this crisis can perhaps be regarded as the first really solid and all-pervasive crisis in the capitalist world.

And what of the devaluation which inevitably results? If the devaluation is to function effectively, according to our theory, then it must leave behind a use value which can be used as the basis for further development. When many of the American states defaulted on their debts in the early 1840s, they failed to meet their obligations on the British capital market but kept the canals and other improvements which they had built. This was, in effect, expropriation without compensation—a prospect which the United States government treats with great moral indignation when some third-world country threatens it today. The great railroad booms of the nineteenth century typically devalued capital while littering the landscape with physical assets which could usually be put to some use. When the urban mass transit systems went bankrupt at the turn of the century because of chronic overcapitalization, the mass transit systems were left behind as physical assets. Somebody had to pay for the devaluation of course. There were the inevitable attempts to foist the costs onto the working class (often through municipal expenditures) or onto small investors. But big capital was not immune either, and the problems of the property companies in Britain or the real estate investment trusts in the United States at the present time are exactly of this sort (although the involvement of pension funds and insurance companies affects individuals). The office space is still there, however, even though the building that houses it has been devalued and is now judged a non-earning asset. The history of devaluations in the built environment is spectacular enough and fits, in general, with the theoretical argument.

2. The Contradictory Character of Investments in the Built Environment

We have so far treated the process of investment in the built environment as

The Urban Process under Capitalism

a mere reflection of the forces emanating from the primary circuit of capital. There are, however, a whole series of problems which arise because of the specific characteristics of the built environment itself. We will consider these briefly.

Marx's extensive analysis of fixed capital in relation to accumulation reveals a central contradiction. On the one hand, fixed capital enhances the productivity of labour and thereby contributes to the accumulation of capital. But on the other hand, it functions as a use value and requires the conversion of exchange values into a physical asset which has certain attributes. The exchange value locked up in this physical use value can be re-couped only by keeping the use value fully employed over its lifetime, which for simplicity's sake we will call its "amortization time". As a use value the fixed capital cannot easily be altered and so it tends to freeze productivity at a certain level until the end of the amortization time. If new and more productive fixed capital comes into being before the old is amortized, then the exchange value still tied up in the old is devalued. Resistance to this devaluation checks the rise in productivity and, thus, restricts accumulation. On the other hand the pursuit of new and more productive forms of fixed capital—dictated by the quest for relative surplus value—accelerates devaluations of the old.

We can identify exactly these same contradictory tendencies in relation to investment in the built environment, although they are even more exaggerated here because of the generally long amortization time involved, the fixity in space of the asset, and the composite nature of the commodity involved. We can demonstrate the argument most easily using the case of investment in transportation.

The cost, speed and capacity of the transport system relate directly to accumulation because of the impacts these have on the turnover time of capital. Investment and innovation in transport are therefore potentially productive for capital in general. Under capitalism, consequently, we see a tendency to "drive beyond all spatial barriers" and to "annihilate space with time" (to use Marx's own expressions).[6] This process is, of course, characterized typically by "long waves" of the sort which we have already identified, uneven development in space and periodic massive devaluations of capital.[7]

We are here concerned, however, with the contradictions implicit in the process of transport development itself. Exchange values are committed to create "efficient" and "rational" configurations for spatial movement at a particular historical moment. There is, as it were, a certain striving towards spatial equilibrium, spatial harmony. On the other hand, accumulation for accumulation's sake spawns continuous revolutions in transportation technology as well as a perpetual striving to overcome spatial barriers—all of which is disruptive of any existing spatial configuration.

We thus arrive at a paradox. In order to overcome spatial barriers and to annihilate space with time, spatial structures are created which themselves act as barriers to further accumulation. These spatial structures are expressed in the form of immobile transport facilities and ancillary facilities implanted in the landscape. We can in fact extend this conception to encompass the formation of the built environment as a whole. Capital represents itself in the form of a physical landscape created in its own image, created as use values to enhance the progressive accumulation of capital. The geographical landscape which results is the crowning glory of past capitalist development. But at the same time it expresses the power of dead labour over living labour and as such it imprisons and inhibits the accumulation process within a set of specific physical constraints. And these can be removed only slowly unless there is a substantial devaluation of the exchange value locked up in the creation of these physical assets.

Capitalist development has therefore to negotiate a knife-edge path between preserving the exchange values of past capital investments in the built environment and destroying the value of these investments in order to open up fresh room for accumulation. Under capitalism there is, then, a perpetual struggle in which capital builds a physical landscape appropriate to its own condition at a particular moment in time, only to have to destroy it, usually in the course of a crisis, at a subsequent point in time. The temporal and geographical ebb and flow of investment in the built environment can be understood only in terms of such a process. The effects of the internal contradictions of capitalism, when projected into the specific context of fixed and immobile investment in the built environment, are thus writ large in the historical geography of the landscape which results.

V. CLASS STRUGGLE, ACCUMULATION AND THE URBAN PROCESS UNDER CAPITALISM

What, then, of overt class struggle—the resistance which the working class collectively offers to the violence which the capitalist form of accumulation inevitably inflicts upon it? This resistance, once it becomes more than merely nominal, must surely affect the urban process under capitalism in definite ways. We must, therefore, seek to incorporate some understanding of it into any analysis of the urban process under capitalism. By switching our window on the world—from the contradictory laws of accumulation to the overt class struggle of the working class against the effects of those laws—we can see rather different aspects of the same process with greater clarity. In the space that follows I will try to illustrate the complementarity of the two viewpoints.

In one sense, class struggle is very easy to write about because there is no theory of it, only concrete social practices in specific social settings. But this immediately places upon us the obligation to understand history if we are to understand how class struggle has entered into the urban process. Plainly I cannot write this history in a few pages. So I will confine myself to a consideration of the contextual conditions of class struggle and the nature of the bourgeois responses. The latter are governed by the laws of accumulation because accumulation always remains the means whereby the capitalist class reproduces itself as well as its domination over labour.

The central point of tension between capital and labour lies in the workplace and is expressed in struggles over the work process and the wage rate. These struggles take place in a context. The nature of the demands, the capacity of workers to organize and the resolution with which the struggles are waged, depend a great deal upon the contextual conditions. The law (property rights, contract, combination and association, etc.) together with the power of the capitalist class to enforce their will through the use of state power are obviously fundamental as any casual reading of labour history will abundantly illustrate. What specifically interests me here, however, is the process of reproduction of labour power in relation to class struggle in the workplace.

Consider, first, the quantitative aspects of labour power in relation to the needs of capitalist accumulation. The greater the labour surplus and the more rapid its rate of expansion, the easier it is for capital to control the struggle in the workplace. The principle of the industrial reserve army under capitalism is one of Marx's most telling insights. Migrations of labour and capital as well as the various mobilization processes by means of which "unused" elements in the population are drawn into the workforce are manifestations of this basic need for a relative surplus population. But we also have to consider the costs of reproduction of labour power at a standard of living which reflects a whole host of cultural, historical, moral and environmental considerations. A change in these costs or in the definition of the standard of living has obvious implications for real-wage demands and for the total wage bill of the capitalist class. The size of the internal market formed by the purchasing power of the working class is not irrelevant to accumulation either. Consequently, the consumption habits of the workers are of considerable direct and indirect interest to the capitalist class.

But we should also consider a whole host of qualitative aspects to labour power encompassing not only skills and training, but attitudes of mind, levels of compliance, the pervasiveness of the "work ethic" and of "possessive individualism", the variety of fragmentations within the labour force which derive from the division of labour and occupational roles, as well as from older fragmentations along racial, religious and ethnic lines. The ability and urge of workers to organize along class lines depends upon the creation and maintenance of a sense of class consciousness and class solidarity in spite of these fragmentations. The struggle to overcome these fragmentations in the face of divide and conquer tactics often adopted by the capitalists is fundamental to understanding the dynamics of class struggle in the workplace.

This leads us to the notion of *displaced* class struggle, by which I mean class struggle which has its origin in the work process but which ramifies and reverberates throughout all aspects of the system of relations which capitalism establishes. We can trace these reverberations to every corner of the social totality and certainly see them at work in the flows of capital between the different circuits. For example, if productivity fails to rise in the workplace, then perhaps judicious investment in "human capital" (education), in cooptation (homeownership for the working class), in integration (industrial democracy), in persuasion (ideological indoctrination) or repression might yield better results in the long run. Consider, as an example, the struggles around public education. In *Hard Times*, Dickens constructs a brilliant satirical counterpoint between the factory system and the educational, philanthropic and religious institutions designed to cultivate habits of mind amongst the working class conducive to the workings of the factory system, while elsewhere he has that archetypal bourgeois, Mr. Dombey, remark that public educaton is a most excellent thing provided it teaches the common people their proper place in the world. Public education as a right has long been a basic working-class demand. The bourgeoisie at some point grasped that public education could be mobilized against the interests of the working class. The struggle over social services in general is not merely over their provision, but over the very nature of what is provided. A national health care system which defines ill health as inability to go to work (to produce surplus value) is very different indeed from one dedicated to the total mental and physical well-being of the individual in a given physical and social context.

The socialization and training of labour—the management of "human capital" as it is usually called in the bourgeois literature—cannot be left to chance. Capital therefore reaches out to dominate the living process—the reproduction of labour power—and it does so because it must. The links and relations here are intricate and difficult to unravel. I will consider various facets of activity within the dwelling place as examples of displaced class struggle.[8]

1. Some Remarks on the Housing Question

The demand for adequate shelter is clearly high on the list of priorities from the standpoint of the working class. Capital is also interested in commodity production for the consumption fund provided this presents sufficient opportunities for accumulation. The broad lines of class struggle around the "housing question" have had a major impact upon the urban process. We can trace some of the links back to the workplace directly. The agglomeration and concentration of production posed an immediate quantitative problem for housing workers in the right locations—a problem which the capitalist initially sought to resolve by the production of company housing but which thereafter was left to the market system. The cost of shelter is an important item in the cost of labour power. The more workers have the capacity to press home wage demands, the more capital becomes concerned about the cost of shelter. But housing is more than just shelter. To begin with, the whole structure of consumption in general relates to the form which housing provision takes. The dilemmas of potential overaccumulation which faced the United States in 1945 were in part resolved by the creation of a whole new life style through the rapid proliferation of the suburbanization process. Furthermore, the social unrest of the 1930s in that country pushed the bourgeoisie to adopt a policy of individual homeownership for the more affluent workers as a means to ensure social stability. This solution had the added advantage of opening up the housing sector as a means for rapid accumulation through commodity production. So successful was this solution that the housing sector became a Keynesian "contra-cyclical" regulator for the accumulation process as a whole, at least until the *debacle* of 1973. The lines of class struggle in France were markedly different (see Houdeville, 1969). With a peasant sector to ensure social stability in the form of small-scale private property-ownership, the housing problem was seen politically mainly in terms of costs. The rent control of the inter-war years reduced housing costs but curtailed housing as a field for commodity production with all kinds of subsequent effects on the scarcity and quality of housing provision. Only after 1958 did the housing sector open up as a field for investment and accumulation and this under government stimulus. Much of what has happened in the housing field and the shape of the "urban" that has resulted can be explained only in terms of these various forms of class struggle.

2. The "Moral Influence" of Suburbanization as an Antidote to Class Struggle

The second example I shall take is even more complex. Consider in its broad outlines, the history of the bourgeois response to acute threats of civil strife which are often associated with marked concentrations of the working class and the unemployed in space. The revolutions of 1848 across Europe, the Paris Commune of 1871, the urban violence which accompanied the great railroad strikes of 1877 in the United States and the Haymarket incident in Chicago, clearly demonstrated the revolutionary dangers associated with the high concentration of the "dangerous classes" in certain areas. The bourgeois response was in part characterized by a policy of dispersal so that the poor and the working class could be subjected to what nineteenth-century urban reformers on both sides of the Atlantic called the "moral influence" of the suburbs. Cheap suburban land, housing and cheap transportation were all a part of this solution entailing, as a consequence, a certain form and volume of investment in the built environment on the part of the bourgeoisie. To the degree that this policy was necessary, it had an important impact upon the shape of both British and American cities. And what was the bourgeois response to the urban riots of the 1960s in the ghettos of the United States? Open up the suburbs, promote low-income and black homeownership, improve access via the transport system . . . the parallels are remarkable.

3. The Doctrine of "Community Improvement" and Its Contradictions

The alternative to dispersal is what we now call "gilding the ghetto"—but this, too, is a well-tried and persistent bourgeois response to a structural problem which just will not disappear. As early as 1812, the Reverend Thomas Chalmers wrote with horror of the spectre of revolutionary violence engulfing Britain as working-class populations steadily concentrated in large urban areas. Chalmers saw the "principle of community" as the main bulwark of defense against this revolutionary tide—a principle which, he argued, should be deliberately cultivated to persuade all that harmony could be established around the basic institutions of community, a harmony which could function as an antidote to class war. The principle entailed a commitment to community improvement and a commitment to those institutions, such as the church and civil government, capable of forging community spirit. From Chalmers through Octavia Hill and Jane Addams, the "moral reformers" in France and the "progressives" in the United States at the end of the nineteenth century, through to model cities programmes and citizen participation, we have a continuous thread of bourgeois response to the problems of civil strife and social unrest.

But the "principle of community" is not a bourgeois invention. It has also its authentic working-class counterpart as a defensive and even offensive weapon in class struggle. The conditions of life in the community are of great import to the working class and they can therefore become a focus of struggle which can assume a certain relative autonomy from that waged in the factory. The institutions of community can be captured and put to work for working-class ends. The church in the early years of the industrial revolution was on occasion mobilized at the local level in the interests of the working class much as it also became a focus for the black liberation movement in the United States in the 1960s and is a mobilization point for class struggle in the Basque country of Spain. The principle of community can then become a springboard for class action rather than an antidote to class struggle. Indeed, we can argue that the definition of community as well as the command of its institutions is one of the stakes in class struggle in capitalist society. This struggle can break open into innumerable dimensions of conflict, pitting one element within the bourgeoisie against another and various fragments of the working class against others as the principles of "turf" and "community autonomy" become an essential part of life in capitalist society. The bourgeoisie has frequently sought to divide and rule but just as frequently has found itself caught in the harvest of contradictions it has helped to sow. We find "bourgeois" suburbanites resisting the further accumulation of capital in the built environment, individual communities in competition for development producing a grossly inefficient and irrational spatial order even from the standpoint of capital at the same time as they incur levels of indebtedness which threaten financial stability (the well-publicized current problems of New York are, for example, typical for the historical experience of the United States). We find also civil disorder within the urban process escalating out of control as ethnic, religious and racial tensions take on their own dynamic in partial response to bourgeoisie promptings (the use of ethnic and racial differences by the bourgeoisie to split the organization in the workplace has a long and ignoble history in the United States in particular).

4. Working-Class Resistance and the Circulation of Capital

The strategies of dispersal, community improvement and community competition, arising as they do out of the bourgeois response to class antagonisms, are fundamental to understanding the material history of the urban process under capitalism. And they are not without their implications for the circulation of capital either. The direct victories and concessions won by the working class have their impacts. But at this point we come back to the principles of accumulation, because if the capitalist class is to reproduce itself and its domination over labour it must effectively render whatever concessions labour wins from it consistent with the rules governing the productivity of investments under capitalist accumulation. Investments may switch from one sphere to another in response to class struggle to the degree that the rules for the accumulation of capital are observed. Investment in working-class housing or in a national health service can thus be transformed into a vehicle for accumulation via commodity production for these sectors. Class struggle can, then, provoke "switching crises", the outcome of which can change the structure of investment flows to the advantage of the working class. But those demands which lie within the economic possibilities of accumulation as a whole can in the end be conceded by the capitalist class without loss. Only when class struggle pushes the system beyond its own internal potentialities, is the accumulation of capital and the reproduction of the capitalist class called into question. How the bourgeoisie responds to such a situation depends on the possibilities open to it. For example, if capital can switch geographically to pastures where the working class is more compliant, then it may seek to escape the consequences of heightened class struggle in this way. Otherwise it must invest in economic, political and physical repression or simply fall before the working-class onslaught.

Class struggle thus plays its part in shaping the flows of capital between spheres and regions. The timing of the "long waves" of investment in the built environment of Paris, for example, is characterized by deep troughs in the years of revolutionary violence—1830, 1848, 1871 (see Figure 5). At first sight the rhythm appears to be dictated by purely political events yet the typical 15-25-year rhythm works just as well here as it does in other countries where political agitation was much less remarkable. The dynamics of class struggle are not immune to influences stemming from the rhythms of capitalist accumulation, of course, but it would be too simplistic to interpret the politial events in Paris simply in these terms. What seems so extraordinary is that the overall rhythms of accumulation remain broadly intact in spite of the variations in the intensity of working-class struggle.

But if we think it through, this is not, after all, so extraordinary. We still live in a capitalist society. And if that society has survived then it must have done so by imposing those laws of accumulation whereby it reproduces itself. To put it this way is not to diminish working-class resistance, but to show that a struggle to abolish the wages system and the domination of capital over labour must necessarily look to the day when the capitalist laws of accumulation are themselves relegated to the history books. And until that day, the capitalist laws of accumulation, replete with all of their internal contradictions, must necessarily remain the guiding force in our history.

VI. A CONCLUDING COMMENT

I shall end by venturing an apology which should properly have been set forth at the beginning. To broach the whole question of the urban process under capitalism in a short article appears a foolish endeavour. I have been forced to blur distinctions, make enormous assumptions, cut corners, jump from the theoretical to the historical in seemingly arbitrary fashion, and commit all manner of sins which will doubtless arouse ire and reproach as well as a good deal of opportunity for misunderstanding. This is, however, a distillation of a framework for thinking about the urban process under capitalism and it is a distillation out of a longer and much vaster work (which may see the light of day shortly). It is a framework which has emerged as the end-product of study and not one which has been arbitrarily imposed at the beginning. It is, therefore, a framework in which I have great confidence. My only major source of doubt, is whether I have been able to present it in a manner which is both accurate enough and simple enough to give the correct flavour of the potential feast of insights which lie within.

NOTES

1. Gottlieb (1976) provides an extensive bibliography on the subject as well as his own statistical analysis. The question of "long waves" of various kinds has recently been brought back into the marxist literature by Mandel (1975) and Day (1976).

2. The main source of information is Brinley Thomas (1972 edition) which has an extensive bibliography and massive compilations of data.

3. The whole question of the capital surplus in the eighteenth century was first raised by Postan (1935) and subsequently elaborated on by Deane and Cole (1967). Recent studies on the financing of turnpikes and of canals in Britain by Albert (1972) and Ward (1974) provide some more detailed information.

4. The best study is that by Parry Lewis (1965).

5. The study by Girard (1952) is truly excellent.

6. I have attempted a much more extensive treatment of the transport problem in Harvey (1975).

7. See Isard (1942) for some interesting material.

8. The account which follows is a summary of Harvey (1977).

REFERENCES

Albert, W. 1972: *The turnpike road system in England.* London: Cambridge University Press.

Day, R. 1976: The theory of long waves: Kondratieff, Trotsky, Mandel. *New Left Review* 99, 67-82.

Deane, P. and Cole, W. A. 1967: *British economic growth, 1688-1959: trends and structure.* London: Cambridge University Press.

Girard, L. 1952: *Les politiques des travaux publics sous le Second Empire.* Paris: Armand Colin.

Gottlieb, M. 1976: *Long swings in urban development.* New York: NBER.

Harvey, D. 1975: The geography of capitalist accumulation: a reconstruction of the marxian theory. *Antipode* 7 (2), 9-21.

Harvey, D. 1977: Labour, capital and class struggle around the built environment in advanced capitalist societies. *Politics and Society* 6, 265-95.

Houdeville, L. 1969: *Pour une civilisation de l'habitat.* Paris: Editions Ouvrières.

Isard, W. 1942: A neglected cycle: the transport building cycle. *Review of Economics and Statistics* 24, 149-58.

Lewis, J. Parry, 1965: *Building cycles and Britain's growth.* London: Macmillan.

Mandel, E. 1975: *Late capitalism.* London: New Left Books.

Marx, K. edn. 1967: *Capital* (three volumes), New York: International Publishers.

Marx, K. edn. 1967; 1968 and 1971: *Theories of surplus value.* Moscow: Progress Publishers.

Marx, K. edn. 1973: *Grundrisse.* Harmondsworth: Penguin.

Postan, M. 1935: Recent trends in the accumulation of capital. *Economic History Review* 6, 1-12.

Rougerie, J. 1968: Remarques sur l'histoire des salaires à Paris au dixneuvième siècle. *Le Mouvement Sociale* No. 63, 71-108.

Thomas, B. edn. 1973: *Migration and economic growth: a study of Great Britain and the Atlantic economy.* London: Cambridge University Press.

Ward, J. R. 1974: *The finance of canal building in the eighteenth century.* London: Oxford University Press.

14

Capital Accumulation and Urbanization in the United States

Richard Child Hill

INTRODUCTION

Students of urban life are preoccupied with understanding the structure and functioning of cities, the dynamics of urban growth and decay, and the fundamental sources and implications of the contemporary urban crisis. Many of us also wish to contribute to the development and implementation of alternative urban arrangements designed to fulfill the unmet needs of urban residents. My own research and reflection over the past few years has centered upon declining central cities, the urban fiscal crisis, and urban based political movements for social change in the United States.[1] Given my location, I have focused particular attention on Detroit.[2] But I have come to realize that the plight of stagnating central cities like Detroit is but a manifestation of contradictions rooted in the larger economic and political order of this society. Only by locating the central city in the overall anatomy and physiology of urbanization on the one hand, and analyzing the dynamic interconnections between urbanization and the developing political economy

---

From *Comparative Urban Research*, Vol. 4 (1977), pp. 39-60. Reprinted by permission of Transaction Periodicals Consortium, Inc.

on the other, can we hope to reach an understanding of the plight of declining central cities and glimpse the future alternatives in store for them. This is an enormously broad and complex task. My limited aim in this essay is to outline a conceptual framework and pose some focal problems for research and reflection.[3]

This paper is divided into three parts. I begin by outlining concepts and assumptions fundamental to the framework of an urban political economy. Next I schematically analyze how two laws of motion of capitalist development have structured the dynamics of the contemporary urbanization process in the United States. I conclude with an illustration of how contradictions emanating from the dynamics of contemporary capitalist development are expressed through the urbanization process.

PRELIMINARY CONCEPTS AND ASSUMPTIONS

Following Marx, I assume that every historical mode of production has its own special laws of urbanization valid within that epoch's limits alone.[4] And the place to begin the analysis of urbanization in a capitalist society is with the structure and functioning of the capitalist mode of production.

The Capitalist Mode of Production[5]

A mode of production consists of those elements, activities and social relationships which are necessary to produce and reproduce material life in a society. People possess capacities to work with tools (means of production) on natural materials (objects of production) in order to create products (results of production). These human capacities, tools, objects, products—and the manner in which they are integrated at the work site—are all forces of production.

In a capitalist society, the forces of production are shaped by the social relationships that workers have with those who own and control the means of production. Ownership of the means and objects of production confers upon one class the power to organize the labor of another class (e.g., the level of employment and unemployment, the pace and hours of work, the division of labor within the enterprise, the degree and manner of utilization of machinery), all to the purpose of producing a surplus product. The surplus product (surplus value in Marxian terminology) is that part of the total value of production which is left over after constant capital (means of production, raw materials and instruments of labor) and variable capital (labor power) have been accounted for. Under capitalist conditions, surplus value is realized in the forms of rent, interest and profit as well as in excessive salaries, fringe benefits and the like.

Yet while labor produces value, it does not realize value. Until the worker's product is sold, it has no exchange value. Surplus value must be realized on the market, which requires, in addition to production, the distribution and exchange (circulation) of commodities. Variations in market conditions influence the exchange value of a worker's product by pushing prices up or down. The governing principle of capitalism is that no use value or exchange value will be produced unless the exchange value of labor power falls below the exchange value of the product created. Labor power is used to produce use values only insofar as it can be used to produce exchange value and surplus value.

Capital accumulation, the production of surplus value, is the driving force of a capitalist society. By its very nature, capital accumulation necessitates expansion of the means of production, expansion of the size of the wage labor force, expansion of circulation activity as more products become commodities, and expansion of the realm of control of the capitalist class. Each is but a stream in the same historical tide of capitalist development.

The survival of a society means the perpetuation of its mode of production. Hence those who control a mode of production must create the conditions for its perpetuation through time. The reproduction of these conditions becomes as important as production itself. This means the development and perpetuation of political, juridical, and other institutional forms which are consistent with the mode of production as well as the perpetuation of the various relationships within the mode of production itself.

However, every class society also contains within itself inherent contradictions which permit and ultimately necessitate change. Marx suggested that the fundamental source of change in all class societies emanates from the contradiction between the forces and relations of production. A society in which production is organized by one class with the purpose of exploiting the producing class fosters endemic structural tensions. The exploiting class seeks to define the relationships which the producers have with one another. The producing class seeks to establish its own internal relationships. The struggle between the exploiting and producing classes over the distribution of the product of work and the organization, objects, conditions and results of labor, is the enduring contradiction between the productive forces and the production relations in a capitalist society. This contradiction is grounded within the mode of production but it permeates every institutional realm.

Any mode of production will tend to exhaust its own potentialities with respect to either the natural or institutional conditions within which it subsists. The exhaustion of institutional possibilities or the depletion of the natural resource base will necessitate adaptations or the total transformation of a mode of production. Adaptations within the existing mode of production may open up new potentialities for economic expansion. Changes of this sort frequently bring political, legal and other institutional relationships into conflict with the evolving structure of the mode of production. These "secondary contradictions" may be resolved through changes in institutional arrangements without fundamental transformation in the mode of production. But internally generated contradictions may bring a new mode of production into being and with it new institutional forms necessary for its own persistence through time.

Urbanization

In a capitalist society urbanization and the structure and functioning of cities is rooted in the production, reproduction, circulation and overall organization of the capital accumulation process. Since the process of capital accumulation unfolds in a spatially structured evironment, urbanism may be viewed provisionally as the particular geographical form and spatial patterning of relationships taken by the process of capital accumulation.

Capital accumulation requires: (1) fixed investment of part of the surplus product in new means of production; (2) production and distribution of articles of consumption to sustain and reproduce the labor force; (3) stimulation of an effective demand for the surplus product produced; and thus (4) additional capital formation through ever-increasing product innovation, market penetration and economic expansion.[6] Correspondingly, the capitalist city is a production site, a locale for the reproduction of the labor force, a market for the circulation of commodities and the realization of profit, and a control center for these complex relationships. Thus the capitalist city functions as a spatial "generative center" through which growing quantities of surplus product are extracted. And continued economic expansion necessitates "both a willingness and an ability for those in the urban center to put surplus value back into circulation in such a way that the city functions as a growth pole for the surrounding economy."[7] In sum, as Castells has succinctly put the matter, the urban system may be described as the "structure of relations between the process of production and the process of consumption in a given geographical area, through a process of exchange and a process of management of their relations."[8]

In all of this the notion of an urban *system* must be emphasized. A particular city cannot be divorced from the encompassing political economy within which it is embedded and through which it manifests its particular functions and form. In a capitalist society, the circulation of surplus is constantly shifting to new channels as new opportunities are explored, new technologies achieved and new resources and productive capacities are opened up. Correspondingly, the prestige and vitality of individual cities come to rest largely upon their location with respect to the geographic circulation of the surplus. Therefore, as David Harvey has suggested,

> ... the geographical pattern in the circulation of surplus can be conceived only as a moment in a process. In terms of that moment, particular cities attain positions with respect to the circulation of surplus which, at the next moment in the process are changed. Urbanism, as a general phenomenon, should not be viewed as the history of particular cities, but as the history of the system of cities within, between, and around which the surplus circulates ... the history of particular cities is best understood in terms of the circulation of surplus value at a moment of history within a system of cities.[9]

There have been several stages in the development of capitalism in the United States and in the total global system. Each major phase of capitalist expansion has been organized around a particular set of forces. Samir Amin has labeled this constellation of forces an accumulation model. Amin has suggested that each accumulation model embodies, among other things, particular propelling industries, forms of competition, types of business enterprises, patterns of geographical expansion and spatial division of labor, types of class alliances, class struggles and political activity.[10] But at the same time, the shape of successive stages of capitalist expansion appear to be molded by invariant "laws of motion" of capitalist development. Correspondingly, the urbanization process and the structure and functioning of cities change with each transition in the process of capital accumulation while simultaneously expressing the underlying laws of motion of capitalist development.

Finally, there is every reason to expect that the urbanization process and the structure and functioning of cities in particular capitalist countries will express the laws of motion of capitalist development in somewhat different ways. Each capitalist country has its own specific urban history which is shaped by a host of forces not the least of which is the period and manner in which a country enters the global capitalist system. That is, variations in the urbanization experiences of individual countries reflect the historical development of the global capitalist system as a whole.

CAPITAL ACCUMULATION AND URBANIZATION IN THE UNITED STATES

We can distinguish three periods of urbanization in the United States— mercantile, industrial and metropolitan—which correspond to phases in the process of capital accumulation. Each period is characterized by a dominant type of city and a particular pattern of relationships among cities within the evolving urban system.

The earliest cities in the United States were mercantile outposts of an agrarian periphery whose exploitation was linked to the first phase of capitalist expansion in the developing urban centers of Western Europe. Autonomous urbanization in the United States came at the end of the eighteenth century as the city became an outlet for capital accumulated in commercial agriculture and a bridgehead for colonial penetration of the continental interior. Regional growth was predicated on a deepwater port serving as the nucleus of an agricultural hinterland adapted to the production of a staple commodity in demand on the expanding Western European market. Thus the dominant city during the mercantile period was typically "a port at a strategic location on long-distance oceanic or riverine trade routes, providing a range of mercantile services, and determining the terms of trade."[11] This pattern of urban mercantile exploitation of an agrarian hinterland established "a geography of markets, transport routes, and labor forces that conditioned the succeeding stages of urban growth" in the United States.[12]

The industrial period of capitalist accumulation was based upon the railway and the steel industry. New resources became important from the middle of the nineteenth century onwards, and new locational forces emerged. Of greatest importance was a rising demand for iron, then steel, and a concomitant acceleration in the development of productive technologies. Railways and the rapid expansion of commercial export agriculture extended the area of capitalist expansion. The periphery continued to supply agricultural commodities but the new propelling industry, steel, now obtained raw materials from within the center itself.

The juxtaposition of bountiful agricultural resources, coal and iron ore, with markets and transportation linkages established in the mercantile period, fostered manufacturing and urban growth in the Northeastern and Northcentral United States. The "heartland" of the U.S. manufacturing belt developed westward from the financial and entrepreneurial centers of the Northeastern seaboard to the area bounded by Lake Superior iron ores and the Pennsylvania coalfields. This region developed into the heavy industrial center of the country and the urbanized center of the national market.[13]

As agricultural production and population diffused over the continent, the periphery attracted servicing and processing activities and experienced urban growth. But the urban centers in the industrial belt set the basic conditions for urban growth in outlying regions. The burgeoning industrial cities were the levers for the successive development of newer peripheral regions. While the industrial core experienced cumulative urban growth, the cities dotting the periphery were relegated to narrow and intensive specialization governed by the input demands of the manufacturing belt. Thus, urban growth in the periphery was determined by the vitality of its export base. Diversification and urban expansion outside the industrial core was contingent upon reaching a threshold in market activity sufficient to support profitable local capital accumulation. Flows of raw materials inward to the heartland and finished commodities outward to the periphery articulated the industrial urbanization process. The great industrial centers of the Northeastern and Northcentral manufacturing belt dominated the urban scene.[14]

Industrial urbanization lost its primacy in the Great Depression of the 1930's but it was not until the close of World War II that the metropolitan urbanization process came into its own. The transformation from industrial to metropolitan urbanization manifests the emergence of a new type of dominant urban complex. The economic base of the dominant urban region is no longer indexed by the output of its manufacturing firms but rather is expressed, Wilbur Thompson informs us, "in the creativity of its universities and research parks, the sophistication of its engineering firms and financial institutions, the persuasiveness of its public relations and advertising agencies, the flexibility of its transportation networks and utility systems, and all the dimensions of 'infrastructure' that facilitate the quick and orderly transfer from old dying bases to new growing ones."[15]

The dominant centers in the metropolitan urban system, Berry has argued, are those which have developed the organizational capacity for invention, innovation and "self-sustained" growth. New, rapid-growth, high-wage industries provide the income and markets for indigenous expansion in public infrastructure, housing stock, commercial and service facilities. In the process, a new urban periphery emerges as less innovative areas become the receptacles of downward filtering, slow-growth, less profitable "classical" industries.[16]

The contemporary "urban crisis" in the United States, starkly manifested in the plight of stagnating central cities, is rooted in the transition from industrial to metropolitan urban formations. But this transformation in the urban system, and the contradictions attending it, are themselves manifestations of the dynamics of capital accumulation. In particular, I would like to focus on how the anatomy and physiology of metropolitan urbanization expresses two laws of motion of capitalist development.

The Law of Increasing Firm Size and the Metropolitan Hierarchy of Cities

The Law of Increasing Firm Size suggests that the increasing concentration and centralization of capital accumulation is intrinsic to the process of capitalist growth.[17] In a precapitalist society, economic activity is individualistic, small in scale, widely scattered and unproductive. But the embryonic workshops operating in the crevices of the feudal economic structure foreshadowed the transformation of precapitalist society. With sufficient funds to buy raw materials and forward wages, an entrepreneur could gather workers within a single worksite and obtain the fruits of increased productivity resulting from social production. Reinvestment of profits steadily increased entrepreneurial capital holdings opening the way to further division of labor

Capital Accumulation and Urbanization

and the introduction of machinery into the production process. Enormous increases in productivity and output gave birth to unprecedented opportunities for urban growth.

Evolution of business enterprise from the small workshop to the family firm represented the first phase in the development of capitalist industrial organization. But as total capital accumulated, the size of the individual concentrations composing it continuously expanded, and so did the vertical division of labor. By the early 20th century, the rapid growth of the U.S. economy and the great merger movement had consolidated many small family enterprises into large national corporations. Yet no sooner had the national corporation become consolidated than it began to blossom into a multi-divisional apparatus engaging in many functions over many regions. Large size, a multi-divisional structure, and technical advances in communications and transportation, gave U.S. corporations a global outlook as well as new sources of competition. The late 1950's saw serious challenges from Europe and Japan. The outward movement to establish sales and production in foreign territories, which began at the turn of the century, now evolved into a way of life for large U.S. enterprises. The multi-national corporation emerged as the dominant form of capitalist business enterprise.

With each step—from workshop to factory to national corporation to multi-divisional corporation to multi-national firm—business enterprises acquired a more complex administrative skeleton to coordinate activities and a more expansive and dynamic central nervous system to plan for survival and growth. Each step witnessed a progressive concentration and centralization of capital and an elaboration and extension of hierarchical systems of authority and control.[18]

The family enterprise, in which day-to-day operations, the coordination of supervision over work, and the determination of goals and planning were embodied in the person of the entrepreneur, gave way to the administrative pyramid of the corporation. The functions of business administration—finance, personnel, purchasing, engineering, and sales to deal with capital, labor, purchasing, manufacturing, and marketing—were divided horizontally into departments. The need to integrate departments and administer geographically dispersed operations led to the creation of vertical administrative structures which distinguished field offices from head offices. The field offices managed local operations, the head office supervised the field offices. To meet the challenges of a constantly changing market in the economic boom following World War II, business enterprise decentralized horizontally into several divisions, each concerned with one product line and organized with its own head office. At a higher level, a general office was created to coordinate the division and to plan for the enterprise as a whole. At the pinnacle of the modern, multi-divisional, multi-national corporation, the modern captains of industry man a powerful general office allocating corporate resources, planning and organizing the growth of corporate capital and presiding over a global corporate empire.[19]

Stephen Hymer[20] and Robert Cohen[21] have applied location theory to the administrative structure of the modern capitalist enterprise and have suggested that the corporate hierarchy of administration and control corresponds to the emergence of a metropolitan hierarchy of cities. The day-to-day operations of business enterprises spread themselves over the nation and the globe in response to the pull of laborpower, markets and raw materials. At this lowest level of the urban hierarchy we witness the proliferation of specialized small to moderate sized *production and marketing* cities. Production and marketing cities may be concentrations of industrial branch plant production, or wholesale and retail distribution centers. Frequently they contain important transportation facilities. While they may specialize in a particular service (e.g., university, retirement and resort communities), they are rarely characterized by diversified service activities, communication or information processing functions, capital markets, media offices or government agencies.

Since their marketing domains are similar, corporations from different industries tend to place their coordinating offices in the same city. Consequently, coordinating activities are far more spatially concentrated than day-to-day production and marketing activities. *Regional* cities, the location for coordinating activities for the production and marketing cities, are characterized by concentrations of communications and information processing white-collar workers and service industries. But regional cities contain few important capital markets, media offices or high-level government agencies.

The general corporate offices—in which goal determination and planning set the framework in which the lower levels operate, and where operations at each level of the corporate pyramid are overseen and coordinated—tend to be even more spatially concentrated in *national* and *world* cities. Goal determination and planning (command activities) require close proximity to the capital market, the media and the government as well as to key business services which facilitate the national and global movement of capital (e.g., accounting, legal, investment, advertising and public relations firms). Top level supervision and coordination of the corporate pyramid (intermediation activities) also require the support of information and processing enterprises and large wholesale and brokerage firms. Spatially, command activities are concentrated in the highest offices of the multi-national corporations and are located in the world's major capitalist centers of high-level strategic planning (e.g., New York, London, Paris, Bonn, Tokyo). Intermediation activities are based in world cities but also spread out in a network that embraces key national cities supplementing the links between the world cities and the international economy.[22]

Thus the structural transformation from industrial to metropolitan urban formations is rooted in the rise and development of national and multinational business enterprise and the increasing concentration, centralization and global extension of capital. Metropolitan urbanization comes to be characterized by the dialectical interaction between the centralization of corporate control over capital, technology and organization, and the decentralization of production, employment and commerce facilitated by advances in the productive forces (particularly transportation and communication) throughout the metropolitan domain. Dominant metropolitan centers become the locus of corporate administration and control, product innovation, development and diffusion, service and quaternary employment. The periphery becomes more differentiated and stratified as it provides the agricultural and industrial products necessary for the maintenance and expansion of metropolitan regions.

The Law of Uneven Development and Urban Growth and Decay

The Law of Uneven Development refers to capitalism's endemic tendency to produce unemployment as well as employment, poverty as well as wealth, underdevelopment as well as development.[23] Contemporary patterns of uneven development are rooted in the evolution of the U.S. market since the Civil War.

By the second half of the 19th century, competition among industrial enterprises all too frequently culminated in bankruptcy. The railroad magnates were the first to respond by forming pools to control competition. Other industrialists, quick to recognize the benefits accruing from the termination of cutthroat competition, soon followed suit. Industry after industry organized along monopolistic lines. The aftermath of the depression of the 1890's heralded the formation of international cartels, engineered to control marketing on a world wide scale.[24]

As capital accumulated, business faced a choice between expanding labor proportionately to the growth of capital or substituting capital for labor. Stephen Hymer has suggested that by the first decade of this century most of the inventions needed for the cheap mass production of the major items of basic consumption had been developed. Theoretically, Hymer argues, mass production systems could have been expanded to make basic consumer goods broadly available throughout the nation and the world. The capital-labor ratio could have been kept constant and labor accumulated in proportion to the accumulation of capital. This "horizontal accumulation" of capital would have absorbed the labor force of any particular country, and then capital would have flowed to foreign countries or labor would have emigrated to industrial centers. Under this production system, earnings per employed worker and the composition of output would have remained stationary as goods were produced on a wider and wider basis.[25] But this trajectory of economic expansion was never seriously entertained.

Since the Civil War, capital and labor had been locked in a largely one-sided class struggle. However, the restrictions on immigration following World War I facilitated the organization of labor and undercut management's tactics of strike-breaking. With the widely successful CIO organizing drives during the 1930's, organized labor was here to stay and the issue now came to revolve around the manner in which unions and industry would interact. In this context, expanding employment in line with capital accumulation would have greatly enhanced the strength of the organized working class. Therefore, the industrial giants developed a strategy of capital deepening instead of capital widening in the productive sector of the economy. Capital per worker was raised and the rate of expansion of the industrial labor force was slowed down. Wage hikes in line with productivity increases were granted to unions in return for an agreement from organized labor to bridle opposition to mechanization. The monopolistic position of the corporate giants allowed them to pass these wage hikes on to consumers through price increases. Advances in technology provided the opportunity, class struggle provided the incentive, and monopoly control provided the means for the implementation of this "capital deepening" strategy of economic growth.

As Harry Braverman has noted, the practical consequences of this policy can be seen in any analysis of U.S. employment in manufacturing industries over any reasonable period of time. Thus:

> ... in the United States between 1947 and 1964, the output of the textiles industry grew by more than 40 percent, but employment was cut by one-third. Other industries such as iron and steel foundries, lumber and wood products, malt liquors and footwear showed production increases of from 15 to 40 percent accompanied by employment drops of 10 to 25 percent. The petroleum industry poured five-sixths more product at the end of the period than at the beginning but its employment was one-fourth lower. Even the construction industry, which by the nature of its production process is notably resistant to technological change, doubled its output while adding only 50 percent to its labor. Only the most rapidly growing industries showed substantial increases in employment. Thus electrical machinery and motor freight added some 50 and 70 percent respectively to their employment, but in the process roughly tripled their output. The aluminum industry more than doubled its employment, but this was the result of a quadrupled output. An extreme case is that of air transport, which enlarged its output some eight times while increasing employment by only one and one-third times.[26]

The uneven growth of per capita income and the imbalance between productive capacity and employment growth, confronted the evolving capitalist production system with chronic problems of underconsumption (i.e., inadequate effective demand for the goods capable of being produced). The response of the industrial giants was to concentrate on continuous product innovation for the more advantaged segment of the population, the introduction of new consumption goods even before the old ones were fully marketed, the development of elaborate credit systems and planned obsolescence. Operating on the basis of standard volume, in a framework of administered policies and prices, competition in oligopolistic markets became largely a matter of styling, advertising and imagery.[27]

The primary target of industry's consumer blitz was the unionized workers and, in particular, the expanding professional and technical labor force. In an economy of shared monopoly and administered prices, the repeated cycle of union wage gains and consumer price hikes was one that large-scale industry could seemingly sustain. Members of the crafts and professions, unable to organize along industrial lines, combated the vicissitudes of the market through a variety of devices to reduce competition and stretch the available work. Craft unions limited entry to the sons of relatives and friends, required long apprenticeships and refused to adopt labor-saving devices. Professional and technical workers used their organizations to establish standards and increase fees through restricting entry. Unorganized workers in less productive and more competitive industries did not have this kind of bargaining strength. Yet, in the absence of comparable wage increases for unorganized workers their purchasing power declines and unemployment rises.[28] Increasingly dependent upon welfare transfer payments for survival, the reserve army of the un/underemployed became a tool for the manipulation of effective demand through government fiscal policies.

But government welfare programs contracted the availability of cheap labor to less productive industries. No longer able to import cheap labor, the labor-intensive industries began to export themselves, first to the non-union, low-wage, low-tax areas of the country and then increasingly to labor-surplus, low-wage countries abroad. In the process the U.S. has been exporting large segments of some of its oldest industries (e.g., leather working and textiles). More ominously, some new industries (e.g., transistors) as well as an increasing proportion of jobs in the more productive industries are moving abroad as well.[29]

Patterns of uneven development rooted in the evolving system of capitalist production correspond to patterns of uneven urban development—simultaneous urban growth and decay—in the evolving metropolitan urban system. Brian Berry has suggested that cities in the metropolitan urban hierarchy are integrated through spatial relationships along three axes: (1) between metropoli and regional hinterlands; (2) between higher and lower urban centers in the hierarchy; and (3) between each urban center and its surrounding urban field.[30] These spatial relationships imply three trajectories of uneven urban development in the United States: (1) between metropolitan regions and the relatively unurbanized periphery; (2) among metropolitan centers themselves; and (3) between central city and the suburban and exurban fringes of its urban field.

The uneven development between metropolitan areas and outlying regions, as well as the concentration of impoverished segments of the labor force in aging central cities, is a spatial expression of the capital deepening strategy of economic growth forged in the early decades of this century. However, the massive suburban development of the urban field of aging central cities is to a significant degree a product of the consumer oriented accumulation strategy developed in response to the underconsumption crisis of the 1930's. In sum, the underdevelopment of the periphery, the development of aging central cities, and the expansion of the suburbs are all interrelated manifestations of the evolving political economy of late capitalism in the United States.

Metropolis and Periphery. Currently so-called "backward" and "traditional" peripheries of the metropolitan United States (e.g., Appalachia and the Upper Great Lakes region) are areas whose economies have historically revolved around three main sectors: agriculture, the railroads, and primary manufacturing (minerals and lumber). Resource depletion and the resulting international expansion of capital to new resource peripheries, corporate concentration, the routinization and mechanization of production, and patterns of government subsidy have burdened these areas with poverty, inordinately high levels of unemployment and underemployment, and deficiencies in education, health and welfare.[31]

Between 1920 and 1970 an estimated 40 million persons left farms for the cities. Southern blacks, who generally worked the smallest farms on the most marginal lands, and were heavily dependent upon farm work for employment, were dealt a particularly severe blow by corporate concentration and the mechanization of agriculture. Conot, for example, has noted that:

> When a minimum wage of $1.25 an hour for farm labor was established in 1967, plantations in the Mississippi Delta intensified their use of machinery. Approximately 8,000 families, with 54,000 members were left jobless and homeless. The use of hand labor was all but eliminated. On one plantation, between the mid-1950's and 1960's, machines replaced 446 out of 450 cotton choppers. In Florida, orchards switched to mechanical pickers for citrus fruit. In California, (where Mexican Americans were primarily affected) the harvesting of tomatoes was mechanized. Every increase in the cost of human labor brought more use of machinery. The few who were left would be better off, but the many would join the "redundant population."[32]

Drawn by the more progressive social welfare legislation[33] and the hope for industrial employment, surplus agrarian labor streamed from rural areas of the North and South into the urban areas of the North and West during the post World War II period. But this migration disproportionately culled out young to middle aged adults and left behind the old and the young and the declining number of workers still able to find employment in the capital-intensive primary industries. In the process those forced to bear the costs of economic expansion became concentrated in the stagnating intermetropolitan peripheries and the deteriorating inner cores of aging central cities.

The basic regional distinction today, Berry has suggested, is between the "self-sustaining" growth of the metropoli, and the "hand-me-down" intermetropolitan periphery condemned to development characterized at best by "lagged emulation and second-hand growth." The key determinant of differential growth, according to this line of argument, is the relative capacity of areas to invest and innovate, to create new rapid growth, high-wage industries. Impulses of economic change are then transmitted in order from higher to lower centers in the urban hierarchy with continued innovation in the large metropolitan complexes the critical factor in the extension of growth over the entire system.[34]

Thus large urban regions combine a favorable mix of growth industries with a declining share of the various older, "classical" industries. Over time, growth industries, originating in the higher level metropolitan centers, become routinized, their skill requirements decline, and their costs of production increase. In search for cheap labor and lowered production costs, older industries "filter down" the metropolitan urban hierarchy to lesser urban centers, smaller towns within and just beyond metropolitan growth zones, into rural areas and abroad. Growth in lower level urban centers and in the peripheries becomes tied to capturing a share of downward filtering industry, slow in growth and yielding lower returns.[35]

But it is misleading to suggest that the basic regional distinction is between the "self-sustaining" growth in service, quaternary and governmental activities in the metropolis and the "backward" traditional periphery. In an increasingly interdependent space economy, the burgeoning metropolis is no more "self-sustaining" than any other part of the system. Metropolitan growth has been and remains dependent upon the increased labor productivity of the primary and "classic" secondary industries whose mechanization and concentration have provided both the economic surplus and the "floating labor force reserve" requisite to the expansion of service, quaternary and government employment. What has begun to evolve is a new spatial division of labor in which the periphery and lower levels of the metropolitan urban hierarchy are coming to produce the primary products and "classical" industrial goods necessary to the maintenance of service and quaternary and government employment in the control centers of the metropolitan urban hierarchy.

City and Suburb. While uneven growth characterizes relationships among metropolitan centers in the urban hierarchy and ties between metropolis and periphery, a major line of differentiation simultaneously develops between the aging central city and suburban and exurban areas in its surrounding urban field. The urban field of the contemporary megalopolis frequently stretches out one hundred miles or more. In the process decentralization of capital and labor replaces centralization and core orientation, and residential differentiation and segregation dispel the mythology of the melting pot. Thus, in Brian Berry's lucid description of the urban field:

> High status neighborhoods seek out zones of superior residential amenity near water, trees and higher ground, free from the risk of floods and away from smoke and factories, and increasingly in the furthest accessible peripheries. Middle-status neighborhoods press as close to the high-status as possible. To the low-status resident, least able to afford costs of commuting, are relinquished the least desirable areas adjacent to industrial zones radiating from the center of the city along railroads and rivers, the zones of highest pollution and the oldest, most deteriorated homes. In the cores of the ghettos, widespread abandonment of properties marks the extreme of neglect.[36]

What has fostered this relentless pattern of uneven development within the metropolis in the United States? Edward Banfield has succintly stated the prevailing explanation:

> Much of what has happened—as well as of what is happening—in the typical city or metropolitan area can be understood in terms of three imperatives. The first is demographic: if the population of a city increases, the city must expand in one direction or another—up, down, or from the center outward. The second is technological: if it is feasible to transport large numbers of people outward (by train, bus and automobile) but not upward or downward (by elevator), the city must expand outward. The third is economic: if the distribution of wealth and income is such that some can afford new housing and the time and money to commute considerable distances to work while others cannot, the expanding periphery of the city must be occupied by the first group (the "well-off") while the older, inner parts of the city, where most of the jobs are, must be occupied by the second group (the "not well-off") . . . The word imperative is used to emphasize the inexorable, constraining character of the three factors that together comprise the logic of metropolitan growth. Indeed . . . given a rate of population growth, a transportation technology, and a distribution of income, certain consequences must inevitably follow: that the city and its hinterland must develop according to a predictable pattern and that even an all-wise and all-powerful government could not change this pattern except by first changing the logic that gives rise to it.[37]

Unfortunately, this explanation of unbalanced metropolitan growth remains at the surface of events and thus fails to illuminate the essential forces shaping the contemporary metropolis. The logic of metropolitan growth is the logic of capital accumulation for private profit rather than social use and has been forged out of the dynamic interplay between the forces and relations of production in the United States. If the uneven spatial development between metropolis and periphery, and the concentration of the un/underemployed in aging central cities is directly linked to the capital deepening strategy developed by monopoly capital in the first few decades of this century, then the massive post World War II suburbanization and uneven development within the metropolis emanates in large measure from the response of corporate capital and federal government to the resulting underconsumption crisis of the 1930's.

The contemporary North American suburb is designed to stimulate consumption. As David Harvey has persuasively argued, the prevailing pattern of suburbanization

> ... is to be interpreted as one of several responses to the underconsumption problems of the 1930's. And it is in these terms, too, that we can interpret how the financial superstructure, itself created in response to the crisis conditions of the 1930's, so mediated the flow of investment into urban infrastructure ... that its mediations served to transform cities once fashioned as the workshops of industrial society into cities for the artificial stimulation of consumption.[38]

The massive suburbanization following World War II is predicated on the interrelated stimulus of the automobile, the freeway, the suburban home, and the shopping center. The emergence of the automobile as a widely owned commodity in the 1920's, and then following World War II, underpinned the prosperity of both periods.[39] But the mass production and consumption of the automobile would not have been possible in the absence of massive government investments in supporting infrastructure, particularly in freeways.[40]

Suburban home construction joins the automobile and the freeway as part of the suburban growth trajectory of the post World War II period. Suburban home purchases, the most salient consumption item for millions of North Americans, requires complementary investments in transportation, household equipment, public facilities as well as recurrent capital costs (e.g., mortgage interest payments) and operating expenses (e.g., outlays on energy). As with the development of freeways, the construction of middle class suburban housing was no historical accident, but rather was systematically guided by government policy. Fiscal policy underwrites numerous subsidies to homeowners.[41] FHA and VA insurance secures the mortgage market for homeownership, stimulating investment in middle-income, single-family dwelling units. FNMA, a direct response to the crisis conditions of the 1930's, backs FHA insured mortgages in the secondary mortgage market. The special treatment afforded to federal savings and loan associations, as intermediaries in housing finance, is yet another of the measures taken during the 1930's to ensure the stability of financial institutions while simultaneously channeling funds to preferred borrowers in order to stimulate the economy.[42]

Rounding out the suburban growth trajectory has been the immense commercial investment embodied in the suburban shopping center. Numbering less than 100 in 1950, shopping centers now number over 13,000. While department stores and supermarkets of central cities are closing, shopping centers are going up at a rate of over 600 a year. Armed with their own trade association—the International Council of Shopping Centers which oversees the interrelated activities of land developers, retail firms, and sources of finance—the shopping center industry now dominates commercial growth in the United States.[43]

In sum, sustained capital accumulation requires expansion in effective demand at an accelerating rate in a capitalist economy. Since World War II, the urban fields of metropolitan centers in the United States have been promoted as "consumption artifacts" as a response to the underconsumption crisis of the 1930's. Metropolitan growth has come to be characterized by suburban sprawl, and an assumption on the part of industrial corporations, commercial enterprises, local governments, and land speculators alike that urban sprawl was inevitable. In a class society, marked by sharp racial divisions, the result has been uneven and segregated patterns of urban development within the metropolis.

URBAN CONTRADICTIONS AND THE FISCAL CRISIS OF THE STATE

The process of urbanization both expresses and exacerbates contradictions emanating from the evolving capitalist mode of production in the United States. The State, which is increasingly responsible for managing the "structure of relations between the process of production and the process of consumption in a given geographical area" has become a repository for many of these contradictions. I would like to conclude this essay with a schematic outline of how contradictions generated in the urban system by the dynamics of capital accumulation become expressed in fiscal dilemmas facing various governmental levels of the U.S. capitalist State.

With the emergence and growth of monopoly capitalism, the state takes on an active, rapidly expanding and increasingly central role in the economy and society. Following the pathbreaking lead of James O'Connor, we can view state expenditures as having a dual character corresponding to the state's two basic and frequently contradictory functions in a capitalist society.[44] On the one hand, *social capital* outlays are state expenditures required for profitable private *accumulation* and are indirectly productive of surplus value. There are two kinds of social capital: (1) social investment (social constant capital) which consists of projects and services that increase the rate of profit (e.g., transportation and research-and-development facilities, utility projects, industrial parks); and (2) social consumption expenditures (social variable capital) consisting of projects and services that lower the private reproduction costs of labor, and (other things equal) also increase the rate of profit (e.g., schools, commuter, hospital and medical facilities, unemployment and health insurance). On the other hand, *social expenses*, the second category of state expenditures, consist of projects and services which are required to *maintain social order* (e.g., welfare and military outlays). Social expenses are not even indirectly productive of profitable private accumulation.

O'Connor has persuasively argued that there is a reciprocal relationship between the expansion of the capitalist state and growth in the monopoly sector and total production. State absorption of the costs of constant and variable capital rises over time and increasingly is needed for profitable accumulation by monopoly capital. But because the growth of the monopoly sector is accompanied by unemployment, poverty and economic stagnation, the state, in order to ensure order and maintain legitimacy, faces pressures to meet the various needs and demands of those who bear the costs of economic growth. In sum, with the development of late capitalism, "the growth of the state sector is indispensable to the expansion of private industry . . . particularly monopoly industries . . . and the growth of monopoly capital generates increased expansion of social expenses. The greater the growth of social capital, the greater the growth of the monopoly sector, and the greater the growth of the monopoly sector, the greater the state's expenditures on the social expenses of production."[45]

As the capitalist state becomes increasingly responsible for the capital investment requisite to profitable private accumulation, and expense outlays necessary to maintain social order in a class society, the contradictions inherent in capitalist development are increasingly played out in the arena of the state. Although the state has socialized more and more capital costs and absorbs more and more expenses of production, the social surplus continues to be appropriated privately. The increasing socialization of costs and the continued private appropriation of profits creates a fiscal crisis: a "structural gap" between state expenditures and state revenues. The result is a tendency for state expenditures and expenditure demands to increase more rapidly than the means of financing them, resulting in economic, social and political crises.[46] Fiscal crisis becomes the state budgetary expression of class struggle in a monopoly capitalist society.

The current fiscal crisis of central city governments illustrates how contradictions in the political economy of late capitalism in the United States are expressed through the evolving urban system. There are sound reasons for suggesting that the quantity and quality of government investments in urban infrastructure geared to enhance the private accumulation of capital is a key factor governing the outcome of competition between urban centers for a dominant position in the metropolitan hierarchy. Aging central cities in the industrial belt are burdened with obsolete infrastructure and an inability to generate sufficient local government revenues to modernize to attract large-scale capital investment. At the same time, they have become the place of residence for a majority of the reserve army of the un/underemployed, entailing massive increases in social expense outlays to maintain a semblance of social order in the urban core. The results have been the familiar spiraling pressures for expenditure outlays far exceeding available tax revenues, further deterioration, and fiscal crisis.[47]

The contemporary relationship between the metropolis and the periphery also illustrates the contradictory and escalating pressures placed upon the state budget by the dynamics of the evolving urban political economy. The development of a national growth and community development policy to combat underdevelopment in the periphery has become a focal item on the agenda of the federal government. A "growth center strategy" is now in the process of development and application in the Appalachian Regional Commission, the Department of Transportation and the U.S. Department of Agriculture. This growth strategy has entailed state investments in "human capital," transportation linkages to metropolitan regions, and public services and facilities to provide the necessary supporting infrastructure for private investments in manufacturing plants and services in the periphery. State policy planners have also recommended industry grants and loan guarantees, liberalized investment tax credits and accelerated depreciation schedules.[48]

Yet, at the same time it has been recognized that the kinds of industry likely to be attracted to Appalachia are those seeking a low-wage, semi-skilled labor force. All of these attempts to attract private capital through state expenditures would be of little consequence for an industry seeking cheap labor if the metropolitan-periphery wage-differential was not maintained. For this reason, policy planners have also recommended dipping into the state's coffers to provide wage subsidies in the form of deductions on wages and salaries for those firms willing to locate in the designated growth center areas.[49] Thus, the simultaneous pressures on the state budget to meet the demands of accumulation and legitimation are thrown into stark relief in the Appalachian development guidelines.

CONCLUSION

I have attempted, in a highly schematic fashion, to elucidate the dynamic connections between capital accumulation and urbanization in the United States. In particular, I have argued that two laws of motion of capitalist development—The Law of Increasing Firm Size and the Law of Uneven Development—correspond to the development of a hierarchy of cities and simultaneous urban growth and decay in the contemporary metropolitan urban systems in the United States. I have illustrated how contradictions between the forces and relations of production, composing the capitalist mode of production, are manifested in the metropolitan urban system through contradictory and spiraling fiscal pressures placed upon the state. The result has been an escalating urban fiscal crisis. Emanating from the dynamics of contemporary capital accumulation, urban contradictions generate pressures for urban change and thus merit systematic comparative urban research.[50]

NOTES

This is a revised version of a paper entitled, "Observations on the Political Economy of Urban Systems in the United States," prepared for discussion at a roundtable session on communities, annual meeting of the American Sociological Association, San Francisco, 1975.

1. Cf. Richard Child Hill, "Black Struggle and the Urban Fiscal Crisis," paper prepared for presentation at the Conference on Urban Political Economy, New School for Social Research, New York, N.Y., February 15, 1975. Versions of this paper will appear in William Tabb and Larry Sawyers, eds., *Marx and the Megalopolis* (forthcoming), and *Kapitalistate*, #4 (forthcoming).

2. Cf. Richard Child Hill, "The Fiscal Crisis of the State: A Case Study of Education in Detroit," paper prepared for presentation at the State and Economy session, Eighth World Congress of Sociology, Toronto, Canada, August 21, 1974; and "The Paradoxes of Power: Corporate Liberalism and the Urban Crisis," unpublished m.s.

3. In my observations to follow I am deeply indebted to the pathbreaking work of Manuel Castells, David Harvey, Stephen Hymer and James O'Connor.

4. Marx's statement on the population question appears equally applicable to the urbanization process: "... every special historic mode of production has its own special laws of population, historically valid within its limits alone. An abstract law of population exists for plants and animals only, and only in so far as man has not interfered with them." Karl Marx, *Capital*, volume 1. N.Y.: International Publishers, 1967, p. 632.

5. My discussion of the capitalist mode of production closely follows James O'Connor's fascinating exposition in "Capital and the Class Struggle," forthcoming in *Class Struggle*, copyright 1974 by James O'Connor.

6. David Harvey, *Social Justice and the City*. Baltimore: Johns Hopkins University Press, 1973, p. 202.

7. Ibid., p. 249.

8. Manuel Castells, "Vers une theorie sociologique de la planification urbaine," *Sociologie du Travail*, 1969, p. 423, as quoted in Brigitte Brette and Francois D'Arcy, "On Recent Urban Research in France: The Marxist View," *Comparative Urban Research*, number 6/Winter 1974-75, p. 23.

9. Harvey, *Social Justice and the City*, op. cit., p. 250.

10. Samir Amin, "Toward a Structural Crisis of World Capitalism," *Socialist Revolution*, Number 23 (April 1975), pp. 7-44.

11. Brian J.L. Berry, *Growth Centers in the American Urban System*, volume 1. Cambridge, Mass.: Ballinger Publishing Company, 1973, p. 4.

12. Ibid.

13. Ibid.

14. Ibid., p. 5.

15. Wilbur Thompson, *A Preface to Urban Economics*. Baltimore: Johns Hopkins University Press, 1968, as quoted in Berry, op.cit., p. 9.

16. The prevailing view of the causes of this transformation in the anatomy of urbanization in the United States places emphasis on the rapid rise in service and quaternary sectors of the economy and the increasing significance of government expenditures. Thus Berry's findings (op.cit. pp. 17-21) on population changes in "daily urban systems" between 1960 and 1970 indicate that: (1) growth rates are inversely related to dependence on primary economic activities; (2) as earnings from secondary sources in the manufacturing industries increase, the growth rate stabilizes around the national average; and (3) the greater the share of local earnings from tertiary, government and quaternary sources, the greater the local growth rate.

17. Stephen Hymer, "The Multinational Corporation and the Law of Uneven Development," in J.S. Bhagvati, ed., *Economics and the World Order*. N.Y.: World Law Fund, 1971, pp. 113-140.

My discussion in this section owes more to Hymer's pathbreaking work than mere footnotes can indicate.

18. Cf. Alfred D. Chandler, *Strategy and Structure*. Cambridge, Mass.: MIT Press, 1962.

19. Ibid.

20. Hymer, op. cit., pp. 123-125.

21. Robert B. Cohen, "Urban Effects of the Internationalization of Capital and Labor," paper presented at the Conference on Urban Political Economy, New School for Social Research, N.Y., N.Y., February 15, 1975.

22. Extensive empirical support for this metropolitan hierarchy formulation will be found in Beverly Duncan and Stanley Lieberson, *Metropolis and Region in Transition*. Beverly Hills: Sage, 1970; Berry, op.cit.; and Otis Dudley Duncan et al., *Metropolis and Region*. Baltimore: John Hopkins Press, 1960.

23. Barry Bluestone, "Economic Crises and the Law of Uneven Development," *Politics and Society* (Fall 1972), pp. 65-66.

24. Robert Conot, *American Odyssey*, N.Y.: William Morrow, 1974, p. 633.

25. Hymer, op.cit., p. 119. This is admittedly an oversimplification but a heuristic one nonetheless.

26. Harry Braverman, "Work and Unemployment," *Monthly Review* (June 1975), p. 27.

27. Paul Baran and Paul Sweezy, *Monopoly Capital*. N.Y.: Monthly Review Press, 1966, chapters 1-7.

28. The increasing gap between the income of poor and nonpoor families is well documented in Herman P. Miller, "A New Look at Inequality, Poverty, and Under-employment in the United States Without Rose-Colored Glasses," *The Review of Black Political Economy*, 3 (2), Table 8, p. 32.

29. As Conot, op.cit., p. 635 points out, "The average Ford worker earns more than $40 a day in the United States, but only $8.80 a day in Mexico."

30. Berry, op.cit., p. 8.

31. For example, Berry, op.cit., p. 43 notes that "thirty-five years ago 10 percent of Appalachia's labor force (approximately 476,895 men) worked in the mines ... by 1960 the mines only accounted for 3.5 percent of Appalachian employment of 198,488 jobs."

32. Conot, op. cit., p. 639.

33. Unable to find jobs in the local economy, displaced families had no choice but to turn to welfare. Yet the Southern states and many of the rural counties of the North staunchly rebuffed pressures to increase their welfare budgets. In 1967, for example, Alabama allocated $85 a month to a family of four. Mississippi calculated the minimum need per person—and then allocated payments at 31 percent of that need. The average Mississippi allotment per child was $9 per month with a maximum family allotment of $90. Cf. Conot, op. cit., p. 639.

34. Berry, op. cit., pp. 8-9.

35. Ibid., p. 10.

36. Ibid., p. 39.

37. Edward Banfield, *The Unheavenly City*. Boston: Little Brown, 1968, pp. 23-24.

38. David Harvey, "The Political Economy of Urbanization in Advanced Capitalist Societies: The Case of the United States," in Gary Gappert and Harold M. Rose, eds., *The Social Economy of Cities*. Beverly Hills: Sage Publications, 1975, p. 139.

39. According to Dowd, the automobile "accounts for the following percentages of the gross market consumption of the following products: Steel 21%, Aluminum 10.4%, Lead 54.7%, Nickel 14.3%, Natural Rubber 68.8%, Zinc 36.5%. Automobiles represent about a quarter of all retail sales. The industry estimates that one out of every six jobs in America is dependent upon the automobile—it is responsible for 16 percent of the work force, 13 percent of GNP, involving more than eight hundred thousand businesses." Cf. Douglas F. Dowd, *The Twisted Dream*. Cambridge, Mass.: Winthrop, 1974, p. 179.

40. As Dowd, ibid., has noted it is the auto, oil and major construction companies who are the most powerful supporters of this investment policy. "These groups have been the moving force behind the Highway Trust Fund which has spent $32 billion on highways since 1956. Its supporters claim another $300 billion will be needed over the next fifteen years, ten times the rate since 1956. For every $1.00 the federal government has spent on mass transit, $50 has been spent on highways."

41. For example, it is estimated that permitting homeowners tax deductions on mortgage interest and property tax payments cost the federal government $6 billion in 1973. The most glaring example of government stimulation of consumption through housing tax provisions is the provision allowing homeowners to defer capital gains on the sale of a home provided the owner moves to another house of equal or greater value. This provision cost the government an additional $1.3 billion in foregone taxes; Cf. Harvey, "The Political Economy of Urbanization...," op. cit., pp. 131-132.

42. Harvey, "The Political Economy of Urbanization...," op. cit., pp. 132-133.

43. Milton Moskowitz, "The Shopping Center Civilization," *San Francisco Chronicle*, February 2, 1971.

44. James O'Connor, *The Fiscal Crisis of the State*. N.Y.: St. Martins Press, 1973.

45. Ibid., p. 8.

46. Ibid., p. 8.

47. Cf. Hill, "Black Struggle and the Urban Fiscal Crisis," op. cit.

48. Berry, op. cit., chapter 2.

49. Ibid.

50. For one tentative attempt in this direction, Cf. Hill, "State Capitalism and the Urban Fiscal Crisis," op. cit.

15

Class-Monopoly Rent, Finance Capital and the Urban Revolution

David Harvey

In a stimulating and provocative work, Lefebvre argues that we ought to interpret the industrial revolution of the nineteenth century as a precursor to the "urban revolution" of the twentieth. He explains that by "urban revolution" he means: "the total ensemble of transformations which run throughout contemporary society and which serve to bring about the change from a period in which questions of economic growth and industrialization predominate to the period in which the urban problematic becomes decisive" (Lefebvre, 1970, p. 13).

Lefebvre is not explicit as to what is meant by "the ensemble of transformations" nor does he explain how and why capitalism is transformed so that questions of urbanization come to replace questions of economic growth and industrialization. Nor is Lefebvre very explicit when he argues that "the proportion of global surplus value formed and realized in industry declines" while the proportion realized "in speculation, construction and real estate development grows" (Lefebvre, 1970, p. 212). The thesis that this "secondary circuit of capital" is supplanting "the primary circuit of capital in

---

Reprinted with permission from *Regional Studies,* Vol. 8, David Harvey, "Class-Monopoly Rent, Finance Capital, and the Urban Revolution." Copyright (1974), Pergamon Press, Ltd. Reprinted by permission of Pergamon Press, Ltd. and D. Harvey.

production" is startling in its implications and obviously requires very careful consideration before being accepted or rejected. In this paper, therefore, I shall attempt to shed some light on Lefebvre's hypotheses by examining how rent, and in particular class-monopoly rent, arises in the context of the urbanization process.

1. THE CONCEPT OF RENT IN AN URBANIZED WORLD

I take it as axiomatic that *value* arises out of those processes that convert naturally occurring materials and forces into objects and powers of utility to individuals in specific social and natural environments. In its simplest form, we can say that value arises out of production and is realized in consumption (Marx, 1967 edn.). But production and distribution cannot take place without (1) an elaborate social structure (encompassing the division of labour, the provision of socially necessary services, and so on), (2) a structure of social institutions through which individual and group activities can be coordinated, and (3) a certain minimum of physical infrastructure (communication links, utilities and the like). Any system of production and distribution requires, consequently, certain transfer payments to be made out of value produced to support socially necessary institutions, services and physical infrastructures.

The history of the rental concept is strewn with arguments for and against the legitimacy of the transfer payment that rent represents (Keiper *et al.*, 1961). In recent years, however, many appear to have been persuaded that rent is a kind of rationing device through which a scarce factor of production—land and its associated resources—is rationally and efficiently allocated to meet the productive needs of society (Wicksteed, 1894). Rent is justified, according to this view, as a necessary coordinating device for the efficient production of value. The problem with this neoclassical argument is, however, that rent is regarded as a payment to a scarce "factor" (which is a "thing" concept) rather than as an actual payment to people. This reification may be convenient for purposes of analysis but actual payments are made to real live people and not to pieces of land. Tenants are not easily convinced that the rent collector merely represents a scarce factor of production. The social consequences of rent are important and cannot be ignored simply because rent appears so innocently in the neoclassical doctrine of social harmony through competition (Barnbrock, 1974).

There is a further point to be considered. In order for payments to be made certain basic institutions are required. In our own society, private property arrangements are crucial; rent is, in effect, a transfer payment realized through the monopoly power over land and resources conferred by the institution of private property. Consequently, any examination of how rent originates and is realized cannot proceed without evaluating the performance of these supportive institutions.

But what is rent a payment for? The simplest answer is that it is a payment made by a user for the privilege of using a scarce productive resource which is owned by somebody else. But how does scarcity arise? Ever since production began to be organized systematically, human societies have recognized that many natural resources (understood as technical and cultural evaluations of nature [Firey, 1960; Spoehr, 1956]) are limited. There is a tendency, therefore, to think of scarcity as something inherent in nature and on this basis we may be willing to concede that more should be charged for the use of productive fields and mines than for fields and mines of average productivity. On reflection, however, this conception of "natural wealth" and "scarcity" appears less satisfactory. There is little "natural wealth" that has not been prepared prior to production—the field has to be cleared and the mineshaft has to be dug. Relatively permanent improvements—such as the terracing of hillsides, the building up of soil fertility and the draining of marshlands, may with time come to be regarded as "natural" resources for human use. In an urbanized world this problem becomes even more serious. Urbanization creates relatively permanent, man-made resource systems (Harvey, 1973, Chapter 2). Human effort is, as it were, incorporated into the land as fixed and immobile capital assets that may last hundreds of years. Consequently, the high rent for a piece of land in the centre of London may be due to its higher productivity, but that productivity has been created by the construction of the vast man-made resource system that is London. Because these relatively permanent fixed capital assets are highly localized in their distribution, the urbanization process has created scarcity where there was none before. If rent is a transfer payment to a scarce factor of production, then the urbanization process has also multiplied the opportunities for realizing rent.

The blurring of the distinction between natural and artificially created scarcity, makes it difficult to distinguish between rent and profit. Are houses, for example, to be regarded as relatively permanent improvements incorporated into the value of the land or are they better regarded as commodities commanding a profit on the capital outlay required to produce them? The answer to this question depends on what is meant by "relatively permanent." Housing has to be produced and it has to be paid for as a commodity. Once this is done, however, the house may be regarded as a relatively permanent improvement incorporated into the value of the land. Buckingham Palace is a permanent improvement whereas the suburban house just built is not yet in that happy state. It seems reasonable to think in similar fashion about other elements in the built form of the city—offices, shops, transport links, and so on.

The distinction between a mere transfer payment—rent—and profit on productive capital investment is difficult to keep in mind. The individual investor does not particularly care about the distinction; the overall rate of return on financial outlays is what matters. Money is put, therefore, where the rate of return is highest irrespective of whether productive activity is involved or not. If rates of return are high in real estate and property markets, then investment will shift from the primary productive circuit of capital to this secondary circuit in a manner that would be consistent with Lefebvre's thesis. From the investor's point of view there is nothing to prevent such a shift. What has to be explained, however, is how returns can be higher on the secondary circuit over any length of time. For the fact that the distinction between productive and unproductive investment has disappeared from the investor's calculus does not negate the significance of such a distinction as a social fact. If all capital chases rent and no capital goes into production, then no value will be produced out of which the transfer payment that rent represents can come.

2. CLASS-MONOPOLY RENT, URBANIZATION AND CLASS-MONOPOLY POWER

Rent can be charged for a variety of reasons. Marx's categories of differential, absolute and monopoly rent, to which Walker has recently added redistributive rent, are useful if only because they force us to consider the different kinds of situations out of which rent can arise (Harvey, 1973, Chapter 5; Walker, 1974). In this paper I will be concerned with what I shall call "class-monopoly rent." Whether this form of rent should be included in Marx's categories of absolute or monopoly rent is not clear. The resolution of this question depends upon the solution of the celebrated "transformation problem" which arises out of the relationship between values and prices in the Marxian schema.[1] I am of the opinion that class-monopoly rent is best treated as one form of absolute rent. But since this is a contentious and as-yet unresolved problem I will stick to the neutral term "class-monopoly rent" in what follows.

Class-monopoly rents arise because there exists a class of owners of "resource units"—the land and the relatively permanent improvements incorporated in it—who are willing to release the units under their command only if they receive a positive return above some arbitrary level (Marx, 1967 edn., Chapter 45). As a class these owners have the power always to achieve some minimum rate of return. The key concept here is *class power*. If landlords could not or would not behave in accordance with a well-defined class interest, then class-monopoly rents would not be realized. Landlords gain their class power in part from the fact that individually they can survive quite well without releasing all of the resource units under their command.

In nineteenth century Europe landlord power was essentially a residual from feudalism. Marx observed that it would be very much in the interest of the capitalist class to bring land and other productive resources under state ownership since this would relieve the capitalist of the obligation of making any transfer payment to landed property (Marx, 1968 edn., Part 2). It was unlikely, however, that capitalists would challenge the private property arrangements that allowed rent to be realized (and which provided the basis for the class power of landlords) since these arrangements also provided the necessary legal framework for entrepreneurial activity. But in an urbanized world, the distinction between capitalist and landlord has blurred concomitantly with the blurring of the distinctions between land and capital and rent and profit. We need, therefore, to adapt our categories to deal with the new complexities of extensive man-made resource systems. But the same questions arise: are there owners of resource units (be they natural or artificial) who can and do behave so as to make it possible to realize rent? If so, what is the basis of their class power, how are they defining "class interest" and how are we to interpret their role in relation to the structure of social class in society as a whole? We can begin to answer these questions by examining two examples that clarify the meaning of "class interest" in the sense in which that term is being used here.[2]

(a) Landlords Versus Low-Income Tenants

Suppose there exists a class of people who, by virtue of their income, social status, creditworthiness and eligibility for public assistance, are incapable of finding accommodation as homeowners or as residents in public housing. The existence of such a class is readily demonstrable in any large American or European city. This class of people has no alternative but to seek accommodation in the low-income rental market; they are trapped within a particular housing sub-market. The needs of this class are provided for by a class of landlords. Landlordism varies, of course, from the old lady who rents an attic to the large scale professional business operation. For purposes of exposition, let us assume that all rental accommodation is provided by a class of professional landlord-managers. This class has certain options as to where it puts its money but much of its capital exists in the form of housing. On the basis of the potential yield of money on the capital market, professional landlords may set their expected rate of return on the estimated market value of their fixed capital assets at, say, 15 per cent per annum. Suppose there is an abundance of low-income units in a particular city for some reason and that rates of return are in fact as low as 5 per cent. A rational landlord strategy is to reduce maintenance, milk properties of value and actively disinvest, using the money so extracted on the capital market where it earns, say 15 per cent. With declining maintenance, the housing deteriorates in quality and eventually the worst units will be taken out of use—scarcity is successfully produced. Rents will gradually rise until the 15 per cent rate of return is obtained (and there is nothing to stop rents going higher if circumstances allow). The class interest of the landlord is to obtain a minimum of 15 per cent or else to find some way to get out of the market.

The class interests of landlord and tenant are clearly opposed to each other. If the quality of housing deteriorates and rents rise, tenants may seek accommodation elsewhere, but since they are, for the most part, trapped in this sub-market their power is limited in this respect. If they have some political power, they may seek to offset the class-monopoly power of landlords by imposing minimum housing standards or rent controls. If the effect of such legislation is to reduce landlord profits, landlords will respond by trying to transform the fixed capital (the house) into money to be used on the capital market. If prices are low it will not be worthwhile to sell. Social, legal and political pressures may make it difficult for the landlord to disinvest without severe social and fiscal penalties. Under these conditions the landlord may well compromise and settle for a much lower rate of return. The tenants will then have achieved some kind of partial victory vis-a-vis the class-monopoly power of landlords. If, on the other hand, tenants are politically weak, there is a shortage of suitable accommodation (because of in-migration or redevelopment) and if landlords can easily sell or transform to different uses (e.g. upper-income tenancies), then the landlord class will have very considerable power and will be able to raise their rate of return to well above 15 per cent. With rising rents eating into an already limited disposable income, low-income tenants can respond only by subdividing space with the inevitable consequences—over-crowding and slum formation.

Class-interest conflict of this sort between tenants and landlords can be documented in any capitalist city (Chatterjee, 1973; Sternlieb, 1966; Milner-Holland Report, 1965). The rate of return set through the working out of this conflict is best interpreted as a class-monopoly rent even though the landlord usually thinks of it as a rate of return on capital investment. The realization of this rent depends upon the ability of one class-interest group to execute its power over another class-interest group and thereby to assure for itself a certain minimum rate of return.

(b) Speculator-Developers and Suburban Middle- and Upper-Income Groups

We now turn to a case that is rather more complex but which indicates that class-monopoly rents can be realized in all sectors of the housing market. Upper-income groups have a wide range of choice of housing as far as their income is concerned. But if their sense of social status and prestige is highly developed, then the producers of housing (who actively promote such thoughts on the part of the buyer) have an opportunity to realize a class-monopoly rent as these consumers vie with each other for prestigious housing in the "right" neighborhoods. Middle-income groups may have less choice. In many American cities, for example, they have moved to suburbia in part because they were hooked on the suburban dream, but also because social changes in the city—the influx of a low-income "lumpenproletariat," the decline of city services, falling property values, the withdrawal of financial support for whole neighbourhoods, and declining employment opportunities—have given them a hefty push by a process that I have elsewhere dubbed "blow-out" (Harvey, 1973, Chapter 5).

The realization of a class-monopoly rent depends, however, on the existence of a class of speculator-developers who have the power to capture it.[3] In a free market economy, speculator developers perform a positive service. They promote an optimal timing of land-use change, ensure that the current value of land and housing reflects expected future returns, seek to organize externalities to enhance the value of their existing developments, and generally perform a co-ordinating and stabilizing function in the face of considerable market uncertainty (Neutze, 1968; Hall et al., 1973). The role of speculator-developer is, in fact, integral and essential to the workings of a capitalist economy. Since the urbanization process relates to economic growth in general, the speculator-developer who is, in effect, the promoter of urbanization, plays a vital role in promoting economic growth. Certain institutional supports are necessary, however, if this role is to be performed effectively. The exact nature of these supports will vary from country to country but they must do two things: (1) they must reduce the uncertainty in land-use competition usually through some form of governmental regulation—planning or zoning controls, provision of infrastructure, etc.; and (2) they must encourage wealthy groups—those who can afford to wait for land to "ripen"—to participate as speculator-developers usually by offering convenient and advantageous tax arrangements. The first support permits speculator-developers to form reasonable expectations about the future, while the second ensures that only people with sufficient resources undertake the task of coordinating and stabilizing land-use change.

Class-monopoly rents can be realized by speculator-developers only if they possess mechanisms for expressing their collective class interest. The necessary institutional supports in fact provide these mechanisms. In the United States, for example, speculator-developers usually realize monopoly-rents through the manipulation of zoning decisions. Political control of suburban jurisdictions by speculator-developers is quite general in the United States; as Gaffney notes, suburban jurisdictions provide one of the most effective of all cartel arangements with respect to land-use decisions (Gaffney, 1973). Political corruption also plays a role which, in a market economy, can be viewed positively since it frequently loosens up the supply of land from the excessive rigidities of land-use regulation by bureaucratic fiat. Without a certain minimum of governmental regulation and institutional support, however, the speculator-developer could not perform the vital function of promoter, co-ordinator and stabilizer of land-use change. Without such an interest group to perform these functions, suburban development would degenerate into chaos and finance capital would be forced to withdraw investment from the suburbanization process. The effect of such a withdrawal upon economic growth in general, effective demand in general and the capitalist market system as a whole would, of course, be catastrophic.

The level of class-monopoly rent realized by speculator-developers depends upon the outcome of the conflict of interest between them and the various consumer groups who confront them in the market. If the speculator-developer can persuade upper-income groups of the virtues of a certain kind of housing in a particular neighbourhood, gain complete control over the political process, and so on, then the advantage lies with the speculator-developer. If consumers are unimpressed by the blandishments of the speculator-developers and have firm control over the political mechanisms for land-use regulation and the provision of infrastructure, then the class-monopoly power of the speculator-developers will be contained. But if certain minimum rates of return are not realized, the speculator-developer will pull out of the business until rates of return rise. What the minimum must be is difficult to say—but in the United States a 40 per cent rate of return is not regarded as abnormal.

The two cases we have examined—the landlord versus the low-income tenant and the speculator-developer versus the middle- and upper-income consumer—provide us with certain insights into the meaning of class-monopoly rent and class-monopoly power in the context of urbanization. Firstly, this form of rent appears inevitable in capitalistically organized land and housing markets. Second, the transfer payments that result from class-monopoly rents are structured in certain important respects. Suppose the landlord lives in suburbia and as a resident there gives up a class-monopoly rent to the speculator-developer? Notice, that the rent realized from a low-income tenant has been passed on, in this example, to the speculator-developer via the landlord. It is unlikely, bordering on the impossible, for rent realized by the speculator-developer to be passed on to the low-income tenant. It seems reasonable to postulate, therefore, an hierarchical structure of some sort through which class-monopoly rents percolate upwards but not downwards. At the top of this hierarchy sit the financial institutions. And so the question arises, how does this hierarchy arise and what is its *raison d'être*?

3. THE HIERARCHICAL INSTITUTIONAL FRAMEWORK FOR CO-ORDINATING ACTIVITIES IN THE HOUSING MARKET

I shall begin by stating a general proposition: the hierarchical institutional structure through which class monopoly rents are realized is a necessity if housing market activity is to be co-ordinated in a way that helps to avoid economic crisis. The problem with seeking to validate this proposition is that institutional arrangements vary markedly from country to country. But all capitalist economies must, of necessity, possess elaborate devices to integrate national and local aspects of economies, to integrate individual decisions with the needs of society as a whole. Any society must possess, in short, formalized human practices which resolve the social aggregation problem (Harvey and Chatterjee, 1974). These formalized human practices are manifest in a structure of financial and governmental institutions which, I shall argue, create the basis for class-monopoly power in the land and property markets. To explore this proposition I will examine institutional structures in the United States and consider how these affect events in Baltimore in particular.

National institutions of government and finance do not operate without a purpose; they seek, by and large, to ensure the reproduction of society and to deal with any problems that may arise in an orderly and non-disruptive manner. In a capitalist society this means a policy directed towards the orderly accumulation of capital, economic growth and the reproduction of the basic social and political relationships of a capitalist society. In the housing market these general concerns are translated into three typical concerns for national housing policy:

1. To ensure orderly relationships between construction, economic growth and new household formation;
2. To ensure short-run stability and iron out cyclical swings in the economy at large by using the construction industry and the housing sector as a partial Keynesian regulator; and
3. To ensure domestic peace and tranquility by managing the distribution of welfare in society through the provision of housing.

In the United States these concerns have been embedded in policy goals which have, by and large, been successfully met since 1930.[4] Economic growth has been accompanied and to some degree accomplished by rapid suburbanization—a process that has been facilitated by national housing policies conducted through the Federal Housing Administration. Much of the growth in GNP, both absolute and per capita, since the 1930s has been wrapped up in the suburbanization process (taking into account the construction of highways and utilities, housing, the effective demand for automobiles, gasoline and so on). Cyclical swings in the economy have been broadly contained since the 1930s and the construction industry appears to have functioned effectively as a major counter-cyclical tool. The evident social discontent of the 1930s has largely been defused by a government policy which has created a large wedge of middle-income people who are now "debt-encumbered homeowners" and consequently unlikely to rock the boat. The discontent of the 1960s exhibited by the blacks and the urban poor, provoked a similar political response in the housing sector—a response that has not provided a "decent house in a decent living environment" (as Congressional legislation perennially puts it) for many of the poor but which has successfully created a debt-encumbered class of black homeowners; the social instability of the 1960s certainly appears to have been defused. It appears, then, that national policies are designed to maintain the existing structure of society intact in its basic configurations, while facilitating economic growth and capitalist accumulation, eliminating cyclical influences and defusing social discontent.

How are these national policies transmitted to the locality and how do individuals come to incorporate them into their decisions? Federal, State and local government form a three-tiered political hierarchy and an independent bureaucracy is attached to each level. The Federal bureaucracy is itself hierarchically organized, however, so that it is in a position to relate national policies to local housing markets. The Federal Housing Administration (FHA) administers a wide range of government programmes and operates autonomously from bureaucracies created at the State and local levels. But in the United States the main mechanism for co-ordinating national and local, individual and societal activities lies in the hierarchical structure of financial institutions operating under governmental regulation. This structure is exceedingly complex and I shall not attempt to detail it here.[5] It is important to note one feature of it, however. Certain kinds of institution—the State and Federally chartered savings and loan institutions—operate solely in the housing sector. They were initially designed to "promote the thrift of people locally to finance their own homes and the homes of their neighbours."[6] Some of these institutions are community-based, depositor controlled and operate on a non-profit basis. They are, of course, affected by money market conditions and government regulation. These institutions contrast with the mortgage banks, savings banks and commercial banks which are oriented to profits or to the expansion of their business. All of these institutions, however, operate together to relate national policies to local and individual decisions and, in the process create localized structures within which class-monopoly rents can be realized.

The Baltimore situation demonstrates the point. The metropolitan area has a population of approximately two million; 900,000 live in Baltimore City and 600,000 live in the largest suburban jurisdiction—Baltimore County— which surrounds Baltimore City on almost all sides. The political machine in Baltimore County has been dominated by speculator-developer interests who have, until recently, been able to manipulate the zoning laws more or less at will in order to realize speculative gains. Political corruption is usual (Agnew was once County Executive). All that is necessary for the realization of class-monopoly rents is some generally sustained demand for new housing (through population increase or new household formation). There is a further point to be considered, however. The investment climate is radically different in Baltimore County and Baltimore City. All of the institutions look collectively on the former as an area of growth and expansion compared to the City which is looked upon as an area that is at best stable and at worst in the process of rapid decline. The consequent channelling of investment funds

FIGURE 1

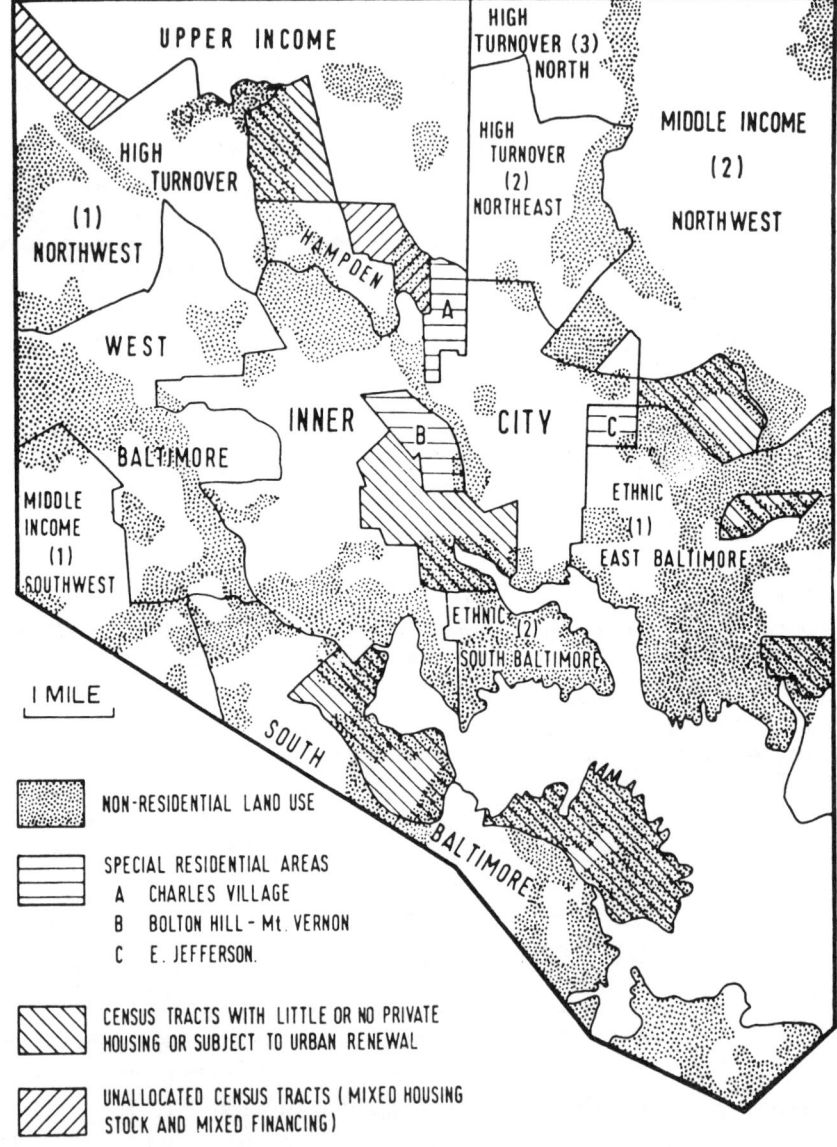

Class-Monopoly Rent and Finance Capital 261

to the County and the general reluctance to invest in the City turns out to be a self-fulfilling prediction to which middle-income groups are forced to respond by migrating from the City to the County, where the speculator-developer eagerly awaits them. In this fashion the conflict between city and suburb in the United States contributes to the realization of class-monopoly rents on the suburban fringe.

But there is also a geographical structure to the housing market in Baltimore City which further contributes to the potential for realizing class-monopoly rents. This geographical structure is produced by the interacting policies of financial and governmental institutions. To demonstrate this point Baltimore City is divided into 13 sub-markets which can be further aggregated into eight sub-market types (see Fig. 1). Data concerning the financing of housing in each of these sub-markets, together with some socioeconomic information, is presented in Tables 1 and 2. It is evident that the housing market in Baltimore City is highly structured geographically with respect to the type of institutional involvement as well as with respect to the insurance of home purchases by the Federal Housing Administration (FHA). Let us consider the main features of this structure.

(i) The *inner city* is dominated by cash and private loan transactions with scarcely a vestige of institutional or governmental involvement in the used housing market. This sub-market is the locus of that conflict between landlord and low-income-tenant to which we have already alluded. There is currently a surplus of housing in this sub-market which is leading to active disinvestment (there are several thousand vacant structures in this submarket). Professional landlords are anxious to disinvest but they still manage to get a rate of return around 13 per cent (Chatterjee, 1973). The tenants are low-income and for the most part black. They are poorly organized, exercise little political control and are effectively trapped in this sub-market. Class-monopoly rents are here realized by professional landlords who calculate their rate of return to match the opportunity cost of their capital.

(ii) The white *ethnic areas* are dominated by homeownership which is financed mainly by small community-based, savings and loan institutions which operate without a strong profit orientation and which really do offer a community service. As a consequence little class-monopoly rent is realized in this sub-market and reasonably good housing is obtained at fairly low purchase price, considering the fairly low incomes of the residents.

(iii) The black residential area of *West Baltimore* was essentially a creation of the 1960s. Low- to moderate-income blacks did not possess local savings and loan associations, were regarded with suspicion by all other financial institutions and in the early 1960s were discriminated against by the FHA. The only way in which this group could become homeowners was by way of something called a "land-installment contract" which works as follows. A

TABLE 1
Housing Sub-Markets—Baltimore City, 1970

	Total Houses Sold	Sales Per 100 Properties	% Transactions by source of funds:								% Sales Insured		Average Sale Price ($)**
			Cash	Pvt	Federal S. & L.	State S.&L.	Mortgage Bank	Community Bank	Savings Bank	Other*	FHA	VA	
Inner City	1199	1.86	65.7	15.0	3.0	12.0	2.2	0.5	0.2	1.7	2.9	1.1	3498
1. East	646	2.33	64.7	15.0	2.2	14.3	2.2	0.5	0.1	1.2	3.4	1.4	3437
2. West	553	1.51	67.0	15.1	4.0	9.2	2.3	0.4	0.4	2.2	2.3	0.6	3568
Ethnic	760	3.34	39.9	5.5	6.1	43.2	2.0	0.8	0.9	2.2	2.6	0.7	6372
1. East Baltimore	579	3.40	39.7	4.8	5.5	43.7	2.4	1.0	1.2	2.2	3.2	0.7	6769
2. South Baltimore	181	3.20	40.3	7.7	7.7	41.4	0.6	-	-	2.2	0.6	0.6	5102
Hampden	99	2.40	40.4	8.1	18.2	26.3	4.0	-	3.0	-	14.1	2.0	7059
West Baltimore	497	2.32	30.6	12.5	12.1	11.7	22.3	1.6	3.1	6.0	25.8	4.2	8664
South Baltimore	322	3.16	28.3	7.4	22.7	13.4	13.4	1.9	4.0	9.0	22.7	10.6	8751
High turnover	2072	5.28	19.1	6.1	13.6	14.9	32.8	1.2	5.7	6.2	38.2	9.5	992
1. North-West	1071	5.42	20.0	7.2	9.7	13.8	40.9	1.1	2.9	4.5	46.8	7.4	9312
2. North-East	693	5.07	20.6	6.4	14.4	16.5	29.0	1.4	5.6	5.9	34.5	10.2	9779
3. North	308	5.35	12.7	1.4	25.3	18.1	13.3	0.7	15.9	12.7	31.5	15.5	12,330
Middle Income	1077	3.15	20.8	4.4	29.8	17.0	8.6	1.9	8.7	9.0	17.7	11.1	12,760
1. South-West	212	3.46	17.0	6.6	29.2	8.5	15.1	1.0	10.8	11.7	30.2	17.0	12,848
2. North-East	865	3.09	21.7	3.8	30.0	19.2	7.0	2.0	8.2	8.2	14.7	9.7	12,751
Upper Income	361	3.84	19.4	6.9	23.5	10.5	8.6	7.2	21.1	2.8	11.9	3.6	27,413

*Assumed mortgages and subject to mortgage.
**Ground rent is sometimes included in the sale price and this distorts the averages in certain respects. The relative differentials between the sub-markets are of the right order however.

Source: City Planning Department Tabulations from Lusk Reports.

TABLE 2
Housing Sub-Markets—Baltimore City, 1970 (Census Data)

	Median Income*	% Black Occupied d.u.'s	% Units Owner Occupied	Mean $ Value of Owner Occupied	% Renter Occupied	Mean Monthly Rent
Inner City						
1. East	6259	72.2	28.5	6259	71.5	77.5
2. West	6201	65.1	29.3	6380	70.7	75.2
	6297	76.9	27.9	6963	72.1	78.9
Ethnic						
1. East Baltimore	8822	1.0	66.0	8005	34.0	76.8
2. South Baltimore	8836	1.2	66.3	8368	33.7	78.7
	8785	0.2	64.7	6504	35.3	69.6
Hampden	8730	0.3	58.8	7860	41.2	76.8
West Baltimore	9566	84.1	50.0	13,842	50.0	103.7
South Baltimore	8941	0.1	56.9	9741	43.1	82.0
High turnover						
1. North-West	10,413	34.3	53.5	11,886	46.5	113.8
2. North-East	9483	55.4	49.3	11,867	50.7	110.6
3. North	10,753	30.4	58.5	11,533	41.5	111.5
	11,510	1.3	49.0	12,726	51.0	125.1
Middle Income						
1. South-West	10,639	2.8	62.6	13,221	37.5	104.1
2. North-East	10,655	4.4	48.8	13,470	51.2	108.1
	10,634	2.3	66.2	13,174	33.8	103.0
Upper Income	17,577	1.7	50.8	27,097	49.2	141.4

*Weighted average of median incomes for census tracts in sub-market.

Source: 1970 Census.

speculator purchases a house for, say, $7000, adds a purchase and sales commission, various financing charges and overhead costs, renovates and redecorates the property and finally adds a gross profit margin of, say, 20 per cent. The house is then sold for, say, $13,000. To finance the transaction, the speculator interposes his credit rating between that of the purchaser and the financial institutions, takes out a conventional mortgage up to the appraised value of the house (say, $9000), borrows another $4000, and then packages a $13,000 loan for the buyer. The speculator retains title to the property to secure the risk but permits the "buyer" immediate possession. The monthly payments cover the interest charges on the $13,000 plus the administrative charges and a small part is put to redeeming the principle. When the purchaser has redeemed $4000 (after, say, 10 or 15 years) a conventional mortgage at the appraised value of $9000 may be obtained. At that juncture the purchaser will get title and can start to build equity in the house.[7]

This procedure is perfectly legal and it was in effect the only way in which low- or moderate-income blacks could become homeowners in the early 1960s. There were many transactions of this sort in West Baltimore. The problem was that a comparable house sold to a person in a comparable income bracket in white ethnic areas cost $7000 compared to the $13,000 registered in the black community. Blacks consequently regarded themselves as exploited and paying "the black tax," which was nothing more nor less than class-monopoly rent realized by speculators as they took advantage of a particular mix of financial and governmental policies compounded by problems of racial discrimination. But a new sub-market was formed in West Baltimore by means of the land-installment contract; and in the process strong pressures were exerted on white middle class groups to move to suburbia where the speculator developers waited, all too willing and able to accommodate them.

The political conflict over the use of the land-installment contract in Baltimore came to a head in the late 1960s. In the process the black communities learned that the speculator was creeping in where financial and governmental institutions refused to tread and that the problems of speculation could not be divorced from the activities of the financial and governmental institutions. Since the 1960s the land-installment contract has declined as a form of financing. But the speculator has not disappeared from the scene; rather, he now has other instrumentalities at his disposal.

(iv) The areas of *High Turnover* are serviced mainly by a combination of mortgage banker finance and FHA insurance which were doing in 1970 what the land installment contract did in the 1960s. Various programmes were initiated in the late 1960s to try and create a debt-encumbered, socially stable class of homeowners amongst the black and the urban poor. These programmes, together with administrative directives to end discriminatory practices against blacks, led to the creation of an FHA insured, mainly black, fairly low income, housing sub-market. The main tool in Baltimore was the FHA 221(d)(2) programme (D2s) which permits the financing of home-ownership for low- or moderate-income groups who have no money for a down-payment. FHA insurance in Baltimore in 1970 was, for the most part, of the D2 variety (see Table 1).

In the high turnover sub-markets created by these programmes there are plenty of opportunities for the speculator to realize a class-monopoly rent. Operating through the D2 programmes makes it less easy to extract the "black tax" but if whites move (as they are likely to do if a low-income black family moves in), speculators can pick up houses cheaper than appraised value, put in some cosmetic repairs to meet FHA quality standards, and sell through the D2 programme. If FHA quality control standards are poor (or if speculators can corrupt the administration of them) then class-monopoly rents can be realized as a white "exit tax" and a black or low-income "entry tax." In some cities, such as Detroit, New York and Philadelphia, the windfall profits to speculators have been enormous largely through the corruption of FHA programmes (Boyer, 1973). In Baltimore, the sub-market created by the land-installment contract in the 1960s is now being extended in areas of high turnover by speculator activity in conjunction with mortgage banker finance and the FHA D2 programmes.

(v) The *middle-income* sub-markets of North-East and South-West Baltimore are typically the creation of the FHA programmes of the 1930s. By the 1960s homeownership was being financed conventionally by Federal savings and loan institutions and some of the smaller ethnic savings and loan institutions which have helped to finance migration from the older ethnic areas of the city to the newer housing of North-East Baltimore. The inner edge of this sub-market is under some pressure, however, and financial institutions are extremely sensitive about risks in these areas. As a consequence they tend to withdraw support from an area if they perceive it to be threatened in any way. By so doing they create a vacuum in housing finance into which the speculator moves backed by the FHA programmes and mortgage banker finance. There is a good deal of political friction in these boundary zones and a political struggle to preserve the middle-income sub-markets from erosion at the edges—an erosion that inevitably leads middle income groups to search for housing opportunities in the suburbs.

(vi) The more affluent groups make use of savings banks and commercial banks to much greater degree and rarely resort to FHA guarantees. Such groups usually have the political and economic power to fend off speculative incursions and it is unlikely that they will move except as the result of their own changing preferences or from declining services. Class-monopoly rents are realized in this sub-market largely because of prestige and status considerations.

This geographical structure of sub-markets in Baltimore forms a decision environment in the context of which individual households make housing choices. These choices are likely, by and large, to conform to the structure and to reinforce it. The structure itself is a product of history. In the long-run we find that the geographic structure of the city is continuously being transformed by conflicts and struggles generated by the ebb and flow of market forces, the operations of speculators, landlords and developers, the changing policies of governmental and financial institutions, changing tastes, and the like. But in the short run the geographic structure is rather fixed and it is this rigidity which permits class-monopoly rents to be realized within sub-markets (as classes of providers face classes of consumers) and between sub-markets as a variety of processes seek to erode the boundaries of the sub-markets themselves (every sub-market has its speculator-developer fringe). In some parts of the city these conflicts may be dormant at times—boundaries may be stabilized (often with the help of natural or artificial barriers) and accommodation between opposing forces may be reached within sub-markets. But it would be rare indeed to find a city in which no such conflicts were occurring.

4. CLASS-MONOPOLY RENT, ABSOLUTE SPACE AND URBAN STRUCTURE

Class-monopoly rents arise because the owners of resource units have the power always to extract a positive return. Ricardo thought that *absolute* rent could exist only on an island where all resource units were employed and on which there was an absolute scarcity. The Baltimore materials indicate that the man-made resource system created by urbanization is, in effect, a series of man-made islands on which class monopolies produce absolute scarcities. Absolute spaces, created by human practices, are essential, it seems, to the realization of class-monopoly rent. Absolute spaces can be constructed by dividing space up into parcels and segments each of which can then be regarded as a "thing in itself" independent of other things (Harvey, 1973, Chapter 5). The private property relation is, of course, the most basic institution by means of which absolute spaces are formally created. Political jurisdictions define collective absolute spaces which may then be carved up by the bureaucratic regulation of land use. All of these forms of absolute space create the possibility to realize class-monopoly rents. But it is primarily through the informally structured absolute spaces of sub-markets that such rents are realized.

The implications of this for residential structure are of interest. Residential differentiation in urban areas has long been explained in terms of social ecological processes, consumer preferences, utility-maximizing behaviours on the part of individuals, and the like. The Baltimore evidence suggests that financial and governmental institutions play an active role in shaping residential differentiation and that the active agent in the process is an investor seeking to realize a class monopoly-rent. The relationship between traditional explanations of urban residential differentiation and this interpretation is complex. The small neighbourhood savings and loan institution in Baltimore, for example, is in effect a community institution that fits neatly into a social ecological view of urban community structure. But most housing finance comes from institutions seeking profits or the expansion of business. Faced with a choice between supporting a risk-absorbing landlord operation and a vulnerable homeowner in the inner city, business rationality dictates support of the former at the expense of the latter. Not all financial institutions exhibit a totally cold market rationality—they will grant personal favours (usually to people of the same social class, however) and they will sometimes actively support neighbourhoods (often to procure a desirable stability in a particular sub-market). But the options of the profit-maximizing or expansion-conscious financial institution are limited. The hidden hand, and in particular the prospects for realizing class-monopoly rents, will inexorably guide them in certain directions. And as a result these institutions become a fundamental force in shaping the residential structure of the city.

This is not to say that considerations of race and ethnicity, social status and prestige, life-style aspirations, community and neighbourhood solidarity, and the like, are irrelevant to understanding residential differentiation. Ironically, all of these features *increase* the potential for realizing class-monopoly rent because they help to maintain the island-like structure, to create the absolute space of the parochially-minded community. Indeed, a strong case can be made for regarding consumer preferences as being produced systematically rather than as arising spontaneously (as neo-classical economic doctrines appear to envisage via the myth of consumer sovereignty). The simplest manifestation of this is the use of techniques of persuasion to convince upper-income people of the virtue of living in a "smart" house in the "right" neighbourhood. But there is a deeper process at work. Financial institutions and government manage the urbanization process to achieve economic growth, economic stability and to defuse social discontent (see Section 3). If these aims are to be realized, then new modes of consumption and new social wants and needs will have to be produced whether people like it or not. If these new modes of consumption and new social wants and needs do not arise spontaneously, in a manner that fits with the overall necessities of capitalist society, then people will have to be forced or cajoled to accept them. The urbanization process achieves this end quite successfully. By structuring and restructuring the choices open to people, by creating distinctive decision environments, the urbanization process forces new kinds of choice independently of spontaneously arising predilections.

If the dynamic of urbanization is powered by financial and governmental institutions, mediated by speculator-developers and speculator-landlords in pursuit of class-monopoly rent, and necessitated by the over-riding requirement to reproduce the capitalist order, then it may not be too fanciful to suggest that distinctive "consumption classes," "distributive groupings" or even "housing classes" may be produced at the same time (see Giddens, 1973; Rex and Moore, 1967). Individuals can, of course, strive or choose to join one or another "distributive grouping" or shift (if they can) from one "consumption class" to another. In like manner they can strive or choose (depending on their circumstances) to move from one housing sub-market to another. What individuals cannot choose, however, is the structure of the distributive grouping or the structure of the housing sub-markets—these are dictated by forces far removed from the realms of consumer sovereignty. The general proposition we are here led to is an intriguing one: in producing new modes of consumption and new social wants and needs, the urbanization process concomitantly produces new distributive groupings or consumption classes which may crystallize into distinctive communities within the overall urban structure. This topic will be taken up again in Section 5.

The Baltimore materials suggest another startling conclusion. The class-monopoly rent gained in one sub-market is not independent of its realization elsewhere and certain strong multiplier effects can be detected. Suppose, for example, that there is a speculative boom in the inner city through which new sub-markets are formed out of existing neighbourhoods and that the old residents of these neighbourhoods are forced to seek housing opportunities in suburbia. Then, the greater the class-monopoly rent earned by the inner-city speculator, the greater the opportunity to realize rent on the suburban fringe. Multiplier effects of this sort may be captured by the same financial institutions or, in some cases, by the same entrepreneur. If there is no conscious collusion to generate the multiplier effect, the calculus of profits and losses, of expectations and perceived risks, will function as a hidden-hand regulator to achieve the same results.

These conclusions are, of course, geographically and institutionally specific to Baltimore and the United States. But a cursory examination of the literature suggests that they may be generalized to all advanced capitalist nations.[8] Whether or not this is the case must be proved by future research. It seems likely, however, that the processes are general but that the manifestations are particular because the institutional, geographical, cultural and historical situations vary a great deal from place to place. In other words, the processes are general, but the circumstances are unique to each case and so, consequently, are the results.

If the multiplier effects to the realization of class-monopoly rents are general, then we have a partial explanation of how investment can shift continuously over time from the primary to the secondary circuit of capital as Lefebvre hypothesizes. Governmental and financial institutions are forced to operate in certain ways if individual behaviours are to be co-ordinated and integrated with national and societal requirements. Urbanization, itself a product of these requirements, creates islands of opportunities for realizing class-monopoly rents. And the quest for this rent generates a multiplier effect that makes it even more profitable in the short run to shift investment into the land, housing and property markets. Such a shift helps to explain the industrial stagnation, particularly evident since the late 1960s, in the advanced capitalist nations as investment shifts from the production of value to the attempt to realize it. In the short run such a shift is possible because it is possible to milk value produced in past periods for purposes of current realization (which means, however, a continuous decay in the quality of urban environments). But in the long run such a shift is doomed to failure for if value is not produced, then how can it possibly be realized?

5. CLASS SYSTEM, CLASS STRUCTURE, CLASS INTEREST IN THE POLITICAL ECONOMY OF URBANISM

We will now consider the relationship between the concept of class interest as it arises in the context of urbanization (and as it is used in this paper) and more general concepts of class structure and class antagonism. It is useful to distinguish at the outset between the concept of *subjective* class which describes the consciousness which different groups have of their position within a social structure and the concept of *objective* class which, in Marx's schema, describes a basic division within capitalism between a class of producers and a class of appropriators of surplus value (for a recent discussion on this topic, see Giddens, 1973). The former class includes both productive labour and that labour which is socially necessary but unproductive (for example, labour contributing to circulation, realization, administration and the provision of socially necessary services). The meaning attached to class interest in this paper stems from the fact of certain conflicts around the realization of class-monopoly rent. We are, therefore, working at the level of subjective class interest and the task is to relate these diverse class interests to the concept of objective class.

Traditionally, rent is viewed as a transfer payment from capitalist producers to a rentier class which gains its power as a residual of feudalism. But we are here concerned with rent extracted from the community out of the consumption process rather than out of the production process. This extraction generates a species of community conflict which has become widespread with the progress of urbanization in advanced capitalist countries. This kind of conflict contrasts, superficially at least, with the more traditional work-based conflicts over the immediate production of value. We can observe as a consequence some curious dichotomies. Community-based organizations rarely offer support in a work-based conflict (such as a strike) and work-based organizations (such as the trade unions) rarely offer active support to community groups in conflict over, for example, the realization of class-monopoly rent. Individuals may in fact switch roles with respect to such conflicts—a work-based radical may be a community-based conservative (and vice versa). The place of work also tends to be male-dominated space compared with the female-dominated residential space. Sex roles may get intertwined as a male work-based radical acts conservatively with respect to a female community-based radical. Such conflicts may be internalized within the family. The geography of human activity within large metropolitan areas appears to generate curious transformations and inversions to create a complex geography of subjective class consciousness. The expression of class interest around community issues cannot, therefore, be interpreted as a simple reflection of class interest at the point of production.

Yet class interest can be equally strong and express analogous goals at the point of production and within the community. Workers may seek for worker-control while residents may seek for community control. Both goals express a basic felt need on the part of individuals to control the social conditions of their existence. But under urbanization the two goals become divorced from each other. A far more cohesive basis for political power exists when community-based and work-based interests coincide (for example, in mining communities and in other situations characterized by *industrial* rather than *advanced urban* forms of social organization). Marx thought that large concentrations of population would heighten class-awareness. But under urbanization class-consciousness appears to have become fragmented.

Community-based class interest always tends to be parochialist in its perspectives. The community is regarded as a "thing-in-itself" independent of other things—it is regarded as an absolute space, as something to be preserved and defended against external threat. From such a standpoint flows a form of community conflict which is essentially internecine—it pits community against community so that the average condition of communities is not altered one whit. What one community gains another loses. The sequence of wins and losses merely serves to perpetuate the defensiveness and competitiveness of the communities concerned—a situation which permits even more class-monopoly rents to be realized since speculators so easily feed off community antagonisms. Parochialist community-based class interest can never be an adequate surrogate for objective social class, for it ignores the essential fact that the survival of the community depends, given the enormous complexity in the division of labour, upon commodity exchanges on a global scale and because it ignores the links in the production and circulation of value in society.

Yet certain kinds of community-conflict lead to the formation of non-parochialist horizons. In Baltimore, for example, community groups enraged at the use of the land-installment contract, gradually came to realize that financial institutions, by denying conventional mortgage funds while financing speculator-landlords, were the controlling influence in the situation. The community group began to unravel the skein of argument presented in this paper through a process of political exploration. And at the end of the road, the community came face to face with what appears to be the dominant power of finance capital.

Curiously enough, there are hints that work-based conflict may lead to the same confrontation. The traditional conflict between worker and industrialist is being ameliorated in certain sectors by the growing integration of workers into management leading, perhaps, to worker control under certain conditions. But worker control over the factory, brings the worker face to face with the power of finance capital to exercise an external control over the activities of industrial enterprise. In much the same way that Marx thought it possible (but unlikely) that land and resources could be brought under state ownership to the advantage of the capitalist, so it appears possible (but unlikely) to nationalize industrial production, introduce decentralized worker control, without in any way necessarily touching or diminishing the power of finance capital. Worker control has to be viewed, therefore, as a transitional step that fails unless finance capital is also controlled.

The conclusion from the standpoint of both the community and the work place is that the ultimate power to organize the production and realization of value in society lies in the hands of finance capital. To sustain this conclusion, however, we have to show the necessity for an inner transformation of capitalism such that finance capital comes to exercise a hegemonic power over industrial production as well as all other aspects of life. All that I have space to do here, is to provide some clues as to where we might look for the logic of such an inner transformation.

The changing role of money itself provides one such clue. Without money there could be no integrated commodity production, no elaborate division of labour, no price-fixing markets, no universalized exchange values, no medium for the accumulation of capital, no urbanization, and so on. Money in its role of mediator of exchange consequently mediates all significant social interactions. Marx argued that:

> The need for exchange and for the transformation of product into pure exchange value progresses in step with the division of labour, i.e., with the increasingly social character of production. But as the latter grows, so grows the power of money, i.e., the exchange relation establishes itself as a power external to and independent of producers. What originally appeared as a means to promote production becomes a relation alien to producers. As the producers become more dependent on exchange, exchange appears to become independent of them, and

the gap between the product as product and the product as exchange value appears to widen. Money does not create these antitheses and contradictions; it is, rather, the development of these contradictions and antitheses which creates the transcendental power of money (Marx, 1973 edn. *The Grundrisse*).

The "increasingly social character of production" (the increasingly complex division of labour), the constant expansion of capitalist social relations and the increasing integration of society on a world-wide basis, have, since Marx's time, greatly increased the "transcendental power of money." But this power, if it is to be exercised, requires an institutional framework for its expression and a class of people willing and able to make use of it. Marx again provides a clue to the former when he argues that the joint stock company is an institutional response to the inherent instability of competitive capitalism— an instability which required the concentration of first, industrial, and later, finance capital. This new arrangement transforms "the actually functioning capitalist into a mere manager, administrator of other people's capital and . . . the owner of capital into a mere owner, a mere money capitalist" (Marx, 1967 edn., Vol. 3, p. 436). As a result, interest—"the mere compensation for owning capital that now is entirely divorced from the actual process of reproduction" is substituted for profit. Marx saw all this creating a transitional mode of production in which new institutions would be increasingly social in character:

> This is the abolition of the capitalist mode of production within the capitalist mode of production itself, and hence a self-dissolving contradiction, which *prima facie* represents a mere phase of transition to a new form of production . . . It establishes a monopoly in certain spheres and thereby requires state interference. It reproduces a new financial aristocracy, a new variety of parasites, in the shape of promoters, speculators, and simply nominal directors . . . It is private production without the control of private property (Marx, 1967 edn., Volume 3, p. 438).

Marx did not elaborate much on these remarks but history has. Industrial corporations have attempted to maintain their independence of financial institutions by generating funds internally, but this has led them to diversify and to take on many characteristics of financial institutions—ITT is almost purely a financial holding company now and General Motors is steadily moving in that direction. Financial institutions equal and perhaps surpass the industrial corporations in economic power (U.S. House of Representatives, 1968, 1971; Herman, 1973). State power has grown remarkably and functions to support, by appropriate budgetary, fiscal and monetary policies, the operations of finance capital. The State is also active in managing both production and consumption (Miliband, 1969). Finance capital, operating through State, corporate and financial institutions, effectively co-ordinates all social activity into one coherent whole. An industrial capitalism based merely on the immediate production of goods has evolved to a finance form of capitalism which seeks to create and appropriate value through the production, not only of goods, but of new modes of production and new social wants and needs (see the important passages on this point in Marx, 1973 edn., p. 92). But in so doing, new institutions are founded on the power of money, which is the appearance but not the substance of wealth. Hence arises, in Marx's view, the contradictory character of finance capitalism and its historical necessity as a transitional form.

Financial institutions can accumulate by a variety of techniques. Operating competitively they frequently try to accumulate off each other (by takeovers, asset-stripping and the like). In aggregate, however, finance capital accumulates out of production in the immediate sense (a work-based exploitation), out of the production of new modes of consumption and the production of new social wants and needs (both of which lead to community-based exploitation). And as finance capital seeks to manage and control the totality of the production process so there emerges a certain indifference as to whether accumulation takes place by keeping wages down in the immediate production process or by manipulations in the consumption sphere (varying from the manipulation of pension funds to accumulation by means of the processes described in this paper).

We have already suggested (Sections 3 and 4) that urbanization serves to produce new modes of consumption and new social wants and needs. The roles of speculator-landlord and speculator-developer are crucial to the dynamics of urbanization and therefore to the maintenance of effective demand; and a structure of sub-markets through which class-monopoly rents can be realized provides the necessary incentive to play these roles with profit. But at the same time the potential to realize these rents provides the possibility for rapid accumulation of capital out of the land and property markets when the occasion demands it. When industrial demand lags and industrial profits decline, financial institutions will compensate by moving into the land and property markets (ITT has extracted millions out of the Florida real estate boom, for example). But many communities will resist these external forces controlling the conditions of their existence—hence the community conflict typical of advanced urban societies. This analysis suggests a certain underlying unity to community-based and work-based conflict and herein may lie a clue to the definition of objective classes under advanced urbanization. If objective classes are still to be defined in terms of the production and appropriation of surplus value, then it is now production as a totality (including the production of new modes of consumption and new social wants and needs) rather than immediate production which defines the division between producers and appropriators of surplus value. Marx's theory of surplus value is founded in the analysis of immediate production (with modes of consumption and wants and needs held constant) (see Marx, 1973 edn., Vol. 1). Exploitation can arise out of the creation of new modes of consumption and the imposition of new social wants and needs—whether or not this exploitation can be interpreted in terms of the surplus value concept or not is a matter of debate (I am inclined to the view that the theory of surplus value ought to be embedded in a general theory of exploitation). But we are on safer ground when we assert that the growing hegemonic power of finance capital over the totality of production, circulation and realization of value in society, produces a dichotomy between work-based and community-based conflict at the same time as it demonstrates its underlying unity.

This view is reinforced when we turn back to the possibility, broached in Section 4, that the processes described in this paper also serve to generate specific "distributive groupings" or "consumption classes" which in turn define community characteristics in housing sub-markets. It is also the case that the production and reproduction of labour power occurs in the community (Giddens, 1973, pp. 109-110; Bunge, 1973). The reproduction of the social relations of capitalism requires the production of a population which, from the standpoint of employment opportunities and the wages system, will ultimately become fragmented into subjective classes, each prepared to take on certain social roles and to acquire certain technical skills, appropriate to its particular position within the overall social structure of a constantly expanding capitalist society. The structure of "consumption classes" and "distributive groupings" may, in this fashion, become related to the production of a stratified labour force. All urban areas exhibit considerable variation in opportunity to acquire education, social status, social services, and the like (to acquire what Giddens calls "market capacity") (1973, pp. 103-110). And while there may be considerable individual mobility, it appears that the structure of sub-markets which we have identified and the distinctive distributive groupings that occupy them, when combined with the differential distribution of resources to acquire market capacity within the urban system,[9] function to reproduce the social relations of labour under capitalism. These social relations achieve a greater stability precisely because communities, differentiated by social relations, become self-replicating. Objective classes have to be defined, therefore, in terms of a totality of the production process which includes (1) the immediate production of value, (2) the production of new modes of consumption, (3) the production of new social wants and needs, (4) the production and reproduction of labour power, and (5) the production and reproduction of the social relations of capitalism.

6. FINANCE CAPITAL AND THE URBAN REVOLUTION—A CONCLUSION

We are now in a position to reflect back upon Lefebvre's fundamental thesis. We can provide a comprehensible inner logic for Lefebvre's "ensemble of transformations" through which industrial society comes to be superseded by urban society. In the early years of capitalism, production in particular (the organization of industrial production) was the main focus of attention. In late capitalism, production in all of its facets predictably becomes more and more important. Since the industrialist is adept at immediate production but has little control over the totality of production, finance capital (operating through industrial, financial and governmental institutions) has emerged as the hegemonic force in advanced capitalist societies. Urbanism has consequently been transformed from an expression of the production needs of the industrialist to an expression of the controlled power of finance capital, backed by the power of the State, over the totality of the production process. Herein lies the significance of urbanization as a mode of consumption and as a producer of new social wants and needs. Concomitantly, the urban realm becomes the locus for the controlled reproduction of the social relations of capitalism. But there also emerges a new definition of objective class interest which is manifest both in work-based and community-based conflicts. In the community these conflicts are over the production of new modes of consumption, new social wants and needs, and over the production and reproduction of both labour power and the social relations of capitalism. It seems, however, that the finance form of capitalism, which has emerged as a response to the inherent contradictions in the competitive industrial form, is itself unstable and beset by contradictory tendencies. Of necessity, it treats money as a "thing in itself" and thereby constantly tends to undermine the production of value in pursuit of the form rather than the substance of wealth. The alien but "transcendental" power of money and the institutions created to facilitate the operation of finance capital are not tied to the production of value and hence we may explain the shift of investment into the secondary circuit of capital at the expense of the primary productive circuit. The perpetual tendency to try to realize value without producing it is, in fact, the central contradiction of the finance form of capitalism. And the tangible manifestations of this central contradiction are writ large in the urban landscapes of the advanced capitalist nations.

The ensemble of transformations of which Lefebvre speaks are far more complex than he imagines. But then so also are the processes of transformation in capitalist society when compared to our ability to grasp them. This complexity cannot be used as an excuse, however, for our almost studied ignorance on the crucial interconnections between the processes of urbanization, economic growth and capitalist accumulation and the structuring of social classes in advanced capitalist societies. This gap in our thinking is quite odd when the literature on the Third World is so explicit in its dealing with these kinds of relationships. It is rather as if we have succumbed to the illusion that because we are both "advanced" and "urbanized" there is no need to examine the crucial relations through which we arrived in our contemporary state and which also serve to sustain us in it. To make these relations more explicit is an urgent task to which this paper seeks to make a modest beginning.

NOTES

I would like to acknowledge the helpful criticism provided in seminars at Darwin College, University of Kent, Department of Planning, The University of Toronto as well as the critical discussion of these ideas by various individuals associated with The Johns Hopkins University or from the Baltimore community.

1. There is an extensive literature on "the transformation problem" most of which is cited in Laibman (1973); the relationship between this transformation and rent is spelled out by Marx (1967 edn., Vol. 3, Chapter 45), and critically examined by Emmanuel (1972).

2. It may be objected to that I am using the concepts "class" and "class interest" far too freely and loosely. In what follows I will use these concepts to refer to any group that has a clearly defined common interest in the struggle to command scarce resources in society. I will use the phrase social class or class structure when referring to more general concepts of class in society. The notion of class-monopoly is made use of by Marx (1967 edn., Vol. 3, pp. 194-195).

3. The term "speculator-developer" is here used generically to refer to all those individuals and institutions that operate in the land and property markets with a view to realizing gains through ultimate sale or change in land use. In practice there may be considerable division of labour in this activity, while different institutions operate under different constraints [see, for example, the difference between entrepreneurs and the relics of the feudal order—the Crown, the Church, etc.—described in CIS Anti-Report on the Property Developers, 1973, *The Recurrent Crisis of London* (London)].

4. The views expressed in this paragraph can be documented in detail from *The Douglas Commission Report* (1968).

5. More detail is provided in Harvey and Chatterjee, (1974).

6. *Ibid*.

7. The details of this are explained in Grigsby *et al*. (1971, Chapter 6).

8. For comparable materials on London see, for example, Hall *et al* (1973), *The Milner-Holland Report* (1965), Pahl (1970), C.I.S. (1973) and Marriott (1967). The point here is, of course, that the large number of vacant houses in the centre of Baltimore is a vivid contrast with the situation in London; but the process of "gentrification" in London is as much a manifestation of the process of realizing class-monopoly rent as is the land-installment contract and speculation with the D2's in Baltimore.

9. For more on these points, see Harvey (1973, Chapter 2).

REFERENCES

Barnbrock, J. (1974) Prologomenon to a debate on location theory: The case of Von Thunen, *Antipode* 6 (No.1), 59-66.

Boyer, B.D. (1973) *Cities Destroyed for Cash*. New York.

Bunge, W. (1973) The point of reproduction (unpublished). Department of Geography, York University, Ontario, Canada.

Chatterjee, L. (1973) Real Estate Investment and Deterioration of Housing in Baltimore, Ph.D. Dissertation, Department of Geography and Environmental Engineering, The Johns Hopkins University, Baltimore.

C.I.S. (1973) Anti-Report on the Property Developers, *The Recurrent Crisis of London*.

Douglas Commission Report (1968) *Building the American City.* Washington, D.C.
Emmanuel, A. (1972) *Unequal Exchange: A Study of the Imperialism of Trade.* New York.
Firey, W. (1960) *Man, Mind and the Land. A Theory of Resource Use.* Glencoe, Illinois.
Gaffney, M. (1973) Releasing land to serve demand via fiscal disaggregation, in Clawson, M. (ed.), *Modernizing Urban Land Use Policy.* Washington, D.C.
Giddens, A. (1973) *The Class Structure of the Advanced Societies.* London.
Grigsby, W., Rosenberg, L., Stegman, M. and Taylore, J. (1971) *Housing and Poverty*, Chapter 6. Institute for Environmental Studies, University of Pennsylvania, Philadelphia.
Hall, P., Gracey, H., Drewett, R. and Thomas, R. (1973) *The Containment of Urban England*, Vol. 2, Chapter 6. London.
Harvey, D. (1973) *Social Justice and the City*, Chapter 2. London.
Harvey, D. and Chatterjee, L. (1974) Absolute rent and the structuring of space by financial institutions, *Antipode* 6 (No. 1), 22-36.
Herman, E. (1973) Do bankers control corporations? *Monthly Rev.* 25 (No. 2), pp. 12-29.
Keiper, J.S., Kurnow, E., Clark, C.D. and Segal, H.H. (1961) *Theory and Measurement of Rent.* Philadelphia.
Laibman, D. (1973) Values and prices of production: the political economy of the transformation problem, *Science and Society* 37, 404-436.
Lefebvre, H. (1970) *La Revolution Urbaine*, p. 13. Paris.
Marriott, O. (1967) *The Property Boom.* London.
Marx, K. (1967 edn.) *Capital* (Three Volumes). International Publishers, New York.
Marx, K. (1968 edn.) *Theories of Surplus Value*, Part 2, p. 44. Moscow.
Marx, K. (1973 edn.) *The Grundrisse*, p. 146. Penguin, Harmondsworth.
Miliband, R. (1969) *The State in Capitalist Society.* London.
Milner-Holland Report (1965) *Report of the Committee on Housing in Greater London.* H.M.S.O., Cmnd. 2605. London.
Neutze, M. (1968) *The Suburban Apartment Boom.* Baltimore.
Pahl, R.E. (1970) *Whose City?* London.
Rex, J. and Moore, R. (1967) *Race, Community and Conflict.* London.
Spoehr, A. (1956) Cultural differences in the interpretation of natural resources, in Thomas, W. (ed.). *Man's Role in Changing the Face of the Earth.* Chicago.
Sternlieb, G. (1966) *The Tenement Landlord.* New Brunswick, New Jersey.
United States House of Representatives (1968) Committee on Banking (Staff Report), *Trust Banking in the United States* (The Wright-Patman Report). Washington, D.C.
United States House of Representatives (1971) Judiciary Committee (Staff Report), *Report on Conglomerates.* Washington, D.C.
Walker, R.A. (1974) Urban ground rent: Building a new conceptual framework, *Antipode* 6 (no.1), 51-58.
Wicksteed, P.H. (1894) *The Co-ordination of the Laws of Distribution.* London.

16

Toward A Theory of Gentrification: A Back to the City Movement by Capital, Not People

Neil Smith

Following a period of sustained deterioration, many American cities are experiencing the gentrification of select central city neighborhoods. Initial signs of revival during the 1950s intensified in the 1960s, and by the 1970s these had grown into a widespread gentrification movement affecting the majority of the country's older cities.[1] A recent survey by the Urban Land Institute (1976) suggests that close to half the 260 cities with over 50,000 population are experiencing rehabilitation in the inner city areas. Although nationally, gentrification accounts for only a small fraction of new housing starts compared with new construction, the process is very important in (but not restricted to) older northeastern cities.

As the process of gentrification burgeoned so did the literature about it. Most of this literature concerns the contemporary processes or its effects: the socioeconomic and cultural characteristics of inmigrants, displacement, the federal role in redevelopment, benefits to the city, and creation and destruction of community. Little attempt has been made to construct historical explanations of the process, to study causes rather than effects. Instead, explanations are very much taken for granted and fall into two categories: cultural and economic.

Cultural. Popular among revitalization theorists is the notion that young, usually professional, middle-class people have changed their lifestyle. According to Gregory Lipton, these changes have been significant enough to "decrease the relative desirability of single-family, suburban homes"(1977, p. 146). Thus, with a trend toward fewer children, postponed marriages, and a fast rising divorce rate, younger homebuyers and renters are trading in the tarnished dream of their parents for a new dream defined in urban rather than suburban terms. Other researchers emphasize the search for socially distinctive communities as sympathetic environments for individual self-expression (Winters 1978), while still others extend this into a more general argument. In contemporary "post-industrial cities," according to D. Ley, white-collar service occupations supersede blue-collar productive occupations, and this brings with it an emphasis on consumption and amenity not work. Patterns of consumption come to dictate patterns of production; "the values of consumption rather than production guide central city land use decisions" (Ley 1978, p. 11). Inner-city resurgence is an example of this new emphasis on consumption.

Economic. As the cost of newly constructed housing continues to rise and its distance from the city center to increase, the rehabilitation of inner- and central-city structures is seen to be more viable economically. Old but structurally sound properties can be purchased and rehabilitated for less than the cost of a comparable new house. In addition, many researchers stress the high economic cost of commuting—the higher cost of gasoline for private cars and rising fares on public transportation—and the economic benefits of proximity to work.

These conventional hypotheses are by no means mutually exclusive. They are often invoked jointly and share in one vital respect a common perspective—an emphasis on *consumer preference* and the constraints within which these preferences are implemented. This they share with the broader body of neoclassical residential land use theory (Alonso 1964; Muth 1969; Mills 1972). According to the neoclassical theory, suburbanization reflects the preference for space and the increased ability to pay for it due to the reduction of transportational and other constraints. Similarly, gentrification is explained as the result of an alteration of preferences and/or a change in the constraints determining which preferences will or can be implemented. Thus in the media and the research literature alike, the process is viewed as a "back to the city movement." This applies as much to the earlier gentrification projects, such as Philadelphia's Society Hill (accomplished with substantial state assistance under urban renewal legislation), as it does to the later schemes, such as

Baltimore's Federal Hill or Washington's Capitol Hill (mainly private market phenomena of the 1970s). All have become symbolic of a supposed middle- and upper-class pilgrimage back from the suburbs.[2] But as yet it remains an untested if pervasive assumption that the gentrifiers are disillusioned suburbanites. As early as 1966, Herbert Gans declared: "I have seen no study of how many suburbanites were actually brought back by urban-renewal projects" (1968, p. 287). Though this statement was made in evidence before the Ribicoff Committee on the Crisis of the Cities, Gans's challenge seems to have fallen on deaf ears. Only in the late 1970s have such studies begun to be carried out. This paper presents data from Society Hill and other revitalized neighborhoods, examines the significance of these results in terms of the consumer sovereignty theory, and attempts to deepen our theoretical understanding of the causes of gentrification.

A RETURN FROM THE SUBURBS?

Once the location of William Penn's "holy experiment," Society Hill housed Philadelphia's gentry well into the nineteenth century. With industrialization and urban growth, however, its popularity declined, and the gentry together with the rising middle class, moved west to Rittenhouse Square and to the new suburbs in the northwest and across the Schuylkill River. Society Hill deteriorated rapidly, remaining in slum condition until 1959. In that year, an urban renewal plan was implemented.

Within ten years Society Hill was transformed and—"the most historic square mile in the nation" according to Bicentennial advertising—it again housed the city's middle and upper classes. Few authentically restored houses now change hands for less than $125,000. Noting the enthusiasm with which rehabilitation was done, the novelist Nathanial Burt observed that "remodeling old houses is, after all, one of Old Philadelphia's favorite indoor sports, and to be able to remodel and consciously serve the cause of civic revival all at once has gone to the heads of the upper classes like champagne" (1963, pp. 556-57). As this indoor sport caught on, therefore, it became Philadelphia folklore that "there was an upper class return to center city in Society Hill" (Wolf 1975, p. 325). As Burt eloquently explains:

> The renaissance of Society Hill . . . is just one piece in a gigantic jigsaw puzzle which has stirred Philadelphia from its hundred-year sleep, and promises to transform the city completely. This movement, of which the return to Society Hill is a significant part, is generally known as the Philadelphia Renaissance (1963, p. 539).

By June 1962 less than a third of the families purchasing property for rehabilitation were from the suburbs[3] (Greenfield & Co. 1964, p. 192). But since the first people to rehabilitate houses began work in 1960, it was generally expected that the proportion of suburbanites would rise sharply as the area became better publicized and a Society Hill address became a coveted possession. After 1962, however, no data were officially collected. The following table presents data sampled from case files held by The Redevelopment Authority of Philadelphia; the data is for the period up to 1975 (by which time the project was essentially complete) and represents a 17 percent sample of all rehabilitated residences (Table 1).

TABLE 1

The Origin of Rehabilitators in Society Hill, 1964-1975

City	Percent City Dwellers	Percent Suburbanites
Philadelphia Society Hill	72	14
Baltimore Homestead Properties	65.2	27
Washington, D.C. Mount Pleasant	67	18
Capitol Hill	72	15

Source: Baltimore City Department of Housing and Community Development (1977), Gale (1976, 1977).

It would appear from these results that only a small proportion of gentrifiers did in fact return from the suburbs; 14 percent in the case of Society Hill, compared with 72 percent who moved from elsewhere within the city boundaries. A statistical breakdown of this latter group suggests that of previous city dwellers, 37 percent came from Society Hill itself, and 19 percent came from the Rittenhouse Square district. The remainder came from several middle- and upper-class suburbs annexed by the city in the last century—Chestnut Hill, Mt. Airy, Spruce Hill. This suggests a consolidation of upper- and middle-class white residences in the city, not a return from the present day suburbs.[4] Additional data from Baltimore and Washington, D.C. on the percentage of returning suburbanites support the Society Hill data (Table 2).

In Philadelphia and elsewhere an urban renaissance may well be taking place but it is not a significant return from the suburbs as such. This does not disprove the consumer sovereignty hypothesis but suggests some limitations and refinements. Clearly, it is possible—even likely—that younger people who moved to the city for an education and professional training have decided

TABLE 2

The Origin of Rehabilitators in Three Cities

Year	Same Address	Elsewhere in The City	Suburbs	Outside SMSA	Unidentified	Total
1964	5	9	0	0	0	14
1965	3	17	7	0	0	27
1966	1	25	4	0	2	32
1969	1	9	2	0	0	12
1972	1	12	1	2	0	16
1975	0	1	0	0	0	1
Total	11	73	14	2	2	102
Percentage By Origin	11	72	14	2	2	100

against moving back to the suburbs. There is a problem, however, if this is to be taken as a definitive explanation, for gentrification is not simply a North American phenomenon but is also happening in numerous cities throughout Europe (see, for example, Pitt 1977) where the extent of prior middle-class suburbanization is much less and the relation between suburb and inner city is substantially different.[5] Only Ley's (1978) more general societal hypothesis about post-industrial cities is broad enough to account for the process internationally, but the implications of accepting this view are somewhat drastic. If cultural choice and consumer preference really explain gentrification, this amounts either to the hypothesis that individual preferences change in unison not only nationally but internationally—a bleak view of human nature and cultural individuality—or that the overriding constraints are strong enough to obliterate the individuality implied in consumer preference. If the latter is the case, the concept of consumer preference is at best contradictory: a process first conceived in terms of individual consumption preference has now to be explained as resulting from cultural unidimensionality. The concept can be rescued as theoretically viable only if it is used to refer to collective social preference, not individual preference.

This refutation of the neoclassical approach to gentrification is only a summary critique and far from exhaustive. What it suggests, however, is a broader conceptualization of the process, for the gentrifier as consumer is only one of many actors participating in the process. To explain gentrification according to the gentrifier's actions alone, while ignoring the role of builders, developers, landlords, mortgage lenders, government agencies, real estate agents, and tenants, is excessively narrow. A broader theory of gentrification must take the role of producers as well as consumers into account, and when this is done, it appears that the needs of production—in particular the need to earn profit—are a more decisive initiative behind gentrification than consumer preference. This is not to say in some naive way that consumption is the automatic consequence of production, or that consumer preference is a totally passive effect caused by production. Such would be a producer's sovereignty theory, almost as one-sided as its neoclassical counterpart. Rather, the relationship between production and consumption is symbiotic, but it is a symbiosis in which production dominates. Consumer preference and demand for gentrified housing can be created after all, and this is precisely what happened in Society Hill.[6] Although it is of secondary importance in initiating the actual process, and therefore in explaining why gentrification occurred in the first place, consumer preference and demand are of primary importance in determining the final form and character of revitalized areas—the difference between Society Hill, say, and New York's SoHo.

The so-called urban renaissance has been stimulated more by economic than cultural forces. In the decision to rehabilitate an inner city structure, one consumer preference tends to stand out above the others—the preference for profit, or, more accurately, a sound financial investment. Whether or not gentrifiers articulate this preference, it is fundamental, for few would even consider rehabilitation if a financial loss were to be expected. A theory of gentrification must therefore explain why some neighborhoods are profitable to redevelop while others are not. What are the conditions of profitability? Consumer sovereignty explanations took for granted the availability of areas ripe for gentrification when this was precisely what had to be explained.

Before proceeding to a more detailed explanation of the process, it will be useful to step back and examine gentrification in the broader historical and structural context of capital investment and urban development. In particular, the general characteristics of investment in the built environment must be examined.

INVESTMENT IN THE BUILT ENVIRONMENT

In a capitalist economy, land and the improvements built onto it become commodities. As such they boast certain idiosyncrasies of which three are particularly important for this discussion. First, private property rights confer on the owner near-monopoly control over land and improvements, monopoly control over the uses to which a certain space is put.[7] From this condition we can derive the function of ground rent. Second, land and improvements are fixed in space but their value is anything but fixed. Improvements on the land are subject to all the normal influences on their value but with one vital difference. On the one hand, the value of built improvements on a piece of land, as well as on surrounding land, influences the ground rent that landlords can demand; on the other hand, since land and buildings on it are inseparable, the price at which buildings change hands reflects the ground rent level. Meanwhile land, unlike the improvements built on it, "does not require upkeep in order to continue its potential for use" (Harvey 1973, pp. 158-59) and thereby retains its potential value. Third, while land is permanent, the improvements built on it are not, but generally have a very long turnover period in physical as well as value terms. Physical decay is unlikely to claim the life of a building for at least twenty-five years, usually a lot longer, and it may take as long in economic (as opposed to accounting) terms for it to pay back its value. From this we can derive several things: in a well-developed capitalist economy, large initial outlays will be necessary for built environmental investments; financial institutions will therefore play an important role in the urban land market (Harvey 1973, p. 159); and patterns of capital depreciation will be an important variable in determining whether and to what extent a building's sale price reflects the ground rent level. These points will be of central importance in the next section.

In a capitalist economy, profit is the gauge of success, and competition is the mechanism by which success or failure is translated into growth or collapse. All individual enterprises must strive for higher and higher profits to facilitate the accumulation of greater and greater quantities of capital in profitable pursuits. Otherwise they find themselves unable to afford more advanced production methods and therefore fall behind their competitors. Ultimately, this leads either to bankruptcy or a merger into a larger enterprise. This search for increased profits translates, at the scale of the whole economy, into the long-run economic growth; general economic stability is therefore synonymous with overall economic growth. Particularly when economic growth is hindered elsewhere in the industrial sector, the built environment becomes a target for much profitable investment, as is particularly apparent with this century's suburbanization experience. In this case, spatial expansion rather than expansion *in situ* was the response to the continual need for capital accumulation. But suburbanization illustrates well the two-sided nature of investment in the built environment, for as well as being a vehicle for capital accumulation, it can also become a barrier to further accumulation. It becomes so by dint of the characteristics noted above: near-monopoly control of space, the fixity of investments, the long turnover period. Near-monopoly control of space by landowners may prevent the sale of land for development; the fixity of investments forces new development to take place at other, often less advantageous, locations, and prevents redevelopment from occurring until invested capital has lived out its economic life; the long turnover period of capital invested in the built environment can discourage investment as long as other sectors of the economy with shorter turnover periods remain profitable. The early industrial city presented just such a barrier by the later part of the nineteenth century, eventually prompting suburban development rather than development *in situ*.

During the nineteenth century in most eastern cities, land values displayed the classical conical form—a peak at the urban center, with a declining gradient on all sides toward the periphery. This was the pattern Hoyt (1933) found in Chicago. With continued urban development the land value gradient is displaced outward and upward; land at the center grows in value while the base of the cone broadens. Land values tend to change in unison with long cycles in the economy; they increase most rapidly during periods of particularly rapid capital accumulation and decline temporarily during slumps. Since suburbanization relied on the considerable capital investments in land, construction, transportation, etc., it too tended to follow this cyclical trend. Faced with the need to expand the scale of their productive activities, and unable or unwilling for a variety of reasons to expand any further where they were, industries jumped out beyond the city to the base of the land value cone where extensive spatial expansion was both possible and relatively cheap. The alternative—substantial renewal and redevelopment of the already built up area—would have been too costly for private capital to undertake, and so industrial capital was increasingly sent to the suburbs. This movement of industrial capital began in force after the severe depression of 1893-97, and was followed by a substantial migration of capital for residential construction. In the already well-established cities, the only significant exception to this migration of construction capital was in the central business district (CBD) where substantial skyscraper office development occurred in the 1920s. As will be shown, the inner city was adversely affected by this movement of capital to the suburbs where higher returns were available. A combination of neglect and concerted disinvestment by investors, due to high risk and low rates of return, initiated a long period of deterioration and a lack of new capital investment in the inner city.

Land values in the inner city fell relative to the CBD and the suburbs, and by the late 1920s Hoyt could identify for Chicago a newly formed "valley in the land-value curve between the Loop and outer residential areas" (see Figure 1). This valley "indicates the location of these sections where the buildings are mostly over forty years old and where the residents rank lowest in rent-paying ability" (Hoyt 1933, pp. 356-8). Throughout the decades of most sustained suburbanization, from the 1940s to the 1960s, this valley in the land value curve deepened and broadened due to a continued lack of productive capital investment. By the late 1960s the valley may have been as much as six miles wide in Chicago (McDonald and Bowman 1979). Evidence from other cities suggests that this capital depreciation and consequent broadening of the land value valley occurred throughout the country's older cities (Davis 1965; Edel and Sclar 1975), producing the slums and ghettos that were suddenly discovered as "problems" in the 1960s by the long gone suburban middle class.

FIGURE 1

**The Evolution of Land Values in Chicago
(After Hoyt 1933)**

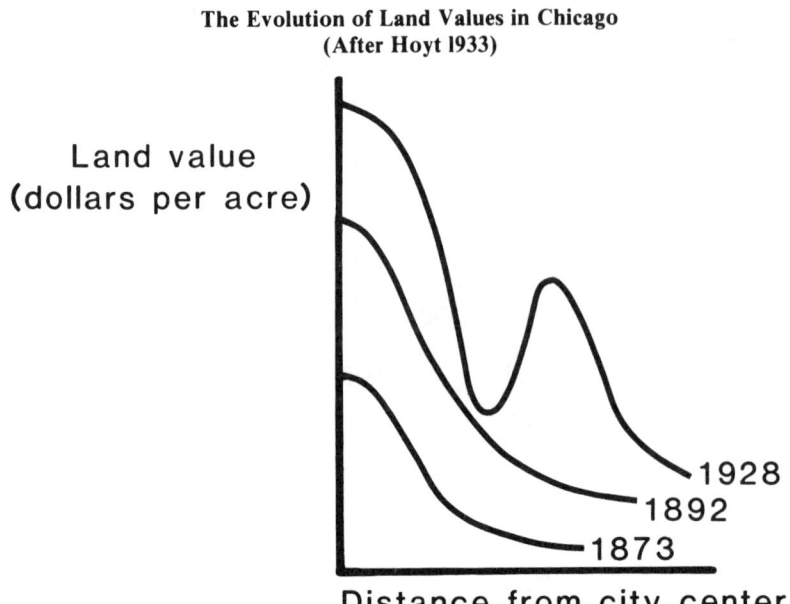

A theory of gentrification will need to explain the detailed historical mechanisms of capital depreciation in the inner city and the precise way in which this depreciation produces the possibility of profitable reinvestment. The crucial nexus here is the relationship between land value and property value. As they stand, however, these concepts are insufficiently refined. Land value for Hoyt, was a composite category referring to the price of undeveloped plots and the expected future income from their use; the type of future use was simply assumed. Property value, on the other hand, is generally taken to mean the price at which a building is sold, including the value of the land. To elaborate the relationship between land value and the value of buildings in fuller detail, then, it will be necessary to disaggregate these two measures of value into four separate but related categories. These four categories (house value, sale price, capitalized ground rent, potential ground rent) remain fully or partially obscure and indistinguishable under the umbrella concepts land value and property value.

House Value. Consistent with its emphasis on consumer preference, neoclassical economic theory explains prices as the result of supply and demand conditions. But if, as suggested above, the search for a high return on productive investments is the primary initiative behind gentrification, then the specific costs of production (not just the quantity of end-product—supply) will be central in the determination of prices. In opposition to neoclassical theory, therefore, it will be necessary to separate the value of a house from its price. Following the classical political economists (Smith, Ricardo), and after them Marx, this paper takes as axiomatic a labor theory of value: the value of a commodity is measured by the quantity of socially necessary labor power required to produce it. Only in the market place is value translated into price. And although the price of a house reflects its value, the two cannot mechanically be equated since price is also affected by supply and demand conditions. Thus, value considerations (the amount of socially necessary labor power) set the level about which the price fluctuates. With housing, the situation is more complex because individual houses return periodically to the market for resale. The house's value will also depend, therefore, on its rate of depreciation through use, versus its rate of appreciation through the addition of more value. The latter occurs when further labor is performed for maintenance, replacement, extensions, etc.

Sale Price. A further complication with housing is that the sale price represents not only the value of the house, but an additional component for rent since the land is generally sold along with the structures it accommodates. Here it is preferable to talk of ground rent rather than land value, since the price of land does not reflect a quantity of labor power applied to it, as with the value of commodities proper.

Ground Rent and Capitalized Ground Rent. Ground rent is a claim made by landowners on users of their land; it represents a reduction from the surplus value created over and above cost-price by producers on the site. Capitalized ground rent is the actual quantity of ground rent that is appropriated by the landowner, given the present land use. In the case of rental housing where the landlord produces a service on land he or she owns, the production and ownership functions are combined and ground rent becomes even more of an intangible category though nevertheless a real presence; the landlord's capitalized ground rent returns mainly in the form of house rent paid by the tenants. In the case of owner occupancy, ground rent is capitalized when the building is sold and therefore appears as part of the sale price. Thus, sale price = house value + capitalized ground rent.

Potential Ground Rent. Under its present land use, a site or neighborhood is able to capitalize a certain quantity of ground rent. For reasons of location, usually, such an area may be able to capitalize higher quantities of ground rent under a different land use. Potential ground rent is the amount that could be capitalized under the land's "highest and best use." This concept is particularly important in explaining gentrification.

Using these concepts, the historical process that has made certain neighborhoods ripe for gentrification can be outlined.

CAPITAL DEPRECIATION IN THE INNER CITY

The physical deterioration and economic depreciation of inner-city neighborhoods is a strictly logical "rational" outcome of the operation of the land and housing market. This is not to suggest it is at all natural, however, for the market itself is a social product. Far from being inevitable, neighborhood decline is

> the result of identifiable private and public investment decisions... While there is no Napoleon who sits in a position of control over the fate of a neighborhood, there is enough control by, and integration of, the investment and development actors of the real estate industry that their decisions go beyond a response and actually shape the market (Bradford and Rubinowitz 1975, p. 79).

What follows is a rather schematic attempt to explain the historical decline of inner-city neighborhoods in terms of the institutions, actors, and economic forces involved. It requires the identification of a few salient processes that characterize the different stages of decline, but is not meant as a definitive description of what every neighborhood experiences. The day-to-day dynamics of decline are complex and, as regards the relationship between landlords and tenants in particular, have been examined in considerable detail elsewhere (Stegman 1972). This schema is, however, meant to provide a general explanatory framework within which each neighborhood's concrete experience can be understood. It is assumed from the start that the neighborhoods concerned are relatively homogeneous as regards the age and quality of housing, and, indeed, this tends to be the case with areas experiencing redevelopment.

1. New Construction and the First Cycle of Use

When a neighborhood is newly built the price of housing reflects the value of the structure and improvements put in place plus the enhanced ground rent captured by the previous landowner. During the first cycle of use, the ground rent is likely to increase as urban development continues outward, and the house value will only very slowly begin to decline if at all. The sale price therefore rises. But eventually sustained depreciation of the house value occurs and this has three sources: advances in the productiveness of labor, style obsolescence, and physical wear and tear. Advances in the productiveness of labor are chiefly due to technological innovation and changes in the organization of the work process. These advances allow a similar structure to be produced at a lower value than would otherwise have been possible. Truss frame construction and the factory fabrication of parts in general, rather than on-site construction, are only the most recent examples of such advances. Style obsolescence is secondary as a stimulus for sustained depreciation in the housing market and may occasionally induce an appreciation of value, many old styles being more sought after than the new. Physical wear and tear also affects the value of housing, but it is necessary here to distinguish between minor repairs which must be performed regularly if a house is to retain its value (e.g., painting doors and window frames, interior decorating), major repairs which are performed less regularly but require greater outlays (e.g., replacing the plumbing or electrical systems), and structural repairs without which the structure becomes unsound (e.g., replacing a roof, replacing floor boards that have dry rot). Depreciation of a property's value after one cycle of use reflects the imminent need not only for regular, minor repairs but also for a succession of more major repairs involving a substantial investment. Depreciation will induce a price decrease relative to new housing but the extent of this decrease will depend on how much the ground rent has also changed in the meantime.

2. Landlordism and Homeownership

Clearly the inhabitants in many neighborhoods succeed in making major repairs and maintaining or even enhancing the value of the area's housing. These areas remain stable. Equally clearly, there are areas of owner-occupied housing which experience initial depreciation. Homeowners, aware of imminent decline unless repairs are made, are likely to sell out and seek newer homes where their investment will be safer. At this point, after a first or subsequent cycle of use, there is a tendency for the neighborhood to convert to rental tenancy unless repairs are made. And since landlords use buildings for different purposes than owner occupiers, a different pattern of maintenance will ensue. Owner occupiers in the housing market are simultaneously both consumers and investors; as investors, their primary return comes as the increment of sale price over purchase price. The landlord, on the other hand, receives his return mainly in the form of house rent, and under certain conditions may have a lesser incentive for carrying out repairs so long as he can still command rent. This is not to say that landlords typically undermaintain properties they possess: newer apartment complexes and even older accommodations for which demand is high may be very well maintained. But as Ira Lowry has indicated, "undermaintenance is an eminently reasonable response of a landlord to a declining market" (1960, p. 367), and since the transition from owner occupancy to tenancy is generally associated with a declining market, some degree of undermaintenance can be expected.

Undermaintenance will yield surplus capital to be invested elsewhere. It may be invested in other city properties, it may follow developers' capital out to the suburbs, or it may be invested in some other sector of the economy. With sustained undermaintenance in a neighborhood, however, it may become difficult for landlords to sell their properties, particularly since the large financial institutions will now be less forthcoming with mortgage funds;

sales become fewer and more expensive to the landlord. Thus, there is even less incentive to invest in the area beyond what is necessary to retain the present revenue flow. This pattern of decline is likely to be reversed only if a shortage of higher quality accommodations occurs, allowing rents to be raised and making improved maintenance worthwhile. Otherwise, the area is likely to experience a net outflow of capital, which will be small at first since landlords still have substantial investments to protect. Under these conditions it becomes very difficult for the individual landlord or owner to struggle against this decline. House values are falling and the levels of capitalized ground rent for the area are dropping below the potential ground rent (see Figure 2.). The individual who did not undermaintain his property would be forced to charge higher than average rent for the area with little hope of attracting tenants earning higher than average income which would capitalize the full ground rent. This is the celebrated "neighborhood effect" and operates through the rent structure.

FIGURE 2

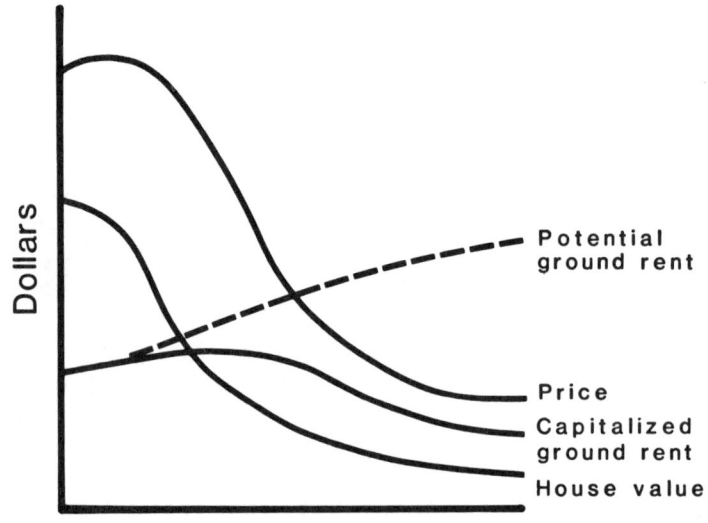

The Depreciation Cycle of Inner-City Neighborhoods

3. Blockbusting and Blow Out

Some neighborhoods may not transfer to rental tenancy and they will experience relative stability or a gentler continuation of decline. If the latter occurs, it is the owner occupants who undermaintain, though usually out of financial constraints rather than market strategy. With blockbusting, this decline is intensified. Real estate agents exploit racist sentiments in white neighborhoods that are experiencing declining sale prices; they buy houses relatively cheaply, and then resell at a considerable markup to black families, many of whom are desperate to own their first home. As Laurenti's research suggests, property values are usually declining before blockbusting takes place and do not begin declining simply as a result of racial changes in ownership (Laurenti 1960). Once block busting has taken place, however, further decline in house values is likely due to the inflated prices at which houses were sold and the consequent lack of resources for maintenance and mortgage payments suffered by incoming families. Blow out, a similar process, operates without the helping hand of real estate agents. Describing the process as it operated in the Baltimore housing market during the 1960s, Harvey et al. (1972; see also Harvey 1973, p. 173) point to the outward spread of slums from the inner city (the broadening of the land value valley) and the consequent squeezing of still healthy outer neighborhoods against secure upper middle-class residential enclaves lying further out. Thus squeezed, owner occupants in an entire neighborhood are likely to sell out, often to landlords, and flee to the suburbs.

4. Redlining

Undermaintenance gives way to more active disinvestment as capital depreciates further and the landlord's stake diminishes; house value and capitalized ground rent fall, producing further decreases in sale price. Disinvestment by landlords is accompanied by an equally "rational" disinvestment by financial institutions which cease supplying mortgage money to the area. Larger institutions offering low downpayment, low interest rate loans find they can make higher returns in the suburbs with a lower chance of foreclosure and less risk of declining property values. Their role in the inner city is taken over initially by smaller, often local organizations specializing in higher risk financing. Redlined by larger institutions, the area may also receive loans insured by the FHA. Though meant to prevent decline, FHA loans have often been ineffectual and have even contributed to decline in places (Bradford and Rubinowitz 1975, p. 82). The loans allow properties to change hands but do little to encourage reinvestment in maintenance so the process of decline is simply lubricated. Ultimately, medium and small-scale investors also refuse to work the area, as do mortgage insurers.

Vandalism further accelerates depreciation and becomes a problem especially when properties are temporarily vacant between tenants (Stegman 1972, p. 60). Even when occupied, however, it may be a problem, especially if a building is being undermaintained or systematically "milked." Subdivision of structures to yield more rental units is common at this stage. By subdividing, the landlord hopes to intensify the building's use (and profitability) in its last few years. But eventually landlords will disinvest totally, refusing to make repairs and paying only the necessary costs —and then often only sporadically—for the building to yield rent.

5. Abandonment

When landlords can no longer collect enough house rent to cover the necessary costs (utilities and taxes), buildings are abandoned. This is a neighborhood phenomenon, not something that strikes isolated properties in otherwise stable areas. Much abandoned housing is structurally sound and this seems paradoxical. But then buildings are abandoned not because they are unuseable, but because they cannot be used *profitably*. The final act of abandonment may be triggered (but not caused) by a variety of events, including the strict enforcement of the building code by the city housing department. Also at this stage of decline, there is a certain incentive for landlords to destroy their own property through arson and collect the substantial insurance payment.

GENTRIFICATION—THE RENT GAP

The previous section presented a summary explanation of the process commonly but misleadingly referred to as filtering. It is a common process in the housing market and affects many neighborhoods but is by no means universal. It is included here precisely because gentrification is almost always preceded by filtering, although the process need not occur fully for gentrification to ensue. Nor should this decline be thought of as inevitable. As Lowry quite correctly insists, filtering is not due simply "to the relentless passage of time" but to "human agency" (1960, p. 370). The previous section has suggested who some of these agents are, and the market forces they both react to and help create. That section also suggests that the objective mechanism underlying filtering is the depreciation and devaluation of capital invested in residential inner-city neighborhoods. This depreciation produces the objective economic conditions that make capital *revaluation* (gentrification) a rational market response. Of fundamental importance here is what I call the rent gap.

The rent gap is the disparity between the potential ground rent level and the actual ground rent capitalized under the present land use (see Figure 2). In the case of filtering, the rent gap is produced primarily by capital depreciation (which diminishes the proportion of the ground rent able to be capitalized) and also by continued urban development and expansion (which has historically raised the potential ground rent level in the inner city). The valley which Hoyt detected in his 1928 observation of land values can now be understood in large part as the rent gap. Only when this gap emerges can redevelopment be expected since if the present use succeeded in capitalizing all or most of the ground rent, little economic benefit could be derived from redevelopment. As filtering and neighborhood decline proceed, the rent gap widens. Gentrification occurs when the gap is wide enough that developers can purchase shells cheaply, can pay the builders' costs and profit for rehabilitation, can pay interest on mortgage and construction loans, and can then sell the end product for a sale price that leaves a satisfactory return to the developer. The entire ground rent, or a large portion of it, is now capitalized; the neighborhood has been "recycled" and begins a new cycle of use.

Once the rent gap is wide enough, gentrification may be initiated in a given neighborhood by several different actors in the land and housing market. And here we come back to the relationship between production and consumption, for the empirical evidence suggests strongly that the process is initiated not by the exercise of those individual consumer preferences much beloved of neoclassical economists, but by some form of collective social action[8] at the neighborhood level. The state, for example, initiated most if not all of the early schemes, and though it plays a lesser role today, is still important. More commonly today, with private market gentrification, one or more financial institutions will reverse a long standing redlining policy and actively target a neighborhood as a potential market for construction loans and mortgages. All the consumer preference in the world will amount to nought unless this long absent source of funding reappears; mortgage capital is a prerequisite. Of course, this mortgage capital must be borrowed by willing consumers exercising some preference or another. But these preferences are not prerequisites since they can be socially created, as was seen above. Along with financial institutions, professional developers have acted as the collective initiative behind gentrification. A developer will purchase a substantial proportion of the properties in a neighborhood, rehabilitate them, then sell them for profit. The only significant exception to this predominance of collective action occurs in neighborhoods adjacent to already gentrified areas. There indeed, individual gentrifiers may be very important in initiating rehabilitation. Their decision to rehabilitate followed the results from the previous neighborhood, however, which implies that a sound financial investment was uppermost in their minds. And they still require mortgage capital from willing institutions.

Three kinds of developers typically operate in recycling neighborhoods: (a) professional developers who purchase property, redevelop it, and resell for profit; (b) occupier developers who buy and redevelop property and inhabit it after completion; (c) landlord developers who rent it to tenants after rehabilitation.[9] The developer's return on investment comes as part of the completed property's sale price; for the landlord developer it also comes in the form of house rent. Two separate gains comprise the return achieved through sale: capitalization of enhanced ground rent, and profit (quite distinct from builder's profit) on the investment of productive capital (see Smith 1979). Professional and landlord developers are important—contrary to the public image, they were by far the majority in Society Hill—but occupier developers are more active in rehabilitation than they are in any other sector of housing construction. Perhaps the main reason for this can be traced to the very nature of gentrification and the characteristics of investment in the built environment discussed above. Urban renewal, like rehabilitation, occurs where a rent gap has been opened up, but in the case of renewal either the dilapidated stock is unsound structurally, or the remaining structures are unsuitable for new uses. While the technical and spatial requirements for industrial and commercial buildings have altered substantially in the last hundred years, those for residences have not, and structurally sound town houses are quite useable given the right economic conditions. But since the land has already been developed and an intricate pattern of property rights laid down, it is difficult for the professional developer to assemble sufficient land and properties to make involvement worthwhile. Even landlord developers tended to be rehabilitating several properties simultaneously or in sequence. The fragmented structure of property ownership has made the occupier developer, who is generally an inefficient operator in the construction industry, into an appropriate vehicle for recycling devalued neighborhoods.

Viewed in this way, gentrification is not a chance occurrence or an inexplicable reversal of some inevitable filtering process. On the contrary, it is to be expected. The depreciation of capital in nineteenth century inner-city neighborhoods, together with continued urban growth during the first half of the twentieth century, have combined to produce conditions in which profitable reinvestment is possible. If this rent gap theory of gentrification is correct, it would be expected that rehabilitation began where the gap was greatest and the highest returns available, i.e., in neighborhoods particularly close to the city center and in neighborhoods where the sequence of declining values had pretty much run its course. Empirically, this seems to have been the case. The theory also suggests that as these first areas are recycled, other areas offering lower but still substantial returns would be sought out by developers. This would involve areas further from the city center and areas where decline was less advanced. Thus in Philadelphia, Fairmount and Queen Village are the new "hot spots" (Cybriwsky 1978; Levy 1978), and the city's triage policy for allocating block grant funds makes part of North Philadelphia a likely candidate for future redevelopment.

The state's role in earlier rehabilitation schemes is worthy of note. By assembling properties at fair market value and returning them to developers at the lower assessed price the state accomplished and bore the costs of the last stages of capital devaluation, thereby ensuring that developers could reap the high returns without which redevelopment would not occur. Today, with the state less involved in this process, developers are clearly able to absorb the costs of devaluing capital that has not yet fully depreciated. That is, they can pay a relatively high price for properties to be rehabilitated, and still make a reasonable return. It seems, then, that the state has been successful in providing the conditions that would stimulate private market revitalization.

To summarize the theory, gentrification is a structural product of the land and housing markets. Capital flows where the rate of return is highest, and the movement of capital to the suburbs along with the continual depreciation of inner-city capital, eventually produces the rent gap. When this gap grows sufficiently large, rehabilitation (or for that matter, renewal) can begin to challenge the rates of return available elsewhere, and capital flows back.

CONCLUSION

Gentrification has demonstrated that contrary to the conventional wisdom, middle- and upper-class housing is capable of intensive land use. Just how intensive is not clear, however. There is significant evidence that the once steep rent gradient (see Figure 1) is flattening out (Yeates 1965, Edel and Sclar 1975); and if this is the case, potential ground rent in inner-city neighborhoods may actually have decreased, presumably due to efficient transportation links to the suburbs and excessive crowding downtown. What this might mean for gentrification or for the commercial and recreational redevelopment that is also happening in some cities ought to be a topic for further research. Another topic for empirical investigation is the extent to which capital depreciation must occur in an area before gentrification can occur. This all assumes the filtering process to be the fundamental source of the rent gap, and while this is certainly so in the U.S. it may not be elsewhere. Although capital depreciation and filtering prepared the way for gentrification in Islington (Pitt 1977), in general, one would not expect it to be so prevalent in the U.K. housing market where much working class housing is produced by local government action, not the private market. In this case, rising ground rent levels due to urban expansion and development may be more important in accounting for the rent gap.

Gentrification is a back to the city movement all right, but of capital rather than people. The people taking advantage of this returning capital are still, as yet, from the city. If the city continues to attract productive capital (whether for residential or other construction) we may witness a fundamental restructuring of urban space comparable with suburbanization. Then, indeed, it would become a back to the city movement by people too—middle-and upper-class people, that is—while the working class and the poor would inherit the old declining suburbs in a cruelly ironic continuation of the filtering process. They would then be trapped in the suburbs, not the inner city. As was emphasized in the discussion of suburbanization, investment in the built environment is a major vehicle for capital accumulation. This process is cyclical and, because of the long life and fixity of such investments, new cycles of investment are often associated with crises and switches of the location of accumulation (Harvey 1978). Seen in this context, gentrification and other kinds of urban renaissance could be the leading edge (but in no way the cause) of a larger restructuring of space. According to one scenario this restructuring would be accomplished according to the needs of capital; a restructuring of middle-class culture may well accompany and influence it, but would be secondary. According to a second scenario, the needs of capital would be systematically dismantled, to be displaced by the social, economic, and cultural needs of people as the principle according to which the restructuring of space occurs.

NOTES

An earlier version of this paper was presented at the Annual Conference of the Association of American Geographers in Philadelphia, April 25th, 1979. Special thanks are due to Michele LeFaivre for her critical reading of the paper.

1. Gentrification is the process of converting working class areas into middle-class neighborhoods through the rehabilitation of the neighborhood's housing stock.

2. That the earlier projects required substantial state initiative and subsidy did not exclude them from being explained in terms of consumer preference. In Philadelphia, for example, the Greater Philadelphia Movement (GPM) was responsible for getting the state to implement Society Hill's renewal plan, and it consistently claimed that the demand to revitalize was ever-present but the cost constraints and risk were too great for private capital and individuals. It was the responsibility of the state, they argued, to use the available federal legislation to subsidize the project, thereby removing the constraints and serving a broader civic cause. On GPM's role in Society Hill, see Adde (1969, pp. 33-6). For the purposes of this paper, I am distinguishing between gentrification and urban renewal not according to whether the process is privately or publicly funded, but according to whether it is a rehabilitation process or purely new construction. As should become clear from the main argument of the paper, the distinction between public and private funding simply represents (in this context) two different mechanisms for carrying out the one essential process.

3. By suburbs I mean here the area outside the present city boundary but inside the SMSA. The older suburbs that now appear inside the city due to consequent annexations are therefore counted as sections of the city. This definition is justified here since one of the main selling points of gentrification is that it will bring additional tax revenues to the city. Clearly, annexed suburbs already pay their taxes to the city.

4. This kind of consolidation may be experienced by other cities. Several of the cities examined by Lipton (1977) display a similar consolidation.

5. For further discussion of the cross-Atlantic comparison, see Smith (1979).

6. Advertising is a primary means of creating demand. In Society Hill, the Old Philadelphia Development Corporation employed a Madison Avenue professional to sell the project (Old Philadelphia Development Corporation 1970).

7. Certainly zoning, eminent domain, and other state regulations put significant limits on the landowner's control of land, but in North America and Western Europe, these limitations are little more than cosmetic. Within these limitations, the property market continues to operate quite freely.

8. By "collective social action" I mean simply activity that is carried on jointly and simultaneously by people, not by individuals acting alone.

9. I omit speculators here for the obvious reason that they invest no productive capital. They simply buy property in the hope of selling it at a higher price to developers. Speculators do not produce any transformation in the urban structure.

REFERENCES

Adde, L. 1969. *Nine cities: anatomy of downtown renewal.* Washington, D.C.: Urban Land Institute.

Alonso, W. 1964. *Location and land use.* Cambridge: Harvard University Press.

Baltimore City Department of Housing and Community Development, 1977. *Homesteading —the third year, 1976.* Baltimore: the Department.

Bradford, C. P., and Rubinowitz, L.S. 1975. The urban-suburban investment-disinvestment process: consequences for older neighborhoods. *Annals of the American Academy of Political and Social Science* 422, November: 77-86.

Burt, N. 1963. *The perennial Philadelphians.* London: Dent & Son.

Cybriwsky, R.A. 1978. Social aspects of neighborhood change. *Annals of the Association of American Geographers* 68, March: 17-33.

Davis, J.T. 1965. Middle class housing in the central city. *Economic Geography* 41, July: 238-51.

Edel, M., and Sclar, E. 1975. The distribution of real estate value changes: metropolitan Boston, 1870-1970. *Journal of Urban Economics* 2: 366-87.

Gale, D.E. 1976. The back-to-the-city movement . . . or is it? Occasional Paper, Department of Urban and Regional Planning, George Washington University.

Gale, D.E. 1977. The back-to-the-city movement revisited. Occasional Paper, Department of Urban and Regional Planning. The George Washington University.

Gans, H. 1968. *People and plans.* New York: Basic Books.

Greenfield, A.M. & Co. 1964. New town houses for Washington Square East: a technical report on neighborhood conservation. Prepared for the Redevelopment Authority of Philadelphia.

Harvey, D. 1973. *Social justice and the city.* Baltimore: Johns Hopkins University Press.

Harvey, D. 1978. The urban process under capitalism: a framework for analysis. *International Journal of Urban and Regional Research* 2: 101-131.

Harvey, D. et al. 1972: *The housing market and code enforcement in Baltimore.* Baltimore: City Planning Department.

Hoyt, H. 1933. *One hundred years of land values in Chicago.* Chicago: University of Chicago Press.

Laurenti, L. 1960. *Property values and race.* Berkeley: University of California Press.

Levy, P. 1978. *Queen Village: the eclipse of community.* Philadelphia: Institute for the Study of Civic Values.

Ley, D. 1978. *Inner city resurgence and its societal context.* Paper presented to the Association of American Geographers Annual Conference, New Orleans.

Lipton, S.G. 1977. *Evidence of central city revival.* Journal of the American Institute of Planners 43, April: 136-47.

Lowry, I.S. 1960. Filtering and housing costs: a conceptual analysis. *Land Economics* 36: 362-70.

McDonald, J.F. and Bowman, H.W. 1979. Land value functions: a reevaluation. *Journal of Urban Economics* 6: 25-41.

Mills, E.S. 1972. *Studies in the structure of the urban economy.* Baltimore: Johns Hopkins University Press.

Muth, R. 1969. *Cities and housing.* Chicago: University of Chicago Press.

Old Philadelphia Development Corporation. 1975. Statistics on Society Hill. Unpublished report.

Pitt, J. 1977. *Gentrification in Islington*. London: Barnsbury Peoples Forum.
Smith, N. 1979 (forthcoming). Gentrification and capital: theory, practice and ideology in Society Hill, *Antipode* 11.
Stegman, M.A. 1972. *Housing investment in the inner city: the dynamics of decline*. Cambridge: MIT Press.
Urban Land Institute. 1976. *New opportunities for residential development in central cities*. Report No. 25. Washington, D.C.: The Institute.
Winters, C. 1978. Rejuvenation with character. Paper presented to the Association of American Geographers Annual Conference, New Orleans.
Wolf, E. 1975. *Philadelphia: portrait of an American city*. Harrisburg; Stackpole Books.
Yeates, M.H. 1965. Some factors affecting the spatial distribution of Chicago land values, 1910-1960. *Economic Geography* 41, 1: 57-70.

Suggestions for Further Reading

GENERAL OVERVIEWS

Bassett, Keith and Short, John. *Housing and Residential Structure: Alternative Approaches* (London: Routledge and Kegan Paul, 1980).

Bater, J.H. *The Soviet City: Ideal and Reality* (Beverly Hills, CA: Sage, 1980).

Berry, Brian J.L. *Comparative Urbanization: Divergent Paths in the Twentieth Century* (New York: St. Martin's Press, 1982).

Bourne, Larry S. *The Geography of Housing* (New York: John Wiley, 1981).

Bourne, Larry S. "Alternative perspectives on urban decline and population deconcentration," *Urban Geography*, Vol. 1 (January-March 1980) 39-52.

Bunting, Trudi and Guelke, Leonard. "Behavioral and perception geography: a critical appraisal," *Annals of the Association of American Geographers*, Vol. 69 (September 1979) 448-462.

Castells, Manuel. "Is there an urban sociology?" in C.G. Pickvance (ed.), *Urban Sociology: Critical Essays* (New York: St. Martin's Press, 1976), pp. 33-59.

Duncan, S.S. "Housing policy, the methodology of levels, and urban research: the case of Castells," *International Journal of Urban and Regional Research*, Vol. 5 (1981) 213-254.

Duncan, S.S. "Research directions in social geography: housing opportunities and constraints," *Transactions of the Institute of British Geographers*, Vol. 1 (1976) 10-19.

Eyles, John and Lee, Roger. "Human geography in explanation," *Transactions of the Institute of British Geographers*, Vol. 7 (1982) 117-122.

French, R.A. and Hamilton, F.E. (eds.), *The Socialist City: Spatial Structure and Urban Policy* (New York: John Wiley, 1979).

Gregory, Derek. *Ideology, Science and Human Geography* (New York: St. Martin's Press, 1978).

Harvey, David. *Explanation in Geography* (New York: St. Martin's Press, 1969).

Harvey, Milton E. and Holly, Brian P. *Themes in Geographic Thought* (London: Croom Helm, 1981).

Johnston, R.J. "On the nature of explanation in human geography," *Transactions of the Institute of British Geographers*, Vol. 5 (1980) 402-412.

Johnston, R.J. *Geography and Geographers* (London: Edward Arnold, 1979).

Keat, Russell and Urry, John. *Social Theory as Science* (London: Routledge and Kegan Paul, 1975).

Kuhn, Thomas. *The Structure of Scientific Revolutions* (Chicago: University of Chicago Press, 1970).

Ley, David. "Social geography and the taken-for-granted world," *Transactions of the Institute of British Geographers*, Vol. 2 (1977) 498-512.

Ley, David and Samuels, Marwyn. (eds.) *Humanistic Geography: Prospects and Problems* (Chicago: Maaroufa Press, 1979).

Saunders, Peter. *Social Theory and the Urban Question* (New York: Holmes and Meier, 1981).

Smith, M.P. *The City and Social Theory* (New York: St. Martin's Press, 1979).

Smith, Neil. "Geography, science, and post-positivist modes of explanation," *Progress in Human Geography*, Vol.3 (September 1979) 356-383.

THE NEO-CLASSICAL TRADITION

Alonso, William. *Location and Land Use* (Cambridge, MA: Harvard University Press, 1964).

Alonso, William. "A reformulation of classical location theory and its relation to rent theory," *Papers of the Regional Science Association*, Vol. 14 (1967).

Ball, Michael. "A critique of urban economics," *International Journal of Urban and Regional Research*, Vol. 3 (September 1979) 309-323.

Berry, Brian J.L. "Internal Structure of the City," *Law and Contemporary Problems*, Vol. 30 (1965) 111-119.

Berry, Brian J.L. "Cities as systems within systems of cities," *Papers of the Regional Science Association*, Vol. 13 (1964) 147-163.

Bourne, Larry S. and Hitchcock, J.R. *Urban Housing Markets: Recent Directions in Research and Policy* (Toronto: University of Toronto Press, 1978).

Brigham, Eugene F. "The determinants of residential land values," *Land Economics*, Vol. 41 (1965) 326-334.

Fales, R.L. and Moses, Leon F. "Land use theory and the spatial structure of the 19th Century city," *Papers of the Regional Science Association*, Vol. 28 (1972) 49-80.

Fisch, O. "Dynamics of the housing market," *Journal of Urban Economics*, Vol. 4 (1977) 428-447.

Ingram, Gregory K. (ed.) *Residential Location and Urban Housing Markets* (Cambridge, MA: Ballinger, 1978).

Kain, John F. *Essays on Urban Spatial Structure* (Cambridge, MA: Ballinger, 1975).

McDonald, John F. "An empirical test of a theory of the urban housing market," *Urban Studies*, Vol. 16 (1979) 291-297.

Mieszkowski, Peter and Straszheim, Mahlon. (eds.) *Current Issues in Urban Economics* (Baltimore: Johns Hopkins University Press, 1979).

Moses, Leon F. and Williamson, Harold F. "The location of economic activity in cities," *American Economic Review*, Vol. 57 (1967) 211-222.

Muth, Richard. "Recent developments in the theory of urban spatial structure," in M. Intriligator (ed.), *Frontiers of Quantitative Economics*, Vol. III-B (Amsterdam: North Holland, 1977), pp. 387-397.

Richardson, H.W. *The New Urban Economics: and Alternatives* (London: Pion, Ltd., 1977).

Senior, M.L. "Approaches to residential location modelling: urban economic models and some recent developments," *Environment and Planning*, Vol. 6 (1974) 369-409.

Solow, Robert. "On equilibrium models of urban location," in M. Parkin (ed.), *Essays in Modern Economics* (London: Longman, 1973), pp. 2-16.

Weinberg, Daniel; Friedman, Joseph and Mayo, Stephen K. "Intraurban residential mobility: the role of transaction costs, market imperfections and household disequilibrium," *Journal of Urban Economics*, Vol. 9 (1981) 332-348.

Wendt, Paul F. "Theory of urban land values," *Land Economics*, Vol. 33 (1957) 228-240.

Wheaton, William. "Income and urban residence: an analysis of consumer demand for location," *American Economic Review*, Vol. 67 (1977) 620-631.

Wilson, Alan. *Urban and Regional Models in Geography and Planning* (New York: John Wiley, 1974).

Yeates, Maurice. "The congruence between housing space, social space, and community space, and some experiments concerning its implications," *Environment and Planning*, Vol. 4 (1972) 395-414.

HUMAN ECOLOGY

Berry, Brian J.L. "Comparative factorial ecology," *Economic Geography*, Vol. 47 (1971).

Berry, Brian J.L. and Kasarda, John D. *Contemporary Urban Ecology* (New York: Macmillan, 1977).

Burgess, Ernest W. "The growth of the city: an introduction to a research project," in Robert E. Park, Ernest W. Burgess, and R.D. McKenzie (eds.), *The City* (Chicago: University of Chicago Press, 1925), pp. 47-62.

Caruso, Douglas and Palm, Risa. "Social space and social place," *The Professional Geographer*, Vol. 25 (August 1973) 221-225.

Cornwell, David A. "The management of tensions between conflicting usages of a public place," *Sociological Review*, Vol. 21 (May 1973) 197-210.

Damer, Sean. "Wine alley: the sociology of a dreadful enclosure," *Sociological Review*, Vol. 22 (May 1974) 221-248.

Duncan, James S. "Landscape tastes as a symbol of group identity," *Geographical Review*, Vol. 63 (July 1973) 334-355.

Entrikin, J. Nicholas. "Robert Park's human ecology and human geography," *Annals of the Association of American Geographers*, Vol. 70 (March 1980), 43-58.

Gerson, Elihu M. and Gerson, M. Sue. "The social framework of place perspectives," in Gary T. Moore and Reginald G. Golledge (eds.), *Environmental Knowing: Theory, Research and Methods* (Stroudsburg, PA: Dowden, Hutchinson and Ross, 1976), pp. 196-205.

Hugill, Peter. "Social conduct on the golden mile," *Annals of the Association of American Geographers*, Vol. 65 (June 1975) 214-228.

Hunter, Albert. *Symbolic Communities* (Chicago: University of Chicago Press, 1974).

Logan, John and Schneider, Mark. "Stratification of metropolitan suburbs," *American Sociological Review*, Vol. 46 (1981) 175-186.

Park, Robert E. "The city: suggestions for the investigation of human behavior in the urban environment," *American Journal of Sociology*, Vol. 20 (March 1915) 577-612.

Schwirian, Kent. (ed.) *Comparative Urban Structure: Studies in the Ecology of Cities* (Lexington, MA: D.C. Heath, 1974).

Short, James F. (ed.) *The Social Fabric of the Metropolis* (Chicago: University of Chicago Press, 1971).

Suttles, Gerald. *The Social Construction of Community* (Chicago: University of Chicago Press, 1972).

Suttles, Gerald. *The Social Order of the Slum* (Chicago: University of Chicago Press, 1968).

Theodorson, George A. (ed.) *Studies in Human Ecology* (New York: Harper and Row, 1961).

Timms, Duncan. *The Urban Mosaic* (Cambridge, MA: Harvard University Press, 1971).

Turner, Ralph H. (ed.) *Robert E. Park on Social Control and Collective Behavior* (Chicago: University of Chicago Press, 1967).

POWER AND LOCATIONAL CONFLICT

Cox, Kevin R. *Conflict, Power and Politics in the City* (New York: McGraw-Hill, 1973).

Cox, Kevin R. (ed.) *Urbanization and Conflict in Market Societies* (Chicago: Maaroufa Press, 1978).

Cox, Kevin R. "Residential location and political behavior: conceptual model and empirical tests," *Acta Sociologica*, Vol. 13 (1970) 40-53.

Cox, Kevin R. and McCarthy, Jeffrey. "Neighborhood activism in the American city: behavioral relationships," *Urban Geography*, Vol. 1 (January-March 1980) 22-38.

Cox, Kevin R. and Reynolds, David (eds.) *Locational Approaches to Power and Conflict* (New York: John Wiley, 1974).

Edelman, Murray. *Politics as Symbolic Action* (New York: Academic Press, 1971).

Edelman, Murray. *The Symbolic Uses of Politics* (Chicago: University of Chicago Press, 1964).

Hays, S.P. "The changing political structure of the city in industrial America." *Journal of Urban History*, Vol. 1 (1974) 6-38.

Hirschman, Albert O. *Exit, Voice and Loyalty: Response to Decline in Firms, Organizations, and States* (Cambridge, MA: Harvard University Press, 1970).

Hoch, C. "Social structure and suburban spatio-political conflicts in the United States," *Antipode*, Vol. 11 (1979) 44-55.

Janelle, D. "Structural dimensions in the geography of locational conflicts," *Canadian Geographer*, Vol. 21 (1977) 311-328.

Lowe, P.D. "Amenity and equity: a review of local environmental pressure groups in Britain," *Environment and Planning*, Vol. 9 (January 1977) 35-58.

Molotch, Harvey. "Capital and neighborhood in the United States," *Urban Affairs Quarterly*, Vol. 14 (1979) 289-312.

Molotch, Harvey. "The city as a growth machine: toward a political economy of place," *American Journal of Sociology*, Vol. 82 (September 1976) 309-332.

Orbell, John M. and Uno, Toru. "A theory of neighborhood problem solving: political action vs. residential mobility," *American Political Science Review*, Vol. 66 (June 1972) 471-489.

Wolpert, Julian; Mumphrey, A. and Seley, J. *Metropolitan Neighborhoods: Participation and Conflict Over Change*, AAG Resource Paper No. 16 (Washington, D.C.: Assocation of American Geographers, 1972).

INSTITUTIONAL CONSTRAINTS

Abrams, Charles. *The City is the Frontier* (New York: Harper and Row, 1965).

Barnekov, Timothy K. and Rich, Daniel. "Privatism and urban development: an analysis of the organized influence of local business elites," *Urban Affairs Quarterly*, Vol. 12 (June 1977) 431-460.

Bassett, Keith and Short, John. "Patterns of building society and local authority mortgage lending in the 1970s," *Environment and Planning*, Vol. 12 (1980) 279-300.

Boddy, Michael J. "The structure of mortgage finance: building societies and the British social formation," *Transactions of the Institute of British Geographers*, Vol. 1 (1976) 58-71.

Bradford, Calvin. "Financing homeownership: the Federal role in neighborhood decline," *Urban Affairs Quarterly*, Vol. 14 (March 1979) 313-335.

Clark, William A.V. "Judicial intervention as policy: impacts on population distribution and redistribution in urban areas in the United States," *Population Research and Policy Review*, Vol. 1 (1982) 79-100.

Feagin, Joe R. "Urban real estate speculation in the United States: implications for social science and urban planning," *International Journal of Urban and Regional Research*, Vol. 6 (March 1982) 35-59.

Flowerdew, Robin. (ed.) *Institutions and Geographical Patterns* (New York: St. Martin's Press, 1982).

Foley, Donald L. "Institutional and contextual factors affecting the housing choices of minority residents," in Amos H. Hawley and Vincent P. Rock (eds.), *Segregation in Residential Areas* (Washington, D.C.: National Academy of Sciences, 1973).

Ford, Janet. "The role of the building society manager in the urban stratification system: autonomy vs. constraint," *Urban Studies*, Vol. 12 (1975) 295-302.

Form, William. "The place of social structure in the determination of land use: some implications from a theory of urban ecology," *Social Forces*, Vol. 32 (May 1954) 317-323.

Harvey, David. "Government policies, financial institutions, and neighborhood change in U.S. cities," in Michael Harloe (ed.), *Captive Cities* (New York: John Wiley, 1977), pp. 123-139.

Lake, Robert W. and Winslow, Jessica. "Integration management: municipal constraints on residential mobility," *Urban Geography*, Vol. 2 (December 1981) 311-326.

Leonard, Simon. "Urban managerialism: a period of transition?" *Progress in Human Geography*, Vol. 6 (June 1982) 190-215.

McNamara, P.F. "Property development, financial institutions, and the state," *Antipode*, Vol. 11 (1979) 56-66.

Pahl, Ray E. "Sociopolitical factors in resource allocation," in D.T. Herbert and R.J. Johnston (eds.), *Social Problems and the City* (New York: Oxford University Press, 1979), pp. 33-46.

Pahl, Ray E. "Managers, technical experts, and the state: forms of mediation, manipulation, and dominance," in Michael Harlow (ed.), *Captive Cities* (New York: John Wiley, 1977), pp. 49-61.

Pahl, Ray E. *Whose City?* (second ed.) (New York: Penguin, 1975).

Palm, Risa. "Financial and real estate institutions in the housing market," in D.T. Herbert and R.J.Johnston (eds.), *Geography and the Urban Environment*, Vol. 2 (New York: John Wiley, 1979), pp. 83-124.

Paris, C. "Urban renewal in Birmingham, England: an institutional approach," *Antipode*, Vol. 6 (1974) 7-15.

Rich, Richard C. "Neglected issues in the study of urban service distributions: a research agenda," *Urban Studies*, Vol. 16 (1979) 143-156.

Smith, T.R. and Mertz, R. "An analysis of the effects of information revision on the outcome of housing market search, with special reference to the influence of realty agents," *Environment and Planning*, Vol. 12 (1980) 155-174.

Vance, James. "Institutional forces that shape the city," in D.T. Herbert and R.J. Johnston (eds.), *Social Areas in Cities* (New York: John Wiley, 1978), pp. 97-126.

Wheaton, William L.C. "Public and private agents of change in urban expansion," in Melvin M. Webber *et al, Explorations into Urban Structure* (Philadelphia: University of Pennsylvania Press, 1964), pp. 154-196.

Williams, Peter. "Building societies and the inner city," *Transactions of the Institute of British Geographers*, Vol. 3 (1978) 23-34.

MARXIST APPROACHES

Blackmar, Betsy. "Re-walking the 'walking city': housing and property relations in New York City, 1780-1840," *Radical History Review*, Vol. 21 (Fall 1979) 131-148.

Burawoy, M. "Contemporary currents in marxist theory," *The American Sociologist*, Vol. 13 (1978) 50-64.

Castells, Manuel. *The Economic Crisis and American Society* (Princeton: Princeton University Press, 1980).

Castells, Manuel. *City, Class and Power* (London: Macmillan, 1978).

Castells, Manuel. *The Urban Question* (London: Edward Arnold, 1977).

Dear, Michael and Scott, Allen J. (eds.) *Urbanization and Urban Planning in Capitalist Society* (New York: Methuen, 1981).

Duncan, James and Ley, David. "Structural Marxism and human geography: a critical assessment," *Annals of the Association of American Geographers*, Vol. 72 (March 1982) 30-59.

Harloe, Michael. (ed.) *Captive Cities* (New York: John Wiley, 1977).

Harvey, David. "Labor, capital, and class-struggle around the built environment in advanced capitalist societies," *Politics and Society*, Vol. 6 (1976) 265-275.

Harvey, David. "Class structure in a capitalist society and the theory of residential differentiation," in R. Peel, M. Chisholm, and P. Haggett (eds.), *Processes in Physical and Human Geography* (London: Heinemann, 1975).

Harvey, David. "The political economy of urbanization in advanced capitalist societies: the case of the United States," in Gary Gappert and Harold Rose (eds.), *The Social Economy of Cities* (Beverly Hills, CA: Sage, 1975), pp. 119-163.

Harvey, David. *Social Justice and the City*. (Baltimore: Johns Hopkins University Press, 1973).

Harvey, David. *Society, the City and the Space-Economy of Urbanism*, AAG Resource Paper No. 18 (Washington, D.C.: Association of American Geographers, 1972).

Peet, Richard. "Inequality and poverty: a marxist-geographic theory," *Annals of the Association of American Geographers*, Vol. 65 (1975) 564-571.

Pickvance, C.G. (ed.) *Urban Sociology: Critical Essays* (New York: St. Martin's Press, 1976).

Pickvance, C.G. "Housing, reproduction of capital, and reproduction of labor power: some recent French work," *Antipode*, Vol. 8 (1976) 58-68.

Sawyers, Larry. "Urban form and the mode of production," *Union of Radical Political Economy*, Vol. 7 (Spring 1975) 52-68.

Scott, Allen J. *The Urban Land Nexus and the State* (London: Pion, Ltd., 1980).

Smith, Neil. "Gentrification and capital: practice and ideology in Society Hill," *Antipode*, Vol. 11 (1979) 24-35.

Stone, Michael E. "The housing crisis, mortgage lending, and class struggle," *Antipode*, Vol. 7 (September 1975) 22-37.

Tabb, William K. and Sawers, Larry. (eds.) *Marxism and the Metropolis: New Perspectives in Urban Political Economy* (New York: Oxford University Press, 1978).

INDEX

abandonment, 292
Abrams, Charles, 185
absolute space, 266-69
accumulation, Chapter 13 *passim* (197-227), Chapter 14 *passim* (228-49)
    class struggle and, 220-26
    investment in the built environment and, 210-18
    laborers and the implications of, 198-99
    laws of, 199-204
    urban process and, 208-20
    also see fixed capital; consumption fund; investment(s)
Addams, Jane, 224
Adde, L., 296
Adorno, Theodore, 120
aesthetics/quality of life
    as a cause for gentrification, 279, 282
    as a factor in land use controversies, 133, 135-36, 137, 140
agricultural land theory, 1, 2-5
Alihan, Milla, 74
Alonso, William, 30, 52
American Bankers Association, 186
American Transit Association, 19
Amin, Samir, 232
anthropology: social, 145, 147, 155; *also see* sociology
Appalachia, 246, 248
Associated General Contractors, 187

Bahr, H. M., 89
Bailey, Martin, 116
balance of nature, 56-58
Baltimore, Maryland, 258, 259-66, 266-67, 268, 271, 276, 279-80, 281, 291
Banfield, Edward, 242
banks, 163-64, 165
Banks, Arthur S., 76
Barclays Bank, 163
Barrows, H. H., 61
Berry, Brian J. L., 79, 234, 239, 241, 242, 247
Bittner, E., 102
Blauner, Robert, 79
Blietz, Irvin, 181

blockbusting, 290-91
blow-out, 256, 291
Boal, F. W., 116
Bohannon, David, 181
Boston, Massachusetts, 26
bourgeois, *see* class struggle; Marx, Karl; middle class; accumulation
Bourne, L., 125
Braverman, Harry, 238
Bristol, England, 148
Britain, *see* Great Britain
Brixton, England, 171
builders/building corporations, *see* developers/development corporations
Building Products Institute, 187
building societies and financial agencies (Britain), 160-66, 171
Building Society Work Explained, 161
built environment, Chapter 13 *passim* (197-227); *also see* investment(s); accumulation
Burawoy, Michael, 81
bureaucracy: theory of, 119
Burgess Concentric Zonal Hypothesis, *see* Burgess, Ernest: theory of
Burgess, Ernest: theory of, 65-66, 74
Burney, Elizabeth, 148-49
Burns, Fritz, 181
Burns, T., 154
Burt, Nathaniel, 280
business land use, 6

California, 121, 140
Camden, England, 166
Canada, 114
capital/capitalism, Chapter 13 *passim* (197-227), 256, 258
    circulation of, 204-208
    class struggle and, 81-82, 220-26
    contradictions of, 198, 199, 209, 219-20
    devaluation of, 211-12, 218, 219
    development of, 232-34
    finance, Chapter 15 *passim* (250-77)
    forms of crisis under, 207-208
    gentrification and, 283-94, 295-96

308

Index

investments and, 202-204, 205, 207, 208
social, 244-45
also see class-monopoly rent; class-monopoly power; Marx, Karl
Capital, Das, see Marx, Karl
capital gains, 115, 168
Castells, Manuel, 82, 152, 231
CBD, *see* central business district
central business district (CBD), 34-36, 39, 43, 44, 47, 49, 59, 118, 285;
also see Vancouver, British Columbia
central cities, 173, 185, 189, 228-29, 240, 245, 278, 285
historical decline of, 288-92
central place theory, 22
Chalmers, Reverend Thomas, 224
Chamber of Commerce (United States), 186
Chambliss, W. J., 100
Chicago, Illinois, 97, 115, 144, 285
South Shore community of, 26, 66, 67, 68, 70
Hyde Park-Kenwood community of, 68-69
Chicago School, 74, 83
Christian natural law, 89, 91
Clark, Colin, 11, 25
class
conflict: land use conflict as an urban manifestation of, 119;
stratification, *see* social stratification
struggle, 197, 199, 204, 205, 207, 220-26, 238, 254-55, 269-74
also see social stratification; class struggle
class-monopoly power, 253-57, 266
class-monopoly rent, Chapter 15 *passim* (250-77)
classical political economists and gentrification theory, 287
Clay Products Association, National, 187
Cleveland, Ohio, 26
clustering (socioeconomic) and residential location, 36
Cohen, Robert B., 236
Cole, Albert, 188
collective social action, *see* community involvement/citizens groups
Columbus, Ohio, 116
community (concept of) and class struggle, 224-25, 270-74
community involvement/citizens groups in land use controversy in
Vancouver, B.C., 130, 134, 135, 137, 138, 139; *also see* political action/processes
competition, 54, 55-56, 57-58, 61, 198-99, 205, 237, 239, 245
for space, Chapter 5 *passim* (65-72), 148
political, Chapter 6 *passim* (73-85), 103, 107
also see symbiosis
concentric zones, 118, 131, 139; *also see* Burgess, Ernest: theory of
conflict theory, 119; *also see* land use: conflict over; class struggle
Conot, Robert, 240
construction, housing, 176-77, 178, 182, 184-85;
also see Levitt and Sons; suburbanization; developers
consumer demand for housing, *see* preference, housing
consumption, 121, 122, 209, 244, 267-68
as a factor in gentrification, 279, 281-83, 293
forces of, 120, 140-41
politics of, Chapter 9 *passim* (118-42)
suburbanization and, 240, 243, 244

Development, Law of Uneven, *see* Law of Uneven Development
Dickens, Charles: *Hard Times*, 222
displacement, 278
distribution (residential), *see* location, residential
dominance, 58-59
Donnison, D. V., 148-49
Douglas, J. W. B., 151
Dowd, Douglas F., 248, 249
Dunham, H. W., 93

economic(s), 61, 118, 119, 283
causes for gentrification, 279-80, 283-95, 296
as a factor in land use controversies, 135-36, 137, 139, 140
Economist, 168
education, 111, 112-13, 148, 151, 222
Electors Action Movement, *see* TEAM
elite theory, 119
Elton, Charles, 56, 57
empirical and theoretical studies, 138-39
employment, 37-38, 77-78, 118, 121, 148-49, 223-24, 238; *also see* occupation
England, *see* Great Britain; name of individual city or area
ensemble of transformations, *see* Lefebvre, H.

Epstein, A. L., 145
estate agents, 166-68
Europe: gentrification in, 282
Evans, Alan, 116
Evening Standard (England), 168
exclusionary policies, *see* social stratification; zoning; class struggle

Fairview, British Columbia, *see* Vancouver, British Columbia
False Creek, British Columbia, *see* Vancouver, British Columbia
family size and residential distribution, 42-46
federal government: role of, 203, 204, 243, 258-59, 272, 278, 294-95; *also see* transportation; Federal Housing Authority; housing policies: federal
Federal Housing Authority (FHA), 180, 183-84, 185-86, 187-88, 190, 243, 258, 259, 261, 264-65, 291
FHA, *see* Federal Housing Authority
filtering theory, 114, 292, 293, 295
finance capital, Chapter 15 *passim* (250-77)
financing of housing, 180, 189-90, 243, 261-65, 267, 293
 in Britain, 160-68
 also see land installment contract; Federal Housing Authority
Firey, Walter, 74
fiscal crisis of the United States, 244-46
fiscal externality, 114
Fishman, Maurice, 181
fixed capital, 201-202, 203, 205, 207, 208, 211, 219, 225; *also see* investments; accumulation; capital/capitalism
Florida, 273
Foley, Raymond, 188
Foote, C., 100
Fortune, 178
Foster, J., 152
France, 218, 223
Fraser River, British Columbia, *see* Vancouver, British Columbia

Gaffney, M. 256
Gans, Herbert, 189, 280
GDP, *see* gross domestic product
Gelfand, Mark, 185
Gellert, Carl, 181
General Motors, 272
gentrification, Chapter 11 *passim* (157-72), Chapter 16 *passim* (278-98)
 capitalism and, 283-94, 295-96
 causes for, 278-80, 282, 283-95, 296
 consumer preference and, 279, 282, 293
 definition of, 170, 296
 developers and, 293-95, 297
 federal role in 294-95
 historical and structural context of, 283-95
 home ownership and, 289-90
 middle class impact on, 279, 280, 281-82, 295, 296
 production/consumption as factors in, 279, 281-83, 293
 rental housing and, 289-90
 also see social stratification; zoning
GI Bill of Rights, 180
Glasgow, Scotland, 148
Glass, Ruth, 143, 144, 152
Gluckman, M., 145
GNP, *see* gross national product
Goffman, Erving, 96, 97, 153
Goldthorpe, J. H., 147
Gomery, J. Douglas, 110
Gottlieb, M., 214, 226
Great Britain, 53-54, 103, 143, 144, 146, 147, 150, 159, 295
 education in, 111, 112-13
 home ownership in, 160-68
 housing preference in, 110-11
 immigration and housing in, 159, 163-64, 167
 investments in the built environment in, 214-18
 political processes in, 106, 110-13, 150-51
 also see name of individual city or area
gross domestic product (GDP), 76
gross national product (GNP), 258
"growth center strategy," 246
ground rent, 287, 288, 291, 292, 295; *also see* rent gap
Grundrisse, *see* Marx, Karl
Guardian (Manchester, England), 168
Gugler, J., 145

Habib, Jack, 77
Haeckel, Ernst H., 55
Haig, R., 1
Hard Times, *see* Dickens, Charles
Harvey, David, 81, 82, 231-32, 243, 291
Hawley, Amos, 65, 66, 74-75
Haymarket Riot (1877) in Chicago, Illinois, 223

Index

Highway Trust Fund, 249
highway and mass transit program, *see* transportation
Hill, Octavia, 224
historical decline of the central city, 288-92
Hollingshead, A. B., 74
Home Builders, National Association of (NAHB), 186, 187
home ownership, 132, 223, 243, 249
    federal housing policy and, 184-85
    gentrification and, 289-90
    in Baltimore, 261-65
    in Britain, 160-68
    political processes and, 107-108
    suburbanization and, 186, 188-90
    also see property; Federal Housing Authority
Houdeville, L., 223
House Purchase and Housing Act (1959), 164
"House That Jack Built," 54
house value, 286-87, 288-89, 291
household consumption of space, *see* space, household consumption of
housing, 25, 243, 222-23,
    class-monopoly rents and, 254-57
    consumption and, 267-68
    hierarchical institutional framework and coordination of, 257-66
    in Vancouver, British Columbia, 132-33, 137
    also see home ownership; preference, housing; housing policies: federal; housing market
Housing Act (1949), 182, 183, 187, 188
Housing Act (1954), 182, 183, 184
Housing and Home Finance Agency, 184-85
housing demand, *see* preference, housing
housing: financing of, *see* financing of housing
housing market, 29-30, 148-49, 151
    control of the, 105, 107, Chapter 11 passim (157-72)
    factors of the, 157-58
    suburbanization and the, 174-75, 177-78
    welfare and the, 108-11
housing policies: federal, 182-88, 191, 258; *also see* name of individual agency or act
housing preference, *see* preference, housing
housing rehabilitation, 279, 280, 283, 293, 294
Housing Situation in 1960, Report of the, 163, 171

Housing Survey of England and Wales (1964), 163, 164, 171
housing technology, *see* technology, housing
Hoyt, H., 285, 286, 292
human ecology, *see* population; competition; dominance; planning and human ecology; succession
Hurd, R. M., 1
Huxley, Julian, 60
Hymer, Stephen, 236, 237

identity, 96-97
immigrant(s)/immigration, 238, 278
    in Britain, 159, 163-64, 167
    in Vancouver, British Columbia, 121-22
income, 13, 39, 48-49, 75, 115-16, 238-39
    occupation, employment, and, 38-42, 149
    of people in Vancouver, British Columbia, 122, 132-33
    space, family size, and, 19, 23, 30, 39-46, 110, 148
    also see occupation; social stratification
Increasing Firm Size: Law of, *see* Law of Increasing Firm Size
individual(s)/individualism and capitalism, 198, 202, 203, 204-205, 207
individuality and consumer preference, 282, 293
industrial urbanization, 233-34
industry/industrialization
    as part of land use controversy in Vancouver, B.C., 130, 139
    gentrification and, 285
institutions, role of
    in Britain, Chapter 11 *passim* (157-72)
    in the United States, Chapter 12 *passim* (173-96)
insurance companies, 163, 165, 171
integration, *see* racial segregation/integration
investment(s), 205, 206, 259-61, 268-69
    capitalism and, 202-204, 205, 207, 208, 245
    in the built environment, 210-20
    science and technological, 203, 206, 208
    also see fixed capital; consumption fund
Ireland, Northern, 116
Islington, London, England, Chapter 11 *passim* (157-72), 295
ITT (International Telephone and Telegraph), 272, 273

Janelle, D., 126
Japan, 110

journey to work, *see* transportation costs
"Juglar cycles," 214

Kitsilano, British Columbia, *see* Vancouver, British Columbia
"Kondratieffs," 214
Kruskal-Wallis, H., 15-16
Kuznets cycles, 214

labor systems and system of places, 81
laborers and the implications for accumulation, 198-99, 220-26
labourer/laborer, *see* Marx, Karl; capital/capitalism; labor systems and system of places; middle class; class struggle
land installment contract, 261-64, 265, 271
land use
    aesthetics/quality of life as a factor in the determination of, 133, 135-36, 137, 140
    as an urban manifestation of class conflict, 119
    change and, 131, 132, 314, 139
    concentric zones and, 118, 131, 139
    economics as a factor in determination of, 135-36, 137, 139, 140
    in Vancouver, British Columbia, 123-38; *also see* Vancouver, British Columbia
    industrial use as a factor in controversy over, 130, 139
    models and employment, 118
    values in determination of, 130, 139-40
land use: conflict over, Chapter 9 *passim* (118-42)
    concept of, 118-19
    grounds for involvement in, 135-36
    news media influence on, 126, 128
    participants in, 134-35
    patterns of resolution of, 136-38
    variables in, 131-33
land use theory, 2-6, 118, 119, 121, 138
    neoclassical economics and, 118-19, 279, 282, 283, 286
    residential, 6-8, Chapter 2 *passim* (11-26)
land values, 59, 119, 283-84, 285-86
landlords, *see* class-monopoly power
Laurenti, L., 291
Law of Increasing Firm Size, 234-37, 246
Law of Uneven Development, 237-41, 246
"laws of motion," 232
Lean, W., 166
Leasehold Reform Act (1967), 159, 164, 169

Lefebvre, H., 250-51, 253, 269, 274-75
Levitt, Abraham, Jr., 178
Levitt, Abraham, Sr., *see* Levitt and Sons
Levitt, Alfred, 181
Levitt and Sons, 178-81, 192
Levitt, William, 178
Levittown, New York, 178, 179, 180-81
Levittown, Pennsylvania, 181, 190
Levittowns, *see* Levitt and Sons
Ley, D., 279, 282
Lipton, Gregory, 279, 296
lobbyists in land use controversy in Vancouver, B.C., 130, 134, 137, 139
Local Education Authorities (L.E.A.), 148
Local Government in England, Report of the Royal Commission on, 150
location
    determination of, 12, 18-19, 23, 26
    residential, 6-7, Chapter 3 *passim* (27-52), 109
    theory, 236
location rent, Chapter 1 *passim* (1-10), 31-36, 46-48
locational conflict, *see* land use, conflict over
locational structuring, *see* preference, housing
London, England, 112, 163, 168, Chapter 11 *passim* (157-72), 276
London, Ontario, Canada, 126
London Property Letter (L.P.L), 159, 167-68, 171
London, University of, 144
Long Island, New York: suburban inequalities on, 75
Los Angeles, California, 26, 178, 214
Lowrey, Ira S., 289, 292

Macpherson, C. B., 99-100
Maisel, Sherman, 176, 181
Manheim, E., 143, 144
"manipulated city" thesis, 119
marginality, Chapter 7 *passim* (86-102)
market equilibrium: concept of, 118, 119
Martindale, D., 143, 144
Marx, Karl, 81, 119-120, 198, 200-204, 206, 207, 221, 247, 269, 270, 271-73, 273-74, 276, 287
    categories of rents of, 253-54
    concept of society of, 99, 230
    division of labor theory of, 209-210
    on fixed capital, 212, 219
    on modes of production, 229, 230, 247

Index

also see capital/capitalism; middle class; accumulation; surplus value
Marxism, Mason, Norman, 188
Mayer, P., 145
McKenzie, R. D., 74
mediation in land use controversies, 121, 134, 139, 140
mercantile urbanization, 232-33
methodology and land use theory, 138
metropolitan hierarchy of cities, 234-37, 240-41, 245; *also see* urban-rural dichotomy
metropolitan urbanization, 234-37
middle class
    impact on gentrification, 279, 280, 281-82, 295, 296
    impact on urban development, 120, 121, 140
    also see political action/processes; social stratification; class struggle
migration, 80-81, 189, 261; *also see* suburbanization; urban-rural dichotomy
Milner Holland Inquiry (1965), 159
Minneapolis-St. Paul, Minnesota, 14
Mitchell, J. C., 145
Molotch, Harvey, 77
money: changing role of, 271-72, 273
Moore, R., 152
moral order, 88-89
    class struggle, suburbanization and the, 223-24
    politcal action and, 87-88
    property and, 89, 92, 97, 104-105
    social stratification and, 108-109
    urban space and, 87-88
Mortgage Bankers Association of America, 186
Mount Pleasant, British Columbia, *see* Vancouver, British Columbia
Mowbray, John, 181
multi-national corporations, 235-36, 237
Murray, Gilbert, 63

NAHB, *see* Home Builders, National Association of
NAREB, *see* Real Estate Boards, National Association of
Nashville, Tennessee, 15, 18
Nassau-Suffolk Counties, New York, 75
negative-exponential hypothesis, 11, 13, 14, 23, 25
Nelson, Herbert V., 192
neoclassical approach to rent and land use theory, 118-19, 251, 267, 279, 282, 283, 286
New Haven, Connecticut, 15
New York, New York, 14, 78, 81, 225, 265, 283
news media influence on land use conflicts, 126, 128
Nichols, J. D., 181
Non-Partisan Movement, *see* NPA
NPA (Non-Partisan Movement), 122-23, 134, 140

Observer (London, England), 167
occupations, 38-49, 76-77, 148, 151, 168
O'Connor, James, 82, 244-45, 247
Option Mortgage Scheme (1967), 164
Orange County, California, 178
organization theory and urban sociology, 153-54
overaccumulation, *see* accumulation

Paris, France, 223, 226
Park Forest, Illinois, 178
Park, Robert E., 65, 66, 74, 99, 144
Philadelphia, Pennsylvania, 26, 100, 189, 190, 265, 294
    Society Hill, 279, 280-81, 283, 296
Pittsburgh, Pennsylvania, 15
place, *see* system of places
planning and human ecology, Chapter 4 *passim* (53-64), Chapter 5 *passim* (65-72), 73-76
political action/processes, 75, Chapter 8 *passim* (103-17), 121
    as a method of mediating land use decision making, 121, 134, 139, 140
    competition for spaces and, 77-78
    in Britain, 106, 110-13, 150, 151
    moral order and, 87-88
    services and, 148, 149
    social movements and, 79-80; *also see* migration
    structure of, 104-107
    system of places and, Chapter 6 *passim* (73-85)
    use of space and, 97, 118, 120-21
political economy, 118, 119-20, 269-74
population, 35, 175, 178, 247
    human ecology and, Chapter 4 *passim* (53-64)
    distribution of urban, Chapter 2 *passim* (11-26), 173
    of Baltimore, Maryland, 259
    of Vancouver, British Columbia, 121
preference, housing/consumer, 6-10, 109-110,

113, 116, 157, 158, 175, 267, 282
  gentrification and, 279, 282, 293
  in Britain, 110-11
  Levitt and, 180, 190
  social stratification and, 116, 148-49
  suburbanization and, 173, 174, 175, 178, 189-91
  welfare and, 110-11
  also see location; land use
Price, James, 181
Producers Council, 187
production, Chapter 13 *passim* (197-227), Chapter 14 *passim* (228-49);
  rent and, 251-52
  also see consumption
production/consumption as factors in gentrification, 279, 281-83, 293
productivity, 205-206
profit, 205, 242, 252-53, 265
property, Chapter 7 *passim* (86-102), 110
  moral order and, 89, 92, 97, 104-105
  also see home ownership; space
property value, 286, 291
Proposition 13 (California), 140
public housing, 183, 184, 187, 188
public safety, 113, 116

quality of life, *see* aesthetics/quality of life

racial integration/segregation/discrimination, 36, 50, 66-67, 68, 70, 79, 185, 224-25, 242, 244, 264-65
racism, *see* blockbusting; blow out; redlining
Real Estate Boards, National Association of (NAREB), 186, 187
Realtor's Washington (D. C.) Committee, 187
redlining, 185, 291-92, 293
Reissman, L., 144
renaissance, urban, *see* Chapter 16 *passim* (278-98)
rent
  concept of, 251-53
  control, 223
  location, Chapter 3 *passim* (27-52)
  theory, Chapter 1 *passim* (1-10)
  types of, 253
  also see class-monopoly rent
Rent Act (1957), 171, 159
rent gap, 292-93, 295, *also see* ground rent
rental housing and gentrification, 289-90
residential preference, *see* preference, housing; location: residential
Retail Lumber Dealers, National Association of, 187
Rex, J. A., 152
Rhodes-Livingstone Institute, Lusaka, 145
Ribicoff, Abraham, *see* Crisis of the Cities, Committee on the
Ricardo, David, 266
Rooney, J. F., 99
Royal Institute of Chartered Surveyors (R.I.C.S.), *see* Surveyors, Royal Institute of Chartered
Rubenstein, J., 88, 93
rural-urban dichotomy, *see* urban-rural dichotomy

San Francisco Bay Area, California, 14, 176
safety, *see* public safety
savings and loans institutions, 259, 261, 265, 267
Savings and Loan League, United States, 186
savings and location rents, 32-33
scarcity and rent, 252
Scholz, Donald, 181
Schnore, Leo, 189
science and technology/technological: investments in, 203, 206, 208
sectoral patterns and land use change, 131, 134, 139
services
  as part of land use controversy in Vancouver, B.C., 130
  availability of, 59, 70, 77-78, 114, 148, 149, 151
  household preferences for, 27-28, 43, 50
sex differences and work/residence patterns, 37-38
shopping centers, 243-44
Shopping Centers, International Council of, 244
Simmel, G., 61
Sjoberg, G., 144
Small Dwelling Acquisitions Act, 171
Smolensky, Eugene, 110
social capital, 244-45
social class, *see* social stratification
social mobility, Chapter 6 *passim* (73-85), 87, 151, 189; *also see* social stratification
social movements, *see* political actions/processes
social stratification, 75, 96, 119, 148, 183
  capitalism and, 81-82
  functionalist theory of, 74-75

Index

housing preference and, 116, 148-49
in Vancouver, British Columbia, 120-21, 133
moral order and, 108-109
occupation and, 76, 152
strategies for attaining, 104, 105, 106
suburbanization and, 188-89
system of places and, 76-77
urban space and, 8-9, 69-70
also see Islington, London, England; gentrification; class struggle
social values, 152-53; *also see* space: social value of
society: definition, function, goals and organization, 63-64, 88, 99, 119
sociology: urban, Chapter 10 *passim* (143-156)
space, 50, Chapter 5 *passim* (65-72), 74, 77-78, Chapter 6 *passim* (73-85), Chapter 7 *passim* (86-102), 148
   absolute, 266-69
   consumption of, 12, 13, 18, 19, 23, 30-31, 36, 46-48, 104-105, 120-21
   family size and, 42-46
   income and, 30-31, 39-46, 148
   location rent and, 35, 46-49
   moral order and, 87-88
   social stratification and, 69-70
   social value of, 91-94, 97
   types of, 91-95
   also see land use
Spain, 224
spatial development of the built environment, 214-15, 219-20, 231, 239-40, 242-43
spatial differential, Chapter 6 *passim* (73-85)
Spearman's coefficient of rank correlation, 15, 16, 40
speculators/speculation, 217, 218, 255-57, 259, 264-65, 276, 297; *also see* developers/development corporations
Spencer, Herbert, 55
Spilerman, Seymour, 77
Spradley, J. P., 90, 92
St. Louis, Missouri, 115, 116
status, social, *see* social stratification
Strauss, A., 152
Stoneson, Ellie, 181
substitution effect, 48-49
suburbanization, Chapter 12 *passim* (173-96), 223-24, 241-44, 258-59, Chapter 16 *passim* (278-98)
succession, 59-60

Sun (Vancouver, British Columbia), 126
supply and demand, 5, 118, 141, 148, 200, 205, 286
surplus capital and the built environment, 217-18, 219
surplus value, 197, 198, 200, 205, 207, 229-30, 231, 244, 250, 273-74
Surveyors, Royal Institute of Chartered (R.I.C.S.), 167, 168
Suttles, G. D., 100
symbiosis, 62-64
system of places and political processes, Chapter 6 *passim* (73-85)

tax policies, 104, 106, 186
Taylor, Waverly, 181
TEAM (Electors Action Movement), 122-23, 133, 134, 140
technology, housing, 175, 177, 179-80, 288
tenant, *see* class-monopoly power
transfer payment, *see* rent; class-monopoly rent
theoretical and empirical studies, 138-39
Third World countries, 144, 145, 275
Thomas, Brinley, 227
Thompson, J. Arthur, 53, 54-55
Thompson, Wilbur, 234
Times (London, England), 167, 168
Tobin, Gary, 116
transportation costs and determination of residential location, 12, 18-19, 23, 26, Chapter 3 *passim* (27-52), 148, 186, 218, 219, 243, 249, 279
Toronto, Canada, 133

unions, 239
United States
   fiscal crisis of the, 244-46
   investments in the built environment in, 214-18
   overaccumulation in, 223
   urbanization in the, 232-44
urban/urbanization, Chapter 14 *passim* (228-49)
   contradictions and the fiscal crisis, 244-46
   revolution, Chapter 15 *passim* (250-77)
   types of, 232-34
Urban Land Institute, 278
urban land market, Chapter 1 *passim* (1-10)
urban renaissance, 183-86, 188, Chapter 16 *passim* (278-98)
urban-rural dichotomy and the urban process, 209-10, 240-41

urban system, 231-32, 245
Utica, New York, 18
value
    profit as, 205
    labor theory of, 287
values in determining land use, 130, 139-40
Vancouver, British Columbia, 121-38
    demography of, 121-22
    land use controversy in, 123-138
    redevelopment of, 122, 123, 125, 134
    income of people in, 122, 132-33
Vancouver Sun, 126
Veblen, Thorstein, 120
Veterans Administration, 180, 187-88, 243
Veterans' Emergency Housing Program (1946), 184
von Thunen, J., 1

Walker, R. A., 253

Wallerstein, Immanuel, 81
Washington, D.C., 279, 281
Watson, W., 145
Webb, Del, 181
Weber, Max, 119
welfare programs, 108-111, 238, 240, 248
Wells, G. P., 60
Wells, H. G., 60, 61
West End, British Columbia, *see* Vancouver, British Columbia
Whitehouse, B. P., 168
Whyte, W. F., Jr., 147
Wingo, Lowdon, 26, 30, 52
Wood, Robert, 81
working class, *see* class struggle; Marx, Karl

zoning, 104, 112, 118, 256, 259
Zorbaugh, Harvey, 74